GEORGE V AND THE G.P.O.

STAMPS, CONFLICT & CREATIVITY

GEORGE V AND THE G.P.O.

STAMPS, CONFLICT & CREATIVITY

Douglas N. Muir

THE BRITISH
POSTAL
MUSEUM
& ARCHIVE

Published by the British Postal Museum & Archive

2010

First published 2010

British Postal Museum & Archive
Freeling House
Phoenix Place
London WC1X 0DL

www.postalheritage.org.uk

ISBN 978-0-9553569-2-6

Designed by Colin Goodhew, Lucid Design, London
Manufactured in the EU by L.P.P.S. Ltd, Wellingborough, Northants NN8 3PJ

Acknowledgements to Royal Mail for assistance in the production of this book.
www.royalmail.com/stamps

CONTENTS

Page

PREFACE & ACKNOWLEDGEMENTS

Archaeology is the study of the material remains of the past. Apply that discipline to a recent historical period and you then have written, oral and pictorial evidence as well to draw on to round out the picture. This is the great advantage of modern times. But it is also the danger – too much detail. It still requires the rigour of archaeological and archival investigation to uncover the facts, as opposed to simple acceptance of received wisdom, or opinion, constantly reiterated. And then choice to avoid obscurity.

Much has been written about the philately of King George V. But it tends to be in detail, based on the material remains, the stamps; or a narrow specialism based on some archives. There is no decent, modern overview, with detail highlighted to bring out the essentials. "Can't see the wood for the trees" is an ambiguous phrase. If by "wood" you mean "forest" then the meaning is that you cannot see the overall picture for the detail. On the other hand, if by "wood" you mean the constituent part of the tree, then it is the opposite – you cannot see the detail because of the overview. In the case of the philately and postal history of the era of George V, the complaint is very much the former: too much detail and too narrow; not enough fitting of the same into an overall narrative. No explanation of why in context, but only how or what - and even that is patchy, or very widely spread in learned journals.

The aim of this work is to fill that gap, an overview - with detail to bring out the essentials. It has also been my aim, to present as clear a story as possible of what actually happened, based upon contemporary reports, now to be found in archives, still largely unexplored.

On the other hand, production detail could not be avoided if the resulting stamps were to be properly understood, and this, at times, can be confusing - or rather heavy reading. Equally, when new material was uncovered it was important, if possible, to make it available for specialists. I have tried not only to do this, but to clarify and, wherever possible, lighten the text to make it easier for the more general reader; and to put it into its overall political, and social, context.

Each of the technical sections has been "peer-reviewed" – i.e. read (and commented on) at draft stage by experts in that particular field. Nevertheless, all errors of omission, or commission, in the final version are clearly mine, and mine alone.

I am indebted to many people for help in researching material for this book, and in providing illustrations. Michael Sefi, Keeper of the Royal Philatelic Collection and specialist in Downey Heads, has been of great assistance throughout both in terms of information, criticism and making King George V's collection available, and also providing a Foreword. Illustrations from that collection throughout this book are reproduced by gracious permission of H.M. The Queen, to whom copyright belongs. I must also thank Miss Pam Clark, Registrar of the Royal Archives at Windsor Castle, and her staff for help with stamp correspondence held there and George V's diary. Again, quotations are by gracious permission of H.M. The Queen.

Many others have also helped and I thank them all (in no particular order). Kevin Clancy, Graham Dyer and Joseph Payne of The Royal Mint Museum have been particularly helpful in providing access, images and information on their holdings of plaster models by Bertram

Mackennal, and also providing access to some documentary evidence which they still hold, to do with dies and plates. David Beech, and Paul Skinner in particular, have made registration and black proof sheets from the British Library Philatelic Collection available over a long period. Work on these will be published by the Great Britain Philatelic Society and, in that connection, I am also grateful to Ian Harvey and Allan Jones of that Society.

Dr Alan Huggins gave me access to the Adams Collection at the Royal Philatelic Society and also kindly commented on the section on postal stationery. Geoffrey Eibl-Kaye was most helpful on letterpress printing and providing contemporary illustrations from *The London Philatelist*, Fred Melville's book and others. Similarly, Bryan Kearsley has helped and commented on the section on Seahorses and intaglio printing. Dr Jean Alexander has, at a time of some difficulty, greatly assisted with sections on rolls, and of course has kindly provided the index. Mike Jackson also provided access to unpublished material.

The resources of the BPMA and the National Archives are vast, and vastly under-investigated. Colleagues at the BPMA have been extremely supportive over a period of years. It may be invidious to pick out particular colleagues who have helped. On the other hand, it would be worse not to mention (in despatches) the great help provided by Julian Stray on vehicles, letter boxes and other matters. That saved me a great deal of time, in terms of background and detail, when time was at a premium.

I must also thank my non-philatelic friend Graham Watson who, on this occasion, has had to plough through highly detailed sections on stamp production in an attempt to make them readable for a non-specialist audience. At least one of his comments has saved me from a highly embarrassing mistake.

However, there is one person above all whom I must thank - for guidance, information, supply of papers no longer available (those marked Richmond papers, also Grover documentation), illustrations and much else besides, and that is Leslie Wilkinson. He is the George V co-ordinating expert in the Great Britain Philatelic Society and he has been of invaluable assistance, often on a day-to-day basis for about three years. His contribution has been immense.

This is most certainly not the last word on the stamps and postal history of King George V's reign but I hope that it will enable, and stimulate, further research.

A note on sources
Sources are given at the end of each chapter for all quotations. Those public record files with the department code POST are held by the British Postal Museum & Archive, as are the De La Rue Correspondence Books. Files with codes – AIR, CO, IR, MINT and T – are held by the National Archives at Kew. The code RA refers to the Royal Archives. Published material has the author in bold type.

Douglas N. Muir
March 2010

FOREWORD

BY MICHAEL SEFI

KEEPER OF THE ROYAL PHILATELIC COLLECTION

I am delighted to see this new book on the stamps and era of King George V, especially in this, the centenary, year of his accession. The Royal Philatelic Collection's material of the reign is described here with new information, as well as being extensively used to illustrate the philatelic story of his reign.

Despite the fact that the period of King George V has been investigated a great deal over the years, this book still provides a lot of new information. This is based on a fresh, systematic, examination of surviving files and material in various archives and a huge amount of work tracking the creation and movement of printing plates from a series of registers, the raw data of which will be published by the Great Britain Philatelic Society in works still to come.

Douglas Muir has not relied on existing published material but rather has gone back to the original files, many of which, as I mention, are brought together here for the first time. However, some records seem to have disappeared over the years and here reliable secondary sources (such as R. W. Richmond) have had to be used.

This book is not a detailed record of flaws on stamps! It is an overall history putting material and events into context, something which has not existed before.
Although I have been consulted over much of the work and writing of this book I shall nevertheless be as eager a reader as anyone else interested in George V. It will, I hope, also inspire others to research the period and I also hope the book will provide a base and reference from which to do so.

Douglas writes well – I hope you enjoy this book as much as I will!

1
INTRODUCTION

King George V acceded to the throne on 6 May 1910, rather appropriate for the philatelist king, as it was also the 70th anniversary of the Penny Black. Then aged 44, he reigned for just over 25 years, dying shortly after celebrating his Silver Jubilee. During his reign his Empire reached its zenith, though it also began its transition into Commonwealth. In Europe, World War and revolution were cataclysmic. Yet, of all the major European monarchies his was almost the only one to survive. His biographer noted:

> The reign of Queen Victoria can be regarded as a period of ever-widening stability; the reign of King Edward VII as an interlude of lavish prosperity and power; in the reign of King George, the foundations of stability were shaken, our power and prosperity diminished, and new forces were brought into operation which, within a quarter of a century, changed the structure of the world.[1]

Left: Portrait of King George V 1921, by Arthur Trevithin Nowell (1862-1940)

Reading histories of the period, and biographies of the King, is like experiencing two parallel worlds which, except for brief moments, neither meet nor coincide. Power lay with politicians; symbolic national focus and ceremonial were with the King. Often the former seemed little concerned with the latter (unless, of course, it suited them). The days when monarchs ruled lay decades in the past. Now they merely advised or warned, but had to accept that their advice or warnings were rarely heeded, and that, constitutionally, they had to submit to the government of the day.

But within national symbols came stamps. There, the King's views could safely be imposed without challenge. It was, after all, the *Royal* Mail. And as an avid stamp collector the King had strong, decided views and considerable experience and expertise. As a result, the stamps of the reign of King George V are a close and clear reflection of the man.

In his autobiography *Another Part of the Wood* Kenneth Clark tells this story of the King [2]:

> Next to his people, King George V loved postage stamps. Late in his life he asked me to come and see him. "You're a young man" he said "and I'm an old one – haven't long to live. I want you to make me a promise. Never allow them to make all those fancy issues of stamps like some ridiculous place like San Marino. We invented the postage stamp – all it had on was the sovereign's head and Postage and its value. That's all we want."

That this was not entirely accurate, at least in terms of his earlier views, will be seen later, but the gruff tones of conservatism ring true.

Despite that, the age was one of innovation, creativity and expansion. It was also one of poverty, doom-laden conflict, unemployment and despair. Yet inherent stability was reflected both in the monarchy and the person of the King, and through him in his stamps. For stamps are a microcosm of the age and place. Innovation, and creativity generally, found remarkably more fertile ground in other areas of G.P.O. activities.

Stamp Design & Production

In 1910, De La Rue lost the contract to create and print all British stamps, a contract they had held for 30 years (and another 25 years for all values above 2d). They had been making far too much money. Responsibilities were now divided. Dies and printing plates were to be made by the Royal Mint; the stamps would be printed by Harrison & Sons Ltd. But the Royal Mint had no experience of making dies or plates for stamps and Harrisons had never printed them. On the other hand Herbert Samuel, the Postmaster General, repeatedly demanded that all values be available for issue by Coronation Day, 22 June 1911. The stage was set for disaster, and disaster duly ensued.

The first so-called "Downey Head" stamps, designed by Bertram Mackennal were universally criticised and no amount of tinkering could make them attractive. "Make me look like a stuffed monkey" the King is supposed to have declared, but this to Evelyn de la Rue who was hardly a disinterested witness [3].

Later, with practice and new designs, matters improved.

Despite the King's reported views that postage stamps only required the monarch's head the reign also saw Britain's first pictorial designs and first commemorative stamps, though they were very few in number. At the monarch's instigation, Mackennal's patriotic high value design (Britain's first pictorial stamps featuring Britannia riding the waves) was engraved and printed in the same way as the Penny Black. The design has remained popular with stamp collectors ever since.

Below: Stamp-size artwork for the Colonial Silver Jubilee omnibus

Commemorative stamps first appeared in 1924, appropriately for the British Empire Exhibition at Wembley. The last stamps of the reign were for the King's Silver Jubilee in 1935. Other innovation came in the form of printing technique which changed from letterpress to photogravure, though the rich and subtle possibilities of the latter were never fully exploited during the King's lifetime.

In the Colonial Empire the King's views on stamps were rather more liberal. He was "warmly favourable"[4] to the idea of stamps from every dependency to mark his Silver Jubilee, albeit in a single design. This was to result in a remarkable 176 pictorial stamps from these (44) colonial territories alone (including Newfoundland, not yet incorporated into Canada). They needed the services of three experienced printers to produce them all in time. Interestingly, the League of Nations mandated territories of Palestine and Transjordan were not included because of real, or potential, divisive political difficulties. Neither was the Irish Free State. Dominions, and their dependencies or mandates, India and Southern Rhodesia all produced their own versions. It served to indicate the unity of Empire.

George V & the GPO

As far as British stamps were concerned, all stages of design and production were submitted to the King for his approval. This was because of his known interest and had never happened to any such extent before. Designs, dies, colours and proofs were all examined in detail. Comments were returned - but examples were kept, or later supplied, for the royal collection.

in his diary the King noted: "At 6.0 went with May and Mary to the new Post Office... ...we also visited the Telegraph Office, most interesting all we saw especially as it was Indian Mail night. It is a wonderful organisation."

Connections between monarch and Post Office were close in other areas of postal activity as well. As with many philatelists, King George was also interested in all aspects of the journey of a letter. One of his first official visits as King, even before his coronation, was to the new post office and sorting office of King Edward Building in the City of London. With Queen Mary (and Princess Mary) he spent two hours investigating technicalities and procedures there (on the evening of Friday, 24 March, 1911) and then crossed the road to the Central Telegraph Office, running out of time to see everything. This unprecedented visit caused great excitement in postal officials and staff.[5] How much excitement was felt by the Queen and Princess is not recorded. That night in his diary the King noted: "At 6.0 went with May and Mary to the new Post Office where Mr Samuel (the Post Master General) & other Officials showed us round & we also visited the Telegraph Office, most interesting all we saw especially as it was Indian Mail night. It is a wonderful organisation." [6]

Later, his son Albert with his wife, as Duke and Duchess of York, were to open the new Mount Pleasant sorting office in London in 1934, experiencing the cancelling and sorting of mail for themselves.

Above: Mail sorting and the telegraph service as seen by Barnett Freedman, 1934

The Scale & Range of the GPO

Some statistics will provide the scale of GPO operations. In 1912, having just taken over the National Telephone Company and its staff, the Post Office employed 238,811 people in the United Kingdom (including Ireland) with over 56,000 being (lowly paid) women[7]. At its height in 1913/14 virtually a quarter of a million people made up the vast workforce. This meant that until 1922 the Post Office was the largest employer in the country, only then being pushed into second place by the reorganised railways[8]. By 1936, even without the Irish Free State, the number had risen again to 245,851[9].

Post Office responsibilities encompassed inland and foreign postal services, obviously, but also telephone and telegraph services, the Post Office Savings Bank, postal and money orders, the sale of stamps for various licence fees (especially for dogs and the recent motor car) and the payment of old age pensions. The new National Health Insurance and Unemployment Insurance schemes were also implemented through the Post Office, a government department, with various revenue stamps.

The rapid spread of railways in the 19th century meant ever quicker delivery of mail inland. This was mirrored in the 1920s and '30s by the expansion of airmail services, bringing overseas destinations markedly closer. The world noticeably shrank.

Above: Airmail and the Post Office Underground Railway – Barnett Freedman, 1934

Some five and a half *billion* postal items were delivered in the United Kingdom in 1912, this to a total population of just over 45 million (i.e. on average, 70 letters per head). This compares to only 168 million letters in 1840 (7 per head) when postal reform first took effect. It was normal in central London for there to be 12 deliveries a day from 7 in the morning till after 8 at night. Famously, it is said, people could send postcards in the afternoon saying when they would be home in the evening. Even in Birmingham or Cardiff there were six daily deliveries. And around the country there were a remarkable 47,630 letter boxes, increasing in numbers year on year.[10] Clearly, it was a huge and highly labour-intensive business.

In War

The "Great War" (as it was almost immediately called) traumatised a continent and a generation, and still reverberates today, more than 90 years on. Postal activities, like much else, were dislocated by war. They also became more important. News from home, news from the front were vital to the morale of soldiers and families alike.

Initially, the existing Army Post Office despatched 300 officers and men with the British Expeditionary Force to establish communications. By the end of the war this had risen to nearly 4,000. At its maximum some 12 million letters and a million parcels a week were sent out.[11] All mail was censored but delivery was still rapid, transit normally being within about 2 days. The Home Depot for sorting these mails was situated in the middle of Regents Park in London. It became so large that it was claimed to be the largest wooden building in the world.[12]

At home, thousands of Post Office workers volunteered for the forces. This was particularly marked after October 1915 when the Post Office sent a letter to all male staff urging them to enlist. By the end of the war they amounted to 73,000. They had to be replaced and, as in other industries, their posts were often filled by women.

The Post Office even had its own battalion – the Post Office Rifles – which had existed in various forms since 1867. A month after war broke out so many men wanted to join that a second had to be created. They fought bravely at Ypres, the Somme and Passchendaele, winning 145 awards for gallantry and one Victoria Cross (to Sergeant Knight). Of 12,000 Post Office Riflemen, 1,800 were killed and over 4,500 wounded.

Apart from morale-boosting visits at home, King George V made several visits to the front in France, on one occasion being seriously injured by a fall from his horse. Worn and weary, to escape the burdens he "declared more than once in later years that [stamp collecting] helped him to preserve his health and reason in the nightmare of the War years."[13] There were frequent references in his diary to an hour snatched with Mr Bacon and his stamp collection, described as "brief forgetfulness" by his first biographer.[14]

Innovation & Creativity

Post war, over the next 15 to 20 years the Post Office expanded into such areas as broadcasting, and - under the aegis and inspiration of the aptly-named Sir Stephen Tallents - public relations, artistic educational posters and famous, ground-breaking documentary films, sometimes surrealistic, always experimental.

Endeavouring to cut ever-increasing labour costs, experiments were carried out in mechanising various aspects of the sorting of mail. A relatively few machines should be able to do the work of many men. After many years of failed trials, a successful, if foreign-built and somewhat limited, machine named the Transorma was finally introduced at Brighton in 1935.

In terms of transport, if the Victorian era was one of the development of steam, then that of George V was one of oil (or rather petroleum). The rapid spread of railways in the 19th century meant ever quicker delivery of mail inland. This was mirrored in the 1920s and '30s by the expansion of airmail services, bringing overseas destinations markedly closer. The world noticeably shrank. Even inland transport was motorised, despite it being the golden age of the locomotive. Inland airmail began in a systematic, if wind-swept, fashion in 1934.

To speed the mails within London a remarkable, underground railway was dug with electric, driverless trains on a narrow 2ft gauge. Connecting the West and East Ends of London, this linked sorting offices through 6½ miles of tunnels to main railway stations above ground and opened in December 1927.

Death & Legacy

The last service rendered to the King by the G.P.O. was the provision of telephones and cable for the press to be able to report his final illness and death at Sandringham, in rural Norfolk, in January 1936.

Communication was the G.P.O.'s business. Even so, emergency arrangements were required to lay miles of cables to provide additional telephone and teleprinter lines. Journalists filled the Feathers Inn at Dersingham and 13 phone lines were installed almost overnight, despite the snow drifts. Cable was even delivered by the Cheltenham Flyer from the West Country. The volume of postal, telegraph and telephone traffic at Sandringham and at Buckingham Palace surpassed all previous records.

Lord Dawson, the King's doctor, wrote the famous, simple bulletin "The King's life is moving peacefully towards its close."[15] It was broadcast on the BBC in hushed tones by Stuart Hibberd, having been flashed on G.P.O. lines from Sandringham to London. After his death towards midnight on 20 January, the Court Post Office dealt with over 200,000 words of condolence the following day.[16]

Above: Journalists at The Feathers Inn at Dersingham

Overshadowed by this, Rudyard Kipling, stout defender of Empire and imperialism, had died on Saturday, 18 January, almost unnoticed. "'The King has gone', they said, 'and taken his trumpeter with him.'"[17]

Philatelically, the reign of George V was often rather staid and old fashioned, though also pivotal, a major turning point full of interest. That of his successor was revolutionary. Edward VIII deliberately broke with the traditions of his father. In the stamp field he chose a modern, simple design based on the drawing of a 17-year old. His head was taken from a photograph, well suited to the production process of photogravure. The result created a furore in the press with arguments between, especially, Eric Gill and Edmund Dulac. After the abdication, George VI, equally deliberately, returned to the image of a solid, sculpted head, a model reminiscent of his father, surrounded by the "decoration" which Eric Gill so despised (yet which he created). Continuity of duty and tradition from father to son, rather than the "aberration" of the modernity of his brother. Yet again, stamps reflected, immediately, the people and the times.

1   **Nicholson, Harold** *King George the Fifth – His Life and Reign* 1952 pp 156-7

2   **Clark, Kenneth** *Another Part of the Wood: A Self-Portrait* 1974, pp 237-8

3   **Houseman, Lorna** *The house that Thomas built: The Story of De La Rue* 1968 p 146

4   CO 323/1274/5 Silver Jubilee

5   "Royal Visit to the Post Office" *St. Martin's-le-Grand* July 1911 pp 229-35

6   RA GVPRIV/GVD/1911 24 March

7   *Report of the Postmaster General* [to Parliament] *on the Post Office* 1912

8   **Daunton, Martin J**. *Royal Mail: The Post Office since 1840* 1985 p 193

9   POST 72/61 Headquarters Summary No. 21 [April 1936]

10   *PMG Report* and **Daunton** op cit

11   **Williamson, General F.H.** *Posts and Postal Services* c. 1931, POST 72/211

12   POST 56/5 Historical record of Army Postal Services (1914-1919)

13   **Gore, John** *King George V – A Personal Memoir* 1941 p 159 [1949 abridged edition]

14   ibid p 163

15   **Rose, Kenneth** *King George V* 1983 p 402

16   **Briant, F. Heathcote** "At Sandringham" *The Post Office Magazine* Vol. 3 No 3 March 1936 pp 75-80

17   Quoted in **Smith, F.W.F. (Lord Birkenhead)** *Rudyard Kipling* 1978 p 358

2
"THAT DAMNED FOOL"
THE KING AS STAMP COLLECTOR

After the Penny Black, one of the most famous stamps in the world is the so-called "Post Office Mauritius", or "Blue Mauritius". In fact, as in Britain with the Penny Red (the successor to the Penny Black), there are two stamps - one red, one blue. The latter from Mauritius is the more famous, however, and is even well-known to the general public in Germany – "*der blaue Mauritius*". It is this stamp which might best introduce King George V as a stamp collector, or philatelist.

Crude in appearance, the stamps were produced by a local engraver, Joseph Osmond Barnard, who clearly based them on the British Penny Red and Twopenny Blue. They were the first stamps from elsewhere in the Empire, and were put on sale on 21 September 1847, though they were not discovered by collectors for another two decades. Their philatelic name in English, "Post Office Mauritius", comes from the inscription on the stamps, wording which has given rise to controversy over the years, with various stories, or legends, about its origin. Was it a mistake or deliberate? Later versions had the wording changed to "Post Paid".

Some 500 of each of the original designs were printed but only 15 Penny stamps and 12 Twopenny stamps have survived. "Biographies" of each of them have even been prepared giving their individual histories over the years. Three Penny stamps exist on envelopes used by Lady Gomm, wife of the Governor, for cards of admission to a fancy dress ball at Government House. The stamps are thus exceptionally rare, and a great deal of Victorian romance surrounds their issue, use, discovery and subsequent history in famous collections. Collectors of classic stamps all wanted to obtain an example, particularly of the blue Twopenny (once described as "the acme of philatelic classics"[1]), thus attracting appropriately high prices to the few remaining.

Perhaps the finest example of an unused 2d stamp came up at an auction of Puttick and Simpson in London on 13 January 1904, and this story is told of its sale. Various versions of the tale have been recorded, but as it was retold many times over the years, more than one may be correct. That given here seems the most characteristic.

As reported in *The Times* the stamp had been found stuck to a page of a small album, a collection made by a schoolboy, James Bonar (now the adult vendor), in 1864. When recognised as a genuine rarity it was boiled to remove it from the page, though happily it remained undamaged by this severe treatment (not to be recommended for any others). It was the first Post Office Mauritius of either type to come on to the open market. Bidding started at £500 and stopped at £1,450, a world record price at the time. The sum was enormous then, though, in purely monetary terms, its equivalent a hundred years later (about £125,000) is not. The next day, news of this appeared in the press. The story goes that an equerry, Arthur Davidson, while phoning the Prince of Wales (as he then was) about another matter, asked "Did you happen to see in the newspapers that some damned

Arthur Davidson, while phoning the Prince of Wales (as he then was) about another matter, asked "Did you happen to see in the newspapers that some damned fool had given as much as £1,400 for one stamp?" Back came the reply "I was the damned fool!"

Left: the 2d unused "Post Office" Mauritius

In fact, *The Times* had reported: "Rumour states that it was purchased for the Prince of Wales's fine collection and that the underbidder was acting on behalf of the authorities of the German Postal Museum in Berlin."

fool had given as much as £1,400 for one stamp?" Back came the reply "I was the damned fool!"[2] According to Sir John Wilson (a later Keeper of the Royal Philatelic Collection) George, as King, would delight in telling this story "invariably accompanied by a very hearty laugh."[3]

In fact, *The Times* had reported: "Rumour states that it was purchased for the Prince of Wales's fine collection and that the underbidder was acting on behalf of the authorities of the German Postal Museum in Berlin."[4] This suggests that the tale may have been embroidered somewhat over the years. However, the more detailed story of how George acquired the stamp illustrates how avid a collector he was, and betrays many typical traits common to most collectors.

Above: John Tilleard, the King's philatelic adviser

When the discovery was first announced, the Prince of Wales offered Bonar £1,200 to withdraw the stamp from the auction and sell it to him privately. This was politely refused, as it had already been widely advertised and it would be a breach of faith to withdraw it. The Prince understood the reasons and wrote to John Tilleard, his philatelic adviser since 1893:

> I am still very anxious to have the stamp and now authorise you or an agent to bid for it at the auction up to *£1,550* inclusive. I am particularly keen to buy the stamp although it does seem a great deal of money to give for it.[5]

Later, he asked for the auction catalogue, and wrote to Tilleard yet again, requesting "another catalogue after the sale with the sums that each stamp fetched written against them which would be very interesting". He was still as keen as before about possessing the stamp. "I shall be waiting anxiously after the 13th to hear what you were able to do". Yet another letter suggested the purchase of other classic Mauritius and Newfoundland stamps in the same sale and concluded:

> You can send me a telegram here [York Cottage, Sandringham] on Wednesday if you have secured the 'Post Office'. Better say merely *'Stamp is yours'* & write later full particulars.[6]

The sum paid was clearly to be kept from inquisitive, not to mention recriminatory, eyes. In his diary, after hearing of his success the next day George wrote: "About the rarest stamp in the world & this is a record price."[7] On the same day he wrote to Tilleard, thanking him warmly.

> *£1450* is certainly a great deal of money to give for a stamp, & it is no doubt a record price, but in spite of that I am very pleased to have it in my collection as I believe it is such a fine copy; & I am also very glad that I have kept it in England & prevented it going to Germany. I am glad that the Public are not aware who the purchaser was, although the Times says that they *believe* it was bought for me.[8]

This prize stamp was added to a collection which was already considerable, both in extent and importance.

The Collecting Mind

To the outsider, a collector's passion can be seen as obsession. To those within the fold, the attitude is quite natural. Acquisition and ownership, and a drive to completion, underlie what is, often, a very private hobby. This can lead to small-minded conservatism. However, stamp collecting can also provide an insight into the world, past and present, and thus, like travel, can broaden the mind. Correspondingly, as travel spurs an interest in the locality visited, stamps can be a useful souvenir.

Although most collectors may choose to deny it, money does also come into the equation. Acquiring something "cheaply" satisfies a basic, human trait.

Early Collecting

How does it start? In the case of Prince George, he was travelling around the world with his elder brother as a midshipman on HMS *Bacchante,* when on 3 November 1881, in Osaka Bay, he noted in his diary: "Put some stamps in my book." He was 16. His uncle, Alfred, Duke of Edinburgh was a well-known collector and his tutor, the Reverend John Dalton, who accompanied the princes on their voyages, also seems to have collected stamps. George was a schoolboy recording his travels to rather exotic places. A few months before, he had visited the Government Printing Works in Sydney seeing postage stamps being printed. Later, he served as a lieutenant in the Mediterranean under his uncle and spent quite some time "arranging stamps with Uncle Alfred".[9]

His uncle was Honorary President of the Philatelic Society, London. As such he opened the London Philatelic Exhibition on 19 May 1890 announcing that Prince George was leaving that day in command of HMS *Thrush.* "He is also a stamp collector and I hope he will return with a goodly number of additions from North America and the West Indies".[10] He did, and seems to have spent a lot of his time in port there working on his growing collection.

With the unexpected death of his elder brother Eddy in 1892, his position changed. Now second in line to the throne he was created Duke of York, given rooms in St James's Palace and an annual parliamentary grant. His collecting interests became more serious and more pointed. John Tilleard became his philatelic adviser, and he was elected a member of the Philatelic Society, London. He also married his brother's fiancée, Princess May of Teck. Rare, classic stamps were among the wedding gifts.

His own stamps

When Queen Victoria died in 1901 Prince George became heir to the throne. In March of that year he sailed on the liner HMS *Ophir* for Australia to open its first parliament. The voyage and tour provided ample opportunities for the acquisition of various classic stamps of the Empire, including Ceylon and various Australian States. On his return, his father (now King) arranged for all new printings of stamps of his reign, including essays and proofs, be sent to him by the Inland Revenue. These included not only British stamps but those for the Colonies provided by the Crown Agents.

With these, and the more immediate prospect of him becoming King Emperor, his attitude to his stamp collection changed. In 1904 he gave a paper to the Philatelic Society of London

Above: Prince George's 1891 Stanley Gibbons stamp catalogue

To the outsider, a collector's passion can be seen as obsession. To those within the fold, the attitude is quite natural. Acquisition and ownership, and a drive to completion, underlie what is, often, a very private hobby.

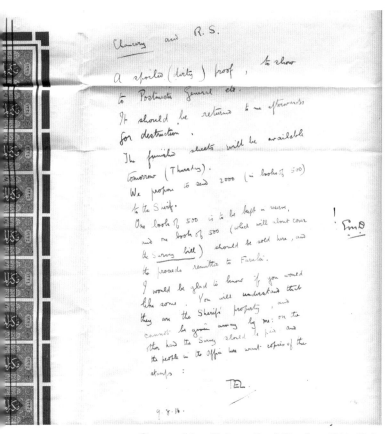

entitled "Notes on the Postal Issues of the United Kingdom during the present reign" (i.e. that of his father) and showed essays, proofs and stamps to illustrate it. In particular, he showed a half sheet of the 1d stamps arranged in tête-bêche format for the forthcoming stamp booklets, the first to be so produced. He also showed the "Post Office" Mauritius stamps which he had recently acquired, the story of which has already been retailed. Shortly afterwards, Prince George decided to dispose of the foreign stamps in his collection and specialise on Great Britain and what would shortly become *his* Empire (with the prospect of his own head appearing on their stamps).

However, he did subsequently collect some foreign stamps – those of the Hejaz created by T.E. Lawrence in Cairo, for example, and the precursors of those German territories occupied by imperial troops during World War I. An interesting example of the latter comes with documentation from the Australian military administrator of what had been German New Guinea. On 9 October 1914, Colonel William Holmes sent examples of captured German stamps for the King's collection.

Above: Proof sheet of the first stamps of the Hejaz annotated by T. E. Lawrence

> Apparently the larger proportion of the stock of Stamps was destroyed on our approach, but the balance I have turned to use by marking on same the Royal Initial letters "G.R.I.", and in some cases amending the values to meet the requirements of the moment.[11]

No mention was made of sending the overprinted versions, though they are in the collection with many of the great rarities.

From the moment he became King on the death of his father, late on 6 May 1910, George availed himself of the opportunity to extend his collection, in particular his specialised section of British stamps. As early as 25 May, less than three weeks after his accession, the Postmaster General, Herbert Samuel, noted:

> In the preparation of the new issues of Postage Stamps, the King wishes to have, for retention by His Majesty, two specimens of all proofs or reproductions of designs in all stages.[12]

Although there was an additional note to Frederick Atterbury at the Inland Revenue asking for two extra specimens of all productions, this does not seem to have been fully implemented, at least in terms of proofs; not, that is, while Tilleard was the King's philatelic adviser. However, Tilleard fell ill in 1913 and died on 22 September. The King mourned his death "not only as one of our leading philatelists, but as a personal friend".[13]

Edward Bacon, Curator

On 13 October 1913, the King's Assistant Private Secretary, Sir Frederick Ponsonby, wrote to Sir Matthew Nathan at the Inland Revenue.

Left: Edward Denny Bacon, King George's stamp curator

> The King desires me to tell you that he has appointed Mr E. D. Bacon to be Curator of his stamp collection.
>
> Any future issue of stamps should therefore be forwarded to E. D. Bacon Esq:, Buckingham Palace, and marked *not to be forwarded.*[14]

Unsaid, but perhaps implied, was that he should be assisted in any request. Bacon was certainly to take that attitude.

Edward Denny Bacon had begun collecting by 1880 as then, aged 20, he joined the Philatelic Society, London (later to become the Royal Philatelic Society, London) and was to serve that Society over many years in several capacities. He retired from the family business at 35 and proceeded to devote his life to stamps. His first task was to mount and describe the collection of his friend Thomas Tapling who had bequeathed his famous collection to the British Museum. Then, he advised both Henry Duveen and the Earl of Crawford, and created the catalogue of the latter's great philatelic library. This was completed in 1911 and so, when Tilleard died, Bacon was not only the obvious choice as his successor, but available.

Four other candidates had proposed themselves, including the Rev. Robert B. Earée of "Album Weeds" fame – even now one of the standard works on early forgeries. However, Earée was born in 1846 and so was already past retirement age.

Once appointed, Bacon proceeded to work in a room at Buckingham Palace two or three days a week for the next 25 years, mounting and describing the King's collection, and gathering more material.

By all accounts, Bacon was a modest man, unassuming and partly deaf. Nevertheless, he attacked his new task with gusto, and persistence. He was extremely acquisitive on behalf of the King. Immediately, and repeatedly, he wrote to all those involved in the production of British stamps - the Royal Mint, the Inland Revenue and the Post Office - for material for the King's collection, visiting each several times in turn and following this up with many requests, carefully written on Buckingham Palace notepaper in his own hand. In character, this seems more like the King, and so may have been at his instigation.

Above: Stamps of German New Guinea as captured by Australian Forces, and overprinted G.R.I. (errors – no stop and large S)

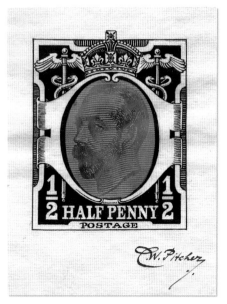

Above: Pitcher's artwork for the postcard stamp signed at the King's request

Just over a month after his appointment Bacon began his quest, responding to a sending of specimens of new stamps, as per the standing arrangement. He wrote in reply to Percy Thompson at the Stamping Department of the Inland Revenue[15]:

> Referring to my interview with you some short time since, I told His Majesty that you had promised to see if you could obtain specimens from the Mint or elsewhere of proofs or trial impressions from the dies and plates made for the various values of postage stamps issued during the last two years or so. I hope you may be successful in obtaining such specimens for His Majesty, who is greatly interested in all kinds of proof impressions.

> P.S. I should be glad if you could let me have any proof specimens you obtain, before December 14th, on which day I have an interview with His Majesty and could lay the specimens before him.

This was to be the first of many such letters carefully invoking the King's name and authority. He then visited the Royal Mint, and Edward Rigg made a note[16] of what occurred:

> Mr Bacon called on Tuesday the 6th inst. and again on the 20th inst & took away all original drawings & sketches we had together with a large number of trial prints, photographs & enlargements of stamp frames & effigies used in the early stages of the new Georgian stamps. Today I have sent him two of these Enlargements to complete a series and the series of all stages of the first penny stamps which I prepared in June 1911 to meet the criticisms passed by the P.M.G. on the Mint work a few days after the Coronation. The necessity for exhibiting this series did not however arise. I am confident that this series is unique.

More essays and drawings were to follow over the years and in November 1915 Rigg, at the Mint, volunteered (having found "in turning out a cupboard") [17]:

1. Early drawing by Mr Mackennal for the halfpenny and three-halfpence-dolphins.
2. Ditto of the first penny-lion couchant.
3. Ditto of the present frame of the twopence, &c.
4. Drawing by Mr Pitcher of the frame for the halfpenny postcard.

A few days later Bacon replied[18]:

> I had the honour of seeing the King today and I shewed him the original sketches of Mr Bertram Mackennal and Mr Pitcher that you gave me yesterday. His Majesty desired me to say how pleased he is to have obtained these sketches and he thanks you for sending them to him.

> His Majesty would much like Mr Pitcher to append his signature to his sketch and I return it to you for this to be done. Mr Mackennal's signature for his sketches, I will see him about myself.

> His Majesty was also pleased with the proofs of the dies of the Postage Due stamps. I told him that there are some other proofs to follow.

Pitcher's signature was duly obtained, as was Mackennal's, and other proofs did, indeed, follow. These were in addition to the blocks of four of issued stamps including the "Control" number in the margin, which indicated the year of printing, which were sent by the Post Office Stores Department.

Probably as a result of Bacon's discussions with the King an enquiry was made by Wigram of Sir Thomas Heath at the Treasury about the 1839 Treasury Competition entries. Some 2,600 suggestions had been made then about postal reform which resulted in the issuing of the world's first postage stamp, the Penny Black. Some had included potential designs.

> Should these papers and designs be forthcoming the King would be very grateful if you would let him have them for this collection together with the letters and description of the designs submitted by the Senders.[19]

Heath replied that, if preserved, they would be at the Public Record Office but he would make enquiries. Subsequently, he reported that the papers had been deposited in the Public Record Office in due course but "they cannot at the present moment be found there."[20] However, he feared that, if recovered, there was no doubt that these papers would have to be regarded as "technically official" in the charge of the Master of the Rolls, who had "no authority to surrender them."[21]

Despite this, there are a large number of Treasury Competition entries in the Royal Philatelic Collection, possibly acquired from the famous collection of the Earl of Crawford. Only a few remain in what is now The National Archives.

In the meantime, Bacon had turned his attention to the archive of registration, or imprimatur, sheets held by the Inland Revenue. In March 1914 he visited Somerset House twice and discussed the Victorian sheets with Seymour Bennett (Controller of Stamping). He then drew up a long list of those where two or more sheets had come from the same printing plate. The implication was that they were duplicate, when in fact they were all different.

> His Majesty desires a specimen cut from one of the corners of each of the "Imprimatur" sheets, showing the marginal plate number and the full margins of the sheet on two sides. In the case of India and the colonial sheets of Mauritius, etc., *if* the plate number is over the second stamp from the corner, it will be best to cut off a pair, so as to get the full margin of the sheet on two sides.[22]

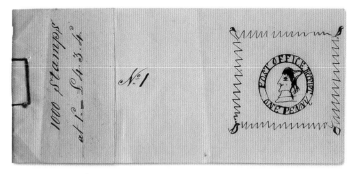

Above: 1839 Treasury Competition entry by John Little, suggesting a stamp booklet

A large package of these was eventually sent at the beginning of May; though yet more requests were to follow, for Telegraph stamps and examples of every die used on embossed postal stationery. There then seems to have been a pause, possibly while all this material was dealt with.

The Royal Household were annoyed at Bacon's direct approach to Government departments, and Sir Frederick Ponsonby (the senior of the two Assistant Private Secretaries to the King) apparently spoke to Bacon about this.[23] So, the next approach in November 1915 was

Right: G. Evelyn Murray, Secretary to the Post Office, 1914-34

through Clive Wigram, the other Assistant Private Secretary, who wrote to the Secretary of the Post Office, G.E.P. Murray:[24]

> Some years ago the Board of Inland Revenue at Somerset House sent the King specimens cut from the series of registration sheets of Postage Stamps, which are now at the General Post Office.
>
> Since that period, sheets of a number of other stamps have been registered, and His Majesty hopes that you will let him have a pair cut from one of the corners, with full margins left on both sides, of each of these sheets, particulars of which I enclose.

The King would also like to be furnished with the dates of registration in each instance, and for the future to have a similar pair sent to him of each sheet registered, with the date, so that his collection may be kept up to date.

This set off a storm within the Post Office, who had, in the meantime, taken over responsibility for stamp production from the Inland Revenue, and thus, also, the care of the collection of past registration sheets. Attitudes in response to such requests were quite different from the more relaxed view taken before.

F. H. Nichols, the officer in immediate charge of stamp records, wrote a stinging (if internal) memo. He pointed out that the Inland Revenue had given the King, when Duke of York, specimens cut from registration sheets up to 1898, but that later ones had not been cut. No mention was made of those Victorian examples obtained more recently by Bacon. He then went on[25]:

> I am strongly of opinion (indeed I do not think the point admits of argument) that the official collection of registration sheets, which is the one and only authentic official record of British Postage stamps, ought to consist of complete sheets of stamps and not of more or less large fragments of sheets (as it unfortunately does for the whole of Queen Victoria's reign). This view is apparently accepted by the King, for in a letter dated 3 March 1914 asking for additional specimens from certain sheets of old stamps, Major Wigram says "His Majesty recognizes that if the sheets had never been cut it would be best to keep them entire, but as several specimens have been detached at various periods he thinks that one more from each sheet can make little or no difference."

However, there was a duplicate collection of registration sheets in the Record Room which was already marked for destruction. Nichols saw no great objection to stamps being cut from these. As regards the future, "if the King insists on specimens from Registration sheets, I think we had better revert to the practice of having a second unperforated Registration sheet on each occasion."[26] This practice of having a second registration sheet had terminated when the Post Office took over the stamp work from the Inland Revenue the previous year.

Herbert Samuel, once again Postmaster General, concurred:[27]

> The mutilation of the standard Registration sheets seems to me to be wholly indefensible. I am at a loss to understand how the Board of Inland Revenue can have permitted it. The books – as they stand – seem to me to be discreditable to that Dept.
>
> I see no objection to registering – on each occasion – a special sheet for His Majesty. I think it is quite a proper thing to do, if Mr Bacon will give us an undertaking that the sheets shall in all cases be kept entire, & shall not leave the King's possession.

As a result Murray replied to Wigram with this diplomatic suggestion[28].

> With reference to your letter of the 17th instant, the registration sheets for all stamps issued in the latter or in the present reign are at present complete and I think it would be a mistake to mar their completeness by detaching individual stamps.

He understood this view commended itself to the King, and quoted Wigram's letter of March 1914. Murray then went on to mention the existing duplicate registration sheets which could be used to provide the imprimaturs required, and suggested that an extra sheet could be provided again in future.

> It is of course important that these stamps should not find their way into the hands of philatelists and I have no doubt that you would make arrangements that any specimens which are not required for His Majesty's purpose would be duly destroyed.[29]

Wigram relayed this to the King who, after thanking the Post Office for all their trouble, suggested that Bacon examine the "surplus" sheets. Subsequently, Wigram wrote officially to Murray agreeing with the proposal for an extra registration sheet in future.[30]

> I explained to the King the gist of our conversation of yesterday. His Majesty quite understands your wish to preserve intact for the Post Office as many individual Registration Sheets as possible, even though, in the past, individual sheets have been mutilated, thereby rendering imperfect a complete collection of sheets. In fact, I told His Majesty that you considered it a slur that the Post Office could not now boast of a complete record of sheets.

As a result of Bacon's examination of the duplicate sheets (of the reign of King Edward VII and his own) the King asked for a corner block of four from each of these, but from those for stamp booklets he preferred a block of four or eight from the centre of the top two rows, to show the tête-bêche printing layout. Wigram then continued:

> With regard to the future, the King desires me to thank you for your suggestion to print a duplicate sheet, which proposal His Majesty accepts with pleasure. As only corner blocks of four Stamps are required for the King's Collection, perhaps you would be good enough to destroy the remainder of the sheets without their leaving the control of the Post Office.[31]

Murray subsequently instructed the Inland Revenue to provide a duplicate registration sheet on each occasion.

A note by Walter Gates, an Assistant Secretary, summed up Post Office irritation at Bacon's activities:[32]

This morning I went to see Mr Murray, the Secretary of the General Post Office, fearing that friction was beginning to arise between Mr Bacon and the Post Office Secretariat, which might lead to some unpleasantness if not smoothed down.

Mr Bacon, being an enthusiastic Philatelist, appeared to be rather grasping as regards some of his demands for stamps.

1919: Proof taken at the Royal Mint after the Die had been retouched. The figures "1" are thicker, etc.

Dies 34, 35.

When I look at these and other papers I cannot help deprecating the considerable amount of trouble which is or has been given to the I.R. and the P.O. by requests which are often only made from what one might term the curiosity-hunting point of view. And I would most respectfully suggest that, if it were possible to give a hint in the proper quarter, requests of this kind might be curtailed for the future.

This may well have been effective. Wigram called and had an interview with Murray, who was "most affable", but he then noted back at the Palace in a memorandum headed "Secret":[33]

George, as Prince and King, kept a daily diary, generally dry and to the point. Meteorological notes begin each day, as befits a former sailor. And there are frequent references, when at Buckingham Palace, to working on his stamp collection, two or three times a week when possible.

Above: Examples of embossed postal stationery dies as proofed, and mounted by Bacon

This morning I went to see Mr Murray, the Secretary of the General Post Office, fearing that friction was beginning to arise between Mr Bacon and the Post Office Secretariat, which might lead to some unpleasantness if not smoothed down.

Mr Bacon, being an enthusiastic Philatelist, appeared to be rather grasping as regards some of his demands for stamps.

A year later, Bacon again wrote direct to Murray, this time clearly at the King's instigation, in connection with a Sinn Fein label, apparently cancelled in the Dublin G.P.O. during the Easter rebellion in 1916. A delay in reply caused Bacon to write again, in umbrage, at this apparent rudeness. This brought the wrath of the Royal Household down on him. Wigram had to explain to the King, to whom Bacon had complained, that he "had no business to write direct to Mr Murray in His Majesty's name and that Sir Frederick Ponsonby had already come to an agreement with Mr Bacon on this point."[34] Bacon was duly contrite, claiming he had misunderstood what the arrangement was. No further correspondence is filed for three years.

However, after the war, Bacon resumed his requests direct to the Royal Mint. This prompted questions as to whether the Post Office had been supplying the same items as the Mint, and so, on 27 August 1919, the Post Office wrote to the Royal Mint to regularise the situation.[35]

The Postmaster General understands that it is the practice of the Royal Mint to supply the Curator of His Majesty's Stamp Collection with

(1) A proof impression in black of each new die, and of any change in the die, prepared for the adhesive postage and 'postage and 'postage due' stamps.

(2) A proof impression in black of each new die, and of any change in the die, made for postcards, letter-cards and wrappers, and of the first embossed die of each value made for stamping envelopes.

Specimens of the colour essays and of the stamps as finally issued are supplied to the Curator by the Post Office, and it has been suggested that it would be convenient if all proofs and specimens for the King's collection were to reach the Curator through one channel.

If you see no objection perhaps you will be so good as to arrange for proofs hitherto supplied by the Royal Mint, including any now ready for transmission, to be forwarded to this Office for transmission by the Postmaster General to the Curator.

This practice was then put into place – a practice which continues to the present day, altered, as appropriate, for different printing processes and printers.

Refuge

When his main biographers said anything at all about George and his stamp collection it tended to be rather disparaging. On one thing, however, they were united. It was, for him, a refuge, what one described as "the solace of stamp album and shotgun".[36]

George, as Prince and King, kept a daily diary, generally dry and to the point. Meteorological notes begin each day, as befits a former sailor. And there are frequent references, when at Buckingham Palace, to working on his stamp collection, two or three times a week when possible. There are particular notes coinciding with times of high excitement or stress. In 1914, on 22 June for example, he detailed, in great spirits, the new arrangements he had experienced Trooping the Colour that morning ("I never saw it better done") and then "Spent all the afternoon with Bacon choosing more stamps...."[37]

Shortly afterwards, on Sunday 28 June:

> A nice hot day 77° in the shade. ....We got the sad news that the poor Archduke Franz Ferdinand & his wife the Duchess of Hohenberg were assassinated this morning at Sarajevo by a Servian with a revolver - they were in a motor car, it will be a terrible shock to the dear old Emperor & is most regrettable & sad. We dined alone. Marked my new stamp catalogue. Bed at 11.30.[38]

The next day ("Very hot, 80° in the shade"), defying protocol, he went to the Austrian Embassy to express his sympathy, and again returned to his stamps.[39] Throughout the terrible War which ensued, when in London, he records that he often worked at his stamps with Bacon "before & after luncheon."[40] He believed that this retreat helped him to preserve his health and reason in the nightmare of the War years – "the most effective means of brief forgetfulness".[41]

Below: Some of George V's 328 three-quarter morocco red leather stamp albums

Extent

At the time of his death, in January 1936, King George's stamp collection comprised some 328 albums containing almost a quarter of a million stamps, all immaculately bound in three-quarter morocco red leather, and described by Bacon in his small, neat hand.

It had become a deliberate, and vast, record of the stamps of the British Empire and undoubtedly the greatest such collection in existence.

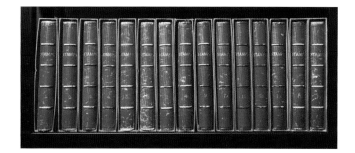

In 1932, an article appeared in *John Bull* about the King's stamp collection, emphasising its imperial nature.[42] Its deference leads the writer into error:

Tremendously enthusiastic as the King is about his collection, there is not one specimen in it that he has not bought with cash or received as a present from a member of his family who has bought it in the ordinary way. He is very strict about that.

From the foregoing, it can be seen that this is not entirely true, though one could regard the King as being clearly entitled to be supplied, as of right, with material bearing his own effigy.

1   **Williams, L.N. & M**. *Stamps of Fame,* 1949, p.22
2   quoted in: **Courtney, N.** *The Queen's Stamps: The Authorised History of the Royal Philatelic Collection* 2004, pp 85-6
3   **Wilson, Sir J.** *The Royal Philatelic Collection* 1952, p.42
4   *The Times* 14 January 1904
5   Tilleard correspondence book, Royal Philatelic Collection
6   ibid
7   RA GV/PRIV/GVD/1904: 14 January
8   Tilleard correspondence op cit
9   **Courtney** op cit, pp.32-3
10   ibid p.35
11   Royal Philatelic Collection
12   POST 33/4595 Arrangement for supply of new issues for HM the King.
13   **Wilson** op cit p.53
14   POST 33/4595
15   POST 33/4595 op cit 24 November 1913
16   MINT 20/545
17   MINT 20/545, 16 November 1915
18   MINT 20/545, 24 November 1915
19   RA PS/PSO/GV/PS/STAMPS/GV/18364/1, 4 March 1914
20   RA PS/PSO/GV/PS/STAMPS/GV/18364/3, 30 March 1914
21   ibid
22   IR 80/8 Postage stamps: colour, design, 11 March 1914
23   Noted in Wigram's later memorandum of 14 December 1915
24   POST 33/4595 17 November 1915
25   POST 33/4595 23 November 1915
26   ibid
27   POST 33/4595 27 November 1915
28   POST 33/4595 30 November 1915
29   ibid
30   POST 33/4595 15 December 1915
31   ibid
32   POST 33/4595 26 November 1915
33   RA PS/PSO/GV/C/O/844/1 14 December 1915
34   RA PS/PSO/GV/C/O/844/3 29 December 1916
35   MINT 20/545. Signed W. G. Gates
36   **Rose, Kenneth** *King George V* 1983 p163
37   RA GV/PRIV/GVD/1914 22 June
38   ibid 28 June
39   ibid 29 June
40   ibid 1915 22 January – a typical example
41   **Gore, John** *King George V A Personal Memoir* 1949 edition p163
42   "The King's Empire History - in Stamps" *John Bull* 26 November 1932.

3
ALL CHANGE!
MONARCH, PRINTERS, P.M.G. ET AL.

1910 was a year of change, not only in the person of the monarch but also for the Post Office and, in particular, the production of stamps.

For 30 years, the family firm of De La Rue Limited had had a virtual monopoly in the contract to print all British postage stamps and most postal stationery. They had exploited this to the full, to such an extent that an investigation discovered that from 1901 payments had run at almost £100,000 per year, or £1 million for the 10-year contract.

For 30 years, the family firm of De La Rue Limited had had a virtual monopoly in the contract to print all British postage stamps and most postal stationery. They had exploited this to the full...

In the history of De La Rue the author castigates the attitude of the then management as "short-sighted" and "pathetic".

> They made no special efforts to maintain their contracts. In spite of decreased manufacturing costs they continued to put in the same prices, thereby making colossal profits. They behaved as if the contracts were a foregone conclusion, and theirs by right.[1]

However, their latest 10-year contract was up for renewal on 31 December that year.

A Committee Appointed

Given the magnitude of the contract, there was an understandable suspicion in Government circles that money might be saved. An enquiry was set up. Officially, it was entitled the "Inter-Departmental Committee on Inland Revenue Contracts". In reality, it was an enquiry into De La Rue's contract. Appointed in January 1910, it was composed of high-ranking officials from the Treasury, the Post Office and the Inland Revenue. Those from the Inland Revenue were Frederick Atterbury, Secretary and Controller of Stamps, and Seymour Bennett, Inspector of Stamping, both intimately concerned with the production of postage stamps. The Committee took evidence from similar officials and swiftly produced a report.

The remit was simple: whether the present prices were reasonable; and if not, what prices ought to be obtainable. And how such prices could best be obtained. The answer to the first question was equally simple: "in the case of the adhesive stamps Messrs De La Rue's prices are extravagantly high".[2] Over 90% of adhesive stamps produced were ½d and 1d postage and revenue stamps, an annual total of nearly 5,000,000,000 stamps. These were supplied at a cost of 2.8d per thousand, with other, lesser used denominations at proportionately higher prices - up to 2s per thousand for the 1s stamp. Watermarked paper was already supplied, so these charges were only for the gumming and milling of that paper, and the printing and perforation of the stamps.

From evidence presented, the Committee concluded that actual cost of production of the ½d and 1d stamps was only 0.8d per thousand. Even allowing for a substantial margin of profit they estimated that the price charged should not be above 1.2d per thousand. In comparison to the 2.8d per thousand actually charged this would represent a saving of over £30,000 per annum, more than 30% of the bill for everything. With regard to higher denominations the sums paid were less considerable but "the relatively higher prices

De La Rue's monopoly
had largely been
based on their supply
of doubly fugitive ink,
where the stamp was
sensitive to attempted
fraudulent cleaning of
both manuscript and
postal cancellation
inks. This had been
regarded as essential,
as stamps were used
for both postal and
revenue purposes.

charged involve a rate of profit scarcely less extravagant."[3] For postal stationery (postcards, letter cards, stamped envelopes and newspaper wrappers) similar savings could be made.

However, to obtain these more realistic prices, there would have to be "free and effective competition", or State manufacture. Any element of monopoly would negate this.

De La Rue's monopoly had largely been based on their supply of doubly fugitive ink, where the stamp was sensitive to attempted fraudulent cleaning of both manuscript and postal cancellation inks. This had been regarded as essential, as stamps were used for both postal and revenue purposes. No other manufacturer could supply these inks. However, the requirement for such specialist inks (only green or purple being available) had been questioned over the years. By 1910 most denominations, and particularly those in greatest use, the ½d and 1d, were printed in singly fugitive inks where only postal cancellations were important. These inks were widely available and not restricted to green and purple. The Committee were satisfied that "any surface-printing ink combined with high-class workmanship would prove sufficiently effective against efforts to remove the Post Office cancellation."[4] So the basis of De La Rue's monopoly was no longer valid.

Apart from the provision of dies and plates, the manufacture of singly-fugitive adhesive stamps involved only gumming, printing and perforating,

> "nothing above the level of high-class commercial work; and it presents no difficulties to any well-equipped firm of experience; while the postal stationery comprises only items of common manufacture. We see no reason, therefore, why the range of possible competition both for singly-fugitive stamps and postal stationery should not be wide, and effective to reduce prices to a level affording a fair trade profit over and above the cost of production."[5]

The Committee then considered three alternatives: private negotiation with De La Rue, the present contractors, open or limited competition, and State manufacture.

Private negotiation was not recommended. Competition was always preferable if practicable. There was no argument against the principle of State manufacture and the Royal Mint were in future to produce impressed stamp dies for the Inland Revenue. They could also produce postage stamp dies and printing plates. It was recognised that this was highly specialised work and involved "processes with which the printing trade is not familiar". If it were to be included in the competitive tender it would narrow the field of competition with "unfortunate results in the matter of prices".[6]

As far as those few items were concerned which required doubly-fugitive ink they could be produced by the Stamping Department of the Inland Revenue (under Bennett at Somerset House). That department already produced larger quantities of impressed postal stationery than had outside contractors.

> "We think it extremely undesirable that it should be made possible for any future contractor to occupy the position which Messrs De La Rue have hitherto held in regard to these stamps."[7]

Registered envelopes had always been manufactured by McCorquodale's and their prices were also found to be excessive, though not by so much. It was recommended that they be included in a separate tender for all stamped postal stationery. The contract with De La Rue was to be terminated ("determined") on 31 December when it was due for renewal, as was that of McCorquodale's.

Strangely, it was on 6 May, the day of King George's accession, that the letter was sent by the Inland Revenue to De La Rue informing them that their contract was to end. They were asked if they wanted to tender for the new separated contracts. Their reply, a few days later, arrogantly pointed out a number of mistakes in the tender forms, especially in the detail of the postal stationery, which the Inland Revenue were then obliged to correct. It cannot have been conducive to a sympathetic reception.

Perhaps still unsuspecting, within three weeks of the death of Edward VII, De La Rue submitted designs for stamps for the new monarch which the Post Office might like to make use of. In a rather self-satisfied manner they added -

> You will notice that in these designs the crowns are in the corners of the stamps, as His Majesty informed our Chairman some years ago that he did not like the crown suspended over the head.[8]

De La Rue's tender was submitted on 10 June, but the firm dictated terms. Prices quoted were dependent upon all work being entrusted to them, especially that of printing the 1d and ½d adhesive stamps. The latter, of course, constituted the vast majority of the contract, and that from which De La Rue had made such great profits in the past. Prices quoted for these included "free of charge" the printing plates required, from dies supplied.

> We feel convinced that plates made by the Mint would cause dislocation of the work, entailing an interruption of the printing for a full day or more, whenever a plate should become defective and require to be taken by one of your officers to the Mint for repair.[9]

On 12 July a terse note from the Inland Revenue announced the bombshell.

> I am directed by the Board of Inland Revenue to express their regret that they are unable to accept the Tender which you have been so good as to furnish for the supply of Adhesive Stamps to His Majesty's Government.[10]

That was all. After 30 years the news devastated the De La Rue family "bursting from a sky which to them had seemed eternally blue."[11] The Chairman, Sir Thomas Andros de la Rue died a few months later, apparently not having recovered from the shock.

The 2d "Tyrian Plum"
The most famous philatelic casualty of the death of King Edward VII was the so-called "Tyrian Plum", the name coming from that of the colour in which the new 2d stamp was printed. It was part of a gradual movement away from bi-coloured designs in doubly fugitive ink where this was no longer considered necessary.

Cost was, of course, the determining factor. To produce a die and plate (480-set) for a single coloured stamp cost £135; for a bi-coloured stamp £185.[12] The cost of the special ink and printing was also correspondingly higher for the two colours. As a result it was proposed to change the colours of the 1½d, 2d and 4d stamps, but not their design. A new denomination of 7d was also required. All were to be in single colours in singly-fugitive ink.[13] In all, a saving of about £200 a month was expected, though this was later estimated at £3,825 a year. The 4d and 7d values were issued, in orange and grey respectively; the 1½d was deferred for a choice of colour, and never appeared.

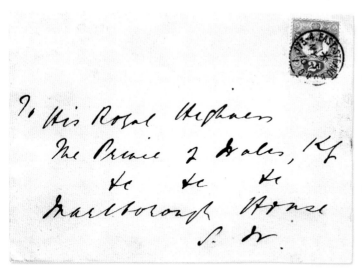

As far as the 2d denomination is concerned De La Rue, whose artists also created all the designs for the postage stamps they printed, suggested that a new version be adopted as "the design of the existing 2d stamp is hardly suitable for reproduction in one colour only".[14] Three designs were submitted by them on 19 August 1909, of which the Postmaster General chose No. 3. A series of 17 colour trials were then produced of the new 2d.[15] That preferred by De La Rue, the "Tyrian Plum", was approved.

Some 197,035 sheets of 240 stamps were now printed by De La Rue and delivered in the last week in April 1910, at the same time as the new 7d. The latter was announced as being ready for issue to the public in a Post Office circular of 3 May "but as there still remains a sufficient stock of the old [2d] bi-colour stamps to provide for the demands of the next four or five weeks, it is not proposed to commence the issue of the new Stamps until after the expiration of that time."[16] However, on 18 May De La Rue received a letter from the Inland Revenue.[17]

The most famous philatelic casualty of the death of King Edward VII was the so-called "Tyrian Plum", the name coming from that of the colour in which the new 2d stamp was printed.

Above The only known used example of the Tyrian Plum sent by Frederick Atterbury to George as Prince of Wales

I have to inform you that the Postmaster General has decided that, in view of the decease of His late Majesty, King Edward VII, the proposed new 1½d and 2d single colour Postage Stamps, bearing the portrait of King Edward, shall not be issued, and that the introduction of the new Stamps is to be deferred until the new series of stamps, bearing the portrait of King George, can be got ready.

The 2d Stamps, which have already been printed, will therefore be destroyed, and no further steps should be taken in the preparation of the die and plate of the new 1½d Stamps.

The cost of this destruction has been estimated at £650. Nevertheless, some few survived, and later "escaped", and are now highly sought after. It has been claimed that these came from examples given to the Postmaster General when those sent to the Universal Postal Union in Bern (for distribution to postal administrations world-wide) were returned and otherwise later destroyed. In official records are the imperforate registration sheet and one perforated sheet, with one stamp removed from the bottom right hand corner.

Only one example was ever used. It was addressed to the Prince of Wales, but arrived the day he became King George V. Cancelled on 5 May with an East Strand London W.C. branch office postmark, the office nearest to Somerset House, the address is clearly in the handwriting of Frederick Atterbury, Secretary and Controller of Stamps at the Inland Revenue. The cover is now in the Royal Philatelic Collection.

New Postmaster General

At the time of the death of Edward VII, the new Postmaster General in Asquith's Liberal government was Herbert Samuel. Many of the difficulties encountered in the creation of the new stamps for George V were because of his repeated insistence on all of them being issued by Coronation Day. In his autobiography he makes no mention of the saga, merely stating:

> The office of Postmaster-General is not one of the more onerous in the Government. The volume of work in the Department is of course enormous; but it is almost all of a routine or technical character, conducted by a highly skilled specialist staff. The Secretary of the Post Office, its permanent head, stands in somewhat the same relation to the Postmaster-General as the general manager of an industrial undertaking to the chairman of the company.[18]

If so, then he was a most demanding and insistent chairman, for (apart from other matters) he was to involve himself intimately, and constantly, with all aspects of the design, colour and production of the new stamps.

Samuel was a rather radical, Liberal politician. Born in 1870 in Liverpool, he came from an orthodox Jewish family. His uncle was the private banker and M.P. Samuel Montagu (the name being reversed by the latter's parents because "there were so many Samuels in Liverpool."[19]) As a young man Herbert Samuel became interested in politics and was appalled by the poverty revealed when canvassing in Whitechapel in London's docklands. Despite coming from a wealthy family, this set his political direction for life. In 1902 he was elected as an M.P. and was appointed to the Home Office four years later, becoming Chancellor of the Duchy of Lancaster, and member of the Cabinet, in 1909. This was the time of the great constitutional struggle with the House of Lords ("Mr Balfour's Poodle"[20]). He was one of those able ministers in the Asquith government described later by Roy Jenkins as of "outstanding intellectual ability".[21]

Samuel took up his post on 19 February, 1910. He was to remain as Postmaster General until February 1914. He then returned in May 1915 for a few months until January 1916. Later, after the War, he was to be the first High Commissioner for Palestine, and thereafter was called upon to provide a report on the British coal industry. It was the lack of implementation of this which was to lead to the General Strike.

There was also a new Secretary to the Post Office, Sir Matthew Nathan, who was established in his post on 17 January 1910. Nathan's father had been a partner in De La Rue for many years.[22] The son had been a soldier in the Royal Engineers and then Governor of Hong Kong and Natal. He was now 48.[23] Later, in July 1911, he was to become Chairman of the Board of Inland Revenue.

Transition

The Postmaster General decided that the new issues of King George V stamps and stamped postal stationery should

Left: The Postmaster General in Asquith's Liberal government was Herbert Samuel

Left: Sir Matthew Nathan, Secretary to the Post Office, 1910-11

It is clear why Harrisons were chosen. On stamps alone the present payment was £63,000 a year as against some £18,000 at the new rates, an estimated saving of £45,000.

commence about 1 March, 1911, and be completed by the date of the coronation in June. Arrangements were made to regulate stocks of King Edward VII issues accordingly. On hand, there was a standard six months' supply of ½d and 1d stamps, and from six to twelve months' supply of higher values. Measures were now taken to reduce any interim orders to De La Rue so that stocks of most values of the Edward VII versions might be exhausted by April or May 1911. De La Rue were delivering about 800,000 sheets monthly of both the ½d and 1d rates. Supplies were now to approximate 420,000 sheets of ½d and 600,000 sheets of 1d stamps for the rest of the period of the contract.[24] Presciently, as far back as the end of May, 1910 the Secretary to the Post Office, noted that "if Messrs De La Rue do not secure the contract, the risk attending a reduction of the reserve stock would be greater, and the difficulty of securing the early introduction of the new stamps will be increased."[25]

However, delay followed delay in the design and production of the new stamps, as will be described in the next chapter. Something had to be done to provide supplies of Edward VII stamps and stationery for the interim. By December 1910 matters had become critical. From 1 January next the new contractors would also have nothing to do and they intimated that they were virtually ready to commence printing. The answer was clear – the new contractors should print from the old De La Rue plates.

Initially, this was for the ½d and 1d denominations urgently required. Later, because of continuing delay and controversy over the new stamps, it was to be extended to other denominations. De La Rue had ceased printing the Edward VII stamps by 11 January 1911 and dies, plates and electros were returned to Somerset House for safe-keeping or onward transmission to the new contractors.

Tenders

Those firms asked to tender for the new stamp contract were: De La Rue, Harrison & Sons, James Truscott & Son, Waterlow Brothers & Layton and Waterlow & Sons (a separate firm). Prices of course varied with De La Rue being by far the most expensive for all items, even though these were lower than their current charges. The lowest, at least for the most important items, were supplied by Harrison & Sons but Waterlow Brothers & Layton also had some competitive quotes. Some comparisons may be instructive. Prices are in each case for a ream of 500 issue sheets:

	De La Rue current contract	De La Rue new tender	Harrison & Sons tender
½d	28s 0d	19s 0d	7s 9d
1d	28s 0d	19s 0d	8s 6d
1½d	117s 6d	27s 6d	10s 0d
4d	35s 0d	25s 0d	9s 11d
9d	207s 6d	84s 0d	12s 0d
1/-	132s 6d	80s 0d	13s 0d

It is clear why Harrisons were chosen. On stamps alone the present payment was £63,000 a year as against some £18,000 at the new rates, an estimated saving of £45,000. For stamped stationery the figures were less dramatic, £33,000 at present, £22,000 at the new rates, a saving of £11,000.

Harrison & Sons Ltd.

Harrison & Sons Ltd of St. Martin's Lane in London, the new contractors for adhesive stamps, were long-established Government printers. They had never printed postage stamps before, though it was later claimed in a parliamentary answer that they had "previously manufactured stamps for one of the small Colonies."[26] No trace of this has ever been found, and is contradicted elsewhere. In their tender they undertook to do the work at St Martin's Lane "or in premises elsewhere specially constructed for the purpose which possibly could be situated to suit the wishes of the Commissioners".[27] Their existing premises could not cope with the huge new contract and the task faced was described in their almost contemporary history as "well-nigh appalling".

> A suitable site had to be found, a large factory built or adapted and equipped with machinery the best and most powerful of its class, all of which had to be specially made, and some of which had to be designed, experimented upon, and perfected. A staff of some hundreds of workpeople had to be organized and trained to their duties, and the whole effectively dovetailed together as a going concern within a period of six months.[28]

A disused factory was found at Hayes and re-built. Machinery was purchased after what was described as a "rapid tour" of European capitals to see how stamps were manufactured. Perforating machinery was purchased from Grovers. On 9 December 1910 Harrisons were able to say:

> Referring to the suggestion that we received to-day that it may be necessary that we commence printing early in the New Year from the plates of the present Stamps, we shall be quite ready to make a start with these on the 1st January as far as the gumming and printing is concerned but it will be necessary to have special Punch Boxes made for the Perforators as we understand from Mr Bennett that the size of new Stamp is slightly altered. The Makers require three weeks from date of order to deliver the first of these and therefore the order must be placed at once in order to secure delivery early in January.[29]

The cost of the extra punch box was £150 which they asked to be reimbursed. This was agreed and meant that the initial printings by Harrisons of the low values was the same perforation as before – perf. 14. However, taking the story forward a little, the Inland Revenue had been experimenting with perforations and as a result recommended that one pin hole be added to the base line making the perforation now 15 x 14.[30] This was accepted on 5 April and later printings by Harrisons, both of the ½d and 1d and other values, were perforated by this new punch box.

Stock on hand of the basic ½d and 1d stamps was meanwhile getting lower and difficulties were encountered commissioning the perforating machinery. Harrisons had been unable to make proper preliminary trials before it was necessary to work it at full pressure. As a result they were instructed on 11 March, 1911 to institute a night shift at their factory at Hayes.

> [The Board of Inland Revenue] are aware that this step will increase the cost of production to your firm of the supplies manufactured under these conditions; but in view of the fact that a position of such urgency has arisen mainly out of delays and changes of policy for which you are in no way responsible, they have consented, subject to the approval of the Treasury, to reimburse you to the extent of the difference

between the cost of production under normal working conditions, and that resulting from the exceptional measures which they desire you to take.[31]

By the end of April reserve stocks were only five weeks. To raise it to the minimum three months' supply would require all-night work at Hayes for at least three months increasing output by 50%. For this Harrisons were to be paid a supplementary price.

In April it also became clear that supplementary stocks of nearly all other values of Edward VII stamps also needed to be obtained. However, several of these were either printed in doubly-fugitive ink or were bi-coloured, or both. Harrisons could not print bi-coloured stamps at Hayes and could not print in doubly-fugitive ink at all. So it was decided to have the bi-coloured stamps printed by the Inland Revenue at Somerset House, but in singly-fugitive ink. This was the "State manufacture" envisaged by the report into De La Rue's contract. The only reason to retain the two colours was to continue with the appearance of the previous issue. Single coloured stamps, or rather those which could also be printed in singly-fugitive ink, were to be printed by Harrisons at Hayes. In practice, Harrisons only printed, additionally, the 2½d, 3d and 4d values from De La Rue plates. All others were printed at Somerset House. Unsurprisingly, all can be differentiated from the original De La Rue printings. Because of yet more delays with the George V values these interim printings were to continue, in some cases, through until 1913.

Somerset House

Somerset House was the headquarters of the Inland Revenue, which had overall responsibility for the production of adhesive postage stamps and postal stationery. It also accommodated a Post Office Stores Department (where the reserve stock of stamps etc was held) and a Stamping Department. The latter was where a large amount of private stationery (cards, wrappers, envelopes, legal documents and the like) were "stamped to order" using the same styles of dies as on stationery officially sold over the Post Office counter. Stationery or documents requiring fees to be paid also had stamps impressed here. Other Stamping Departments were situated around the country, at Edinburgh, Dublin and Manchester, each with their own dies. The manufacture of these dies had only recently been transferred to the Royal Mint. Now Somerset House had the additional task of printing adhesive postage stamps, and fiscal or revenue stamps.

For the interim printings of Edward VII postage stamps, Somerset House were responsible for the 1½d, 2d, 5d, 9d, 10d and 1/-, all of which were bi-coloured; the high values (2/6d, 5/-, 10/- and £1) which were not part of the Harrison contract; and the 6d which needed to be printed in doubly-fugitive ink for revenue purposes. They also printed the new 7d value. These were on uncoated paper, watermarked Crown or Anchor as the case may be, perforated 14. Revenue stamps were on a different watermark.

McCorquodales & Postal Stationery

As decided by the 1910 Committee the contract for adhesive stamps and imprinted postal stationery was split, the latter being combined with the other contract for registration envelopes. Although McCorquodales who held the contract for registration envelopes, were criticised in the report, and their contract terminated on 31 December, they were nevertheless successful in gaining the enlarged contract for all imprinted postal stationery – postcards, letter cards, newspaper wrappers and envelopes.

However, the delays in regard to new designs for adhesive stamps also affected them in terms of designs and dies for postal stationery. So, production of Edward VII postcards, letter cards, wrappers and envelopes was continued at McCorquodales' plant at Wolverton from De La Rue plates, deliveries beginning towards the end of January 1911. At the same time, as will be seen, there was a move to reduce the number of different designs used for the same denomination on different articles.

The Royal Mint

In February 1910 the Mint were given the task of creating the impressing stamp dies for the Inland Revenue. However, this was very similar in nature to the creation of dies for coins and medals which they had undertaken for centuries. Then, with the death of Edward VII the Royal Mint were immediately, and most importantly, concerned with the design and production of coins and medals for his successor. This coincided with the new task of creating letterpress dies and plates for adhesive postage stamps and stationery. As with new plant at Harrisons so the Royal Mint also required extended premises and new machinery. They were situated on Tower Hill, near the Tower of London.

Above: The Royal Mint, near the Tower of London, c1910

In preparation, Edward Rigg, Superintendent of the Operative Department, accompanied by Atterbury and Bennett from the Inland Revenue went to inspect the French Government printing works in Paris from 13 to 15 June, 1910 and then the well-known firm of J. Enschedé & Fils in Haarlem from 21 to 26 July.[32] Immediate steps were taken to obtain the special machinery required and temporary premises were cleared in the new Mechanics' Shop. Some idea of the complexity of the operation can be gained by a description in the Mint's annual report for that year.

> Two rooms on the ground floor, having an area of 835 square feet, at present contain the wax-moulding and electro-depositing plant with suitable transformers, steam boiler, blackleading machine, wax-shaving machine, lye and washing tanks, stereo metal furnace, with backing stand, with all necessary motors and various minor appliances. In a room of 427 square feet on the first floor provision is made for the electrotype finishers' work, and a planing and roughing machine, incline shaving machine, trimming machine, with circular saw and motor, as well as a long bench with minor tools have been set up. Finally on the top floor, in a room of 342 square feet, the engravers and provers are housed with benches, two proving presses, and a transfer press, as well as the minor implements required.[33]

In a temporary wooden shed were two special furnaces to harden mild steel. These used cyanide of potassium and the poisonous fumes had to be kept well away from the rest of the Mint.

Towards the end of January 1911 permanent quarters were started on the south side of the premises and the work of erecting them continued through the year.

A new era

So, it can be seen that what began as a relatively simple matter of stopping excess charging by one printing firm had had huge consequences. New printers, new plate makers, new premises and machinery for both, all having to be staffed by many people, all highly skilled – and all within the space of some six months. All this without printing one new stamp. Then, as will be seen, external designers for the new stamps and new engravers, all combining to create yet more problems. It was indeed a case of "all change!"

1   **Houseman, Lorna** *The House that Thomas Built – The Story of De La Rue* 1968 p142

2   POST 30/2303A Postage stamps and stamped stationery: Report of the Inter-Departmental Committee on Inland Revenue Contracts.

3   ibid

4   ibid

5   ibid

6   ibid

7   ibid

8   POST 54/48 Correspondence regarding the introduction of King George V postage stamps. 26 May 1910.

9   De La Rue Correspondence book I.R. 15 p120

10 De La Rue Correspondence book I.R. 15 op cit p141

11 **Houseman, L.** op cit

12 IR 28/73

13 ibid 24 February 1909. Inland Revenue to De La Rue

14 ibid 19 August 1909. De La Rue to Inland Revenue

15 IR 28/71 12 January 1910, though not approved until 1 April.

16 **Wiseman, W.A.** *GB Journal* July 1978, p 82

17 De La Rue Correspondence book I.R. 15 p108 from H. Birtles

18 **Samuel, Herbert** [Viscount Samuel] *Memoirs* 1945, p77

19 ibid p2

20 Lloyd George speech 1908, and the title of the book *Mr Balfour's Poodle: Peers v. People* by Roy Jenkins 1954

21 **Jenkins, R.** op cit p.13

22 POST 30/2303A Contract with Harrisons, 13 July 1911, Walter Gates to Inland Revenue

23 "The New Secretary" *St. Martin's-le-Grand* 1910 pp 67-8

24 POST 54/48 op cit, 2 September 1910, Inland Revenue to De La Rue

25 POST 30/1995 Postage stamps and stamped stationery: King George V issue, 25 May 1910

26 HC Deb, 13 March 1911, Volume 22 cc1872-3

27 POST 30/2303A op cit

28 **Houseman, L.** op cit p36

29 POST 54/48 op cit

30 Quoted in **Beaumont, K.M. & Easton, John** *The Postage Stamps of Great Britain: Part Three* 1964 pp190-1

31 T1/11338 Terms and conditions of contracts with Messrs Harrison and Sons for the manufacture of stamps and postal stationery: Atterbury to Harrison 11 March 1911

32 MINT 20/418

33 Royal Mint Annual Report 1910-11, 9 August 1911, pp45 ff

> " We invented the postage stamp – all it had on was the sovereign's head and Postage and its value. That's all we want."
>
> Thus George V to Kenneth Clark – but if only it were that simple.

With the death of King Edward VII one of the first tasks for Herbert Samuel as new Postmaster General was the creation of new postage stamps. In terms of design, it was decided to treat the frame and the head of the low-value definitives separately, something which was, unsurprisingly, to lead to endless difficulties. Indeed, George Clausen of the Art Workers Guild, when asked, clearly warned that in his opinion it was "very desirable that (if possible) one artist should design both the head and its framing, so that it is all in accord."[1] He acknowledged, however, that this might be found impracticable (few accomplished figure draughtsmen would have the necessary decorative sense), and went on to provide the names of a number of artists who could draw the head alone. None was subsequently approached. More helpfully, he also suggested a few artists "line engravers, who design and make fine bookplates, and their kind of work lends itself to such design as would be good for framing the head."[2] Two were very good – George W. Eve and C. W. Sherborn.

Above: Suggestions by the Royal Mint to include the country name

Suggestions as to the inclusion of the name of the country of origin were dismissed as being impracticable. "Great Britain and Ireland" would be the full title (according to a discussion with the Inland Revenue) and this was altogether too long in Samuel's opinion, and unnecessary. Nevertheless, a number of stamp-size suggestions were subsequently submitted by the Royal Mint, probably in September, 1910. These used cut-outs of the head of Edward VII from current stamps placed within hand-painted frames incorporating the names "British Postage", "British Kingdom" and even "British Kingdom – Home Isles". The last would have included the Isle of Man and the Channel Islands, but the proposals were not taken any further.

Samuel then wrote (formally, in the third person, and in his own hand) to the King explaining what he proposed [3]:

> After consultation with the President of the Royal Academy and with others, he would submit that the invitations should be addressed to Mr C.W. Sherborn, Mr G.W. Eve

and Mr Garth Jones, all of them designers of repute of book-plates and title-pages, and specially qualified, therefore, for this work, which is of a somewhat analogous kind. Mr Samuel is informed that Mr Eve was the designer of the book-plate of His late Majesty.

It is probable that the stamps would be most effective if the head were re-produced from a plaque prepared by a sculptor and not from a drawing by a painter or draftsman.

He suggested that Mr Mackennal should be commissioned for this purpose as he had been selected to prepare the effigy for coins. If this were unsatisfactory perhaps the King could give sittings to a portrait painter. An outline of the draft instructions to artists was also enclosed. Amongst the detail was the requirement that one at least of the designs should embody a lion *couchant*. These instructions were generally approved by the King, but with a few comments conveyed by Sir Arthur Bigge, his joint Private Secretary (later Lord Stamfordham).[4]

> The King, having had some experience in the designing and preparation of a die for the last Canadian Stamps, would suggest that an indication of the space to be allowed for the head should be given to the Artists, and also, if possible, the mode of reproduction intended to be employed for the printing of the Stamps, as such information would be undoubtedly very useful, and also affect the work in preparing the design.

> As to the head, His Majesty will be interested to see the result of your proposed reproduction from a plaque prepared by a Sculptor, but he is inclined to believe that a more faithful reproduction and a more satisfactory result would be obtained by an engraving made from an actual photograph. This was done in the case of the die for the Canadian Stamps. His Majesty has had photographs taken by Mr Downey for the above purpose, and directs me to send them for your consideration.

The photographs referred to were taken a week or so before by the Court Photographers, W. & D. Downey, mainly for coins and medals. Bertram Mackennal, an Australian sculptor, was preparing the effigies for these, the first of which would appear on the medal to commemorate the new Union of South Africa. A postscript to Bigge's letter read "I think you will agree with the King that the Photographs are excellent. His Majesty and the Queen prefer those showing both eyes."[5] This would be the three-quarter profile, originally with full-dress military uniform, though probably here cropped and retouched to show the head only. Slightly later, it was also submitted to the Mint and Mackennal for coins and medals but was useless in that regard as it was not a true profile. Another photograph, this time a full profile, was then supplied to the Mint, clearly taken at the same time and thus used for coins. These photographs were to prove crucial to the story of the first stamps of George V.

Right: Photograph of the King taken by W & D Downey

Invitations to Artists

The invitation to artists to provide frames for the new stamp designs was sent on 1 July with instructions amended to include the King's pertinent suggestions. It went to G.W. Eve,

A. Garth Jones and C.W. Sherborn with a submission date of 30 July. All agreed to provide designs. The size of drawings, as prescribed by the Inland Revenue, was given somewhat strangely – "not larger than will go in a circle 9 inches in diameter" – though it could be any size smaller.[6]

> A portrait of the King will be separately obtained and the designs for the frame should merely give an outline of the head in profile to indicate the space it is intended to fill which should be about the same as, or only very slightly smaller than, in the present penny stamps, the profile facing in the same direction. For your guidance I am to state that the treatment of the head will be similar to that adopted in the current issues; the background, however, will be solid in all cases and not shaded.

> At least one design must consist of a frame for the portrait with a lion couchant beneath it. The words 'Postage and Revenue' should also appear, though the lettering may be small. No other words, letters or figures should be introduced. It is desirable that a royal crown, of the same type as in the present stamps, should be included, but this is not essential if it is inconsistent with the general character of the artist's design.

The cultivated Samuel was anxious to obtain designs which, while meeting operational requirements efficiently, had "a higher artistic merit than some of the former issues."[7] In view of the outcome, this must be regarded as ironic.

By the end of July three designs each had been received from Sherborn, Garth Jones (sketches only) and Eve. Many incorporated the required lion *couchant*; none were immediately attractive. Samuel forwarded them to the King on 8 August showing a preference for those by Eve. Bigge replied the same day saying that the King "does not care very much for any of them" and suggesting that Mackennal be approached for a fresh design.[8]

Bertram Mackennal

Three days before, Mackennal had had a sitting of the King. In his diary George V noted:

> Saw Mr Macartney (deputy Master of the Mint) about the new coins & medals & then I gave a sitting to Mr Mackennal (a very clever Australian sculptor) who is doing my head for the new coinage & medals.[9]

Clearly, he and Mackennal had got on well. Mackennal later recalled that the King had heard that his work was of the highest artistic merit. He therefore proposed to entrust him with the commission to sculpt his head which would appear on all British coins.

> I'm conscious that I'm not what one would call a particularly handsome man, but I become full of vague apprehension when I think of the kind of portrait that some of the sculptors whose work I have seen might produce. I know I can trust you to make the best of me, and not the worst.[10]

Above: Sketch designs submitted by C W Sherborn, A Garth Jones and George Eve.

Edgar Bertram Mackennal was born on 12 June 1863 near Melbourne, Australia. He was

Above: Portrait of Bertram Mackennal by Ruth Hollick

the third of six children of a Scottish immigrant sculptor, John Simpson Mackennal, from Stranraer, who had come to seek his fortune in the goldfields. At 16 he began his studies in the School of Design in Melbourne but at 19 sailed for England. Later Mackennal described his desire to get to England as "the absorbing passion of his early years."[11] A more objective, if acerbic, assessment of Australian expatriate sculptors of the time was given by R. Jope-Slade. They "mastered the grammar of their art in Melbourne schools, they came to Paris to learn, and finally to London to sell."[12] Mackennal was based in Paris for several years in the 1880s and early 1890s when he exhibited his first major work *Circe,* a nude goddess in the new style. This was to be typical of several of his works, both female and male. While visiting Australia at this time he wrote in a letter: "I love these places where clothes are scarce and flesh plenty and the brutes walk so well".[13]

From 1894 he lived in London, gaining an increasing number of private and public commissions, and in 1904 moved to a spacious studio ("quite swagger" according to a visiting Australian sculptor) in St John's Wood. He was commissioned to create a large pediment for the new Government offices in Whitehall and in 1908 produced classical designs for his first medals – those for the London Olympics of that year. Later, he worked on a large number of sculptures of British royalty and also war memorials, including that for Eton – an overlifesize young male nude which caused both controversy and disapproval. He was to be the first Australian Royal Academician, and was knighted in public by George V. He died suddenly in 1931.

The Post Office now wrote to Mackennal (in August 1910) in the same terms as to the other artists, but a short note came back saying that he was unable to submit designs "under the conditions".[14] Samuel noted that he gave no reasons for declining. In desperation he suggested that Mackennal be approached again.

> If he wishes to submit designs both for the frame and the portrait, that could certainly be agreed to. If it is a question of payment, you would no doubt ascertain what fee he would accept and the matter could be re-considered. If he objects to be put into competition with others, you might explain, confidentially, that three designs were selected, as it was thought that the work was more suited for black-and-white artists, but that none of the designs were quite suitable, and that I am not now inviting any artist other than himself.[15]

Samuel's suspicions turned out to be accurate. Mackennal did not compete. However, when reminded that the King took a particular interest Mackennal relented, agreeing to a fee of 100 guineas. He was now quite keen to take on the work despite being fully occupied with the coins.

> Mr Mackennal suggested that some of the stamps might be larger so as to give more opportunity for the design. He mentioned the French stamps of 45 centimes & upwards.[16]

This was immediately proposed, and agreed, for the high value stamps. Less than one month later Mackennal submitted six designs, one of which was larger in size for the higher values, and two featuring the lion *couchant*. Samuel sent them to the King at Balmoral together with some designs prepared by the Royal Mint incorporating security work. (Because of his signature, the precise spelling of Mackennal's surname varies at this time in typewritten references.)

The size and shape of Mr MacKennal's 5/- [Seahorse] stamp is quite acceptable from a Departmental point of view and if the numeral were taken from the shield, where it is incongruous, and placed upon the label at the bottom, this would I think make a fine stamp for the higher values.

The designs marked A and B [with lion *couchant*] with some slight modifications, such as an alteration in the design of the olive branch, would I think also make good stamps. But possibly Mr MacKennal could make further improvements on these designs.[17]

The King's Views

On 1 October Bigge replied with the King's carefully considered views – some 4¼ typed pages. He asked about the mode of production and suggested line-engraved stamps if possible. He thought it essential, especially for the ½d and 1d stamps "used by the whole community", that the most prominent feature should be the portrait of the King, and the value be expressed in words.

In most of the sketches submitted the design itself, or some special portion of it, is the dominating feature, so that none of them would appear to be quite suitable for the values in question.[18]

He liked Eve's designs, particularly the 2d "Wreath" and 3d "Pillar" ones, but they needed to be seen at stamp size. Further designs might be requested. Mackennal's low value designs needed more room for the head and there were specific suggestions for the larger high value. Comments were also made on the Royal Mint essays but the photographic portrait sent with them was approved. A die should be engraved at that size. The question of the watermark was also raised.

Above and left: Five of Mackennal's first sketches (with sketched profile portrait)

The Mint was informed of the King's comments and asked to modify one of its designs. On 15 October they replied with three versions of design A in green, red and dark blue. Samuel forwarded these to the King but he feared however "that there would be very general disappointment among the public if the design for the denominations of the stamps most generally used did not possess a greater artistic value than would attach to a stamp of this character."[19] He felt that such a design would be regarded "to an even greater degree than the present design for the penny stamp is regarded – as craftsman's work rather than

Samuel thought that the design would meet with general approval and "the symbolism embodied in the lion would be welcome, both at home and throughout the Empire."

Right: Designs from the Royal Mint

as artist's work and that it would be condemned accordingly."[20] The King agreed and did not approve them, but nevertheless kept the examples for his collection.

Eve was asked to provide stamp-size versions and Mackennal was contacted on holiday in the Mediterranean. Eve's designs, slightly modified, were approved on 28 and 31 October for the less urgent denominations of 4d and above.

As a matter of greater urgency Mackennal was asked to alter his lion designs. He replied from Monte Carlo with a revised drawing which the Postmaster General again forwarded to the King. Samuel thought that the design would meet with general approval and "the symbolism embodied in the lion would be welcome, both at home and throughout the Empire."[21] He had been "particularly anxious to be able to submit a drawing… which would stand out as different from the general run of stamps."[22] However, it was still not satisfactory and in his letter Samuel made a number of detailed suggestions.

Above: Revised essay from the Royal Mint with the approved head inserted.

In his reply, Bigge conveyed the King's general agreement.

> More space should be given for the head: the entablature at the bottom bearing the words "one penny" should be made less deep: the Crown should be removed from the top of the oval, and put, as you suggest, at the side, but please be sure it is a proper Tudor Crown: the numerals at the sides could be left out altogether.

The only fresh suggestion that the King would make is with regard to the knot of the oak

Right: First revision by Mackennal of the Lion design sent from Monte Carlo

and laurel leaves in Mr Mackennal's design, which His Majesty thinks want some rearrangement, so as to avoid the appearance of the oak leaf coming out of the lion's head.[23]

Yet more discussion took place within the Secretary's Office of the G.P.O. about how to accommodate the lion, frame and head in a pleasing whole. Samuel then wrote from his constituency in Cleveland:

> I agree that Mr Mackennal should be asked to see that the lion does not have the appearance of being in a cave under the shield. But I am not sure that the shield would look well if it were in mid air, so to speak, and unsupported at the corners.

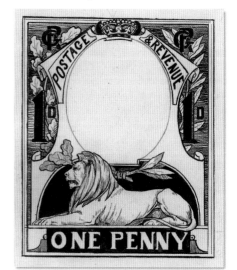

The point should be put to him, but it would be unwise to interfere with his discretion.[24]

This did not stop him making further, more detailed criticisms, however. On his, and Mackennal's, return to London he spoke to him direct. As a result of this meeting further alterations took place with the lion design, but Mackennal was still not happy.

> I cannot quite satisfy myself with the design. You know this stamp has been so altered from my first conception that it is no more my design but more or less a composite work. However I am trying more than one way with it and I am also making a small model of it from which I expect better reproduction result.[25]

It was now November 1910, and time was pressing. No design for the all-important ½d and 1d stamps had been approved and Samuel was still very anxious to have them all available before the Coronation the following June. By the end of the month revisions had been completed to the lion design, and there is first mention of a "dolphin" design. Both of these were sent direct to the King by Mackennal on 28 November.

At Bigge's suggestion the King now sought the advice of his philatelic advisor, still at this time John Tilleard.

> The King is getting quite in despair about the Stamps. I send you Mackennal's last design, and, although evidently the Postmaster-General is anxious to get the matter settled, His Majesty still thinks it may be possible to improve the design.[26]

The revised design showed an alteration suggested by the King, but the more he looked at it "the more does His Majesty fail to appreciate the scroll at all! They look rather like the supports of an oval looking glass!"[27] On the other hand the new design with the "Nautilus" and dolphins was certainly an improvement.

> Can anything be done? As I said before the King is almost inclined to do nothing more. It really was at my suggestion that he appeals once more to you. I am afraid, as it stands now, the stamp will not go forth to the world as a triumph of philatelic art.[28]

Tilleard replied, agreeing, but giving still more suggestions for its improvement. In the meantime, not having heard anything, Mackennal produced yet another design with a wreath which he sent again direct to the King. In replying to Tilleard, Bigge informed him of this and thanked him for his comments.

> [The King] quite sees that it would be hopeless to suggest further alterations in the design containing the Lion, but by this morning's post Mr Mackennal has submitted another design without the Lion, and the King has approved of it. It has not yet been seen by the Postmaster-General, who may still clamour for the introduction of a Lion into the design,

Above: Second and third revisions of the Lion design

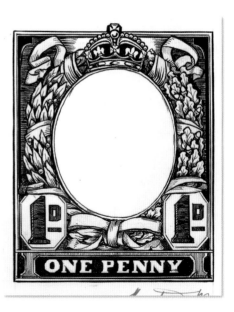

Top: First submitted versions of the Dolphin and Wreath designs

Bottom: Approved versions

but I hope not, as there seems to be little prospect of finality in this matter unless the last design is approved. I wish there had been time for you to see it. It is not altogether unlike King Edward's stamp, a wreath of laurel surmounted by a Crown round the oval.

The King quite agrees with your criticisms about the Lion making the design lopsided.

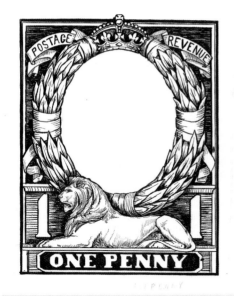

His Majesty has also approved the Nautilus design, but suggested the slight alteration you propose. No doubt Mr Mackennal will carry it out.[29]

Bigge now wrote direct to Mackennal approving both the new "Wreath" and "Nautilus" designs but passing on still more notes from the King. In particular the King pointed out that Mackennal had missed out the words "Postage" and "Revenue" from his "Wreath" design and suggesting that they could be accommodated on the knot at the foot. Bigge also wrote to Samuel to inform him of what had been going on.

> The King has seen a fresh design by Mr Mackennal for the Postage Stamp, and has approved it. There is no Lion in it, which His Majesty fears you may regret, but it seems almost impossible to get an artistic design with the Lion introduced.

> The King has also approved another design for the higher values; both these, of course, will be submitted to you by Mr Mackennal.[30]

It was, of course, Samuel who had instigated the idea of a lion *couchant*. On hearing of this latest development he sent a telegram from Saltburn, Cleveland asking if it was proposed to abandon the lion design. When, shortly afterwards, he saw the designs he said that he liked all three – the dolphin, the wreath *and* the lion. He was clearly not going to give the lion up and arranged to see what they would all look like with the King's head inserted.

Above: Versions of the Lion design for the 1d and 2½d values.

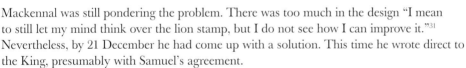

Left: Approved Lion design (top) and Harrison's engraver's sketch (bottom)

Mackennal was still pondering the problem. There was too much in the design "I mean to still let my mind think over the lion stamp, but I do not see how I can improve it."[31] Nevertheless, by 21 December he had come up with a solution. This time he wrote direct to the King, presumably with Samuel's agreement.

I am enclosing for your Majesty's approval an improved design for the lion stamp which has the approval of the Postmaster General. I have adapted it from the wreath

I am enclosing for your Majesty's approval an improved design for the lion stamp...
... I beg to submit that I think it greatly in advance of any of the lion designs which I had the honour to submit to Your Majesty...

design which your Majesty liked and I beg to submit that I think it greatly in advance of any of the lion designs which I had the honour to submit to Your Majesty…

The Postmaster General proposes to use the following designs – 1st The Lion stamp 2nd The Dolphin 3rd The wreath and for all stamps above two & six pence the large design of Britannia with the sea horses.[32]

All the King could do was approve. The final frame design (Dolphin) intended for the ½d and 1½d values and the Wreath design (for the 2d and 3d) were sent to the Mint on 22 December, with the Lion frame for the 1d and 2½d following six days later.

Design Sources

Of those designs by Eve previously approved, design B was of a wreath surmounted by a crown and regional symbols; C, his so-called "Pillar" design featured two caducei – the rod

of Hermes, messenger of the gods, with two wings and entwined with two serpents (not that of Asclepius or Aesculapius, which has only one serpent). Both designs were clearly of bookplate origin, or inspiration, for which Eve was renowned.

Above and right: Dolphins and Nautilus shells at the Old Admiralty building, and Landseer's lion in Trafalgar Square

The source of the Lion design was certainly Samuel's Liberal imperial viewpoint, and it was at his continued insistence that it came to fruition. It could well be argued that inspiration for Mackennal's drawing was Edwin Landseer's famous monumental lions guarding Nelson's Column in Trafalgar Square in London (there since 1867). The pose is almost identical. In its final form the overall Lion design was based on his new "Wreath" version which the King had considered the best of all. But where did the idea for the "Nautilus" design with the dolphins come from?

Mackennal had a meeting with Samuel on 4 November. There are no notes of this but at a subsequent meeting with Samuel's private secretary Kenelm Kerr on 28 November he said that at his interview at the House of Commons Samuel had approved the dolphin design subject to seeing a reduced reproduction. On that same day Mackennal sent the design direct to the King describing it as a fresh design "chosen by the Postmaster General"[33]. The King then referred to it as the "Nautilus" design based on the shell-like frame.

The dolphin in times of heraldry was known as the "king of fish". It was also known as the "sailor's friend". As such it adorns the outside of the Admiralty buildings on Horseguard's Parade in London in particularly lively fashion. These buildings were finished in about 1908 as part of the rebuilding of Government offices in Whitehall. For this, Mackennal had received a prestigious commission for a sculptured pediment in 1904, so he would have been familiar with both the architects and the new buildings. These were also next door to Trafalgar Square with its Landseer's lions used on the penny stamp. Spirited twin dolphins are shown in more than one format on the façade of what is now called the Old Admiralty building, together with Nautilus shells, and this is clearly the source of Mackennal's inspiration. Again the poses are almost identical. There seems to be no record as to the sculptor.

Other Designs

More than one design was also sent in by members of the public, but they were all rather crude and none had any influence on the accepted designs. There is even one submitted by Perkins, Bacon, printers of the Penny Black, showing an almost full-face portrait of the King. Printed by the Printex photographic technique examples are known in different colours. In the Royal Philatelic Collection they are dated by Bacon to October and November 1911, though this is unlikely.

The Downey Head

As has been seen, the head approved for insertion into the accepted frames was based on a three-quarter profile photograph taken by the firm of W. & D. Downey back in June, 1910. William Ernest Downey was the doyen of British professional photographers. He had been

a photographer of royalty for over 40 years, holding royal warrants from Queen Victoria. At the funeral of King Edward VII his firm produced formal portraits of nine European sovereigns. So he would have been well-known to George V, and accepted by him.

Left: Downey photograph reduced and cropped

It was the King who suggested the use of a photograph as origination. This then had to be translated into an engraved die suitable for letterpress printing. Before, this had been accomplished by skilled and experienced, in-house engravers at De La Rue. Now, the Mint, newly responsible for the production of dies as well as plates, had to find one. Their own engravers had no experience of letterpress postage stamp dies, being more used to embossed punches.

The engraver the Mint found was J.A.C. Harrison, no connection to the printing firm with the same name. John Augustus Charles Harrison, to give him his full name, was born in 1872, and came from an engraving family. By the time he was 13 he was working for a firm of line engravers in Birmingham, pupil to his father.[34] At the age of 18 he joined the staff of Waterlow Brothers & Layton, but by about 1900 had become free-lance, specialising in heraldic book-plates and book illustrations. However, his experience was in engraving in intaglio, or recess, not for letterpress.

Below: J.A.C. Harrison at work with engraving tools and mirror.

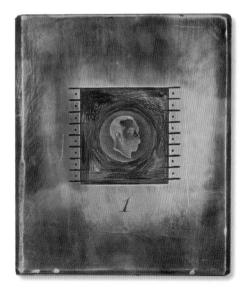

The first documentary mention of his work on the effigy comes on 14 November, 1910 when the Inland Revenue forwarded "two impressions taken from the steel die which has been engraved by the Royal Mint from the photograph of His Majesty King George V".[35] This was the final version of stage 1 of the engraving of the die (1c) with the surround uncleared - there being three stages, and several sub-stages, recognised by specialists.

From Windsor Castle Bigge returned the proofs to Samuel. The regard in which Mackennal was held now became clear.

> The King thinks there must have been some mistake on the part of the Mint in sending them to you until they had been passed by Mr Mackennal, the sculptor who had undertaken to do this in accordance with an understanding with His Majesty.[36]

Mackennal had been at the Castle that weekend and seen the proofs. He thought that "considerable improvement can be made with very little additional work." From the Mint, Macartney was duly apologetic. He claimed he had had no idea the proofs were to be submitted to the King.

> There are so many cooks at this job that it is sometimes difficult to find out the precise stage which has been reached. But you may assure His Majesty that the impression he saw was not from a finished die and that every effort will be made to improve it.[37]

Harrison now cleared the die, cutting away the metal from the surround, and made various improvements. This is stage 2, and as such was approved by the King on 27 December.

Creation of the die

The highly technical and complicated process of creating the die has been minutely described by Richmond.[38]

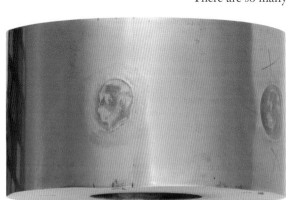

Above: the original master head die and transfer roller, with progressive proofs taken from it

From the Downey photograph J.A.C. Harrison produced a very careful black and white line drawing much larger than the final engraved effigy. This was his engraver's sketch. It showed every line that was to appear on the die in its correct weight, or tone value. This line drawing was photographed down on to a glass plate so that the negative image was the cor-

rect size of the die. The thin photographic film was then
stripped from the glass plate and turned over on to another glass plate so that the image was again right-reading
as the original. The next stage was to transfer the image
to a polished, softened steel block.

The steel block was coated with a solution of
albumen, water and bichromate of ammonia, which
hardens and becomes insoluble in water after being
exposed to light. The photographic plate was placed
with the film side in close contact with the sensitized
steel block and exposed to a powerful light. The
dark lines on the original drawing which were clear
glass on the negative, appeared on the surface of the
steel block as hardened albumen. After applying a
thin film of special ink to the surface the block was
washed in running water and soluble albumen over
the areas which were white on the original drawing
was washed away. The block was then warmed and
dusted with an acid-resisting powder which adhered
to the inked lines, leaving the white portions of the design as unprotected steel. The
back and sides of the block were varnished and it was immersed in acid for a short
period so that the design was lightly etched onto the surface.[39]

After the block had been cleaned, Harrison engraved the die using the lightly etched design
as a guide. This design was now reversed in relation to the original photograph and the
engraver's sketch. The die will be negative, in relief. To achieve this the engraver has to cut
away those parts of the design which are not required to print, as in a wood engraving. A
photograph shows a relatively young Harrison at work at his desk, poring over a steel die,
with a mirror supported in front of him so that he could see the results in reverse; and tools
and pipe to one side.

With the engraving of the head complete, the die was hardened
and it thus became the master head die, with the image in
reverse. As with all master dies, after first use to create replica
surrogates this was kept as pristine as possible. It was placed in
a transfer press where, under great pressure, three impressions
were taken by an employee Mr Macdonald Junior from the
hard steel die on to a softened steel transfer roller. These
impressions were exact replicas of the die but with the image
now right-reading and the non-printing parts of the design
standing up in relief. The roller was then hardened in turn "and
from it eight steel Head Plates were produced in the Transfer
Press each with one impression of the die. These Head Plates were each to become Master
Dies for the various groups of stamp designs."[40] Harrison then etched and engraved the
respective frame designs around these heads, the designs still being in reverse. These then
became the Master Dies for the particular designs and denominations.

*Above: the master
frame die for the
Dolphin design and
transfer roller, with a
proof in green*

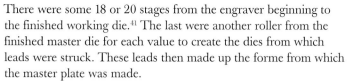

There were some 18 or 20 stages from the engraver beginning to the finished working die.[41] The last were another roller from the finished master die for each value to create the dies from which leads were struck. These leads then made up the forme from which the master plate was made.

At all the various stages proofs, or pulls, were taken to see that no imperfections had crept in. Many of these proofs were taken at the Royal Mint, but Harrison worked at home, and he also took a number of intermediate pulls to check his own progress.

From the Master Dies, plates were created through a remarkable number of stages (as will be described in the next chapter) and then provided to the printers for them to print the stamps.

But Harrison could obviously only work on one die at a time. The Mint and the Inland Revenue had tried their utmost, but could only find the one competent engraver. As the work built up this was to lead to yet more delays. It was not until the end of January 1911 that the head die was agreed (now stage 3) and Harrison began work on engraving the frame of the Dolphin design for the ½d and 1½d values.

Colour

In the meantime, consideration had turned to colour. All stamps had to be immediately distinctive, one from another, so that postal workers could identify the rate without delay. In the past this had come from design, paper and size, as well as colour. But to distinguish different denominations "in the pressure of business – the Counter Officers and the officers employed in Sorting Offices greatly rely upon the colours."[42] Complicating this was the fact that they were often working at night in artificial light, when some inks could be very similar. Colour, thus, became of considerable importance, and discussions were prolonged, diverting attention from lack of progress in creating the dies and plates.

Certain colours, though not necessarily the particular shades, were prescribed by the Universal Postal Union world-wide for "typical rates" equivalent to 5, 10 and 25 centimes.

These were green for the ½d (inland postcard rate etc), red for the 1d (inland letter rate) and dark blue for the 2½d (basic overseas rate). It was recommended, therefore, that these colours be avoided for other denominations. At the same time the 6d value, which was largely used for revenue purposes, needed to be printed in doubly-fugitive ink. This meant a purple colour, and the Inland Revenue wanted this to be retained.

There were 14 different denominations of stamps up to 1/-. First colour specimens, described as "advance proofs" were supplied by Somerset House on 13 December. As yet, no die had been engraved so zinc blocks had been prepared by Carl Hentschel & Co Ltd of the two designs by then approved, those by Eve. The three-quarter head inserted was taken from the first engraving. For the "Pillar" design a 7d rate was created; for the "Wreath" design a 3d.

Above: the master die for the ½d Dolphin design and transfer roller, with final proofs

They were proofed at Somerset House in a total of 48 inks manufactured by Mander Brothers, Slater & Palmer and Winstone & Sons Ltd. For the 3d "Wreath" design there were two versions, one with a white background to the King's head, one with a solid. Not every version was proofed for all three manufacturers and yellow paper was used for two proofs intended for the final 3d denomination, so there were a total of 126 different proofs.

These were not satisfactory. Some images were printed too large, some too small. More importantly Bennett, at the Inland Revenue, pointed out that "the colour of a stamp is affected to some extent by the design, the same colour frequently presenting a different appearance when used for different designs.[43]" A final selection should be postponed until the designs up to 2½d had been approved and specimens obtained. Where there was a solid surround to the King's head the latter unfortunately merged into the background. However, if Harrisons were to print from the Edward VII plates the choice of a colour scheme would not be a matter of such urgency as was previously thought.

New blocks were now made by Hentschel but both artist and Royal Mint stressed that these should *not* be shown to the King. The size of the numerals was too thick ("not yet adjusted to the design" according to Macartney at the Mint[44]) and they could not provide a correct representation of the stamp as it would appear when printed. On the same day Mackennal went further:

> In case you did not quite understand my point on the telephone with regard to the prints of the stamps that the Mint have had made for you. They are only very poor reproductions from photographs and not from an engraved plate.

> And it did not seem wise to me, to make experiments in colour. On these reproductions they would not be much guide and all the work would have to be gone through again. I do not want The King to see them in this state nor for that matter do I want you to see them. And I feel sure you expected the real prints from the plates and not this stuff.[45]

Nevertheless, they were used, though with some of the thicker value figures modified. These images were a step forward and nearer the final intended versions. All were Mackennal's work: the ½d and 1½d featuring the Dolphin frame; the 1d and 2½d the Lion; and the 2d and 3d the Wreath. The more advanced dies utilised the latest stage in the Downey head die (stage 2). Eve's two designs, previously approved, were for the higher values.

Above: Advance proofs of 13 December 1910 from Hentschel zinc blocks

Below: Hentschel block of January 1911 with thicker value

The next set of proofs, again for colour only, was sent on 14 February 1911 and over the next few days. The Tyrian Plum colour requested caused some difficulty but a version was achieved. Higher values had provisional designs by Eve with a much smaller Downey head. By 18 February all values up to 1s had been essayed, there being this time some 177 different proofs in all. Inks came from the same three manufacturers.

The Post Office now made the first of four selections of colours (later called Colour Scheme A) based not upon the proofs submitted but rather, remarkably, on 14 issued Japanese, United States and Canadian stamps which they supplied. When proofs were submitted on 2 March Bennett pointed out that several of the U.S. stamps, in particular, were recess printed rather than surface printed and it would be impracticable to reproduce the same colour effect. Where a similar colour existed in the Edward VII series he had printed that stamp in the same colour beside the new essay "in order to show the colour effect resulting

Above: Proofs for colour of 14 February 1911

from the difference in design."[46] However, a black stamp, such as the Canadian one, would clearly make it difficult to determine whether or not a stamp had been cancelled.

Almost immediately another set of colour proofs was submitted by the Inland Revenue. This was of one proof for each value up to 1s and was later described as Colour Scheme B. From these two schemes the Post Office made a selection allocated to particular values. This selection (now Colour Scheme C) was then provided on 13 March with the top three values on tinted paper. Three days later further variations of tinted paper (four for each value of 9d, 10d and 1s) were also supplied.

At this point Samuel intervened directly[47]:

> I do not like the magenta colour for the 1½d, & would suggest that that stamp should be maroon & that the 8d stamp should be black on green.

He also wanted to see alternative tinted papers as the colours printed were not satisfactory in artificial light. This resulted in yet more proofs, 40 in all, sent on 25 March.

Out of these, and some additions, Nathan, the Post Office Secretary, created a Colour Scheme D. After discussion with Bruce of the London Postal Section as to their advisability he submitted this to Samuel on 1 April, subject to any slight variation when the final dies were approved. Even this was not to Samuel's liking and he amended the choice for the top four values - yet the selection was still provisional. All these trials, both exhaustive and exhausting, were to be far from the end of the matter.

However, this concentration on colour through February and March, with designs apparently available for all values, may have distracted Samuel, and he may not have realised just how slow progress was elsewhere.

The pressure mounts

Back in October 1910 Samuel had emphatically stated that he was committed to having all the stamps available by Coronation Day (22 June 1911). He could not "undertake to defend in Parliament such delay in their issue as is contemplated by the Board [of Inland Revenue]"[48], extending up to 11 or 12 months after the termination of the De La Rue contract, and to a year and a half after the death of King Edward VII. This was reiterated at frequent intervals. On the other hand the Royal Mint, knowing more of the complexities they faced and the amount of work involved in the new coinage, would not guarantee that any value above 6d would be available. Nevertheless, they anticipated to have plates ready for the ½d and 1d stamps by the end of February, 1911.

By 22 February, however, only the dies for the ½d and 1½d values were ready, but still required the values to be engraved. It was thus not until the end of March that the dies for both the ½d and 1d stamps were finalised, after various amendments in consultation with Mackennal and Samuel. Proofs were submitted to the King on 11 April and approved the same day with the statement that he was "much pleased" with them.[49] These proofs, as with all others, had been hand printed and Samuel had qualified them saying that the steel die "tends somewhat to deaden the colour and I am informed that the colours of the actual stamps from the printing plates will be rather brighter than these, particularly in the case of the penny stamp."[50] Nevertheless, the King must have rued his approval later.

Plates still had to be made, and the process was very complicated. Regular visits were now made to the Mint by officers of the Inland Revenue to check on progress, which was slow. Towards the end of April a Post Office memorandum detailed the time spent, and lost, since the death of Edward VII, obtaining new designs and engraving dies. The plates for the ½d and 1d were now promised for the middle of May.

On Samuel's behalf, Nathan wrote to the Mint:

> As you are aware, Mr Samuel regards himself as pledged to the issue of the George V adhesive postage stamps and stamped stationery by Coronation Day; but in view of the rate of progress during the last few months there seems to be grave doubt whether that pledge will be fulfilled. It is true that considerable time was occupied in obtaining satisfactory designs and securing their approval, but the progress made since the designs were approved can scarcely be regarded as satisfactory.[51]

He went on to say that Samuel "trusts that it may even yet be possible to secure the issue of all, or nearly all, of the adhesive stamps and articles of stamped stationery on Coronation Day."

On 1 May, Macartney responded angrily that he was in no way responsible for Samuel's pledge and that he had repeatedly "declined to pledge himself" as to what could be issued by Coronation Day. Recriminations began as to responsibility for the delays.

Expectations were clearly being lowered. Within the Post Office, Nathan thought there was little point in apportioning blame. He felt that little, if any, could be laid at the door of his office; rather the delay, since approval of the designs (a rather important caveat), was "chiefly due to the lack of competent engravers at the Mint, but whether this is the fault or the misfortune of the Mint, we are without materials for judging." He drafted a reply expressing the Postmaster General's regret at the news that not all stamps would be issued on time. Samuel amended this to read his "very great regret".

> The Postmaster General gathers from the statements in your letter that, in the absence of any unforeseen accident, the new ½d and 1d adhesive stamps and the postcards, lettercards and wrappers bearing George V stamps, will certainly be issued on Coronation Day, and that in all probability the adhesive stamps of the values 1½d, 2d, 2½d and 3d will also be issued on that day.

For the higher values, Eve was still finalising the designs which were described as having been "useless for any process here" by Macartney at the Mint.

By the end of May, four working plates of the ½d had been supplied to Harrisons, the printers; by 10 June they had one more, and five plates of the 1d. Setting up the machines and proving the plates had to be rushed through, with no time for trial or experiment, in order to print a supply sufficient for distribution. Any idea of other values being immediately available was abandoned. At this point the 2½d Lion die had just been engraved, but no plate made; the Wreath die was still without value.

On 20 June, two days before the Coronation, the Inland Revenue sent the Post Office specimens of items to be put on sale:

> The Inland Revenue sent yesterday the enclosed specimens of George V stamps and

Above: Proofs for colour of 14 February 1911

45

This page: Colour Scheme
C of 13 March 1911

S.O./3 5273

Green.

S.O./2 5273

Red.

M.B./95 5273

Magenta.

S.O./8 5273

Brown.

S.O./6 5273.

Deep Blue.

S.O./16 5273

Orange Grey

Dutch Red

M.B./91 5273

Dutch Brown
Orange

S.O./10 5273

Pale Blue.

M.B./13 5273

Purple.

S.O./12 5273

Maroon.

S.P./6 5273

Grey.
Dutch Brown

W./98 5273

Black

W./98 5273

Black

W./98 5273

Black.

Green

Red

S.D.
12

Maroon

S.D.
5

Brown

S.D.
6

Blue

S.D.
18

Grey

S.D.
16

Orange

S.D.
10

Light Blue.

M.B.
13

Purple

M.B.
91

Dutch Brown.

9d.

Black

8d.

Verdant Green

9d.

Art Purple
on
Rose

10d.

8d.

Art Purple
on
Blue

1/-

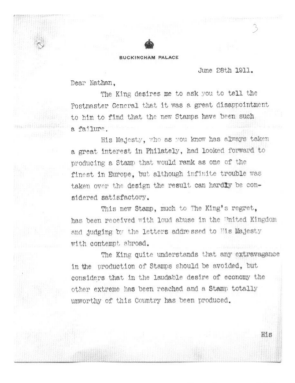

Above: Letter from Ponsonby expressing the King's displeasure

stamped stationery which will be on sale on Coronation Day.

½d adhesive stamps

1d adhesive stamps

Thin postcards

Thin reply postcards

Registered Letter Envelopes.

They also stated that the George V letter cards were expected, and that, if received (as they were), supplies would be issued to London offices for sale on the day.[52] Examples of the stamps were also sent to the King. All the stationery had come from McCorquodales, the struggle for which will be described later.

Disaster

"What awful stamps. I have to suffer for all. I think the lion one ought to be withdrawn. It was not my idea as I think you know, nor the King's."[53]

Thus Bertram Mackennal to Macartney at the Mint. *The Times,* on the day, had been "disappointed". Although Coronation Day was a public holiday some post offices were open and the stamps had been on sale. *The Times* commented that it could "scarcely be said that Mr Bertram Mackennal has excelled himself in the new stamps, and it is doubtful whether they are any material improvement upon Herr Füchs's [sic] much-criticized portrait of the late King." The "diminutive portrait" of the King was "poor and unflattering, and lacks the fine execution which the public has been led to expect." In general, the printing compared unfavourably with the workmanship of De La Rue.

The King was appalled. He thought the "new Stamps have been such a failure." He, as a philatelist, had looked forward to producing a stamp "that would rank as one of the finest in Europe, but although infinite trouble was taken over the design the result can hardly be considered satisfactory." Much to the King's regret the new stamp "has been received with loud abuse in the United Kingdom and judging by the letters addressed to His Majesty with contempt abroad." Despite the laudable desire of economy "a Stamp totally unworthy of this Country has been produced."[54] Behind this comment lay the use of cheap letterpress instead of the more expensive line engraving in intaglio the King had wished.

An urgent meeting was called at the Inland Revenue with Bernard Harrison representing the family printing firm. In view of the general condemnation of the penny stamp in particular there was an urgent necessity of improving the printing.

> Mr Harrison admitted the inferiority of the printing of the first issue of that stamp, but pointed out that perfect printing could not have been expected in the circumstances. The firm was given no opportunity of making experimental printings, but was required to deliver large quantities of stamps at the outset in the brief time available after delivery of the plates. The printing was, however, improving, and was expected to improve still more.[55]

Questions were then raised about the ink, the quality of the paper and of the printing machines used, and these were subsequently to be changed. But although a lot of work was done on the design over the rest of the year it was all to no avail.

Complete lack of experience on the part of the Royal Mint, the printers and the unrealistic demands of a new Postmaster General, combined with the minute and exacting interest of the monarch, had resulted in entirely foreseeable delay and disaster. Each party proceeded to blame the other.

Above: Post Office notice announcing the new stamps

1   POST 30/2136B Postage Stamps: designs for King George V issue, 12 June 1910

2   ibid

3   RA PS/PSO/GV/PS/STAMPS/4130/43 24 June 1910

4   RA PS/PSO/GV/ PS/STAMPS/4130/45 30 June 1910.

5   ibid

6   POST 30/2136B op cit, from Sir Matthew Nathan

7   POST 54/48 Correspondence regarding the introduction of King George V postage stamps; 30 May 1910, Sir Matthew Nathan to the Treasury

8   RA PS/PSO/GV/PS/STAMPS/4130/49

9   RA GV/PRIV/GVD/1910 Friday 5 August 1910

10 *T.P's and Cassell's Weekly*, 24 October 1925, pp. 18, 30. (Quoted in **Tranter, R.R.** *Bertram Mackennal a career*, 2004, p.72).

11 **Edwards, Deborah** "'Adaptability and versatility': Bertram Mackennal – an overview" in **Edwards, Deborah et al** *Mackennal* 2007 p18

12 ibid

13 Quoted in **Peers, Juliette** "Home and away: Bertram Mackennal as sign and visual source in tracking the influence of the New Sculpture in Australia" in *Mackennal* op cit, p93

14 POST 30/2136B op cit, 13 August 1910

15 ibid, 17 August, internal note to A.F. King

16 ibid, 20 August, note by King to Samuel

17 RA PS/PSO/GV/PS/STAMPS/4130/50 15 September 1910, Samuel to Bigge (typed)

18 RA PS/PSO/GV/PS/STAMPS/4130/53

19 RA PS/PSO/GV/PS/STAMPS/4130/55 18 October 1910, Samuel to Bigge

20 ibid

21 ibid

22 ibid

23 RA PS/PSO/GV/PS/STAMPS/4130/56 20 October 1910, Bigge to Samuel

24 POST 30/2136B op cit, 22 October 1910

25 ibid, 18 November 1910, Mackennal to GPO

26 RA PS/PSO/GV/PS/STAMPS/4130/59 30 November 1910, Bigge to Tilleard

27 ibid

28 ibid

29 RA PS/PSO/GV/PS/STAMPS/4130/62 3 December 1910, Bigge to Tilleard

30 RA PS/PSO/GV/PS/STAMPS/4130/64 3 December 1910, Bigge to Samuel

31 POST 30/2136B op cit, 5 December 1910, Mackennal to Samuel

32 RA PS/PSO/GV/PS/STAMPS/4130/68 21 December 1910, Mackennal to the King

33 RA PS/PSO/GV/PS/STAMPS/4130/58 28 November 1910, Mackennal to the King

34 **Mackay, James A.** "The Harrison Collection of Proofs" *Stamp Collecting* 31 January 1964, reprinted in *The Essay-Proof Journal* Vol. 21, No.4 1964, pp 147-152

35 POST 30/2136B op cit

36 ibid 21 November 1910

37 ibid 23 November 1910, & RA PS/PSO/GV/PS/STAMPS/4130/57 Macartney to Bigge

38 **Richmond R. W.** The Letterpress Printed Postage Stamps of K.G.V. *GB Journal* Vol 12 pp 113-4 (1974)

39 ibid

40 ibid

41 Listed in detail in a memorandum by Edward Rigg 16 November 1910, T1/11338

42 POST 30/1967A Postage Stamps: King George V colour scheme, 3 March 1911, London Postal Section to Secretary, GPO

43 POST 30/1967A op cit 14 December 1910 memorandum by F.W. Phillips

44 POST 54/49 Correspondence regarding the introduction of King George V postage stamps, 17 January 1911

45 POST 30/2136B op cit Mackennal to Samuel 17 January 1911

46 ibid

47 POST 30/1957A op cit 14 March 1911

48 MINT 20/418 Dies and plates for Inland Revenue adhesive stamps, A.F. King to Secretary, Inland Revenue 13 October 1910

49 RA PS/PSO/GV/PS/STAMPS/4130/73 Bigge to Samuel

50 RA PS/PSO/GV/PS/STAMPS/4130/72 Samuel to Bigge

51 POST 54/50 Correspondence regarding the introduction of King George V postage stamps, Nathan to Macartney, 8 May 1911

52 POST 30/2136B 21 June 1911

53 MINT 20/450 Decorations and Medals: Jubilee, Coronation and Durbar medals. Coronation Medal King George V. 6 July 1911, Mackennal to Macartney

54 POST 30/2137A 28 June 1911 Ponsonby to Nathan

55 ibid 3 July 1911

5
LETTERPRESS PRINTING
THE PRINTING OF LOW-VALUE DEFINITIVES

The report of the Interdepartmental Committee in 1910 recommended that the production of dies and plates should be entrusted to the Royal Mint. Having no experience of such work Edward Rigg, in charge of the Operative Department at the Royal Mint, accompanied by Frederick Atterbury and Seymour Bennett of the Inland Revenue, visited printing works on the continent to see what would be required. They could hardly ask De La Rue to provide their expertise but there is no record of their asking other security printers in Britain.

On their return from the continent they had to obtain both equipment and staff. They also had to decide precisely how they would manufacture the plates. One aspect became crucial. This was the variation of dimensions in the plates made by De La Rue. The result of that had been increased difficulty in uniform perforation and this had added considerably to the quantity of watermarked paper spoiled in the manufacture of stamps.

> It has therefore been suggested that, in future, the new plates to be made by the Royal Mint should exactly conform to the pattern of a master plate of standard dimensions, and experiments have been made with the object of arriving at a standard for both stamps and plates.[1]

What this meant was the creation of master plates for all formats and denominations, and then working plates produced from these masters. This determined the process to be used and made it doubly complicated. There was also to be a slight change in the size of stamps, gutters and therefore plates, which was to affect the perforating comb required.

Creation of master plates

If the creation of the engraved die was complicated then that of the plates was even more so. As was seen in the last chapter there were some 20 stages in the creation of the die, the last being the striking of the number of "leads" required to make up the forme. One might have expected that to be used for printing but that was not the case. First, a master plate had to be made from these "leads".

After being firmly locked in a shallow metal box or chase and arranged in two panes of 120 images the mould was put into an electrolytic depositing bath to begin the process of creating the plate. Again, as with the dies, Richmond has described this process in great detail.

> Electrodes were attached to the mould and the mould face was blackleaded in order to increase its electrical conductivity. The

Above: Die for striking leads (top) and the holder for it.

Below: electrotyping – backing the shell (left); a mould going into a copper bath (right)

51

Above: wax mould with copper grown on it

Above: nickel shell

Above: working plate with gap for control number

Above: from the printed registration sheet

depositing bath was filled with a solution of copper sulphate and sulphuric acid in which the mould and a sheet of pure copper were totally immersed. The electrodes of the mould were connected to the negative terminal and the copper sheet to the positive terminal of an external power source. The electro-chemical reaction set up in the depositing bath caused a film of copper to be evenly deposited upon the surface of the mould. This process is known as electrotyping and the copper shell so deposited is said to be 'grown' upon the mould. The thickness of this copper shell is dependent upon the time allowed in growing it.[2]

The time in the copper bath varied, but for the first two master plates (for the ½d and the 1d) it was 82½ and 72 hours respectively. When the shell was of the required thickness the mould was re-moved from the bath and the shell separated. The face bore an ex-act replica of the mould, but in reverse. The copper shell was thin and flexible and need to be backed to give it the necessary rigidity. Molten type metal, an alloy of lead, tin and antimony, was poured on to the back of the shell with a ladle, carefully avoiding distortion of the thin shell. The back was then planed and the whole plate slabbed to ensure a perfectly flat surface on the front printing sur-face. The face bearing the images of the stamp (in reverse) was then proofed and any imperfections corrected. This was then the master plate from which all working plates derived.

Whatever format of sheet layout would require a separate master plate. This meant that individual master plates needed to be created for such things as booklets and rolls.

Making the working plate

In total, some 1150 working plates were made for George V stamps, postage and fiscal. The process of making them was complex and varied over time. Initially, they were copper plates with a steel finish. This was found to require frequent repair, so a nickel surface was provided which was much more durable. Finally, after about 1929, there was a further chromium facing.

The 140 or so initial copper plates were described as being "steel-faced". This was misleading. The facing was only a very thin "flash" coating of electrolytically deposited iron. Harrisons, the printers, complained that it wore off and bits of gum were pressed into the copper. On the other hand the coating could be easily removed and the plate re-surfaced in a very short time and this happened frequently. However, after a second visit by Edward Rigg to conti-nental printing works in July 1911 an improvement was introduced, adding a new nickel coating before the copper. The description that follows is of the creation of a working plate from that period.

Firstly, an impression of the master plate was taken by means of a large hydraulic press in warmed black mineral wax, known as "ozokerite". When hard this wax mould was dusted with graphite and then put into a nickel depositing bath, normally for about 48 hours (though this could vary dramatically). Then, it went into the copper bath, as before, for anything from 71 up to 85 hours for a thicker coating of copper. With the wax removed, the shell was then backed and slabbed as with the master plate. The first nickel-faced working plate was received from the Mint on 25 November 1911, although two trial plates of 25-set were created by 23 October.

Each time a mould or deposit is made from an original the image is reversed and it is difficult to visualise the process. When Bacon was sorting out the King's die proofs he asked Rigg at the Mint to explain the process so that he knew which stage the proofs came from. Rigg explained it thus, from the point where the die was engraved with the frame but no duty[3]:

Steel die with frame but no duty	-	Reverse
Roller die taken from it	-	Direct
Die in which duty is added	-	Reverse
Roller taken from it	-	Direct
Die from this roller for leads	-	Reverse
Leads	-	Direct
Master Plate from these leads	-	Reverse
Ozokerit [sic] mould from Master	-	Direct
Working plate from this mould	-	Reverse
Stamps printed from working plate	-	Direct

A diagram helps explain the detail of the plate-making. The printing was from the raised parts of the nickel surface.

Printing presses & printing

There were four processes undertaken by Harrison & Sons Ltd, the stamp printers, at Hayes – the gumming and calendering of the paper, and the printing and perforating of the finished stamps. Both the calendered paper and the printing presses were accused of being, at least part of, the cause of the poor printing. It transpired that, before they had purchased their machinery, Harrisons had also visited the principal stamp printing works on the continent. There they found that the stamp paper was calendered to make it smooth to receive the ink, and so they obtained three rotary machines to do this. With experience, this proved to be a mistake. An Inland Revenue report described what happened.

By the "Calendering" process the printing surface of the paper is obtained by passing the paper between polished steel rollers under power-pressure, a cheap and, for all or-dinary purposes, a sufficiently satisfactory process. But it is a markedly unsatisfactory process in the special case of the paper for British Stamps, as this paper is not only thin but is largely covered by the recessed surfaces of the watermarks, and the effect of the action of the steel rollers is to thin out and distort the paper (and thereby to cause spoil-age in the perforating process), and to break small holes in its surface, especially in the very thin surfaces over the "watermarks". It is this irregular "thinning" of the paper and breakage of its surface which gives the paper of the stamps the markedly poor appear-

1 Die

2 Lead

3 Electro-plated copper

4 Copper shell removed from lead

5 Copper backed by type metal

Above: Five stages in making the master plate

1 Master

2 Wax mould

3 Electro-plated Nickel on wax

4 Copper plated on nickel

5 Shell removed from wax mould

6 Backed with type metal

Above: Six stages in making the working plate

Above: Elliott Wharfedale printing machine at Waterlow Brothers & Layton

ance which has been so severely criticised; and the torsions and distortions set up in the paper by the calendering have been the direct cause of a large proportion of the considerable amount of spoilage of stamps which has taken place while the sheets are being perforated.[4]

To produce a paper surface suitable for the deeply watermarked British paper it needed to be "plate-glazed" rather than calendered. This, however, was more expensive. "Plate-glazing" was a process which consisted of placing each sheet between two plates of metal prior to the application of pressure in a power-driven machine. "Enormous power" was consumed in the process, according to Harrisons, and there was much more wear and tear on the machines, with resulting higher costs in maintenance.[5]

Then there was the question of the printing machines. Harrisons had noted that the French Government printed their stamps by Miehle machines, the most successful of the fast running (or "continuous revolution") machines.[6] So they purchased four of these, regarded as being excellent presses for general printing work. Both the rotary calendering machines and Miehle presses operated very rapidly, and here clearly lay the basis of Harrisons' original low quotations.

> As regards the printing, … a main aim in the construction of high class commercial printing machines is that they shall be fast running, and fast running is opposed to the successful printing of stamps, the machines for which should possess greater rigidity, and a far higher degree of ink-distributing power, than is required for other forms of printing.[7]

Slower running machines, Wharfedale presses, with a more even ink distribution, were used by De La Rue, Waterlow Brothers and Layton (for the Insurance stamps), and also in the Stamping Department of the Inland Revenue. Experiments at Somerset House during 1912 proved that rotary calendering and rapid printing by machines of the Miehle type did not produce stamps equal in quality to those on plate-glazed paper printed by Wharfedale presses.

Wharfedale machines had revolutionised the printing industry when first introduced in 1856. At first a cylinder was combined with a flat bed plate, instead of the traditional method of printing from two flat surfaces. David Payne of Otley in Yorkshire provided the next stage – a stop-cylinder machine with a travelling bed which meant that print could be delivered without the machine having to be stopped. In letterpress, or surface printing, the raised parts of the plate are inked, not the recesses as in intaglio. In the Wharfedale type of machine, the flat forme, with two or four working plates, travelled in turn beneath the inking rollers and the impression cylinder, both of which rotated but in fixed positions. The paper was fed automatically against the impression cylinder, held in place by grippers, and after being printed was again automatically led away to the delivery point.

To improve the printing on the Miehle presses the Inland Revenue required Harrisons to transfer production on to Wharfedales, with plate-glazing rather than calendering of the paper. In order to do so Harrisons demanded more money. The Treasury initially refused authorisation for the extra payment for plate-glazing and the use of Wharfedale machines. This forced the Inland Revenue to provide a detailed explanation of the processes and justification for the changes. Eventually, and very reluctantly, the Treasury agreed to the payment of an extra 1s 3d per ream. The additional payment amounted to about £2,700 a year, still leaving a saving of about £40,000 over the cost under the previous contract. Harrisons agreed to install more Wharfedale presses; they already had one.

However, this was not the first extra payment made to Harrisons. As has been seen they had been required in the first few months to work night shifts at Hayes to raise the reserve to a three-months' supply. For this they were paid double price for every ream supplied over the normal weekly output of 810 good reams. This was initially for three months, but was later extended through 1912. Even this was not enough but had to suffice.

> There can be no doubt that the prices inserted in their tender were quoted without complete knowledge of the cost of producing Stamps, and that, even when normal conditions of manufacture have been reached, there will be little or no profit accruing to the firm during the 10 years the Contract will run.[8]

They anticipated that receipts would barely pay for material and wages leaving nothing for profit. To offset this Harrisons asked to be given the contract for the supply of the paper. This was, unsurprisingly, refused by the Treasury.

Paper Contract

Since Victorian times watermarked stamp paper had been supplied by Messrs R.D. Turner of Roughway Mills, Tonbridge in Kent. They also supplied paper for the India Office and the Colonies. Their current contract had been agreed in 1904 for a period of seven years ending in September 1911, but this was also considered by the 1910 Interdepartmental

Below: Roughway Mills, Tonbridge

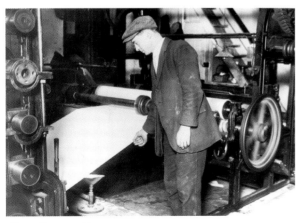

Above: Paper-making from wet (top) through steam drying cylinders (middle) to dry, examining the watermark (bottom)

Committee. As a result, the contract with Turner was extended to 1912 with a view to obtaining tenders from other firms for a replacement.

Some 37 firms were invited to tender in December 1911 but only eight quotations were received.[9] These were from:

> Mr William Nash
> Messrs John Dickinson and Company Limited
> Messrs R.D. Turner and Company (the present contractor)
> Messrs Alexander Pirie and Sons Limited
> Messrs William Joynson and Son
> Messrs Wiggin Teape and Company Limited
> Messrs The Basted Paper Mills Company Limited
> Messrs John Allen and Sons (Ivybridge) Limited

Two were described as being "conspicuous both for merit and cheapness", being the quotes from William Joynson of St Mary Cray (Kent), and John Allen of Ivybridge (Devon). Joynson had already supplied paper for Insurance stamps and that paper, at 12/4d per ream of 500 cut sheets at 5½d a lb, was recommended. This was tested and found to be very satisfactory. It was also a considerable saving on the price then paid to Turner of 21/3d per ream, an annual saving of over £11,000. The Treasury were astonished and delighted, as evidenced by a note they added to this letter:

> The terms seemed at first to me to be too good to be true or too cheap to be good. But Mr Atterbury tells me that the reduction has been effected by the adoption of the [Committee's] recommendation of a continuous watermark with a consequence of less exacting tervvms of contract. The [Inland Revenue] have consulted the Stationery Office all through as to the forms of tender. [Mr Atterbury] says the paper is the best they have had.[10]

Until now the watermark had been that of a crown which was required to be centrally positioned on each stamp image. The new requirement was of an all-over watermark of the GVR cipher and crown which did not need any registration. Savings were immediate, and a two year contract was agreed.

Some allowances had to be paid, however. At Turners, accommodation for the Inland Revenue supervisors had been provided free, but not at Joynsons. Equally, the hours had been from 6 a.m. to 6 p.m. daily finishing at 2 p.m. on Saturday. At Joynsons the papermaking machine was run day and night from 6 a.m. on Monday morning until midday on Saturday and the supervisors needed to be there for the entire time official work was being done. The machine would be run about 10 days in every four weeks, the remainder of the time being taken up with calendering, cutting and sorting.

Joynson paper was first used in September 1912, described as "over-all watermark".

Perforating

Once printed the stamps had to be perforated. The perforating machine was supplied to Harrisons by Grover & Co. Ltd of Stratford in east London. Their type I machine was designed on the "Comb" principle whereby the perforating pins were laid out across the sheet in a comb formation, punching holes at three sides of the stamp, one row at a time. It was found that seven sheets was the optimum number to be perforated in one go. However, rapid adjustments had to be made while the machine was running to meet the changes which occurred through stretch and contraction of the gummed paper due to atmospheric changes.

Above: The first Grover perforating machine

A different punch box was supplied for the Georgian stamps because of a slight difference in size compared to the previous Edwardian ones. Grovers measured it by the number of pins to the side of the stamp. So, for Edwardian stamps they made a box with perforations 17 x 14; for the Georgian stamps the perforations were 17 x 15, and the stamps were perforated sideways in both cases. Stamp collectors measure the number of holes every two centimetres, resulting in different figures in stamp catalogues.

In Grovers' experience it was best to keep the sheet as small as possible and not to attempt to perforate a very large sheet at one operation.

> Owing to atmospheric influence nearly all sheets are distorted, and naturally the larger the sheet the greater the error caused by distortion. It is, therefore, obvious that the waste from large sheets is out of all proportion greater than when smaller sheets are dealt with. This is also the case when the pinning up is erratic, due to the carelessness or inexperience of the operators. British Stamps are usually perforated in 240 "sets", though printed in 960 "sets". At one time 480 "sets" were perforated, but with very indifferent results, and with the "Grover" Machine there is no economy in so doing, as the operators are able with the 240 "sets" to keep up with the speed of the machine, and make good work; and should spoilage occur for any reason, it is much less expensive than with the larger sheets.[11]

Adjustments were thus provided under micrometer control for both the feeding and delivery of the stamp sheets. Operators could perforate some 2,000 sheets an hour. After about 450 reams the pins had to be sharpened or "dressed".

...the Inland Revenue concluded that "no material improvement in the appearance of [the ½d & 1d] stamps is possible while they continue to be printed from the plates at present supplied by the Royal Mint."

Recriminations

No one was immediately prepared to accept the blame for the initial poor printing. There was a climate of recrimination between the printers, the GPO and the plate-makers – the Royal Mint. The Inland Revenue, responsible (acting as controlling agents), were in the middle. Relations between the GPO, the printers and the Royal Mint descended to the acrimonious.

The Royal Mint, in particular, rejected the complaints of the printers. Plates were "out of gauge" – i.e. not precisely the correct size leading to problems with perforating. "Trifling" or "non-existent" was the response of Edward Rigg at the Mint to this charge. "As at present advised I hold that this and the great majority of complaints of similar nature have no real foundation in fact and are but poor excuses to transfer to the Mint blame for [the printers'] own incapacity."[12] Did Harrisons test the plates every morning as had been the practice at De La Rue's?

However, the plates wore out and frequently had to be returned for repair. In the four months to the end of September the Mint had delivered 26 halfpenny plates and 29 penny plates. Halfpenny plates had been returned 35 times, penny plates 31 times.

> A modus vivendi was then agreed upon as to the examination and repair of the plates. It was arranged that the Contractors should examine new plates as to gauge immediately upon receipt, and should return them if out of gauge. As regards repairs Mr Rigg agreed to have all plates which are returned for repair, carefully examined, and to repair all defects found, as well as any pointed out by Somerset House or the Contractors.[13]

One might have assumed that this would have been normal practice. It was nevertheless clear that Rigg had not appreciated the consequences of what he regarded as "trivial" differences. Atterbury and Vivian from the Inland Revenue visited Harrisons' works in person and then met Rigg the next day. They informed Rigg that they had measured an unused ½d plate and found it to be out by 1/32 inch. Even Rigg admitted that this amount of variation was "fatal to good perforation". It was also pointed out that the perforation gutters between stamps on both ½d and 1d plates were too narrow resulting in the stamp images encroaching on the perforations, and thus bleeding.

> This was admitted by Mr Rigg and Mr Evans, and it was agreed that in the preparation of the new ½d and 1d plates, every care should be taken to get the correct gauge and measurement of stamp surface, gutter and plate.[14]

Ellison Macartney, the Deputy Master of the Mint, suggested that both Rigg and Evans should visit the Hayes factory to inspect the various processes, especially the perforating, and this was agreed.

However, the Inland Revenue concluded that "no material improvement in the appearance of [the ½d & 1d] stamps is possible while they continue to be printed from the plates at present supplied by the Royal Mint."[15] They then worked with the new amended dies to produce new master plates.

Improving the plates and dies

With a view to improving the method of plate manufacture Atterbury, Bennett and Rigg again visited state printing works on the continent. On an extended visit in July 1911 they

Below: the 1d stamp as originally issued (top) and the deepened die (bottom)

looked at processes in Berlin, Vienna, Budapest and possibly Turin and Brussels. On their return, the Mint decided to replace steel facing with nickel on their working plates (the nickel being put on as a skin). This was claimed to treble the life of the plates.[16]

However, even before the first stamps were issued the Royal Mint had tried to improve the master plates for both the ½d and the 1d. New master plates from more deeply cut dies with sharper impressions were being created by the middle of June and from these more working plates were brought into use. Stamps from these plates (termed die 1b by collectors) were coming off the presses from the beginning of August. They could be available to the public in six weeks' time.

This was not enough, and the engraver Harrison was then asked to make a number of revisions to both dies. Dies and transfer rollers went backwards and forwards between the Mint and Harrison for various experimental re-engravings. Harrison wrote on 15 September saying that he had taken a few days holiday as he was "feeling the need of a change."[17] Consideration was also given to removing the tint behind the King's head and having a white or solid surround, and essays were produced in October.

Above: colour trial of the amended 1d die

> The question of possible improvements in the artistic quality of the ½d and 1d designs has, however, been exhaustively considered by the Royal Mint in conference with Mr MacKennal, with the result that certain changes have been decided upon and fresh engravings made in accordance therewith. These changes will entail the preparation of new master-plates and working plates, in the manufacture of which an opportunity will be taken to introduce the latest improvements in the engraving of the King's effigy and in the general engraving of the stamp which the Mint have been able to effect upon the plates for some of the other designs.[18]

The changes mentioned were particularly noticeable on the lion of the 1d, adding shading to the lion's body, and the dolphins of the ½d.

Both new dies were ready by the beginning of November, with lettering and some detail to the head touched up by C.G. Lewis, the Mint's engraver. New master plates, the third for each value, were then created and working plates from these subsequently.

Above: Amended ½d

With the new dies a number of colour trials of the 1d, were undertaken at the Stamping Department of the Inland Revenue in November, and 15 sheets were submitted.

> It should be borne in mind, in considering the whole range of shades now submitted, that in accordance as a red approximates in character to a crimson, to that extent it has a tendency to absorb light and exhibit a dull and lifeless appearance, especially after handling; and that in accordance as a red approximates to a scarlet or vermilion to that extent it reflects light, and both possesses and retains brilliance.[19]

At the beginning of December, Samuel approved "Imperial scarlet" (No. 3181 made by Shackell Edwards & Co.), and this was introduced with the new stamps in January. Almost at the same time the new nickel plates came into use.

59

The British 1d Stamp (H.M. Geo. V) printed on Austrian Stamp Paper.

Rose Colour formerly used

Scarlet Colour now used

Top: Downey 1d offset trial

Bottom: Downey 1d trials on Austrian paper

In the midst of all this activity a minor clause of the Government's Finance Act of 1911 transferred statutory powers controlling the manufacture of postage stamps to the Postmaster General. From 1914 the Inland Revenue would no longer be the intermediary between Post Office and Royal Mint or printers.

Printing Experiments

Still trying to effect an improvement in the printing Harrisons, on their own initiative, tried an experiment on the 1d denomination. On 25 January 1912, using one of the new plates on a Miehle machine, Mr Warne, manager of the works at Hayes, made some experimental prints on Crown watermarked paper. Later, when asked to explain, Harrisons stated that he had instructions to improve the printing in every way and to be "on the watch" for anything which might help.

> Our attention having lately been called to the broken appearance of many of the fine lines of the head of the stamp when examined under a glass, our Manager wished to see whether this could be altered if the medium of the impression was changed; and for that purpose he took some impressions of one of the Plates through the medium of a rubber sheet. These pulls were taken and examined in the printing room and no attempt made to make any other use of them.[20]

Taking an impression on to a rubber sheet and then printing from that would have the effect of creating an offset, or reverse, print (in other words offset letterpress). Although Harrisons regarded the result as satisfactory others did not and offset, as a process for printing stamps, was described as being "quite unsuitable". One sheet of these reverse prints has survived and is in the philatelic collections of the British Library.[21]

The Inland Revenue were not at all impressed by these actions, particularly as they had only discovered them by accident, and the printers were duly reprimanded.

Another printing experiment, this time official, took place in March 1912 when the Stamping Department at Somerset House printed the 1d Downey on Austrian stamp paper. This was both coated and unwatermarked and proofs were struck in the rose formerly used and the scarlet in use with the second die.

Other Values

Other low values using Mackennal's designs were also engraved by Harrison. These were the 1½d from the master Dolphin die; the 2½d from the master Lion die; and the 2d and

3d from the master Wreath die. Master plates, and then working plates, as before, had to be made from these dies. As a result of the poor printing of the stamps as issued modifications were made to the new dies.

In particular the Wreath die was altered after the 2d value had been engraved. This continued on the 3d value through August. For the 2½d Lion design a master plate was created in July. However, the spacing of the wording was not satisfactory and this plate was not used. The die was altered and a new master plate made on 4 August. Even then, a new die was engraved on 31 October using the re-engraved 1d die.

Master plates were made by the Mint for all values up to 3d. Working plates were made for the 1½d, 2d and 2½d but not all were satisfactory and only two of the 2d Wreath design and two of the 2½d Lion were received by Somerset House. These were both used to print various colour trials.

Colour Revisited
As Bennett had implied back in December 1910 there was little point in allocating final colours to denominations until the finished die or plate was ready. Designs could alter perceptions of colour considerably. With the working plates of both the 2d and 2½d designs new colour trials were requested.

Bartolozzi Brown.
M.B. 23,759.

Mackennal suggested that the 3d Wreath die would print well with a better colour, but this would have an impact on the colours for other values.

Sheets of the 2d and 2½d in various shades of brown and blue respectively were first supplied on 9 September but the blue was considered too dull and dark. Brighter shades were requested. Maroon had been proposed for the 1½d and brown for the 2d but Samuel thought that this might lead to confusion. The Inland Revenue were therefore informed on 20 October that the 1½d value should be brown, the 2d a vivid orange and the 3d purple.

Further sheets of both the 2d and 2½d were printed on watermarked paper on 24 October, the 2d in six shades of brown, olive green and maroon, and the 2½d in six shades of brighter blue. Yet more shades of blue were requested, still brighter and more vivid but this was then superseded by the cancellation of all work on the Downey head values above 1d.

Problems with Eve's designs
After initial approval in October 1910, little was done with George Eve's designs for the frames for the higher values, as all work concentrated on the ½d and 1d and related denominations. His "Wreath" design was originally intended for the 4d, 5d, 6d and 7d

Top: 24 October 1911. Limited colour scheme for proposed Downey stamps

Above: Colour trial of proposed 2d Downey Head in "Bartolozzi Brown"

Below: Amended Lion die for 2½d, November 1911

H.M.S. MEDINA.

11th Nov. 1911.

Dear Mr Samuel,

There is no disguising the fact that the King is disappointed about the Stamps, and if it were possible he would prefer that nothing further is done in the matter until his return from India, and suggests that Stamps with King Edward's effigy might be used. If you would allow Mr J.A. Millard, "Ivor" Goldhurst Terrace, West Hampstead, NW to show you a stamp which the King approved of for the Crown Colonies, and if this could be adopted by you His Majesty would be quite satisfied.

Yours very truly,

Stamfordham

The Rt. Hon:
Herbert Samuel, M.P.
Postmaster General.

Above: The King says nothing more should be done with the Downey stamps

stamps while his "Pillars" design was approved for the 8d, 9d, 10d and 1/- values. When the head of the King was engraved, it became necessary to modify these designs in order that the head was of the correct proportions to the frame. This work was done through February and March 1911 and then the particular values had to be drawn in. Photographs of lettering being used for the coinage (specially chosen by Mackennal) were supplied by the Mint for this purpose.

It was explained that the tints in his designs would have to be interpreted in lines by the engraver. For the "Wreath" design this was initially done by H.P. Huggill, a young engraver studying at the South Kensington School of engraving. This took place in April, and by May an amended drawing of the 4d was submitted to Eve for his detailed comments. These he provided on 18 May.[22]

> The tint of the upper part of the background is much too dark. It was intended to be as light as the necessities of surface printing would permit and about the weight of the lightest tint on King Edward VII stamp. The tint should be carried through the crown. In the latter the line of the arch should be more marked and the jewel more accurately copied from the original.
>
> The background at bottom is intended to be solid graduating to the top and equal on both sides. The drawing of the border and the drawing and proportions of the lettering are not well copied and the sides of the border are very unequal, a slight discrepancy in the original being exaggerated rather than corrected in the line drawing.
>
> In some respect, no doubt, allowance has been made for cutting down to the actual engraving but it will be well to note the preceding points.
>
> It will be desirable to add a tint to the Shamrocks in the badges as I have now indicated even though it may ultimately be dispensed with.

Right: photograph of Mackennal's chosen lettering for the coinage

Huggill was then employed to engrave this 4d (Wreath) design, with Harrison working on the 9d (Pillars). The work began in August, but Huggill's engraving was not satisfactory, and the 4d Wreath design was handed to the Mint engraver, Lewis. Later these design allocations were to change entirely.

Lewis worked on Eve's Wreath design from August through till October, creating dies for the 4d and 5d values. He was finalising the 6d

ABCDEF
GHJKLM
NOPQRS
TUVWX
YZ·1234
567890

Left: October 1911 – colour trials for the 5d Downey in Eve's Wreath design

denomination when he was ordered to stop. On 27 October Samuel was described as being "very unhappy" with this design, in particular with the size of the Downey head. It was too cramped. Matthew Nathan, now at the Inland Revenue, wrote that he was "advised that for any size smaller than that of the 'approved' head on the 1d – 3d stamps only profile will produce reasonably satisfactory results."[23] Enquiries were then set in train.

The end of the Downey head

On 11 November, the King set sail for his Durbar in India on the new P & O ship *Medina*, now entitled H.M.S. *Medina*. From on board, Lord Stamfordham (the ennobled Arthur Bigge) wrote to the Postmaster General:

> Dear Mr Samuel
>
> There is no disguising the fact that the King is disappointed about the Stamps, and if it were possible he would prefer that nothing further is done in the matter until his return from India, and suggests that Stamps with King Edward's effigy might be used. If you would allow Mr J.A. Tilleard, "Ivor" Goldhurst Terrace, West Hampstead, N.W. to show you a stamp which the King approved of for the Crown Colonies, and if this could be adopted by you His Majesty would be quite satisfied.[24]

Left: Eve's 4d Wreath design engraved by Huggill (in blue) and by Lewis (others)

Below: Eve's 6d unfinished Wreath die

Thus was the Downey head dismissed, and work was stopped on all values above 1d on 15 November. Some work continued on the two lower values, however, and stamps from the new amended dies for the 1d and ½d were registered on 5 and 11 December respectively, being issued to post offices from 30 December 1911.[25]

This was also, perhaps just as importantly, to be the end of the lion design, until now so tenaciously retained by the PMG, Herbert Samuel.

---

1   MINT 20/418 Inland Revenue to GPO 18 October 1910

2   **Richmond R. W.** The Letterpress Printed Postage Stamps of K.G.V. op cit

3   MINT 20/545 Rigg to Bacon 5 February 1914

4   T1/11491 Inland Revenue to Treasury, 2 November 1912

5   ibid Harrisons to Inland Revenue, 28 October 1912

6   ibid 2 November 1912

7   ibid

8   T1/11338 21 October 1911, Inland Revenue to Treasury

9   T1/11523 Joynson paper contract, 25 June 1912, Inland Revenue to Treasury

10   ibid 27 July 1912

11   Grover leaflet, undated but 1920s.

12   POST 54/50 Rigg to Bennett 7 October 1911

13   ibid Memorandum 6 September 1911

14   ibid 10 October 1911

15   ibid Atterbury to GPO 14 October 1911

16   POST 54/50 op cit Atterbury memorandum 26 August 1911

17   Harrison to Eve 14 September 1911; quoted in **Beaumont, K.M. & Stanton, J.B.M.** *The Postage Stamps of Great Britain* Part 4 1957 p231

18   POST 30/2137A Dies and colours for King George V issue. Atterbury to GPO 14 October 1911

19   ibid 29 November 1911

20   POST 30/2303A Contract with Harrisons. Harrisons to Atterbury

21   **Muir, D. N.** "Downey Head Printed Offset – A Mystery Explained" *GB Journal* Volume 46 March/April 2008 pp25-30

22   Eve to Royal Mint, 18 May 1911, in **Beaumont & Stanton** op cit p228

23   POST 54/50 op cit Nathan to King 27 October 1911

24   POST 30/2137A op cit. 11 November 1911

25   [Richmond papers] Atterbury to Rigg 2 January 1912

6
THE KING'S HEAD IN PROFILE
MACKENNAL'S COINAGE & MEDAL HEADS

"T"he King desires me to let you know how delighted he is with your design for his effigy for the African Medal."[1]

This was at the beginning of the close working and personal relationship between Bertram Mackennal and the King. Although Mackennal had been chosen in June 1910 to work on an effigy for coins, British and Imperial, he had also been asked to provide effigies for medals – for the Coronation and various naval, military and civil versions. For this he was to be paid a total of 1,000 guineas, a sum only reluctantly agreed by the Treasury. They reflected that, as the King was taking such a personal interest, there was little they could do.

> As to the amount of the fee, I suppose that having selected our artist we are practically bound to pay him what he asks, though I confess I think 1000 guineas a very large sum to pay for the work to be done. Mr Macartney has a very high opinion of Mr MacKennal's reputation, but I am not sure that that opinion is very widely shared.[2]

However, the most urgent medal required was to be given to those who had helped to create the new Union of South Africa. Their united parliament was due to be opened in November 1910 and the medals were required to be taken out for that occasion. Interestingly, the inauguration of the South African parliament was also the occasion for the first stamp of George's reign to bear his portrait (a three-quarter profile).

The "African Medal" was Mackennal's first, and, as required by the Mint, he based it on the profile photograph by W. & D. Downey taken in June – not the three-quarter profile taken at the same time on which so much time, effort and tears were expended by the Post Office, the Mint and the engraver, for stamps. This plaster model, the final one dated 27 September, was in many ways the basis for all subsequent effigies. The model for the coinage followed on 15 November.

Thereafter came Coronation medals with the King crowned and including a bust of Queen Mary, and then naval and military medals, with the King in appropriate uniform for each. The latter can most easily be distinguished by the epaulettes on the King's uniform on the naval medal, which are lacking on that of the military. These were all being created at the same time as the coinage model which was similar to the South African effigy. More importantly, all these profile heads were available when the crisis

...I suppose that having selected our artist we are practically bound to pay him what he asks, though I confess I think 1000 guineas a very large sum to pay for the work to be done.

Left: Original Downey profile portrait

Below: Mackennal's plaster model for the South Africa medal

Bottom: Mackennal's Coronation medals showing King George V and Queen Mary

came with the Downey three-quarter profile.

Yet another effigy was also created by Mackennal, this time for India. Here he is shown crowned and wearing Indian insignia. This sculpture was used for Indian coins and also Indian stamps and De La Rue claimed this was the basis of their engraved head of the King for Colonial stamps. They were probably referring to photographs of the Coinage head. In truly pompous and self-congratulatory fashion Evelyn de la Rue wrote to the Crown Agents in 1911 only six weeks after the stamps printed by Harrisons had been issued to such disdain:

We have to inform you that, in accordance with the Royal Command received a few hours previously, we on Saturday last waited upon his Majesty at Cowes, and submitted to him various engravings and photographic proofs of his portrait which we happened to have by us. An impression from the steel that you supplied to us a short time since [with the three-quarter Downey portrait] was among their number. His Majesty selected for use on the issues of Colonial stamps a portrait of himself which he initialled as approved. This portrait ...is identical with the design to be used for the India stamps, with the exception that the crown and mantle have been removed...

We may add that his Majesty expressed himself as highly satisfied with this portrait, and wishes to see proofs from the die.[3]

Above: Mackennal's model (in metal) for Indian coins and stamps, with 1 Rupee coin and stamp from 1912

As early as August 1910 the King was first aware of a satisfactory portrait, profile in nature, on the South Africa medal. Later that year, Mackennal had created a series of portrait models for the medals. Now, he saw that it could be translated into a satisfactory engraving. These various effigies were to be the basis of King George V's profile image on stamps, but the story is complex.

Profile head on stamps

The idea of a profile head on stamps was first mooted by the Inland Revenue in connection with the larger, high value design. Referring to a visit to the Mint in August 1911 Atterbury recorded:

A new head will be required. The idea is that Harrison should engrave the King in profile (from an existing photograph, shewn in plaque on the occasion of our visit) for these stamps. Then if the profile is approved by the public and a request is made for it to be inserted in substitution in the lower stamps, this can be done without difficulty.[4]

However, the decision to change to a profile head from the problems of the Downey head seems to have been that of Herbert Samuel and had nothing to do with the high value stamps. He was not happy with the result of inserting the Downey three-quarter profile into the frames by George Eve. Here Clausen's remarks, right at the outset one year previously, that one artist should be employed for the complete design, were being proved correct. Samuel wanted a smaller head, and this could only satisfactorily be provided by a profile.

As Samuel did not approve the dies work was stopped on engraving Eve's Wreath design on 27 October. The Inland Revenue recorded "that he desires that fresh dies be engraved, the design of the present new frames being retained, but a new head of the King, smaller and in profile, being substituted".[5] The Mint were informed and they saw no great difficulty.

> A reduction to the required size of a profile photograph of the King is now being prepared & will be sent to Mr Eve without delay, & with this Mr Eve will be able to make such modifications in his designs as may be required to meet the recent decision of the P.M.G. Mr Eve is not of course required to make any drawing of the King's effigy for use hereafter in the preparation of the plate, as the engraver works directly from the photograph with which the Mint supplies him.[6]

Sources of the profile head on stamps

Samuel now wrote to the King admitting that the existing head on the new stamps "is certainly not as satisfactory as could be wished but in spite of many attempts the Mint seem unable to effect further improvements in the appearance of the portrait."[7] It was to this letter that the reply came from the *Medina* asking that nothing further be done, but also suggesting that Tilleard provide a proof of the head as approved for the Crown Colonies. The proof in the official collection which came from Tilleard is annotated as being for the South African stamps, but this is identical with that for the Crown Colonies, coming, as it does, from De La Rue who created and printed both (and is described as Colonial in contemporary documents). It was left with the G.P.O. on 17 November and was supplied to the Mint a few days later, together with versions of the colonial postcard die and frame.

Earlier the King, quite exasperated, had intervened personally to ensure that South African stamps did not bear the Downey three-quarter portrait. The Cape Parliament had agreed to adopt this but in a letter to Tilleard Sir Frederick Ponsonby, the King's Assistant Private Secretary reported:

> His Majesty however was horrified to think that the mess there has been with the English stamp would be reproduced in South Africa. The King therefore wishes to produce a really good head and at his own expense. He hopes that when this has been adopted in South Africa, the Post Master General will be able to see the difference and so the English stamps will eventually be copied from them.

> The King wishes you to get from Downey the two little photographs which they did last year on purpose for the stamp, one profile and the other three quarters face. Will you thus get the best engraver you know and have a really good engraving done and send this to His Majesty at Balmoral. The King thinks that it would be best to try the profile one to start with.[8]

Above: Downey profile portrait as prepared for coins (top)

De La Rue die proof for South African and Colonial stamps (middle) with South African stamp of 1913

Tilleard consulted De La Rue who had already created a die for Colonial stamps and, with modifications, this was pronounced satisfactory for the South African. No expense was therefore required of the King but this is what was now given to the G.P.O.

The problem faced by all concerned was the variety of frames already approved, with the consequent great variation in the space provided for the King's head. Two or more profile

heads would be required because of this. Various versions were now considered but measuring them vertically was awkward because of different truncations of the neck. As a result, the Mint came up with a remarkable formula for measuring them *horizontally*, which they then used to describe the various heads under consideration. They measured between the tip of the nose and the extreme of the back of the head, and then took this as a percentage of the width of the entire stamp. Thus "41.4" was the size of a head which was 41.4% of the width of the stamp, or 7.7553 mm.

A number of photographs of various profiles were prepared by the Mint. These were:

1. Photograph from life [profile by Downey] with bust stopped out. [cropped]
2. Effigy engraved for Colonial stamps and approved by the King.
3. Effigy of Imperial Coinage in three sizes.

Above: Mackennal's plaster model for British coinage

Right: proof half crown with Mackennal's profile

In a memorandum on re-designing the George V stamps the Mint described these steps in detail. Referring to the Imperial Coinage effigy they stated that "it will at once be seen that the Colonial Stamp Effigy is a mere copy".

If, therefore, we proceed at once to engrave an effigy from the Imperial Coinage Effigy, we shall be executing His Majesty's Commands, and it only remains to determine the exact dimensions of the effigy to be engraved.[9]

Reduced stamp-size photographs were therefore produced incorporating profile heads at sizes ranging from 41.4 to 50.0 by the Mint scheme of measurement. These are now in the Royal Philatelic Collection (dated by Bacon 27 November 1911). First, a photograph of a die of the Colonial head in different sizes; then a profile Downey photograph and lastly a photograph of the plaster model of the Coinage head, again in different sizes.[10]

At a meeting on 21 December at Somerset House it was decided to proceed with an engraving of the Coinage head. When this was conveyed to Rigg at the Mint he at once telephoned Harrison to go there "when I gave him photographs and a plaster cast of the coinage head as well as other items necessary to get to work at once on the

Above: frames with different sized Coinage head photographs

Right: die proofs of the Coinage head

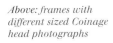

47.4 head".[11] Harrison expected to get it finished before the end of January so "it should be ready to submit to the King immediately on his return" (from India). In his reply to Rigg's letter Atterbury ruefully acknowledged his good wishes for the New Year – "May it see us through all our stamp troubles."[12] It was to be a forlorn hope.

Harrison completed the Coinage head engraving, as requested at 47.4 in size by Mint reckoning, by the beginning of February 1912, although it was subsequently to be slightly modified.

In the meantime, Mackennal had been consulted with a view to altering the frames of his Lion and Wreath designs, enlarging the ovals containing the King's head to give more space for the 47.4 head by reducing the width of the wreath.

> It is quite possible to do this in the wreath design, without harm it could be done at the base of the oval. But in the case of the lion design, if you enlarge the oval in the present design, you will thrust the head of the lion more into the oval containing the head, and make a bad design very much worse.

> You cannot lift the oval as the crown is already on the small size. The whole of this design has been squeezed already, to try and carry the lion, and to me it is a failure. What is suggested will only make it worse. I think if it is the intention now to improve the head it at least deserves a decent frame. My suggestion is to do away with the lion altogether and have another base to this design or a new design altogether.[13]

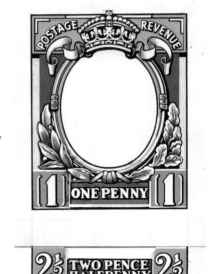

This unpleasant news had to be conveyed to the Postmaster General. It was put to Samuel "in person" by Inland Revenue officials on 17 January 1912. His immediate response was to ask if the new effigy could be truncated, shortening the point of the neck, rather than get rid of his beloved Lion design. This could be done, according to Mackennal, but he had other things in mind.

Alternatives

While Harrison was engraving the Coinage head die Mackennal was working on an alternative frame design to the hated Lion. There is little documentary, or other, evidence extant. What does remain is a finished drawing of oak and laurel leaves supporting a large oval surmounted by a crown. This has the value of One Penny (but there is an additional value tablet of Two Pence Halfpenny). There is also a photograph of a sculpted plaster model of the same, but with a slightly different layout, with a fresh profile portrait of the King inserted into the centre. This was clearly shown by Mackennal directly to the King because the latter initialled it as approved on 21 February, immediately on his return from India. Of the original plaster model or models there is now no trace.

It was Mackennal who conveyed the photograph to the Post Office two days later with the news that it was to be used in place of the Lion design. Samuel's reaction is not recorded. He had been out-manoeuvred.

Mackennal continued to deal directly with the King. In reply to a letter from Sir Frederick Ponsonby, in Stamfordham's absence, about the existing engraved Coinage head die he emphasised that this was *not* the effigy he wished used in his new design for the 1d and 2½d.

Above: artwork by Mackennal for an oak and laurel leaves design

Bottom: initial sculptured model with a smaller Medal head to replace the 1d Lion, approved by the King

Intriguingly, this is not the first dated use of the military medal head. Three weeks before Mackennal's new design for the 1d was submitted to the Mint Lewis began an engraving from a transferred photograph of the military medal.

Right: Mackennal's plaster model for the Naval medal, with medal (top)

The plaster model for the Military medal (without epaulettes) with medal (bottom)

I do not know whether the Postmaster General made it clear to The King that the head shown is not for the penny stamp or the twopence halfpenny but less used values. It is my wish to have the head for the penny stamp made from the design I showed His Majesty.[14]

In fact, Samuel had written the same day to Stamfordham pointing this out. The King could not quite see why more than one head was required but a meeting with Mackennal clarified matters and he accepted Mackennal's wish, agreeing that the Coinage head would be used on other values. An internal Post Office memorandum explained the difference, apart from the question of size.

> The Mint have completed the engraving of the effigy based on the model used for the coinage, of which, I believe, you obtained His Majesty's approval. The effigy in the latest 1d and 2½d design is drawn from the head in the model of the naval and military medals, and the difference between the two is not very great.[15]

About this time Eve drew rough sketches to show what differences there were between the two heads.

As depicted on the medals there were also major differences between the effigies on the naval and military medals. These, however, were in the uniform rather than the head, the military version being "without cloak". The most obvious visual difference is that the naval medal has the King with epaulettes, the military one without. The head would appear to be the same.

Intriguingly, this is not the first dated use of the military medal head. Three weeks before Mackennal's new design for the 1d was submitted to the Mint Lewis began an engraving from a transferred photograph of the military medal. This included the shoulders which makes identification certain. It is possible that Mackennal had already indicated to the Mint that he was using this as the basis for the new design he was working on.

Another alternative was also tried by the Mint. On 15 February the original die for the Edward VII ½d and 1d was proofed at the Mint and enlarged essays were printed from half-tone blocks from another version of King George's head. However, there is no evidence that any of these was seen by the King, and no documentary evidence of their creation or submission.

This all served to delay the engraving by Harrison of an accepted profile head. If the King had not agreed to the use the Coinage head already engraved on some values the Mint were so hard pressed that there was a "great fear of their engraving staff breaking down."[16] That at least was progress.

Work on the new Medal head did not begin until mid April because there was still the question of what size it should be. This was settled by the King as being much larger than the others, 52.5 on the Mint scale and the Inland Revenue were informed on 10 April. A photograph of a plaster model with the larger head exists though it is not clear if Mackennal amended the original model or created a new one. The other Mackennal designs would have the Coinage head as engraved. For Eve's designs Samuel was strongly of the opinion that the 47.4 head was too large but the smaller version was not proceeded with. The head used was to be quite different and it was not agreed until much later.

Harrison worked on the die for the new oak and laurel leaves design at home, beginning with the new Medal head. No master head die as such exists. Rather, on the same piece of steel Harrison added the new frame in stages around this head. There is no evidence that this reached the Mint before the master die was complete on 15 or 16 May. No die proofs are recorded in the Royal Mint proof book which has a day-by-day account of what was done there. Nevertheless, several stages of the engraving of the die survive, clearly proofed by Harrison in his workplace.

The master die was for the two values, the 1d and the 2½d. For the 1d the denomination was first engraved at the end of May though various modifications took it through to 11 July. Thereafter the 2½d die was created by scraping out the 1d value and lettering and re-engraving the new value on another die. The first working plate of the 1d was ready at the beginning of August; the 2½d not until the end of September. Stamps were first issued to the public on 8 and 18 October respectively.

Dies of other values, in the meantime, were prepared for the original Coinage head to be inserted in place of the Downey head. In April and May 1912 the 1½d Dolphin and 2d Wreath designs began to be engraved with the new profile, with the Dolphin frame being re-engraved. The 3d Wreath design followed in July. Working plates were ready for the 2d in July and the other values in September or October. As new Georgian denominations they were quickly made available to the public, but in piecemeal fashion – the 2d on 20 August, followed by the 3d and 1½d in October (9th and 15th respectively). Printing was on the new Joynson paper, watermarked G R V, plate-glazed and on the Wharfedale machine.

Above: Engravings by Lewis from the Military medal (top) and Royal Mint essays based on the Edward VII die

So, by the end of October 1912 the only stamps on sale bearing George V's head were: ½d (Downey Dolphin), 1d and 2½d (Oak leaves), 1½d (Dolphin), and 2d and 3d (Wreath), all with a profile head except the ½d.

71

Problems remained the same with the lack of skilled engravers to engrave the dies. So, progress was slow. This caused the Inland Revenue to look at alternatives which might speed the process up. However, they did it in secret without informing the Royal Mint...

  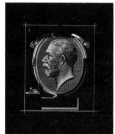 

Right: Progression of the Medal Head die for the 1d, with Coinage Head inserted in Dolphin frame and Mackennal's issued stamps

Work on all values proceeded with both designers, Mackennal and Eve, intimately involved at all stages.

Right: Approved engraver's drawing of the Medal Head

An Experimental Printing Process

Problems remained the same with the lack of skilled engravers to engrave the dies. So, progress was slow. This caused the Inland Revenue to look at alternatives which might speed the process up. However, they did it in secret without informing the Royal Mint of their experiments in any detail. The Post Office, on the other hand, were aware of them. First mention comes on 17 May when Nathan asked Samuel to approve the 4d frame design.

> If you accept the design now submitted it should be possible to issue the stamp, from plates prepared by the new process, in the first days of June.[17]

Eve had submitted photographs of the amended version of his 4d Wreath design on 2 April. Now, rather than have it engraved at the Mint a photographic method was to be tried to create the plates. Samuel reported this to the King on 25 July enclosing a sheet proofed by the process.[18]

In spite of the prolonged delay the Mint are still not ready with the plates for the 4d and higher denomination stamps, and as a possible alternative the Board of Inland Revenue have had plates prepared by what is known as the Motley process. This is a method of etching from a photograph reproduced on the surface of a copper sheet.

The sheet of 4d stamps, which I enclose, has been produced by this method, the result of which is clearly not quite so good as that obtained from plates produced in the ordinary way. ...

The question which has now to be decided is whether it is better to issue at once the higher denomination stamps produced by the Motley process, in spite of its slight inferiority, leaving the plates from the Mint to be substituted later as soon as they are ready; or whether it is better to wait for these plates, possibly for several months.

My own inclination was to the former course, but Mr McKennal [sic], whose opinion I asked, is strongly against issuing the Motley plates, on account of the inferiority of the reproduction of the head, and I agree that there is considerable force in the objection. Perhaps you would ask His Majesty to be good enough to decide which course he would prefer to be taken?

Above: Eve's artwork for the 4d Wreath design, with stamp-size reverse photograph for the Printex process

CONFIDENTIAL.

STAMPING DEPARTMENT 11 JUL.1912

Purple. (Official)

Essays for Colour only

E. 64.

The Motley, or Printex, process was photographic. It was quicker and cheaper than the laborious craft of engraving dies and creating letterpress plates. After a careful, enlarged line drawing was produced in reverse – one such exists on metal – a master photograph was created on glass, positive and reversed. By placing this in a form of step-and-repeat printing machine, a reversed multi-negative was produced. From this a copper plate with a light-sensitized surface was

Left: Colour trial of Eve's 4d Wreath design by the Printex process

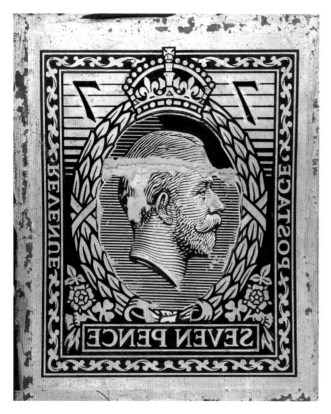

etched after exposure to light through the multi-negative. The British patents for the photographic printing frames (24,487 and 27,264 of 1911) were registered in the joint names of Alfred Henry Motley (hence the name), Clark Aubert Miller and Herbert Morris Pilkington.[19] Later it was produced by the Printex Company. It was to be used as a means of producing colour essays and also a mock "Ideal" 1d stamp design printed at the Jubilee International Stamp Exhibition, held under the auspices of the Junior Philatelic Society (Fred Melville) at the Royal Horticultural Halls in London from 14 to 19 October.

Evidence of the Inland Revenue experiments in printing sheets, rather than blocks of four essays, is held in the British Library philatelic collections. The first rough proof of a sheet of the 4d, 240-set, (by Baderean & Jones) was dated 12 June. Several more amended sheets followed through July, and included 5d and 6d versions. Comparing these with the head on the 2d stamp, traditionally engraved, Mackennal "expressed the opinion that the one was 'dead', flat and blotched, the other 'alive', and clear."[20]

Above: Reverse large-size artwork on metal used to create the Printex blocks of the 7d Eve wreath design

Right: George Eve (1855 – December 1914)

The King concurred. When shown the specimen 4d Wreath sheet, the King was neither amused nor impressed. Stamfordham replied immediately to Samuel's letter:

> the King does not at all like the Stamps which have been produced by the Motley Process, as exemplified by the sheet of 4d Stamps which you sent, and which will not bear comparison with the 2d Stamps from the Mint Plates.

> The King thinks it would be much better to wait, no matter how long, in order to get the best possible stamps obtainable from the plates produced in the ordinary way.[21]

In this, the King was undoubtedly influenced by Mackennal's forthright and adverse opinion. Work was stopped on the Motley sheet proofs on 29 July as a result. Blame was put on the Inland Revenue for the secrecy and the Post Office admitted to the Mint that they "have not treated you well in the matter of the 4d stamp".[22]

Change of 4d Design

The 4d design began life with Eve's Wreath frame. After the Motley experiment there was a reversion to

CONFIDENTIAL.

Gloriosa Blue.

Essays for Colour only.

E.189.

CONFIDENTIAL.

Tyrian Red.

Essays for Colour only.

E.198.

the more traditional approach of engraving at the Mint. This was undertaken by Lewis and his first proof with the same Eve design dates from 17 July. Eve had been seriously ill and this had delayed matters. Work continued on minor detail through till October when a colour proof was submitted to the King. He approved the Wreath design but not the colour. Instructions were given to make a master plate but in the end this was superseded by events.

At the same time Lewis worked on the 8d design which utilised Eve's "Pillar" frame, 8d being a new value not yet in circulation. The die was complete and passed by Eve on 18 September. These two dies of Eve's designs, the 4d Wreath and the 8d "Pillar" were to act as the basis for the other values as then agreed.

However, Samuel had never liked the size of the head in relation to the frames. When a proof was produced for the 4d in May in preparation for the Motley printed sheets he commented that he supposed he would have to put up with it. At that time the King had no objection and thought it a "great improvement". With the rejection of the colour in October Samuel now found support for his view from Atterbury. He shared Samuel's opinion that the head was rather too big for the Wreath frame "and the defect is of course more pronounced in the case of the design for the 8d to 1/- stamps." Rather than alter the frames yet again "it would be better to have the head re-drawn and re-engraved on a slightly smaller scale and used for both designs."[23] A rather smaller head would in any case be required for the Inland Revenue's fiscal stamps. This was, of course, exactly what Samuel had wanted to hear and he immediately agreed. "But the head should not be *much* smaller. Mr Eve might be consulted about this." It would, however, entail delay.

Above: Colour trials by the Printex process showing different backgrounds to the King's head

Conveying this information to Eve, Rigg at the Mint betrayed his growing impatience.

> I believe you have already heard from Atterbury that the P.M.G. has raised further questions in regard to the 4d and 1/- designs from the same old point of the head of the King being too large, and this notwithstanding the fact that he has himself submitted the former to the King and had it approved.[24]

Nevertheless, he enclosed a number of photographs at different sizes for Eve to try in the frames, reiterating the Mint method of measurement. Instead of 47.4

> The new ones, 46 and 45 respectively, are taken from the large hand drawing made by Harrison for the head on the new penny, which we know as the medal head and it is more recent than the other, the coinage head, and generally considered better. It is important to bear in mind that whichever head is chosen it must be suitable for both designs and I gather that they are most nervous about the 8d design on account of the straight sides of the opening.[25]

This was the first suggestion of using the Medal head rather than the Coinage one for Eve's frames.

Before any decision on the head the first of more radical solutions was proposed. In view of the delay why not use *Mackennal's* Wreath design (rather than Eve's) for the 4d as well as the existing 2d and 3d? A 2d die (in the Mackennal Wreath design) on a roller therefore had the value removed and could be used to make a totally new 4d master die. The engraving was regarded as better in appearance than the latest 4d Eve Wreath version. This was agreed and the Inland Revenue so instructed on 28 October.

Now, the allocation of designs for the range of low values stood as follows:[26]

Artist	Design	Denominations			
Mr Mackennal	Dolphins	½d (2481)	1½d (36)		
	Medal head	1d (2484)	2½d (60)		
	Wreath	2d (36)	3d (58)	4d (48)	
Mr Eve	Wreath	5d (24)	6d (67)	7d (8)	
	Pillars	8d (*)	9d (8)	10d (4)	1/- (19)
Mr Mackennal	Sea horses	2/6 (1)	5/- (½)	10/- (¼)	£1 (⅛)

Approximate annual issue in millions shown in brackets

*not yet issued

This was not to be the end, however.

Yet more colours

From the middle of 1912, with the prospect of more designs and values, colour again came to the fore. A scheme (Colour Scheme D) had been provisionally approved in March 1911. But Samuel had already departed from this when he adopted brown for the 1½d, orange for the 2d, and purple for the 3d in November. Through June and July various essays were considered for a new scheme.

Of the low values already engraved, the 2d was supplied on 30 July in various shades of orange. One had already been approved but this would cost more (10/- as against 4/-) than a

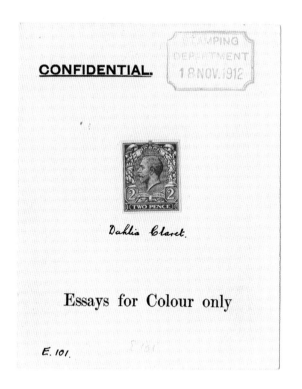

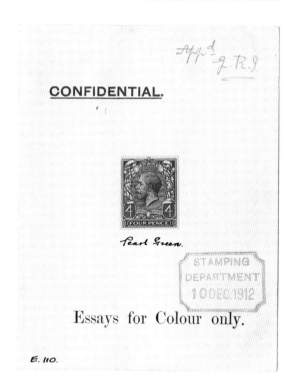

Above: Colour trials for the 4d Mackennal Wreath design, with the 2d die (left) and the finished approved 4d die (right)

rather darker shade. The darker shade was thus then preferred and issued. For the new 1d, eight sheets were submitted on 26 August in various shades of red. These were printed on a Wharfedale machine at Somerset House on the new paper, watermarked G R V, and plate glazed. Bennett had added a solid colour bar in the margin to show the true colour, and an example of an Edward VII 1d stamp for comparison. The sheets were sent to the King at Balmoral and he approved that printed in Manders Brothers ink, M.B. 25602, rather than the Shackell Edwards S E 3181 then in use on the improved Downey. The King then kept all the sheets for his collection.

Sheets of the 3d followed in September. In this case, it was stated that the proposed shade of purple was almost exactly the same as a proof already approved by the King, so there was no necessity to "trouble" him with the sheets. The approved ink was violet M.B. 21731. In October came sheets of the 1½d in five shades of brown. Again one was selected (M.B. 10589/D) without recourse to the King. Similarly, the 2½d was printed in seven shades of blue and SPA 10/12 was approved. The plates of all these values were immediately put to press and the stamps issued within a matter of days. All these sheets were kept in the official collection and were not supplied to the King.

For the 4d value, still at this point in Eve's Wreath frame, a proof was submitted to the King on 10 October in pale blue. While he approved the design, he thought the colour too pale and that it should be of a decidedly deeper tint. As a result the Inland Revenue were asked to provide essays in other colours (not dark blue as this was the international colour for the 2½d).

Above: Bromide of Eve's artwork for the "Pillar" design with value inserted by hand

Possibly Dutch brown, maroon, pearl green, bronze green, or dark grey might be suitable. …. Also, as our choice of a colour for the 4d must depend to some extent upon the colours to be adopted for the 5d, 6d and 7d, I shall be glad if you will let us have specimens of the 4d stamp printed in the colours approved for those denominations, viz. magenta, purple and raw umber.[27]

This was superseded by the decision to change the design but, using the 2d Mackennal Wreath die, some 19 essays were sent by the Inland Revenue on 18 November for a colour to be selected for the new 4d design. These ranged from grey, through maroon and magenta, to "Brilliant Rhone Blue". Pearl green, deep bronze green and grey were initially selected and proofs from the working die were submitted in these colours on 11 December.

Samuel now had to explain to the King why the design had changed. While recommending pearl green as the colour he added:

since proofs of the 4d stamp with a "wreath" frame of Mr Eve's design were submitted to His Majesty in October last, it has occurred to me that the stamp had rather a "crowded" appearance and that its appearance would be much improved if the head were made very slightly smaller, and the opening of the frame slightly wider. Arrangements have been made for these alterations to be carried into effect with all possible speed, but in order to minimise the delay in the introduction of the 4d stamp I would propose to adopt Mr Mackennal's "wreath" design for the frame of that stamp.[28]

On 14 December the King approved pearl green as the colour, thinking it certainly the best. He made no comment as to the change in design. It was issued thus on 15 January.

There remained the question of colours for the values in Eve's two frames. Eve was consulted and made his suggestions but officials thought it best to wait until the dies had been engraved before coming to a decision. An internal Post Office memorandum summed it up.

Experience has shown that it is extremely difficult to settle a colour scheme in advance and to adhere to it. Stamps look different when printed from the actual dies; and there is a risk that a selected colour may not meet with general approval when final proofs are submitted. Further, an alteration in the colour of one denomination frequently necessitates alterations in others. I think it would be well to defer a definite settlement of the colours for the seven outstanding denominations – viz., 5d, 6d, 7d, 8d, 9d, 10d and 1/-, - until the new dies of the two designs to be used (Mr Eve's "wreath" design and "pillars" design, respectively) are ready.[29]

The Inland Revenue should be asked to furnish, as soon as the dies were ready, specimens printed from each of the two dies in all seven colours originally selected, and also in some additional colours, such as deep bronze green, maroon, Dutch brown "and any others the Inland Revenue can suggest." In January 1913, despite this admonition, a series of colour trials for the 7d value (in the Wreath design) was made using dies made by the Printex process (formerly Miller & Motley) with alternative backgrounds to the King's head – one tinted, the other solid. The King's head was still the Coinage head at this point. The original large size artwork for the 7d has survived – drawn in reverse on metal ready for the photographic process. At the end of the month further trials, also using Printex or Motley dies, were made with the 8d value (in the Pillar design). This time there were four different surrounds to the King's head (plain line, graduated line, solid and half solid). Now the King's head had changed to a Medal version.

The King, when asked, preferred the graduated line surround.

Eve's frames switched

However, the same internal memorandum quoted above went on to suggest yet another, radical departure from the original scheme. Because of the colour of the 3d stamp (violet) complaints had been received of similarity with the old 6d (purple) stamp. For technical reasons the 6d had to remain as purple but as a "wreath" design was being used for the 3d, could not Eve's "pillars" design be used for the forthcoming 6d instead of another "wreath"? This would make the difference between the two stamps that much greater, but would also entail a change of design for the new 6d. To regularise this "I would suggest that Mr Eve's "pillars" design be used for the 5d, 6d, 7d and 8d, and his "wreath" design for the 9d, 10d and 1/-."[30]

This seems to have been agreed with little or no discussion, and no reaction from the Inland Revenue or the Mint. The Post Office presumed, apparently correctly, that there would be no difficulty in making that change.

The Second Medal Head

Proceeding in tandem with these developments was the choice of a slightly smaller head to insert into Eve's frames. Rigg, completely exasperated with events, now boiled over.

Left: die proof of Medal Head II

> Very well! If the P.M.G. and the I.R. choose to stick to the triflingly smaller head they may as well, but I utterly dissent from the scheme. This is not likely to distress either of them but I none the less decline to act Sancho Panza to their Don Quixote![31]

Atterbury tried to pacify him with a personal letter. He was sure that Rigg had done his best to expedite matters as far as the 4d was concerned. That would be printed at first at Somerset House "on paper gummed and *plate-glazed* by Harrisons."[32] Then, perhaps trying to put things into perspective, and referring to the more important wider world, he added "We are frightfully busy this week over [Irish] Home Rule or I could come & see you." It was a salutary reminder.

Rigg's outburst had come after he had supplied Eve with prints of the Medal head, with all tint lines removed, at the 46 size, and prints of the Coinage head as used on the 1½d, 2d and 3d stamps already issued. Eve then amended his frames to take the new size of head.

Above: Colour essays for Eve's "Pillar" design

On the advice of his officials Samuel now recommended the use of the Coinage head for Eve's designs, that engraving in the 2d to be copied as closely as possible. At this point Mackennal intervened. He stated categorically to Macartney, Deputy Master of the Mint "that the King prefers *the head on the new penny*"[33] and then wrote to Lord Stamfordham (referring to Eve's designs) that the head had been altered and was not at all good. "When we have a good head which The King approves I cannot understand why it should be touched."[34] The King was for once non-committal, saying that he did not think the head "so bad."[35] This was not said to Macartney who was now convinced that the King preferred the Medal head "as used in the new 1d stamp" and informed the Inland Revenue of such. When told, the Post Office saw no alternative. Quoting Macartney, an internal memorandum reluctantly stated:

> I presume we must agree to the adoption of the 'medal' as a model for the small head required for the 5d to 1/- stamps.[36]

This they immediately did but, because of discussions about the surround to the head (plain, graduated, partially solid, or solid), no engraving took place until February 1913 when the King chose a graduated tint.

Atterbury wrote a resumé explaining the long saga. He ended with -

> the delay has been due partly to the fact that there is only one Mint engraver who is capable of doing the kind of work required, but mostly to the three changes in the size and character of the head to be inserted in the frames. These changes have necessitated

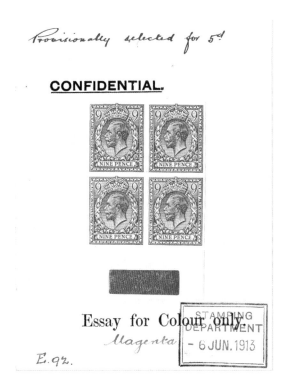

Above: Colour essays for Eve's "Pillar" and "Wreath" designs

many re-drawings of both head and frame for each design, each stage of the process involving interviews and submissions for approval.[37]

Thereafter, matters proceeded more calmly. Eve was given large photographs of his two designs and asked to draw in the values and the lettering for each. Revised dies were submitted to the King on 8 May and were approved the following day by Stamfordham, with the question "Can the King keep them, or must they be returned?"[38]

Designs (and heads inserted) were now allocated for the last time for the low values as follows:

Artist	Design	Denominations	Head	Size
Mackennal	Dolphins	½d , 1½d	Coinage	47.4
	Oak & laurel leaves	1d, 2½d	Large Medal	52.5
	Wreath	2d, 3d, 4d	Coinage	47.4
Eve	Pillars	5d, 6d, 7d	Medal head II	46
	Wreath	8d, 9d, 10d, 1/-	Medal head II	46

Final Colour Selections

Thereafter, final colours had to be selected. For this blocks of four electrotype stamp-pieces were provided by the Mint to the Inland Revenue for each design for colour proofing. Rigg provided these at the end of May in the 5d and 9d denominations, initially as steel-faced copper electros but shortly afterwards in nickel.

STAMPING DEPARTMENT

7 JUN. 19..

CONFIDENTIAL.

Essay for Colour only.

Black on lemon tinted paper

E. 227.

On 6 June the Inland Revenue provided 30 different colour trials in blocks of four in each of the two designs. There were various shades of brown, green, grey, red and blue and three colours provisionally selected – umber for the 7d, magenta for the 5d, and the official purple for the 6d. Further specimens on tinted paper were sent to Eve who made a preliminary selection if they should be required.

A minute to the Postmaster General made a number of points to be borne in mind when choosing the colours:

> Stamps of the same design should be of quite distinctive colour by artificial light as well as by daylight.
>
> Stamps of adjoining denominations should be as distinctive as possible.

It is especially desirable that no stamp should resemble at all closely either the 1d or the ½d stamp.

Stamps representing rates of postage on foreign letters – viz. 2½d, 4d, 7d and 10d – should be distinctive.[39]

The colours recommended, therefore, were:

5d   fawn (215)
6d   purple (222)
7d   deep bronze green (167)
8d   azure blue (6)
9d   agate (130)
10d black on lemon tinted paper (227)
1/-   umber (11)

These were initially approved but, as always, this was not the end of the matter. The 7d was changed from deep bronze green (227) to green (206) by mistake, and 6d essays were supposed to follow. However, Eve suggested that if black were to be used on tinted paper then it would be better if the "Pillars" design were used. Black on lemon paper had been selected for the 10d value which was in the "Wreath" design. So, it was agreed to transpose the colours for the 10d and the 8d which was in the "Pillars" design.

Finally, Samuel approved, but there was still the matter of the 6d purple. Because it was doubly fugitive the Inland Revenue were emphatic that it remain in that colour. However, there was a possible clash with the new 3d stamp, also in purple. Violet was suggested as a substitute for the latter and it was agreed that new printings would be in this ink (234). The 7d reverted to deep bronze green, and a deeper shade of orange was subsequently used for the 2d.

The 5d and 9d values were issued to the public on 30 June. All other values not already issued were held until 1 August. Stamps bearing the head of King George V had thus been issued as follows:

Year	Date	Value	Design	Designer
1911	22 June	½d	Dolphin	Mackennal
	22 June	1d	Lion	Mackennal
	September	½d deepened die	Dolphin	Mackennal
	September	1d deepened die	Lion	Mackennal
1912	1 January	½d re-engraved	Dolphin	Mackennal
	1 January	1d re-engraved	Lion	Mackennal
	20 August	2d	Wreath	Mackennal
	8 October	1d	Oak & Laurel	Mackennal
	9 October	3d	Wreath	Mackennal
	15 October	1½d	Dolphin	Mackennal
	18 October	2½d	Oak & Laurel	Mackennal
1913	15 January	4d	Wreath	Mackennal
	30 June	5d	Pillars	Eve
	30 June	9d	Wreath	Eve
	1 August	6d	Pillars	Eve
	1 August	7d	Pillars	Eve
	1 August	8d	Pillars	Eve
	1 August	10d	Wreath	Eve
	1 August	1/-	Wreath	Eve

It had taken more than three years to produce George V's stamps. From concept to distribution the Penny Black (the world's first postage stamp) took less than five months. Not one word on this sorry tale appears in Samuel's memoirs.

One aspect, however, was much more successful - the Seahorse high values.

Left: Issued stamps with Eve's designs

a1   RA PPTO/PP/GV/MAIN/A/3337 Sir Arthur Bigge to Bertram Mackennal 2 September 1910

2   T1/11478 Treasury note 7 July 1910.

3   CO 323/577 De La Rue to Crown Agents 8 August 1911

4   POST 54/50 Memo by Atterbury re visit to the Mint 25 August 1911

5   POST 30/2137A Atterbury to GPO, 3 November 1911.

6   ibid Macartney to Nathan, 10 November 1911.

7   RA PS/PSO/GV/PS/STAMPS/2090/7 Samuel to Stamfordham 10 November 1911

8   Ponsonby to Tilleard 2 September 1911, quoted in **Goodwyn, C.** "King George V: The Downey and the Colonial Profile Heads" *The London Philatelist* Vol. 106 p111, May 1997

9   19 December 1911. Royal Mint memo on "Re-designing of Georgian Stamps" quoted in *PJGB* June 1970 p48

10   Royal Philatelic Collection, page B 40

11   [Richmond papers] Rigg to Atterbury 1 January 1912

12   [Richmond papers] Atterbury to Rigg 2 January 1912

13   POST 30/2884 Postage Stamps: H.M. King George V Issue. Mackennal to Macartney 10 January 1912

14   RA PS/PSO/GV/PS/STAMPS/2090/11 Mackennal to Ponsonby 5 March 1912

15   POST 30/2884 op cit internal memo to PMG 12 March 1912

16   ibid

17   ibid Nathan to Samuel 17 May 1912

18   ibid Samuel to Stamfordham

19   **Williams, L.N.** & **M.** *Fundamentals of Philately* 1960 p418

20   POST 30/2884 op cit memorandum by F.W. Phillips 24 July 1912

21   POST 30/2884 op cit Stamfordham to Samuel 26 July 1912

22   ibid A.F. King to Macartney 3 July 1912

23   POST 30/2884 op cit memorandum by F.W. Phillips 16 October 1912

24   Rigg to Eve 25 October 1912 in **Beaumont** & **Stanton** op cit pp236-7

25   ibid

26   POST 30/2884 op cit memorandum by F.W. Phillips 25 October 1912

27   ibid A.F. King to Nathan 15 October 1912

28   ibid Samuel to Stamfordham 13 December 1912

29   ibid F.W. Phillips to Walter Gates 19 December 1912

30   ibid

31   Rigg to Eve 9 November 1912 in **Beaumont** & **Stanton** op cit p238

32   MINT 14/53 Stamp Dies Atterbury to Rigg (personal) 19 November 1912

33   Rigg to Eve 14 December 1912 in **Beaumont** & **Stanton** op cit p239

34   RA PS/PSO/GV/PS/STAMPS/2090/30 Mackennal to Stamfordham 16 December 1912

35   RA PS/PSO/GV/PS/STAMPS/2090/31 ms note 18 December 1912

36   POST 30/2884 op cit F.W. Phillips to Walter Gates 20 December 1912

37   IR 79/23 Memorandum by F. Atterbury 20 February 1913

38   POST 30/2884 op cit Stamfordham to Capt Cecil Norton (Assistant Postmaster General) 9 May 1913

39   ibid memorandum by A.F. King 12 June 1913

7

BRITANNIA RULES THE WAVES
HIGH VALUE DEFINITIVES

"The fleet that assembled off Portsmouth for the coronation review of 1911 included thirty-two battleships, thirty-four cruisers and sixty-seven destroyers. Britannia ruled the waves and her sovereign determined that she should continue to do so." [1]

It can be no coincidence that the high value stamps of King George V (issued in 1913) feature Britannia riding the waves in triumph, in a chariot pulled by powerful horses. Conceived by Bertram Mackennal at a time of rising naval tension between Germany and Britain, this was a statement of intent.

Design Origin

The origin of the design has been much debated. In his first comments, the philatelist King observed that "the resemblance of the special feature of the design to some of the Barbados stamps has no doubt been noted."[2] It has to be regarded as unlikely that British postal officials would have known much about the stamps of Barbados, but they did have in their archives examples which had been sent at the time of issue by the Universal Postal Union since 1892. These they retrieved for comparison when considering the finalised design. As Atterbury wrote,

> I expect McKennal knows all about the origin of the Sea-horses etc and that De la Rue could not take exception to our new stamp.[3]

Above: Seal of Barbados on stamps from 1897 [top] and 1916 (with motto)

The Barbados stamps in question featured the seal of the colony, the stamps having been designed and printed by De La Rue from 1892 onwards. This seal had originally been granted in 1663 and showed King Charles II "representing Neptune in a Chariot drawn by two sea horses and robed with his royal robes and crowned, with a trident in his left hand."[4] Later versions depicted a clam-shell chariot with different monarchs. The seal bore a motto, based on a line in Virgil's first Eclogue (written in 37 BC) in which an Italian herdsman expresses his fear of being banished to Britain because it is so cut off from the world: "*et penitus toto divisos orbe Britannos*" – "and the Britons, wholly sundered from the world."[5] Amusingly, and with great ingenuity, the Barbados seal altered only one word so that it now read "*et penitus toto regnantes orbe Britannos*" - that is "and the British *ruling* throughout the whole world".

Below: Copper alloy coin of Antoninus Pius showing Britannia with shield and trident (140-144 A.D.)

This image was then combined with another tradition. "Britannia" was the Latin name for the Roman province of Britain. As an image, Britannia first took female form on coins of the Roman emperor Hadrian (AD 117-138) marking his subjugation of southern Britain. There she was depicted as a captive of the Roman Empire. Later coins of his successor Antoninus Pius (AD 138-161) portray her as a seated warrior complete with spiked shield. Subsequent emperors used similar images on some medallions and coins. This image was revived in the late 16th

century by the publication of William Camden's *Britannia* which illustrated, in slightly later editions, the Roman coins and incorporated the image as part of the title page. With the union of the crowns of Scotland and England under James VI & I in 1603 the name "Great Britain" was coined for the political entity, and Britannia came back into vogue as a symbol.

The first English coins bearing the image of Britannia did not appear until 1672 and the design was modelled quite closely on the classical Roman precursors, but with the shield becoming a baroque cartouche bearing the Union Flag. It was in this form as on contemporary coins that Britannia was finally incorporated into Mackennal's design, in place of a monarch as Neptune.[6] The design was known from the outset as the "Seahorses", though this was no allusion to the marine creature of that name.

Above: UK 1d coin showing Britannia (top)

Silver coin of Syracuse with quadriga

Below: 1908 Olympic medal (top)

Leonard Wyon's 1854 medal

Given the close friendship of Mackennal and the King, and the latter's great knowledge of stamps (and his remarks about the similarity of the design to that of Barbados stamps), there must be a suspicion that artistic inspiration may have had a particular source.

Nevertheless, classical allusions may have been uppermost in Mackennal's mind. He had a fascination for Greek and Roman coins and knew the 5th century BC coins of Syracuse which bore a version of a quadriga, a two-wheeled chariot drawn by four horses abreast. His father, J.S. Mackennal (also a sculptor), had produced a sculpture of Phaethon driving his father's (Apollo's) sun chariot as far back as the 1860s. Apollo, or Phoebus (shining) Apollo, with his own horses and chariot, was the subject of several works by Bertram Mackennal, most importantly the monumental sculpture adorning Australia House in London, begun in 1912. There, he is depicted emerging from the ocean and drawing the chariot of the sun across the heavens. The god can best be seen, however, on the commemorative medal for the 1908 London Olympics, standing naked in a chariot being pulled by four rearing horses. In Mackennal's stamp design they "send the sea foam flying", as Homer put it.[7]

A combination of Britannia and sea horses can be seen on Leonard Wyon's 1854 medal for his father, the great medallist William Wyon. So, there was a considerable heritage of Greek gods, sun chariots, sea horses, coins and medals for Mackennal to draw on, quite apart from the stamps of Barbados.

Mackennal also prepared some sketches featuring Britannia for the low value stamps but these were discarded and never submitted to the Post Office.

Sept 15th 1910. Original sketch by Mr Mackennal for the stamps of 2/6 to £1, signed by him.

Photograph of sketch reduced to stamp size.

POSTAGE
& REVENUE

In regard to Mr
Mackennal's designs –
The sketch for the 5/-
which is so strongly
commended by Mr
Samuel for the higher
value stamps might be
accepted

*Left: Original artwork
by Mackennal*

*Far left: Phaethon
driving sun chariot by
J.S. Mackennal*

The King's comments & intaglio printing

The King's comments on the Seahorse design came as part of his initial critique of the first designs submitted to him in 1910. A larger size had been suggested by Mackennal, similar to current French stamps of 45 centimes and upwards and double the width of the standard low values. This was to "give more opportunity for the design".[8] Interestingly, in the original drawing there is a sketch of a *profile* head already in the space provided. Samuel commended the result to the King noting that the size was "quite acceptable from a Departmental point of view and if the numeral were taken from the shield where it is incongruous and placed upon the label at the bottom, this would I think make a fine stamp for the higher values."[9] The King agreed.

> In regard to Mr Mackennal's designs – The sketch for the 5/- which is so strongly commended by Mr Samuel for the higher value stamps might be accepted, the value being taken off the shield, the crosses of the Union Jack being substituted, and the value added (preferably in words) in the lower tablet as suggested. If, as appears to be the case, the 5/-, 10/- and £1 values are not available for Revenue purposes as apart from postal or telegraphic use, the space occupied by the words "& Revenue" could be used for the words of value, the 2/6 stamp in that case being of a different design in the smaller size.[10]

The design was returned to Mackennal with these suggestions and "that it might be better to have an indication of harness on the sea-horses."[11] The revised version, complete with flag on Britannia's shield and harness on horses, was received in December and approved by the King. However, further revisions were required in February the following year to widen the wreath frame to accommodate the King's head, and also the value tablet.

Referring to all the definitive stamps the King had asked if the method of production had been decided.

Above: Revised drawing with Union Flag in shield

If it were possible, without undue increase of trouble and expense, to work from steel plates (line engraved stamps) these would appear to give the best results judging from a comparison of numerous stamps of all the recognised modes of production. This is a question for the responsible authorities, and it is to be hoped that if the present mode of production [letterpress] be adhered to some means may be found of improving upon the somewhat rough appearance of the present series.

This eventually sparked off a discussion about the merits or otherwise of recess, or intaglio, versus letterpress printing. Of the artistic merits of the former, there was no doubt. An immediate response from the Mint agreed that as far as appearance went it was undoubtedly a better process. Stamps above a shilling were excluded from the printing contract with Harrisons and annual consumption only amounted to approximately two million. Cost of production would be higher but because of the small quantities this would hardly matter. It was estimated at about an extra £150 a year.

There, the question rested while the problems of the low value designs were dealt with. Then in March 1911 Mackennal was free to turn his attention to the high values. A quick note revealed Post Office anxieties about the quality of the low value stamps even then:

> McKennal rings up to say he is anxious that his big stamp shd be *engraved* not surface printed. He says there is enormous improvement in appearance - & as supply is presumably small & difference in cost not great you may wish to consider this. We want at least one *real* success.[12]

But there were the questions of forgery and possible fraudulent re-use of the stamps after cleaning off the cancellation. These were dealt with in summary fashion by Seymour Bennett at the Inland Revenue. He did not think that the stamps could be successfully cleaned of cancellation ink.

> Nor do I think that successful fraud by transfer of the stamps to stone for lithographic printing need be feared. It is not practicable to make such a transfer after the inks of the stamps have dried, as they would do before they were issued from stock. And even if a successful transfer were made from new ink, the prints therefrom would be but *lithographed copies* of the stamps, and therefore they would be so noticeably different from the *engraved originals* that the forgery could not escape early detection.[13]

The only other problem was the 2/6d value which previously had also been used for fiscal purposes and therefore had to be printed in doubly fugitive purple ink. However, this was no longer valid. The duty for which it had been used - 2/6d in Furnished Letting Agreements - had been raised to 5/- and a special Revenue stamp had been provided. So there was no longer any requirement for doubly fugitive ink, nor for the phrase "Postage & Revenue" in the design. When Samuel was informed of this he approved the use of intaglio for printing, being very glad that "this improvement" was practicable, and the inclusion of the word "Postage" only in the design. Dimensions for all four values, 2/6d, 5/-, 10/- and £1, were to be identical - twice the size of a low value stamp.

Photographed 15. 3. 11.

The King's Head

In both Mackennal's original sketch and his revised artwork for the Seahorses, drawn between September 1910 and March 1911, are outlines of the King's head *in profile* – not in the three-quarter profile of the Downey Head then agreed for the low values, but obviously based on Mackennal's work on medals and coins. By the middle of March the embossed profile head for registration envelopes was ready. This had been based by the Royal Mint on a model by Mackennal, again similar to his coin and medal work. It is probably this that Mackennal is referring to when discussing the final revisions to his high value design.

> I have solved the problem of the head. The one already done will fit my space as I am enlarging it. As to the lower part of design where the numeral and lettering goes, I am making arrangements to suit the different stamps by leaving sufficient room & I hope that in no way will the design be harmed.[14]

Above: With profile head at Royal Mint, March 1911

Below: progressive drawings showing shading

Given the nature of the Seahorse design, a profile head was clearly intended from the outset. Here, he can hardly be referring to the three-quarter Downey head which would have looked quite wrong. However, even more intriguing is a note by the recipient of this statement, Kenelm Kerr (Samuel's private secretary), shortly afterwards.

> I visited the Mint to-day and saw Mr Rigg with reference to outstanding questions:…. As regards the large design, high value stamps, …there would be presumably little objection to their production by the process of steel engraving. The die for the stamp head has been completed and hardened and it is anticipated that a proof can be sent to the Post Office to-morrow.[15]

This was still the middle of March 1911 and some confirmation is provided by the Royal Mint proof book for the previous day where there is a photograph of the Seahorse design at stamp size, with a photograph of one of Mackennal's new profile heads inserted – sculpted but not engraved. There seems to be no

I have seen Mr
Mackennal with
regard to the shading
of the effigy of
His Majesty in the
enclosed design for the
10/- stamp. Generally
speaking the whole
of the portrait portion
will be from two and
a half to three tones
lighter.

*Above: Eve's suggestion
for King's head*

*Right: Harrison's
engraving 30 August
1912*

other trace at all of such a profile head engraved for intaglio printing, nor any documentary comment until August. Dies for postal stationery, for issue on Coronation Day, were now given urgent priority.

In August, as already mentioned in connection with the origins of the profile head, Atterbury noted that for the recess high values "A new head will be required.

The idea is that Harrison should engrave the King in profile (from an existing photograph, shewn in plaque on the occasion of our visit) for these stamps."[16] This would seem to contradict the previous statements. Certainly, if there were an earlier engraved head it does not seem to have survived.

Little now happened as work was concentrated elsewhere. In December, Mackennal made the surprising suggestion that "to make the stamp really effective, it ought to be done without the head". It was the only way to make the stamp artistic "and not a jumble as the others are".[17] This was ignored. What his friend, the King, would have thought can easily be imagined.

Then in January 1912 the Mint informed the Inland Revenue that the drawing was nearly ready for work to begin on the engraving.

> I have seen Mr Mackennal with regard to the shading of the effigy of His Majesty in the enclosed design for the 10/- stamp. Generally speaking the whole of the portrait portion will be from two and a half to three tones lighter. The hair especially being much too dark. The engraver will work from the photograph of the coin head which will enable him to produce a much better effect.[18]

A few days later Samuel was told that the head would be the approved Colonial one (the same as the coin head) but specially engraved. The size was to be 47.4 by the Mint's form of measurement.

Production of the die

*Right: Harrison's
engraving 30 August
1912*

The original intention had been that both the high value stamps and the doubly-fugitive 6d be printed at Somerset House by the Inland Revenue. This was to simplify the printing tender eventually won by Harrisons. Now, however, there was considerable congestion at the Mint and, as a result, no likelihood of the high values being produced soon from plates provided by the Mint. The Inland Revenue, therefore, suggested that they be put out to tender.

There are …. several firms expert in the production of recess-printed stamps who could undertake the work efficiently and speedily in all its processes, including the actual engraving of the King's effigy and of the stamp design.[19]

More to the point, the Inland Revenue had no machinery to print the stamps in recess. When Mackennal learnt of this he protested: "he personally would much prefer that the work should be left with the Mint, with the work of whose engraver he is now quite content." So, yet further postponement was agreed. It was not until 31 July (1912) that it was reported that considerable progress had been made – and even then the first proof was not ready until mid August, when it was due to be sent to Mackennal who was now in Naples. Various stages of J.A.C. Harrison's work are recognised by specialists, from 24 August through to 18 September when it was first proofed at the Royal Mint.

Engraving an intaglio die is a much shorter process than for letterpress, but there is also one other major difference. Where the initial letterpress engraving is negative in relief, that for intaglio is negative recessed. In other words, the lines of the drawing are engraved into the steel die rather than standing proud (with the rest of the steel cut away). Harrison was much more experienced at this than with letterpress. This, however, did not stop him getting the Union Flag "heraldically" wrong on Britannia's shield. Rather than re-engrave a completely new die, wasting yet more time, this was left and taken up, wrong as it was, on to a transfer roller. Here, the lines of the design stood proud and could easily be scraped off, which is what happened with the Union Flag. The resulting design, only partly finished, was now rolled out on to four dies, one for each value, with the shield and value tablet blank. Each shield and value were engraved separately and thus differences occur in the shields on each duty. Once fully engraved and hardened these dies became the master dies and transfer rollers from them were used to create the plates. A note at the Royal Mint records:

Above: Harrison's master die with wrong flag (top)

Proof from the die from roller showing blank shield

Right: colour trial from 5s die

Mr Harrison charged £105 cutting the original H.V. Postage die with blank duty panel. (This included cutting King's effigy). His charge for cutting the denomination on each working die was £10 10 0.[20]

The first die to be completed was that for the 5/- and this was used for colour trials in mid October. As was his wont, Mackennal had shown these directly to the King who thought the engraving "admirable in every way"[21] - as long as it could be reproduced exactly as the proof.

Printers

Although the creation of dies and plates had been left to the Mint, and Harrison, the question of printing had been left open. Originally, it had been agreed that more than one tender would be invited but it seems that the Inland Revenue only obtained one – from Waterlow Brothers & Layton Ltd. As they informed the Treasury they were "skilled printers of engraved stamps"[22] and were already the contractors for printing National Health Insurance stamps, though these were printed letterpress. This meant that they already had Inland Revenue supervision on site. At 40-set they would charge £2 per ream in the finest inks. It was proposed to have a two-year contract at the outset, at a total cost of about £500. This was approved, subject to Post Office agreement.

The printing firm of Waterlows went back to the early 19th century, but Waterlow Brothers & Layton came about in 1877 as a result of a family disagreement and was now in competition with Waterlow and Sons.[23] Later, in 1920, they re-united and were to print the low value definitives from 1924 until 1933.

There was now the business of creating the plates which could not happen until various decisions were made. Discussions took place, for example, as to the width of the gutter between the stamps. This was settled at 0.2 inch, to be followed by various technical requirements of the thickness of the plates to achieve the required results on Waterlows' (four-plate) Hoe printing press. Initially, the two top values were to have been in sheets of 20, the lower two 40-set. In the interests of economy and ease of printing it was agreed in November that all the plates should be the same, 40-set, with markings so that the Post Office could easily issue half sheets to counter staff. These decisions were also necessary before Grovers could produce a suitable Punch Box to perforate the sheets. This was already the middle of November 1912.

To create the plates the Royal Mint used a transfer roller from the original dies which had been received from JAC Harrison on 5 November.

The plate-maker started at the top right-hand corner, laying impressions from right to left. The hardened transfer roller, sometimes known as a roller punch, was lowered until it rested in its correct alignment on the soft steel plate; then considerable pressure was applied. The roller punch was rocked in repeatedly, until a perfect impression was obtained. On completing the first impression, the plate was pulled right to receive the next one. After the first horizontal row was laid, the plate was brought back to its original position, the side-lay was moved over by one prescribed step, so work on the second row could begin. And so on, until all ten rows of four impressions each were completed.[24]

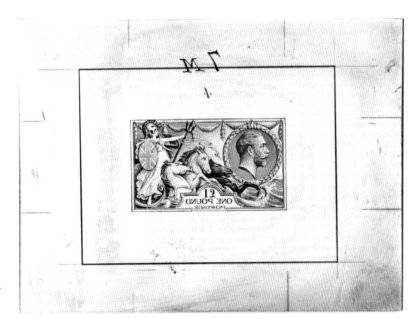

The first flat plate to be created was the 2/6d denomination made by one Mr Macdonald, not an employee, as a demonstration. While still soft, Rigg sent the first proof from this plate to the Inland Revenue on 19 December. At the end of December it was sent to the printers for them to test and proof. A second plate was made by the Mint without the assistance of Macdonald and was regarded as a good first attempt but it was to be held in reserve.

The Printing Process

The underlying principle of the operation of printing from intaglio plates is the fact that the paper must be pressed against the plate with such force that it will be pushed into the troughs or recesses engraved on the plate, and on being peeled off after this operation will bring away on its surface the ink that had already been deposited on the plate.[25]

This was true in 1840 with the Penny Black and remained true for the Seahorses in 1913. To help the removal of the ink it was usual to dampen the paper beforehand (obviously ungummed), leaving it to dry afterwards, and be gummed and perforated later. Waterlow Brothers & Layton had a four-plate Hoe power press. This allowed the three processes of inking the plate, wiping off excess ink and printing to be carried on at the same time.

Above: Master die of the £1 value and transfer roller

Four separate printing plates were provided for, and these were laid on beds connected by an endless chain. The first plate was inked by a roller then moving to the second stage where it was wiped by hand to remove excess ink. Then it moved to the third stage where the sheet of paper was laid on it, thence through the impression rollers where the paper was printed. However, at the same time as this was happening the other plates were following through each of the same stages, so that an operator was removing the printed sheet from the first plate at the same time as the fourth plate was going through the inking roller. And so on. However, it was Waterlow's custom to print from only two plates at a time to produce the best results.

They described the process as taking six days in all, as follows:[26]

Damp the paper	1st day
Print 2 or 3 reams	2nd day
Dry	3rd night
Gum and dry	4th day and night
Perforate	5th day
Deliver	6th day

Below: approved colour standards for 5s and £1 using 2/6 die

This memorandum was annotated in red with corrections, however, bringing the first stage back to the first night, and thus reducing the number of days to four or five days.

WATERLOW BROS. & LAYTON, LTD.

Problems with Paper

Colours had been agreed back in October based on proofs of the 5/- die. It was decided to print the 2/6d in brown, the 5/- in crimson lake, the 10/- in blue and the £1 in green. Precise shades were not approved until they were initialled by Samuel on 7 May 1913 (2/6d, 10s and £1) and 18 June (5s).

Printing trials with the 2/6d plate took place in the early months of 1913 but these were not satisfactory. The question was why. It could be due to the printing, the pigment or the plates. Or the paper. Resolving this was to delay matters through to May.

At this time, the stamp paper contractors were William Joynson of St Mary Cray in Kent. The printers contacted them in February 1913 with specifications for the paper required for intaglio printing (different from letterpress). They supplied an esparto paper sample asking for the same type in rag. "The surface should be a smooth mill finish, not calendered. Anything in the nature of a hard unsympathetic surface is to be avoided."[27] No written instructions were given to the paper-makers by the Inland Revenue, nor any trials undertaken, before 40 reams of watermarked pure rag paper were delivered to the printers. When printing trials took place it was found that the ink spread in the fibres of the dampened paper, especially in the surround to the head, resulting in the fine lines closing up in the printed stamp. Writing to the Mint, the Inland Revenue reported:

This difficulty does not arise with the esparto paper the fibres of which are more flattened out. Waterlow uses esparto paper for the stamps he makes for other countries, but we must use rag paper as we are precluded from the esparto paper by its low breaking strain and its want of permanency…
… Please stop any further work on the rest of the high-value plates.[28]

Trials were carried out on other papers, and George Eve was consulted confidentially about the die. Waterlows then turned to W. Howard of Chartham, Kent who manufactured watermarked paper for the Indian Government. They were able to provide a satisfactory paper and work could resume. The dandy roll for the watermark, made by T.J. Marshall & Co. Ltd. of Stoke Newington, was adapted for Howard's machine and 500 reams of paper ordered.

This was now May 1913 and plates for values other than the 2/6d still had to be made by the Mint. First came the 5s at the beginning of June, the 10s at the end of that month and finally the £1 in July. Only one of each could be provided immediately which caused the printers to complain that their four-plate machine was being run inefficiently and wasting expensive ink, thus causing increased costs in production. Otherwise, matters progressed remarkably swiftly. The first watermarked paper was delivered on 24 June and printing of the 2/6d had already commenced the following day. Both this value and the 5/- were ready for issue on 30 June (together with the 5d and 9d low values) and envelopes with the first examples "to go through the post" were sent to the King that day by Sir Matthew Nathan, now in charge of the Inland Revenue.

The useless Joynson paper was pulped in 1915.

Perforating

However, one problem had not been entirely solved – perforation. There had been no time to test the shrinkage of the new paper after it had dried. This affected the dimensions of the punch box to be supplied by Grover. As the size of the stamps was different a completely new one was required. However, a punch box had been supplied to the Inland Revenue on 21 February for trials there, Grovers measuring it as 16 pins, short way of perforations, by 24 pins long way.[29] In a desperate attempt to get the stamps out to the public, it was decided, as a temporary expedient, to perforate the stamps now at Somerset House. As has been seen, this was achieved, just, requiring the tightest of schedules on the part of both printers and Inland Revenue. This temporary expedient was to continue until 12 December 1913 when Grovers supplied Waterlow Brothers & Layton with a new punch box "jigged" from the one sent to the Inland Revenue.[30] In all, Bennett stated that 82 reams of 500 sheets of stamps were perforated at Somerset House.[31]

Above: the issued stamps

Issue & Public Reaction

The first Seahorse stamps (the 2/6d and 5/-) were issued to the public on 30 June 1913. In the very short time available 100 sheets of the 2/6d and 20 sheets of the 5/- had been supplied. On 1 August the 10/- and (possibly) the £1 were issued in conjunction with the remainder of the low values. As far as the design was concerned *The Times* noted that there would "probably be general agreement that the new design is a great advance in an artistic sense on any British postage stamp at present in circulation".[32] It then went on to comment on the use of line-engraving in the printing and this is what it concentrated on. "In reverting to that process now the authorities will give gratification to many philatelists". This has certainly proved true, even to the present day.

Printing

By the end of 1913, the Mint had provided two plates for each of the values. In the course of their use over the next year and a half a number of complaints caused adverse reports from tests carried out at the Government Laboratory. These were to do with the lack of sufficient gum and the qualities of the ink. Lead was found in the inks of the 2/6d and £1 stamps of the first printings and mercuric sulphide in the 5s. A later printing of the £1 had potassium chromate in the ink and was of a yellowish tint. Delivered in December 1914 they seemed to deteriorate in storage.

After a year and a half, by the end of 1914, the following totals of stamps had been delivered (here compared with consumption):[33]

Value	No. of sheets	Total stamps	Consumption 12 months– 1913 (total)	Issued 1914
2/6d	62,699*	2,507,960	1,304,874…	1,280,160
5s	28,679	1,147,160	599,406	573,640
10s	12,194	487,760	228,810	197,560
£1	6,036	241,440	128,119	80,600

*There was a further printing of 2/6d stamps at Waterlow Brothers & Layton in April 1915, of 13,086 sheets.

Later Printers

The initial contract had only been for two years and there had been no competitive tendering process. After the experience of introducing the stamps, attention turned to the longer term. In June 1915, four printers were invited to submit tenders for future contracts – initially for a further two years. The present printers, Waterlow Brothers and Layton, were invited, as were their family rivals Waterlow and Sons Ltd, and also De La Rue and Bradbury Wilkinson and Co., all experienced in intaglio printing and all known to the Government as a result of work on wartime Treasury banknotes.

Perhaps surprisingly, given history, the tender of De La Rue was accepted. Their prices were later described as "cutting". Plates were to be supplied by the Postmaster General, and so all six of those for the 2/6d, 5/- and 10/- denominations at Waterlow Brothers and Layton were transferred, on 29 July 1915. It was indicated that it was unlikely that there would be any further call for £1 stamps and those two plates were retained by the Director of Stamping. In fact, the only £1 Seahorses ever printed were those by Waterlow Brothers and Layton.

No particular type of printing press was specified in the tender requirements. De La Rue employed a new German press, described by them as "modern" and "expeditious" rather than the Hoe press as used by Waterlow Brothers and Layton. It had a mechanical wipe to remove excess ink, rather than manual as before. Printing of the 2/6d at least was 80-set rather than 40 – i.e. two plates were used simultaneously, side by side. Problems immediately occurred with the existing plates, regarded as too worn, but also with new plates previously unused. Two years of argument ensued.

It began on 14 September 1915 when De La Rue wrote:

> We beg to call your attention to the state of the 2/6 Postage plates. When we commenced printing the plates showed very considerable signs of wear, and in our opinion they are now quite unfit for further use. We have therefore thought it advisable to suspend the printing.[34]

A new plate was created at the Mint, but complaints continued. However, when the plates were tried on the Hoe press results were reasonably satisfactory, but the colour was quite different. New ink was obtained and it was agreed to make this the new standard. It was now July 1916 and De La Rue demanded a 60% increase on the tender price if they had to print on the slower Hoe press. Colour variation remained a problem and it was discovered that ink had been left to harden in the interstices of the plates which they claimed was the cause. Should the money be paid, or were De La Rue to blame for poor maintenance and using the wrong press?

> It is recollected that after the Contract for surface printed stamps had been placed with Messrs Harrison it was agreed to pay them additional remuneration in respect of the substitution of the Wharfedale printing machine for the machine originally used by Messrs Harrison. Do you think this affords a parallel to the present claim? It can hardly be said that the stamps printed with the "Mechanical wipe" by Messrs De La Rue are worse than Messrs Harrison's early productions.[35]

The Post Office refused to pay the extra 60% but allowed further trials on the fast German machine, agreeing to accept those stamps if they came up to standard. They did not, and stamps printed on the Hoe press, if acceptable, were also not very satisfactory.

In November 1917, De La Rue gave six months' notice to terminate the contract.

> We regret we are compelled to do this, as we find the plates furnished to us are not suitable for the printing machines we intended to use for the work.[36]

They had obviously had enough. Nevertheless, De La Rue were asked to tender for a new contract with three other printers. They were not successful and the contract passed to Bradbury Wilkinson & Co. in July 1918. Interestingly, and perhaps as a result of the problems with De La Rue, Bradbury Wilkinson were allowed to make their own plates for rotary printing machines. The master dies were loaned to them, from which they made their own transfer rollers and then plates 80-set (two panes of 40), curved for use on their rotary press.

Although the contract was for three years, with yearly extensions, it in fact ran until December 1933. In that time they produced a total of 11 plates, 80-set, for the 2/6d value, and four each for the 5/- and 10/-, requiring permission to do so on each occasion. Stamps printed from these have been extensively studied but, like all other Seahorse plates, no metal plate has survived, all having been officially destroyed.

Bradbury Wilkinson were also supplied by Grover, on 6 June 1918, with a perforating punch box (De La Rue had apparently used their own). This was based on the one supplied to Waterlow Brothers & Layton – i.e. four stamps across to perforate single panes.[37] Bradbury were printing double panes and so, on 1 January 1920, Grover supplied a new larger box, adjustable rather than solid, over eight stamps or two panes.[38] The margin or

gutter between the panes was laterally adjustable by ¼" between 2 15/16 " and 2 11/16".

In the 15-year period of the Bradbury, Wilkinson contract there was one major innovation in printing. In November 1925, the printers submitted sheets printed by a new dry process. If successful, this had obvious advantages in that the paper would no longer shrink after printing, providing a much better result for perforating. Wastage should be

Above: experimental plate 9-set with proof from larger working plate

considerably reduced, a factor which had been the source of continuing arguments with the Post Office. The new dry process was approved, and new registration sheets taken in January 1926. It was claimed that the appearance of the stamps would improve.

Various paper changes also took place over the period – these are discussed elsewhere.

Experimental Improvements
From 1929, interesting plate-making experiments took place at the Royal Mint. They were still producing all letterpress plates for the low values but had lost the contract for the high values. They now tried to introduce some of the techniques used in letterpress to that of intaglio plate-making. A skin, or shell, might be appropriate for rotary printing. If so, it could be "grown" from a master in the same way as letterpress working plates.

To test this, a special small master plate was made of the 10/- value, 9-set, with an uncompleted extra one-third of an image as well. Using wax and gutta percha moulds, the latter a form of rubber, a number of nickel and copper shells were grown and eventually pronounced satisfactory as printing surfaces. Various experiments continued through until 1934 but there is no evidence of their being brought into use.[39] The Royal Mint did, however, use this to quote unsuccessfully for plates to produce the Seahorses which now needed to be improved.

By 1934, Waterlows had lost the low value contract to Harrisons who introduced the photogravure process with richer colours (see Chapter 17). This had an impact on the high values, whose contract changed at the same time, now being transferred to Waterlows.

> Experiments have been made with a view to improving the High Value Postage Stamps (2/6, 5/- and 10/-), which appear weak in colour in comparison with the new Unified Stamps to be produced by the Photogravure process.
>
> It was found that the desired improvement could not be obtained by the use of new inks

and that the only method of enriching the appearance of the stamps was by deepening the engraved lines and adding shading and cross hatching to the design, principally on the background to His Majesty's head, the horses, and Britannia's apparel. This had been done and proofs from the altered dies are enclosed. They are considered to give a richer and more pleasing stamp without altering the character of the design. A similar enrichment of design by cross hatching was introduced into the £1 Postal Union Congress stamp on the advice of Sir Frank Short.[40]

The dies had been re-engraved by J.A.C. Harrison using an impression from the original master roller with the shield blank. Thus, not only was the image re-engraved but the shields and value tablets were engraved afresh as well. The King "quite approved" of the new specimens in a letter dated 23 February.[41]

Waterlows made their own plates, as had Bradbury Wilkinson, 80-set, curved for rotary printing. There is no record of a perforating punch box being supplied by Grover for these, although they supplied Waterlows for everything else, so that may have been transferred from Bradbury Wilkinson. The new stamps first made their appearance in mid October 1934, and Waterlows continued printing these until January 1939.

Of all the George V definitives the Seahorses were the most successful from an artistic point of view. Maintaining standards of printing continued to provide all the printers with difficulties but combined to make the issued stamps some of the best loved, and most studied, of George V's reign.

1   **Rose, Kenneth** *King George V* 1983, p.158

2   RA PS/PSO/GV/PS/STAMPS/4130/53 Bigge to Samuel 1 October 1910

3   MINT 14/53 Stamp Dies – letters and papers, Atterbury to Rigg 20 September 1912

4   **Shilstone, E M** "The Society's Corporate Seal" The Journal of the Barbados Museum and Historical Society 1. 1933-34
    – quoted by **Hewitt, Virginia** *A distant view – Imagery and imagination in the paper currency of the British Empire 1800 – 1960* in
    Ed. Gilbert, Emily & Helleiner, Eric Nation-States and Money: The Past, Present and Future of National Currencies
    1999. p 112

5   **Virgil.** *Eclogues, Georgics, Aeneid.* Translated by Fairclough, H.R. 1916 - Eclogue 1.

6   **Muir, D.N.** *Britannia Depicta* NPM exhibition brochure, 1993; National Postal Museum *Review of 1993* pp10-11

7   **Homer.** *The Iliad* p88 Penguin Classics edition 1950

8   POST 30/2136B op cit A.F. King to Samuel 20 August 1910

9   RA PS/PSO/GV/PS/STAMPS/4130/50 Samuel to Bigge 15 September 1910

10 RA PS/PSO/GV/PS/STAMPS/4130/53 op cit

11 POST 30/2136B op cit. Notes by Samuel 22 October 1910

12 IR 79/23 Post Office to F.W. Phillips 7 March 1911

13 POST 54/49 28 March 1911

14 POST 30/1995 Mackennal to Kerr 28 February 1911

15 ibid Memorandum by Kerr 16 March 1911

16 POST 54/50 Memorandum by Atterbury 26 August 1911

17 [Richmond papers] Mackennal to Rigg 13 December 1911

18 POST 30/2888 William Ellison-Macartney to Sir Matthew Nathan 11 January 1912

19 ibid Atterbury to GPO 15 March 1912

20 Cost of Stamp Plates, Dies etc [documentation at Royal Mint]

21 POST 30/2888 Stamfordham (at York Cottage) to Cyril Hurcomb, Private Secretary, GPO. 18 October 1912.

22 ibid. Inland Revenue to Treasury, 22 October 1912

23 For more details see **Kearsley, B.** *Discovering Seahorses: King George V High Values,* 2005 p15

24 ibid p31

25 **Easton, J.** *Postage Stamps in the Making* 1949 p111

26 POST 30/2888 Memorandum by Gregg, 19 February 1913

27 ibid. Waterlow Brothers & Layton to Joynson 4 February 1913

28 ibid. Inland Revenue to Rigg, 27 February 1913

29 Grover documentation MP 102/65

30 ibid MP 102/93

31 POST 30/2888 op cit 3 February 1914

32 *The Times* 1 July 1913

33 POST 30/2888 op cit H. Sparkes to Secretary, GPO 18 February 1915

34 De La Rue Correspondence Books, G.P.O.3 p47 De La Rue to Inspector of Stamping 14 September 1915

35 IR 79/2424 November 1916. A.R. Kidner, GPO to Inspector of Stamping

36 De La Rue Correspondence Books, G.P.O. 3 op cit p169 De La Rue to Controller, P.O. Stores Dept, 23 November 1917.

37 Grover documentation M.P. 102/197

38 ibid M.P. 102/233

39 For detail see **Muir, D.N.** "Seahorse Experimental Plates: New Discoveries" *GB Journal* Vol 48, No3 May/June 2010
    pp50-61

40 POST 52/931 High Value George V design, memorandum by W. M. Cook , Controller Post Office Stores Department
    for the King, 19 February 1934

41 Ibid. Quoted in letter from PMG to Napier, his Private Secretary, 23 February 1934.

8
POSTAL STATIONERY
WRAPPERS, CARDS & ENVELOPES

On Coronation Day, 22 June 1911, it was not only the ill-fated Downey Head ½d and 1d adhesive stamps which went on sale. There were also postcards, letter cards and registered envelopes. These had been printed by McCorquodale and Co. Ltd at their Wolverton plant (now part of Milton Keynes) with new imprinted postage stamp designs. Work on the dies for these had taken place at the Royal Mint at the same time as all the other new items – adhesive stamps, coins and medals, all contributing to the rushed disaster of the Downey Head adhesives.

Postal stationery fell into two basic types in terms of production. On the one hand there were postcards, letter cards and newspaper wrappers which were printed letterpress. On the other were registered, and standard, envelopes of different sizes, and telegram forms which were impressed with an embossed stamp. Such embossed stamps of varying values were also used to imprint private stationery submitted by firms or members of the public. With the exception of registered envelopes (and private stationery) all items had previously been printed by De La Rue. There were also other items, such as postal orders and reply coupons, which were dealt with quite separately.

Transition

Back in 1910, where this story began, the Interdepartmental Committee set up to look into the Inland Revenue stamp printing contracts also investigated the printing of postal stationery. Excessive profits were found here as well. Registered envelopes were printed by McCorquodales, and had been since the outset in 1878 at their specially-built factory; the remaining official stationery was printed by De La Rue; and the embossed dies had only just commenced being made by the Royal Mint, although they had also made early Victorian embossed dies.

The Committee recommended that official stationery be removed from the general contract, be amalgamated with registered envelopes, and put out to a separate tender. This was then won by McCorquodales for a period of five years beginning on 1 January 1911 and it was to be extended throughout the reign of George V.

Apart from five sizes of registered envelopes there was a remarkable variety of items of stationery on sale. A member of the London Postal Service reported:

> I found at the Chief Office Counter that the officer selling the letter cards had a general stock consisting of white and buff Post Cards, white embossed 1d envelopes of two sizes, cream coloured reply Post Cards and halfpenny embossed envelopes, among which the blue Letter Card stood out, owing to its colour.[1]

For the ½d and 1d denominations there were three different designs of stamps of each value over the range (four if you included the adhesive stamps). It was decided to reduce these to two (one letterpress and one embossed) and to make the ½d and 1d designs the same. This would have a small saving in terms of money, but a greater saving in time in preparing the new dies. The distinctive blue colour of letter cards would be eliminated, despite counter staff objections. As with the adhesive stamps, Samuel had committed himself to having all items of postal stationery on sale by Coronation Day.

But, as with the adhesive stamps, there were delays in getting the new dies and so when De La Rue ceased printing the stationery Edwardian plates had to be handed over to the new contractors. Rather reluctantly, De La Rue gave up the original stamp dies which they had engraved for stationery and the "steel heads" they had made and used. Apart from the master dies they transferred to the Inland Revenue[2]:

Postcards
½d   300 "steel heads"   Nos. 1 to 300
1d   111 "electros"

Newspaper Wrappers
½d   64 "steel heads"   Nos. 1 to 64
1d   37 "electros"

Letter Cards
1d   108 "electros"

There were also the master embossing dies from ½d to 1/-, the registration die (2d plus 1d postage) and ½d embossed postage dies (11), 1d dies (11) and two 2½d dies. Also listed were three Britannia head dies (small, medium and large) presumably used for trial stamps.

The letterpress electros and "steel heads" must have been transferred to McCorquodales though there is no documentary evidence of this. On 19 January 1911 the Inland Revenue reported that the first consignments were due to be delivered the following week. Until then, deliveries had been in large boxes, with stock-sized packets being made up at Somerset House. For a fee of £1 per 100 parcels this was now changed and McCorquodales made up the final stock packets. This extra charge was saved by the Inland Revenue in staff costs and space now freed up at Somerset House.

Proposed changes in charging for the new Georgian postcards and lettercards now impacted on the supply of the Edwardian ones. It was agreed that the new cards would be sold at face value, which should dramatically increase demand. Prior to this they had been sold at a slight premium. But delays meant that not enough of the new cards would be available on Coronation Day.

> The Contractors have now completed their orders of Edward VII Letter Cards in the old banding; and in the circumstances described above it would appear to be necessary for them to proceed with the manufacture of Edward VII Letter Cards in the new banding, either from the blue material used for the previous supply, or from the white material approved for the George V Letter Cards.[3]

Although McCorquodales still had a supply of blue card in stock they also had the new white material. The end result was that Edwardian letter cards were then printed on white card as well, and all were sold at face value from Coronation Day, with new banding providing the new prices. After various experiments the perforations of the lettercards were also altered.

Letterpress Designs

Herbert Samuel concerned himself just as much with the designs for postal stationery as he did with those for adhesive stamps. Initially, he thought that the accepted designs for adhesives might be used on stationery but he was soon disabused of this.

> The design of the adhesive stamp … would not be suitable for the embossed stamps; and it seems probable that it would not be suitable either for the stamps printed on postcards, lettercards and wrappers. The adhesive stamp design usually contains much fine line work; and the Inspector of Stamping is of opinion that it would look "tawdry" if printed on cards and wrappers the material of which is much stouter than that of the adhesive stamps and the surface rougher. It seems probable that a plainer and more solid design, such as those hitherto adopted, would be better for the cards and wrappers.[4]

In his response Samuel agreed that the present Edwardian designs (which harked back to Victorian ones) were not good "but perhaps the Mint might be able to submit better ones. It does not seem advisable to ask an artist to prepare drawings."[5] It was a pity that things had been left so late. This was 1 November 1910. The Mint duly submitted a design on 23 December in the form of an architectural arch with two pediments on either side, leaving room for the King's portrait in the centre. Although approved by his subordinates this was not artistic enough for Samuel. A.F. King was despatched to the Mint where it was explained that "a simple, even a coarse-drawn, design was necessary, as a fine-drawn design gave only a blurred impression."[6]

Above: design for postcard stamp submitted by the Royal Mint

Samuel turned to his friend Marion Spielmann, whom he had also consulted over the initial adhesive stamp designs. Through him, designs were submitted for postcard headings from one William Pitcher who was described as:

> a man of extreme sensibility, yet *very practical* & used to dealing with awkward & cantankerous people (so *you* are all right); as straightforward, kindly, & gentle as you can meet.
>
> He has a growing malady of the bones of the legs – so if you find him bandy you must not be angry with him.[7]

Pitcher had used bookplate style decoration to produce five designs but these were all to provide decorative headings and not the frame of a stamp. Designs featured St. George and the Royal Coat of Arms to balance the King's head of the stamp. One design was to prove formative.

> Mercury being the accepted patron of commerce, letters & languages, I have taken his Caduceus as a fitting emblem. Entwined with our symbolic Oak & laurel – I shall be interested to hear what *you* think. I have a notion for the stamp itself but haven't had time to work it out yet.[8]

Discussions at length within the Post Office ruled out decorative headings, despite Samuel's appreciation of the "artistic" nature of the designs. A design for the stamp was supplied on 27 January, again through Spielmann. Three days later, Samuel sent a revised version "B" to the King noting that the artist had been highly recommended to him.

> After submitting the first design, marked "A", the artist was informed that the head was too small and the work too fine to be suitable for reproduction upon the relatively coarse textured card or paper which would be used, and that it was preferable that the design should not be architectural in character. He has accordingly furnished a second design marked "B" which I submit for His Majesty's approval.[9]

This design featured the caduceus of Mercury, or Hermes, messenger of the Gods which of course could already be seen on an accepted adhesive design by George Eve. Two caducei stood behind an oval frame, suspiciously reminiscent of Mackennal's "Nautilus" design, also recently approved. There is, however, no documentary evidence that Pitcher had been shown the approved adhesive designs, though this seems likely. The King approved immediately. Samuel noted: "Head of course as in other portrait. To be engraved at once."[10]

There then ensued what was described as "deadlock" between Pitcher and the Royal Mint. The latter maintained that there was not enough room for the head of the King; the former stated that the head should be re-engraved. It was the same dilemma which had occurred with the original adhesive stamp frames.

Kenelm Kerr visited Pitcher at his home in Earls Court with enlarged photographs of both frame and head and explained the problem. Pitcher responded with an amended design and two new ones, all incorporating the Downey head. However, the previous design had already been approved by the King which put Samuel in a predicament. Kerr wrote again

Below: approved design by Pitcher

Far Right: essay for letter card (top) with unadopted arrangement of wording and letter card and foreign reply postcard as issued

> Mr Samuel is very sorry that you should be troubled again in the matter but he is anxious that the alteration from the design approved by the King should be restricted to the minimum necessary to accommodate the authorised head. In any case he prefers the general style of the earlier designs with the relatively plain cartouch [sic] as he fears that when the new design is reduced to stamp size, it may appear somewhat florid in character and crowded with detail.[11]

He asked if it would be possible to adhere more closely to the original design or to adapt one of the others. Amendments went back and forward to arrive at a final drawing which would be suitable for printing. So it was not until the end of March 1911 that arrangements were put in hand at the Mint to engrave the dies. Printing was letterpress so the method of engraving and production was as for the dies for the adhesive stamps – head die, frame, value all being added with intermediary transfer rollers. This took place in May and the ½d die was issued to McCorquodales on 7 June 1911. However there was more than one die, as explained much later to Bacon by Rigg.[12]

> The first issue had the defective caduceus and was first issued, for the use of contractors, on the 7th June 1911. The omission of the period after 'Halfpenny' was intentional and it was done as a distinguishing mark for contractors' dies; those for use at Somerset House having the period added. So far we do not appear to have issued any of these

with the defective caduceus. [On the other card] the oval rule round the Effigy was thinned and regulated, the tint lines modified and the caduceus equalized; the first issue of dies for contractors, that is without period, was made on the 15th May 1912.

In fact three or four variations exist, as do the original metal dies with attendant transfer rollers. Somerset House used the dies with the period to imprint stationery submitted by the public.

So thin postcards, and thin inland reply-paid postcards, both at ½d, together with 1d lettercards were available on Coronation Day alongside the adhesive stamps. The lettercards had not been announced. A memorandum by Phillips dated 30 June explained:

Letter cards bearing George V stamps … are now on sale at many Post Offices, and are being issued by the Inland Revenue at a fairly rapid rate. The issue of these cards was not announced in the Public Notice of the 20th June …, as it was only possible to supply them to London Offices in time for sale on Coronation Day.

The cards seem satisfactory; and it might be well if public opinion could be diverted in some degree from the new 1d adhesive stamps to the new 1d letter cards. Perhaps therefore a brief notice might be sent to the Press respecting the issue of George V letter cards.[13]

Later, stout postcards, reply-paid cards and newspaper wrappers, as well as overseas postcards, were also issued, all with the same design and Downey head. Headings were required for all and a new Royal Arms was agreed early on, but Samuel's wish for more decorative lettering was denied because of the pressing need to get electros made in time. Initially, at least, the old simple format was continued.

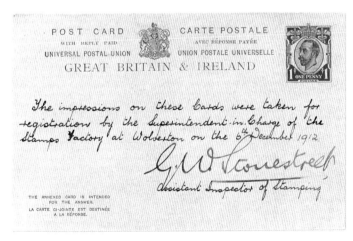

Quantities

Very optimistic forecasts had been made about the reduction of the cost of postcards and lettercards and a resulting increase in sales:

> the Postmaster General originally estimated that when thin postcards are sold at face value their sale will probably amount to something like 330 million a year. This estimate was considered at the time to be somewhat liberal; and moreover, since it was formed, arrangements have been approved for the discontinuance of the sale of thin postcards in uncut sheets, and also for the discontinuance of the fees charged by the Board for impressing postage stamps on private cards presented in large quantities. In view of these facts, and having regard to statistics furnished by the German Post Office respecting the sale of postcards at face value in that country, the Postmaster General is now of opinion that the original estimate of 330 millions a year will probably not be realised, and that the sale is not likely to exceed, say, 240 millions a year.[14]

Production had been arranged accordingly. However, in the event, actual sales were just over 55 million thin postcards. Compensation of more than £3,000 had to be paid to the contractors for lack of promised orders.

Embossing Dies

At the same time as letterpress designs were being considered embossed dies were also required for envelopes and paper stamped to order. This was much more the style of work to which the Royal Mint was used and needed no outside designers. But a head was still required and early on it was made clear that, as for coins and medals, the three-quarter Downey photograph could not be used as a basis.

Given his work on coins, the obvious person to create the effigy was Bertram Mackennal, but it was not until 21 January 1911 that the Mint were able to say "Mr Mackennal has just completed the models for coinage on which he has been engaged for some months and is consequently only now free to commence work on the model for the King's Effigy for the embossed postage stamps."[15]

Above: registration copy of the embossed die for registered envelopes

Samuel and his officials had not realised that nothing had been happening and were furious, but that did not alter the fact of the matter. Mackennal began work on a profile head, initially for registered envelopes. As before, he created a plaster model of the head based on the work he had done for the coinage and this was forwarded to the Mint by 23 February. The embossed head die was complete on 16 March and a lead impression was approved by the King on 31 March. With frame and value added the first die was delivered on 9 June (two more followed the next day) and brought into use immediately, using the same colour of ink as before.

Earlier, the Post Office had asked for the Mint to prepare the frames of the 10 denominations of embossed postage stamps and the 3d registration stamp. Existing Edwardian frames (all different) should be used, but

> Under the provisions of the Postal Union Regulations the values of all postage stamps must be shown in Arabic figures; and it will be necessary, therefore, to make a slight alteration in the frames of the present embossed stamps. In most cases the words now printed on the stamps will have to be moved a little; and figures denoting the value

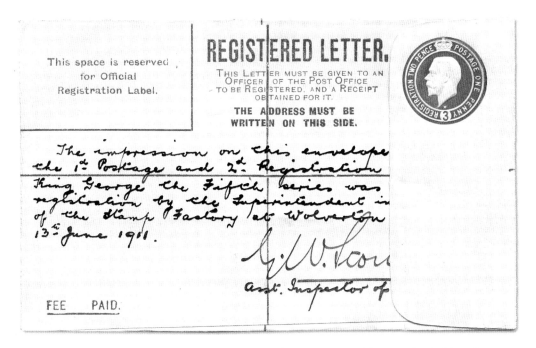

REGISTERED LETTER.

This space is reserved for Official Registration Label.

THIS LETTER MUST BE GIVEN TO AN OFFICER OF THE POST OFFICE TO BE REGISTERED, AND A RECEIPT OBTAINED FOR IT.

THE ADDRESS MUST BE WRITTEN ON THIS SIDE.

The impression on this envelope the 1ᵈ Postage and 2ᵈ Registration King George the Fifth series was registration by the Superintendent in of the Stamp Factory at Wolverton 13ᵗ June 1911.

G. W. Scott Asst. Inspector of

FEE PAID.

Above: registered envelope as issued

Left: drawing of proposed embossed die with Downey head

Below: 1d embossed die partly engraved

should be shown in small "insets", either at the foot, or about midway on both sides of the frame, or in some other appropriate positions.[16]

Frame designs incorporating these were submitted on 21 February. In the Victorian and Edwardian series the ½d design had been smaller than the others. Samuel had regarded this as being particularly poor and had suggested using the 2d frame instead, thus increasing the size of the frame considerably. Subject to minor adjustments he now approved the frames as submitted, but there was then a major hold-up. The designs included engine-turning as a security feature. However, the machine to create this had not yet been delivered. With the pressure to get the ½d and 1d adhesives issued to the public, pressure to which this aspect was contributing, it was decided to delay production of the dies. The delay was to last another two years as adhesive stamps took priority and went through their series of trials.

Work began on the 1d embossed die in November 1911. The head was the same as that used on the registration die. But the introduction of Arabic numerals in the frame caused technical problems

with the lacework of the security printing. The Mint engravers were afraid that the delicate diamond tools used in the engraving might be damaged and they could only be repaired, or replaced, at Darmstadt in Germany. A slight alteration to the frame was proposed, and agreed, to obviate this. The first mock-up in

Suggested Stamp

Sketch of Border of New Design showing numerals in white. and the legend in the type of the present design

Stamp in Present Use.

STAMPING DEPARTMENT 15 DEC.191-

the colour of the new 1d adhesive, Imperial Scarlet, was provided in mid December, with a proof from the completed die on 15 February 1912.

A detailed record was compiled from die sinkers record books many years later of precisely how all the embossed dies were built up, and by whom.[17] For the 1d –

> A matrix was cut with the embossing head in centre. The crown, heads and figure "1" being cut by Whitehouse. The security was cut by Lewis. The figure "1" was taken from £5 obverse (Victoria).

However, progress in bringing the 1d and ½d embossed dies into use was slow. Both dies were initially

Above: comparison of Edwardian and Georgian embossed dies

Right: colour trial for 1d embossed die

ready by June and July 1912. Colour trials took place in October for the ½d (using the 1d die) but not until January 1913 for the 1d. Dies for both were registered on 28 January of that year. They were then brought into use as detailed by Seymour Bennett:[18]

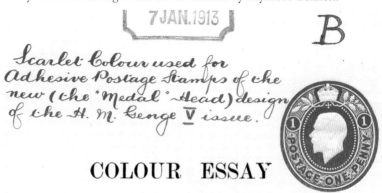

7 JAN.1913

Scarlet Colour used for Adhesive Postage Stamps of the new (the "Medal" Head) design of the H. M. George V issue.

B

COLOUR ESSAY

FOR

1d. Embossed Postage Stamps.

½d and 1d Dies used at *Somerset House* on 17th March 1913.

½d and 1d Dies sent to *Wolverton* on 28th January 1913.

Envelopes first issued to Public:-
"O" size stamped ½d on 12th March 1913
"Commercial" size stamped 1d on 7th May 1913
"A" size stamped 1d on 29th May 1913

From then on dies for use only on private stationery were gradually brought into use in colours generally corresponding to the equivalent denomination in adhesives. Delays were caused by work on plates for the Seahorse high values and there were some initial production problems. Rigg reported that:

> some trouble has been experienced owing to some of our embossed dies having shown signs of scaling in use. This is due either to the composition of the steel we use or the mode of treatment and we are making experiments with a view to overcome the difficulty.[19]

The 2d appeared in August 1914, followed by the 1½d in October. Then, because of war and munitions work at the Mint there was a hiatus until 1915. Colour trials for all other values above 2d were submitted on 22 February (2½d, 3d, 4d, 6d, 10d and 1s). Colour scheme A used colours from the Edwardian series; B approximated the Georgian adhesive stamps. A minute to the Postmaster General (now Charles Hobhouse) noted of colour scheme B:

> Some of the shades are not very pleasing, but I scarcely think it is necessary to obtain alternative proofs in view of the small use which is made of the stamps. Apart from the ½d and 1d stamps, which have already been issued, the embossed stamps are not used on any stationery issued for sale at Post Offices, but only on private covers impressed with stamps by the Inland Revenue Department.[20]

These were then approved without comment. All were of different designs taken from Edwardian models, but with Arabic numerals introduced.

Later that year, there was a need for a 9d value due to the increase of the initial charge for inland telegrams from 6d. A fresh design was sought, but by this time Samuel had returned as Postmaster General. Immediately, he commented on the three proposed designs, and then on the colour of the resulting proof.

> The colour is not a pleasing one, and if there are any future changes in the colours of the stamps generally this one might be altered with advantage, now that the ninepenny

ESSAYS FOR COLOUR ONLY
(NOT FOR DESIGN).

STAMPING DEPARTMENT,
INLAND REVENUE,
SOMERSET HOUSE.

Above: colour essay for 2d embossed die

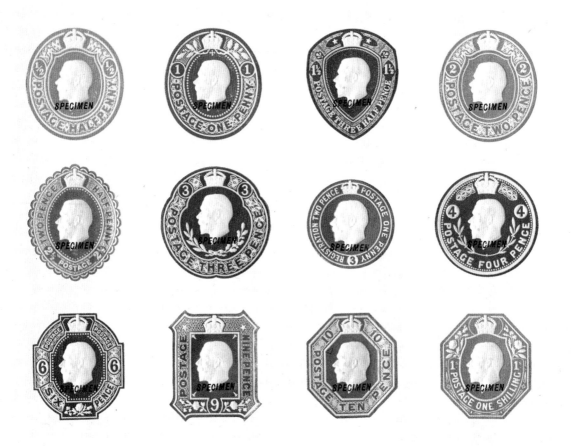

Above: specimens of all values of Georgian embossed dies

stamp has come into more widespread use. But it is advisable that the colour of the embossed stamp should not differ from that of the adhesive stamp of the same value.[21]

It was brought into use on 27 November.

Change of head on letterpress dies

The letterpress dies as approved and brought into use on postcards and wrappers all bore the three-quarter Downey portrait. With the changeover to a profile head on adhesive stamps it was realised that the stationery dies also needed to be changed. In January 1913 the Inland Revenue sent a new design with the same frame but with a profile head.

> I am directed by the Board of Inland Revenue to transmit to you the enclosed sketch of a new design, containing the "profile head" with a blank surround, that has been proposed for the ½d stamp for Post Cards and Wrappers. Subject to the lines of the design being made somewhat coarser than in the sketch, the Board are advised that the design is an improvement on the one at present in use and that it will print satisfactorily. They will accordingly be glad to learn whether it meets with the Postmaster General's approval.[22]

Officials decided to wait until they knew what the King's views were with regard to a tint background to his effigy on the 5d to 1/- adhesive stamps. As he preferred a graduated tint they then asked the Inland Revenue to provide specimens in that style. Nothing happened until August when five variations in Motley prints on specimen cards were supplied, both buff and white. Using the ½d value these ranged from a plain surround through different tints to a solid background. The Inland Revenue noted:

> in addition to its use on official Postal Stationery, this Stamp has to be printed on cards and wrappers presented by the public and the material presented for stamping shews wide variations in quality being not infrequently very coarse and quite unsuitable for a Stamp with fine detail. It is therefore desirable that the design adopted should be one that will print satisfactorily on different qualities of paper.[23]

As a result, the design with the plain white surround was the most satisfactory for printing purposes. However, if a graduated tint were preferred this could be achieved by making the lines on the even tint coarser and more widely spaced. The specimens were submitted to the King and the modified even tint was approved. Subsequently, the die was approved by Samuel without comment. This was 3 November 1913.

Astonishingly, nothing then happened until May 1916. The papers were apparently filed in a cupboard and forgotten. F.H. Nichols found them and was astonished to discover that the three-quarter Downey head was still in use. However, now the Mint were heavily engaged in munitions work and had no time for stamp dies unless it could be proved to be extremely urgent. Nevertheless, the Mint said, when asked via the Inland Revenue, that the ½d dies for official stationery were well advanced and could be brought into use shortly.

Nichols reported:

> The Inland Revenue proposal means that the new "profile head" dies will shortly be brought into use for halfpenny postcards and wrappers printed by Messrs McCorquodale, for sale at Post Offices; but the present "three-quarter" dies will remain in use (apparently until the end of the war) for penny postcards, letter cards and wrappers printed by Messrs McCorquodale, for sale at Post Offices, and for both halfpenny and penny stamps impressed on material for cards and wrappers presented by the public at Somerset House. Thus for a considerable period halfpenny articles bearing stamps of the new design will be on sale at Post Offices concurrently with penny articles bearing stamps of the present design, while all private stationery stamped at Somerset House whether with halfpenny or penny stamps will continue to bear the present design.[24]

Above: essay for profile head postcard die with graduated line behind the King's head

Below: Profile head postcard as issued

There seemed no alternative but to acquiesce in this. But perhaps the new Postmaster General, Joseph Pease, should be told, and perhaps the King. Pease sensibly annotated this minute "No, the less we draw attention to the delay of 3 years in such a simple matter the better."

Colour proofs were submitted, but it was only in December 1916 that an announcement could be made in the *Post Office Circular*.[25]

Introduction of Halfpenny Post-cards and Wrappers bearing a new design of stamp. Post-cards and newspaper wrappers bearing a halfpenny impressed stamp in which His Majesty's head is represented in profile are about to be issued. Reply post-cards of the new pattern will be supplied first, about the date of this Circular.

Ten months went by before anything was heard of the 1d design, when proofs of a postcard and wrapper were submitted.

The colour appears to be a fairly good match with the standard. The fact that it has not quite the same brilliancy is probably due to the difficulties which all ink makers are experiencing with this colour. The printing of the wrapper stamp should improve, particularly as regards the solids, when the form has been running for a time.[26]

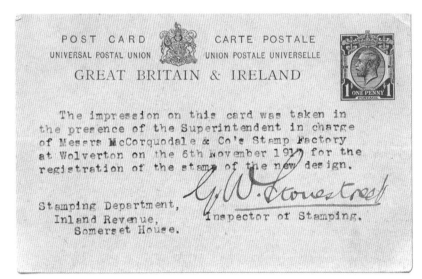

Above: Foreign postcard with profile head as issued

The registration copy of the 1d postcard (for abroad) is dated 6 November 1917. On 13 November a short notice appeared in the *Post Office Circular* simply stating that "Letter-cards, post-cards and newspaper wrappers bearing a penny stamp in which His Majesty's head is represented in profile are about to be issued." They were only four years late, but it is unlikely that many noticed.

Rate changes
Over the course of George's reign there were a number of rate changes, both up and down, which entailed corresponding changes in the stamps used on postal stationery. Where the dies already existed there was no great problem but on some occasions new dies were required. One such was on 3 June 1918 when letter cards went up to 1½d (postcards increasing to 1d and registered envelopes to 3½d). This also caused a new design of the 1½d embossed die. Another was in 1920 when on 1 June the inland letter rate was increased to 2d, though printed and postcard rates remained the same. Clearly, 2d dies would now be required, in letterpress for letter cards and then an embossed 4d for registered envelopes. In contrast to previous experience, a proof of the new 2d letterpress die was ready on 14 April having only been ordered some two days before. These were approved and 24 dies ordered "sufficient to give the Contractors at Wolverton a start."

However, there was also the question of stamping wrappers at Somerset House, perhaps surprising given the basic ½d rate remaining the same.

Above: Unadopted essay for uprating Letter Cards

> There is a considerable and, apparently, a growing demand on the part of the public to stamp material for newspaper &c wrappers with the 2d Postage rate and this has been met up to the present by printing (in one operation) two penny stamps [Downey heads] on each wrapper.[27]

A note supported this stating that in "the past three months 2d duty has been impressed on Wrappers to the extent of 117,540 with the use of two penny dies." As a result 120 2d dies were ordered on 3 August with 18 dies received and issued on 9 September and 12 to follow immediately. However, these did not have the dot distinguishing printings from Somerset House and this needed to be added.

As far as embossing dies are concerned there was no stop after the die number on Somerset House dies. Otherwise, they had no distinguishing features. A remarkable number were created, many being reconditioned during the course of their life. Some were still being made three years after the death of the King and some still used up to 1951.

Embossed dies created

Value	Wolverton	Somerset House	Edinburgh	Manchester	Dublin (till 1922)
½d	32	382	35	18	4
1d	59	48	12	10	4
1½d	342	162	25	6	10
2d	24	16	5	3	3
2½d		6*			
3d		4**			
4d		6			
6d		6			
9d		17			
10d		4			
1s		14			

*one was frequently loaned to Manchester
**one was frequently loaned to Manchester, another to Wolverton for emergency stamping of G envelopes September 1921; this GV die was still in use in 1951

All Dublin dies were returned in December 1922 and re-conditioned for use in the Chief

Office. Threepenny and fourpenny dies were used up till 1951, the 4d in blue from 1950.

Registration Dies created

Value	2d + 1d	2d + 1½d	2d + 2d	3d + 2d	3d + 1½d
Number	96	24	20	12	123

Postal Orders

Postal orders, although sold by the Post Office, were printed by the Bank of England. The design had been more or less fixed since its introduction in 1881, with only a change in the poundage die with the monarch's head. As engraved by J.A.C. Harrison the Downey Head die was now approved in a design produced by the Bank, this pattern also being used for Old Age Pension orders, also printed by the Bank since 1909. The Controller of the Money Order Department, F. Wickham, was insistent that "it has been held that the present pattern should not be interfered with except for the strongest reasons. I have no alteration to suggest at present of a pressing nature."[28]

Below: Unadopted design for postal order poundage die submitted by the Bank of England

This did not stop the Bank of England submitting a completely new design for the poundage die which was duly rejected. It was thus not until the end of August that the new designs were approved, and the orders were issued on 3 November.

Utilising the Downey Head, of course, caused the same problem as with other stationery when it was replaced by a profile on stamps. On 10 June 1913 Wickham, thought that as the "effigy which now appears on postal orders has been superseded in the case of postage stamps it would, I think, be desirable to arrange with the Bank of England for the introduction of the latest approved effigy in future supplies."[29] Because the Mint were so busy with the stamps it was proposed to "postpone this question for a month." That month was to turn into years.

In September 1913 the Mint suggested that, because of its size, it would be better to adopt the profile head to be used for postcards. But that depended on the die for postcards being ready. Despite its non-introduction on the postcards themselves, a pull from that head die was received from the Bank of England in July 1914. Improved proofs were prepared in January 1915 and then modified. The revised designs were finally approved on 27 February, still well in advance of the forgotten postcards. First issue was not until 1 October that year.

Printing by Bank of England continued until 1923 when it was decided to bring everything under Post Office control. The printing contract was then given to McCorquodales. Minor changes took place in later years.

*Above: specimen of
the first Downey Head
type of Georgian postal
orders*

Imperial Reply Coupon

To facilitate the prepayment of a return letter from overseas the Universal Postal Union had created an International Reply Coupon. This was in a standard design printed by Benziger & Co in Einsiedeln in Swizerland, overprinted with the name of the issuing country. In 1926 it was proposed that the British Empire have a similar coupon – an Imperial Reply Coupon. Waterlows were approached to provide a design.

> Without in any way restricting you in the choice of a design the following possible subjects are indicated:
>
> A map in Mercator's projection with Empire in red.
>
> Britannia and a Ship.
>
> The figure of Britannia similar to that on the 10/- Treasury Note.[30]

Treasury Notes had first appeared at the outset of World War I. At the time Bank of England notes were only of £5 and above, but lower values were required to limit the outflow of gold from the country. Almost immediately an improved design by George Eve was printed. Because of forgeries, these designs were then changed and printing techniques made more complex to provide security features. Printed by Waterlow Brothers & Layton the £1 of the third series was issued on 22 February 1917 and the 10s on 22 October 1918. These were designed by Bertram Mackennal and, apart from a large version of his profile head of the King, featured St George and the Dragon on the £1 and Britannia on the 10s. A 5s note was prepared but not issued. The illustrations on the front and reverse of the notes were printed in offset litho, with other parts of the design in letterpress, together with a photogravure security overprint. This was the first use of the photogravure process in security printing in Britain.

After the War these notes had continued in circulation and in 1926 were being printed by Waterlow & Sons Ltd, so they had immediate access to the designs and plates, and were familiar with the printing techniques required. A few days after being invited Mr Rose of Waterlows submitted four sketches by staff artists, one of which "too nearly approached in design the 10/- Treasury Note".

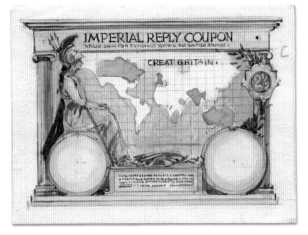

Mr Rose stated that he could print coupons to correspond with either of the sketches, in green and mauve, green and blue and green and brown. It was not possible for reasons of security to introduce red except as a third printing. The type of printing would be off-set litho.[31]

Red had been suggested to pick out the British Empire around the globe, but apart from the printing restriction it was pointed out that many of the dots would have been too tiny to notice, so this was not pursued. Surplus paper for the British Empire Exhibition stamps would be suitable for the printing.

Offset-litho printing

In the files there is a later description of printing these coupons in offset-litho by Harrisons at Hayes.[32] The process at Waterlows was undoubtedly similar and it accords with what is known of their printing of the Treasury Notes.

Firstly, the design is engraved in reverse on a steel or copper plate. This is smeared with ink, and then cleaned so as to leave ink only in the engraved grooves.

> An impression of the design is taken from the plate on a special (coated) transfer paper and transferred to a second transfer paper in order to get the design into reverse again.[33]

This second transfer paper is pasted on to a litho stone and the impression is transferred under pressure. As the stone surface is slightly absorbent the ink sinks in. After cleaning the stone is rubbed with gum and washed with water. This renders the plain part of the surface resistant to the greasy ink used (which includes a high proportion of beeswax). The stone is then rolled with an ink roller and because of the grease only takes to the design impression and not any other part of the surface.

In traditional litho printing this stone could be used in a flat-bed machine to print direct to paper (without one of the previous transfers) but it would have been a laborious process. Here zinc working plates were made for use in a rotary machine (possibly not zinc in the case of Waterlows).

The impression is transferred from the stone to the zinc by means of transfer paper. The zinc is then treated with a salt etch, gum and a final washing with water to render the

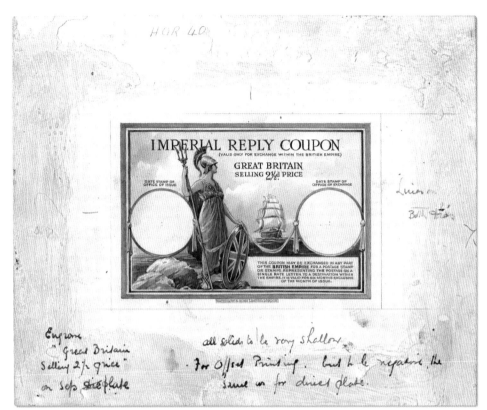

surface (except where the impression lies) resistant to greasy ink. (N.B. The design is not etched into the surface. It is merely a film of ink lying thereon).[34]

During printing, the zinc plate is inked and moistened between each impression but the paper to be printed is not applied direct to the plate. The machine includes a rubber blanket cylinder which takes an offset impression (in reverse) from the zinc plate and applies it to the paper.

The design to be printed in this manner was recommended by General Williamson to Sir Evelyn Murray, Secretary to the Post Office.

> I think the most suitable on general grounds is that marked "A" bearing the figure of Britannia (standing), and no map. Some slight adaptations in respect of detail will be required, e.g. in the size of the date stamp space and the alignment of the superscription; but there should be no great difficulty about this. I think too a steamship would be more appropriate, though less picturesque than a sailing ship.[35]

Murray responded – "I agree, but leave the sailing ship."

After some minor modifications, in September 1926 250,000 coupons were printed, to be overprinted GREAT BRITAIN for use in Britain, and otherwise for use in Dominions and Crown Colonies. By 1933 the stock of the unappropriated coupons was reduced to 25,000 (with some 40,000 overprinted for overseas since 1932). A further supply of 160,000 coupons was produced and then in 1935 225,000 more printed on Postal Order paper.

1   POST 30/3694 Stamped Stationery: H.M. King George V issue, part 1. Bray, L.P.S. to Controller, L.P.S. 11 October 1910

2   De La Rue Correspondence Book I.R. 15 p162

3   POST 54/49 Atterbury to Secretary, GPO 27 March 1911

4   POST 30/3694 op cit. Minute to PMG. 1 November 1910.

5   ibid

6   POST 30/3694 op cit Memo by A.F. King. 12 January 1911

7   ibid Spielmann to Samuel, 21 January 1911

8   ibid Pitcher to Spielmann 22 January 1911

9   RA PS/PSO/GV/PS/STAMPS/4130/70 Samuel to Bigge 30 January 1911

10 POST 30/3694 op cit Bigge to Samuel 31 January 1911

11 POST 30/1995 Kerr to Pitcher 28 February 1911

12 Rigg to Bacon 1917, quoted in **Dagnall, H.** *The Evolution of British Stamped Postcards & Letter Cards: Their History & Documentation* 1985, p132

13 POST 30/3695 Stamped Stationery: H.M. King George V issue, part 2. 30 June 1911

14 POST 30/3694 op cit, A.F. King to Inland Revenue 31 March 1911

15 MINT 20/418 W. Ellison-Macartney, Royal Mint to Inland Revenue 21 January 1911

16 MINT 20/437 Walter G Gates to Inland Revenue, 5 November 1910

17 MINT 15/54 Record of production methods adopted for Postage Embossing Dies Since 1913 – Rates ½d – 1/- (c.1933)

18 IR 79/173 Note by Bennett, 25 September 1913; also IR 79/91A Bennett to Superintendant, Stamping Room 15 March 1913

19 IR 79/23 Rigg to Gregg 23 August 1913

20 POST 30/3695 op cit 27 February 1915

21 ibid 17 November 1915

22 ibid Atterbury to GPO, 15 January 1913

23 ibid Inland Revenue to GPO, 29 August 1913

24 ibid F.H. Nichols to Walter Gates 19 July 1916

25 *Post Office Circular* 19 December 1916

26 POST 30/3695 op cit. G.W. Stonestreet, Inspector of Stamping to Secretary, Inland Revenue. 8 October 1917

27 IR 79/178 Stonestreet to Sparkes 23 July 1920

28 POST 30/3310A Postal Order and Old Age Pension Order forms: H.M. King George V issue. F. Wickham to Secretary, GPO, 24 February 1911

29 ibid 10 June 1913

30 POST 52/658 Imperial Reply Coupons – Unappropriated. W. M. Cook to Waterlows 1 February 1926

31 ibid. Cook memorandum 18 February 1926

32 ibid. 27 October 1937.

33 ibid

34 ibid

35 ibid 17 March 1926

9
POSTAGE & REVENUE
FUGITIVE INKS & POSTAGE DUES

Since 1881 British definitive stamps were described as "Unified". Formerly, there were separate stamps for postage and revenue use. These were now combined. Thus most stamps bore the legend "Postage & Revenue". There were still quite a number of fees which were paid by specific revenue or fiscal stamps, and these were to increase dramatically during the reign of George V.

With postage stamps being available for revenue purposes it was considered that doubly fugitive ink was necessary to print them. This was a security precaution and meant that anyone trying to remove either postal cancellations or writing ink from a stamp already used would damage the image on the stamp, thus making it obvious that it had been tampered with.

De La Rue monopoly

De La Rue's monopoly from 1880 depended upon this apparent necessity for the stamps to be printed in doubly fugitive inks. When they were about to be investigated in 1910 a history of the use of fugitive inks in printing stamps was compiled.

> The fugitive inks used by De La Rue and Company are of two kinds – singly and doubly fugitive. The singly fugitive inks render Stamps used for Postage services proof against a successful removal of the Postage cancellation marks. The doubly fugitive inks, which can be produced in two colours only – purple and green – render adhesive Stamps, used for Postage and Revenue purposes, proof against the successful removal of Postage cancellation marks and, though no doubt in a less efficient degree, also against the successful cleaning of stamps used for Revenue purposes, which have been cancelled by writing…. Another important advantage claimed for both De La Rue's fugitive inks, and which it is alleged other manufacturers' surface inks do not possess, is that Stamps printed in these inks cannot be forged by being directly transferred to stone, from which successful lithographic reproductions of the Stamps can be printed.[1]

All Revenue and Fee stamps had always been printed in doubly fugitive inks and these inks were then used for Unified stamps with the exception of the ½d which was always singly fugitive.

> Since 1901, the 1d. Postage and Revenue Stamp has been printed in singly fugitive ink. This change, which effected a saving of £6,000 a year, was decided upon by the Postmaster General – one of the arguments in favour of adopting the singly fugitive ink being that the introduction of the red colour was necessary to meet the views of the Postal Union Congress.[2]

Some of the Edwardian stamps were bi-coloured, one of the colours being doubly fugitive. On grounds of economy, however, it had recently been decided to change some of the bi-coloured stamps (the 1½d, 2d and 4d) to singly fugitive ink and in one colour only. Others, which were little used for Revenue purposes (5d, 9d and 10d) would follow suit. The high values (5s, 10s and £1) were all singly fugitive, but all Revenue and Fee stamps proper (from 1d to £50) were printed in doubly fugitive inks and it was recommended that this continue.

> The total cost of printing and overprinting adhesive Revenue and Fee Stamps proper is about £600 a year – the extra cost of the doubly fugitive ink, as compared with that of the singly-fugitive ink, being about £50 only.[3]

However, there was a considerable extra cost in printing the 3d, 6d, 1s and 2s 6d stamps in doubly fugitive inks. The 2s 6d was only £9 a year, but the 3d cost £180 (plus an extra £140 for the yellow paper), the 6d £210 and the 1s £555. The 6d was used extensively to denote the Stamp Duty on various agreements and so needed to remain as it was. The others could be printed in singly fugitive inks without any great danger. This was the state of play when the new Georgian stamps came to be considered. When the printing contract was removed from De La Rue the opportunity was taken to except the 6d stamp from the contract, and it was now to be printed under State control by the Inland Revenue at Somerset House. All other stamps would be printed in singly fugitive ink. After some discussion this also applied to the 2s 6d.

Ink and Paper Problems

Throughout the reign of George V there were constant problems with the supply of doubly fugitive inks. For postage and fiscal stamps the specification to the manufacturers was:

> The ink must be clean and free in working, quick drying, fast to sunlight and quite free from any ingredients deleterious to health. It should be of such a character that stamps printed therewith are highly sensitive against any attempts to remove writing and postal ink cancellations and that the ink on such stamps is non-soluble in water.[4]

It was also specified that anything which could be used successfully to remove ordinary writing inks should destroy the proper colour of the stamps.[5] The coating of the paper on which the stamps were printed had to be insoluble in water.

At first, Somerset House printed the 6d Edward VII stamps in doubly fugitive ink, but they had problems with the colour. In March 1913 they made a delivery of 3,000 sheets on coated paper made by Dickinsons which they thought unsatisfactory particularly in terms of matching the shade of previous printings on uncoated paper. This prompted a reply stating that they were not sufficiently bad to justify the destruction of the stock of coated paper. "The shades of 6d stamps printed at different times vary considerably & we have at the present time in stock some stamps at this rate which are not very dissimilar from those now in question."[6] Nevertheless, it became impossible to perforate the stamps because the coating was so hard. Some 100 reams, costing 45/3d a ream, had to be discarded. The result of this was that from March 1913 they turned to De La Rue for supplies of coated, gummed and plate-glazed paper, "as satisfactory as that used by themselves", at a cost of 21/6d per ream. This was to continue until at least 1920, though by then the cost was 49/- per ream.[7]

Two plates for the George V profile 6d became available and were put to press on 16 July 1913.

All batches of ink were sent to the Government Laboratory for testing for sensitivity to treatment for removal of writing ink, postal cancellation, solubility in water and any content in the ink which might be deleterious (such as lead). The purple ink used generally for the

6d was manufactured by the family firm of Mander Brothers Ltd of Wolverhampton "Manufacturers of Varnishes, Fine Colours and Printing Inks". It had been established in 1792 and held a royal warrant. Although supposedly the same make (Manders 27449A) it varied.

> As you are aware the 6d Unified stamps and all the Fiscal adhesive stamps are printed in inks which are supposed to be doubly fugitive in character. Considerable trouble is experienced with these inks which vary in their degree of sensitiveness and lack uniformity of colour, and the coating of the paper is a costly business.[8]

"Safety" paper was tried but this turned blue. Then in 1924 and 1925 experiments were made with ink produced by Winstones and Slater & Palmer. Coated and uncoated papers were also tried and in 1926 it was decided to change over to uncoated paper for the 6d.

> As you are probably aware there has been in the past and always will be, I am afraid, considerable trouble with the doubly fugitive inks used for the sixpenny Unified and for the fiscal stamps. Some time ago many of the reports received from the Laboratory indicated that the inks did not possess the necessary fugitive qualities and that writing ink cancellations could be removed without any material alteration in the appearance of the stamps. We carried out experiments over a period with the result that it was discovered and confirmed by Laboratory test that the ink which we had obtained was more sensitive when used in connection with uncoated paper than with coated paper. The Post Office agreed to the change and some economy was effected. The 6d Unified stamps have been on issue for some time and they appear to be satisfactory.

> The use of the uncoated paper causes the prints to be a little lighter in tint but otherwise good prints are produced and it is hoped that a standard colour will be more easily obtained than has hitherto been the case.[9]

Towards the end of 1927 some fiscal stamps had also been printed on the uncoated paper.

One of the problems was that the fugitive qualities of ink seemed to disappear, as far as writing ink was concerned, after a period of time. Thus stamps printed from the same ink as, say, three months earlier were no longer doubly fugitive. The durability of the purple ink was markedly less than that of the green. This caused many more experiments with different inks to take place especially in late 1928 and 1929. In July 1928 a new ink was

Above: Laboratory trials of 6d doubly fugitive ink

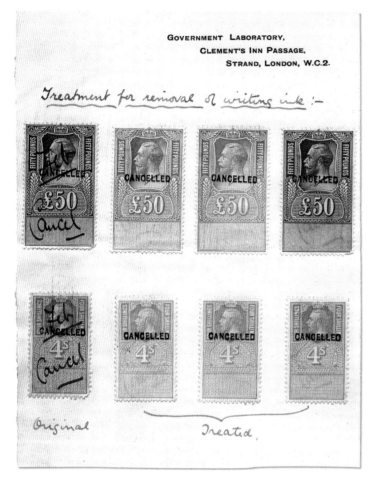

GOVERNMENT LABORATORY,
CLEMENT'S INN PASSAGE,
STRAND, LONDON, W.C.2.

Treatment for removal of writing ink :—

Original

Treated

Above: Laboratory trials of doubly-fugitive inks on fiscal stamps

to be made standard. This new ink (Manders 61871) was registered on 8 April 1929 on super-calendered paper (i.e. still uncoated).

This too proved unsatisfactory and experiments were carried out with ink from Winstones. Then in January another new Manders purple ink (65000) was first used on 1s unappropriated fiscal stamps with excellent results. It used about two thirds of the amount of ink and cleaned up well. The same ink was used in February on 100,000 sheets of 6d Unified with a slightly smaller saving in ink. This was due to the paper, that for the 6d being super-calendered "which is more absorbent than the plate-glazed used for the printing of 1s unappropriated."[10]

The same problems occurred in the green inks used on many revenue stamps, this time the manufacturers being Winstones from 1926.

When the contract for unified stamps was awarded to Harrisons in 1933 the 6d was included for the first time. Harrisons then produced this value letterpress but never succeeded in obtaining a photogravure version. The problems of doubly-fugitive ink for photogravure printing were not solved until the reign of King George VI.

Revenue and Fiscal Stamps

There were two basic types of revenue fee or fiscal stamps. Certain versions had their own designs, such as stamps paying for National Health Insurance (designed by George Eve in 1912), or Unemployment Insurance or Dog Licences. Others used a standard type with the monarch's head in varying values but overprinted, or "appropriated", for a particular service. These were for fees for such matters as Bankruptcy, various court fees and the like. The latter were printed in doubly fugitive inks and were thus, with very few, minor exceptions, printed in either green or purple, all by the Inland Revenue at Somerset House. Unoverprinted ("unappropriated") versions of these had to be created in the same way as postage stamps.

Even though it was decided to retain the existing frames from Edwardian designs, substituting Mackennal's profile head, there was still a considerable delay in producing the necessary dies because of all the troubles with postage stamps. Because of this delay in creating the new dies and plates for the Georgian unappropriated revenue or fiscal stamps new printings took place at Somerset House of the old Edwardian designs in the early part of George's reign. There were different sizes for pence values, shilling values and pounds; thus for each there were different numbers of stamps making up a sheet. Printings of some of these continued until 1920.

Edward VII Unappropriated fiscals

Value	Set	Colour	Registration Date	Notes
6d	240	green	4 January 1915	new colour
1s	168	olive	24 August 1914	
1s	168	Olive green	21 September 1917	
1s 6d	168	olive	21 August 1914	
2s	168	green	1 August 1916	
2s 6d	168	olive	22 July 1915	
4s	168	olive	1 September 1914	
5s	168	olive	9 February 1915	
10s	168	olive	20 August 1914	
15s	168	olive	27 July 1915	
£2	120	purple	1 March 1918	change of ink

Edward VII Unappropriated fiscals: Change from I.R. to I.R. & Orb watermark

Value	Set	Colour	Registration Date
2s 6d	168	green	24 March 1916
4s	168	Olive green	27 March 1916
5s	168	olive	1 March 1916
10s	168	Olive green	21 November 1916
15s	168	green	22 February 1917
£1	120	purple	11 October 1918
£3	120	purple	13 November 1919
£50	120	purple	8 October 1919

George V dies

In the meantime, because of the delays, there was no question of having a Downey Head die. Rather, the first engraved head was the Mackennal profile Medal head but at a different size. The first one was engraved, but not finished, by J.A.C. Harrison by 17 November 1913. This was shown to Mackennal the same month. A trial proof from an unfinished die for a large fiscal stamp head was also ready by the beginning of March 1914. These were then inserted into existing Edwardian frames.

Above: appropriated fiscal, pence type

Dies for the 1d, 2d, 3d and 4d were all ready before the outbreak of war, but that was to slow progress dramatically. The Royal Mint was partly turned over to munitions work and fiscal dies and plates had to wait. The 6d and 9d were engraved by 21 December that year and that completed the small pence values printed in sheets of 240 (other than the 8d which did not appear until 1916).

The shilling dies were printed in sheets of 168. Dies for the particular values were only

Above: appropriated fiscals, shilling and pound types

Right: proof of the new unappropriated 7/6d die

Far right: Somerset House and Harrisons control numbers

slowly engraved between January 1915 and the same month two years later. As can be seen from the continued printings of Edwardian values the pound series (from £1 to £50) printed in sheets of 120 and exclusively in purple was even more delayed. Dies were finished from November 1918 through to November 1920, the last being the highest value.

Printings went through the same vicissitudes as the 6d doubly fugitive Unified stamp, with different watermarks, papers and inks. There was one completely new additional value – 7/6d ordered on 19 December 1922. For this the design was created

by the Royal Mint. It had a background for the King's Head similar to that of the Pound series, but the size of the head is that of the pence and shilling series, described as .41" high.[11] As with all other fiscal printing plates this was grown on leads with no nickel facing. The stamps were first registered on 13 June 1923.

All these were unappropriated dies. Before use they were overprinted for the particular function for which they were required.

From 1934, production of these revenue stamps was taken over by H.M.S.O. and printing plates were transferred there on 7 May that year.

Postage Due

Uncollected revenue was always of concern to the Post Office. If an item was posted without sufficient prepayment it was surcharged and the excess collected by the postman on delivery. But the system in place was complicated and open to abuse and a conference in March 1912 looked at possible reforms.

> An unpaid or insufficiently prepaid packet when detected in the post is marked (usually by means of a metal Surcharge stamp) with the amount to be collected on delivery. From that moment the packet acquires a money value, and has to be accounted for at the several stages through which it passes.[12]

And it passed through a great many stages. There were inadequate checks in the system, with 40% of surcharges having no direct audit by postal headquarters. "There can be no doubt whatever that under this system leakages of one kind or another occur." In other words, the postman or his supervisor sometimes pocketed the money and it was not detected. The system was therefore, in the dry words of the report, "hardly in accord with the well recognised principle of the Service, that temptations to dishonesty should be minimised."[13]

It was proposed that "Postage Due" labels be introduced. These would be accounted for in the same way as postage stamps and therefore a direct check could be maintained. After some discussion within the Post Office this was agreed.

George Eve was invited to create a design along the lines of existing postage due labels of other countries, without the monarch's head.

The labels will be issued in four denominations, viz:- ½d, 1d, 2d, and 5d. The same design will be used for all four denominations, the numerals and words denoting value alone being different. The labels will be of the same dimensions as the 1d postage stamp, but the short edge of the stamp will be from top to bottom and the long edge from left to right. The colours of the labels will probably be the same as those of the corresponding denominations of postage stamps, viz., ½d green, 1d red, 2d orange and 5d fawn.[14]

A fee of 30 guineas was offered. Eve accepted and produced a design in the style of a bookplate with leaves and national symbols, and the words POSTAGE DUE, the following month. An apparently unsubmitted design included two crowns. By 19 December the accepted design had already been engraved by Lewis at the Royal Mint with a 2d denomination. On submission to the Inland Revenue authorities at Somerset House, this die was approved without comment, as indeed were the subsequent values. Clearly, designs without the monarch's head were not highly rated in importance. The ½d, 1d and 5d dies all followed in January and the same process was followed for producing letterpress

plates as was for postage stamps – i.e. leads struck, copper master plate grown and backed and nickel-faced working plates grown from the master. All were created, as with postage stamps, at the Royal Mint. Colour essays used the entire 2d plate, dated at Somerset House 11 February.

First printings of these four values in the approved colours took place on 17 March 1914 or slightly afterwards at Somerset House. Then at the end of March or beginning of April the plates were transferred to Harrisons and re-registered. Printings can only be distinguished by the control number, that for Somerset House being in a serif typeface with a full stop, that for Harrisons sans with no stop. The stamps were issued, and the system begun, on 20 April.

In 1915 a 1s value was added to be printed at Somerset House and not Harrisons, though it was then transferred to Waterlows with the change of contract in 1924. Other values followed – 3d in 1918 and

Above: Postage Due artwork and colour trials for the first issue

Above: colour trials for 1s and 3d additional values

Right: Post Office notice announcing introduction of postage due labels

4d in 1920. The design was not changed other than the denomination and this work was carried out at the Royal Mint. Numbers printed and issued varied with detailed postage rates (and seasonal volumes of mail) but it was clear that while all denominations up to 4d were in demand, the 5d and 1s values were rarely used. Where several thousand 1d or 2d sheets were issued each month it was rare that there were more than 100 sheets of the 5d or 1s.

In October 1921, J.J. Anderson, an Assistant Inspector in Dundee pointed out to the Dundee Postmaster that "As the minimum surcharge on all Foreign correspondence is now 1½d I would respectfully submit that a 1½d Postage due label be issued." This suggestion was passed on to London and agreed, but with a certain amount of hesitation. It was unclear how long the rate would exist but as the total cost of producing 5,000 sheets was only £35 it was decided to go ahead.

No. 5.

SURCHARGES.

INTRODUCTION OF "POSTAGE DUE" LABELS.

On and after the 20th of April all surcharges on letters, parcels and other postal packets, posted unpaid or underpaid, will be denoted by means of "Postage Due" Labels to be affixed to the covers and date-stamped before delivery.

On and after that date no surcharge should be paid on delivery of any letter, parcel, or other postal packet, unless it bears a "Postage Due" label or labels of the face value of the amount demanded.

The new system does not apply to Customs Duty on parcels, to Trade Charges on Cash on Delivery packets, or to Express Fees.

"Postage Due" Labels are of the following denominations and colours:—

½d.—green.　　　2d.—agate.
1d.—red.　　　5d.—brown.

Each label bears at the top the words "Postage Due," in the middle its face value in figures, and at the bottom its face value in words.

By Command of the Postmaster General.

GENERAL POST OFFICE,
14th April, 1914.

[10649] 2500　Printed for His Majesty's Stationery Office by W. P. Griffith & Sons Limited, Prujean Square, Old Bailey, E.C.　4/14 B

> The 5d and 1s labels are undoubtedly white elephants, and each additional line means a certain amount of additional work in the Stores Department and elsewhere.[15]

The colour should follow that of the 1½d postage stamp (brown) and six essays were submitted on 11 August. That chosen was chocolate brown made by Slater & Palmer. Unusually, the plate was struck on leads and had a copper rather than a nickel face. First supplies were issued in December 1922. It was not to last. At the UPU Congress in Stockholm in August 1924 the minimum charge was reduced from 30 centimes (rated at 1½d) to 10 centimes, to come into force on 1 October 1925. There would be no further need of a 1½d value.

However, this was not the last new denomination. The highest denomination so far was 1s. For postal purposes this was regarded as sufficient and its small use would support that. In mid 1923 there was a move for a higher value – of 2/6d – for which there was apparently a need. This was not so much for underpaid postage but rather for the collection of Customs dues. As a result it was proposed that the words POSTAGE DUE should be replaced by TO PAY. To accommodate the value in words on the tablet at the foot of the design Williamson decided it should be HALF CROWN.[16]

At the beginning of September a rough sketch was supplied by the Mint and Somerset House was given a ½d Postage Due working plate in order to produce colour essays. As with most other Postage Due labels it was intended that the colour match the colour of the Unified stamp, in this case green. Five shades of buff or brown were supplied on 12 September using the ½d denomination.

Extraordinarily, Williamson then wrote to the Union of Post Office Workers to ask them for their opinion. They wrote back with a rather pertinent objection:

> With reference to the colour essays which I herewith attach, I think the colour proposed for the 2/6 "To Pay" label is not sufficiently distinctive remembering that it will be used in a number of cases on parcels with brown paper covers. I suggest a colour which would be quite distinctive from brown.
>
> Another objection is that it is not sufficiently distinctive as compared with the "Postage Due" label for 2d.[17]

They took the point. Further essays were required in light pink and in orange (the colour of the 2d Unified stamp) "and also in any other colours which you may consider suitable." The first batch are dated 21 November – four shades of orange, one of green and two of magenta. More followed on 6 December – Royal Scarlet, Dahlia Claret, Purple, Claret Lake, Pansy Lake and Plum – all carefully mounted on brown paper. On 16 January came the reply:

> The Secretary of the Post Office favours the "purple" shade but desires to see further essays in that colour printed on a bright yellow paper which would be readily distinguishable on the covers of parcels. Will you please furnish the essays required as early as possible?[18]

Six essays, still in the ½d value, arrived a few days later. The approved version was printed on Dark Canary paper from Samuel Jones with the ink being Slater & palmer's Purple No. 2034. This would cause problems as the paper suppliers at the time were William Joynson and not Samuel Jones. They found difficulty matching the lemon tint and the resulting paper was not as originally chosen. It was used nevertheless. The plate was made to the pattern required by the new printers, Waterlow & Sons Ltd (without

P.D. 48.

P.D 55

Umbrian Brown. S + P 1114

Above colour trial for 1½d (top), 2/6d (middle) and sketch for 2/6d design (bottom)

Above: colour trial for 2/6d on yellow paper and 2/6d die proof (right)

central gutter, but with indicative arrows in the margins) and put to press on 3 July. Only one plate was ever used.

This was to be the last addition to the series in the reign of George V. Although later monarchs had different watermarks the design was to remain the same right through until 1970.

1 D/S E 746 "Fugitive Inks: History of Use in Adhesive Stamp Manufacture" H. Birtles, Deputy Controller of Stamps 18 January 1910

2 ibid

3 ibid

4 D/S E 746 Specification for Doubly Fugitive Printing Inks, 17 December 1929

5 ibid. Bennett to A.E. Mallaindain, of Park Royal paper mills 30 July 1912

6 ibid. H. Birtles to Stonestreet, 5 March 1913

7 De La Rue Correspondence books G.P.O. 4. De La Rue to Controller, Stores, Somerset House. 28 October 1919

8 D/S E 746 Stonestreet to Government Chemist 13 April 1923.

9 ibid. 27 January 1928. Longley to Osmond

10 ibid. 20 February 1930 A.L. Firth to Longley

11 Royal Mint register – Master Plates and Issued Working Plates register

12 POST 30/3188 Surcharges: Postage Due labels introduced. Report on Unpaid Postage Account Forms and Records. 12 March 1912

13 ibid

14 **Beaumont K.M. & Stanton, J.B.M.** *The Postage Stamps of Great Britain* Part Four 1957, p242 Walter G. Gates to Eve, 28 October 1913.

15 POST 52/1334 Postage Due Labels: introduction of the 1½d value. F.H. Nicholls to Williamson, 15 July 1922

16 POST 52/1332 Postage Due labels: Introduction of 2s 6d To Pay label. Memo by R. Fanshawe 5 September 1923

17 ibid. Secretary, Union of Post Office Workers to Secretary, GPO. 19 October 1923

18 ibid. R Fanshawe, P.O. Stores to Director of Stamping, 16 January 1924

10
PRODUCTION CHANGES
PRINTERS, BOOKS, ROLLS & METERS

O ver the course of 25 years stamp production changed. Contracts for printing adhesive stamps were renewed or "determined" and as a result printing was transferred to another printer. Different printers required different formats of printing plate and paper changed. The printing technique remained letterpress, however, until the final change-over to photogravure in 1934, described later. Postage rates also changed, not only up but also down. This had an immediate impact on the production of the stamps concerned. While the process remained as letterpress for lower value definitives all dies and plates were created at the Royal Mint. Referring to postage dues in 1922, the cost of production of one letterpress plate was estimated at £15. Over 850 were produced of the profile heads alone.

Postage stamps were not only sold over the Post Office counter from sheets. The most-used values also came in other formats. Stamp books had been on sale since 1904 and stamps could also be obtained from stamp-vending machines mainly supplied and operated by the British Stamp and Ticket Automatic Delivery Co. Ltd, of which Mrs Kermode was a director. Rolls of stamps for stamp-affixing machines were also similarly made up from sheets by manufacturers such as the International Stamping Machine Co. Ltd.

Previously, the production of stamps in sheets has been described, but at the same time they had to be printed to be made up into stamp books. This required a different format of plate and this had added to the pressure both at the Mint and at Harrisons.

Stamp Books

Stamp books were a means of buying stamps for future use. As it was thought they would be put into breast pockets, or wallets, the panes of stamps were provided with interleaving so that they did not stick together. When the first books were issued in 1904 they consisted of 24 1d stamps. The cost was 2/0½d, including a surcharge of ½d for the cost of producing the book. Later, ½d stamps were included and the contents changed to amount to 1/11½d worth of stamps and a blank label with a printed cross. As with other items of postal stationery Herbert Samuel wanted these books to be sold at face value when the first Georgian stamps came out. The value was thus written down in manuscript on the front cover.

Special plates were required to print the stamps for books. This was because of two basic requirements:

  (a) The stamps should always be upright when the booklet was opened.
  (b) There would always be a binding margin on the left of each pane.[1]

In practice, this meant that each pane of six stamps (or four with two blank labels used for advertising) had to have a blank margin to its left. To save space on the plate this resulted in one central gutter rather than several narrower margins. However, this entailed the panes being inverted in relation to each other – termed tête-bêche. This, of course, resulted in inverted watermarks on half the stamps from the sheet. Making these plates was an added complication for the Royal Mint when they took over production. Samuel expected

Above: part of the registration sheet for Downey Head books showing tête-bêche arrangement

that stamp books would also be on sale on Coronation Day together with the sheet stamps. He was to be disappointed. The first Downey Head plates for books were only received by the printers in July and the first books were not ready for issue until 10 August 1911. Costing 2s the first George V books had a full 2s-worth of stamps. Interleaving carried Post Office notices and from 1911 there were many different numbered editions, with advertising sold by the agents Messrs Sells to help offset the cost of producing the books. Numbered series of these were created by the Post Office, based upon value and differing content, though they were not consistent. As stamp printing changed over the years (described later in this chapter) so did the stamps contained in the books.[2] For convenience, all major changes in books are listed here.

Series No.	Cost	Content	1st Issue Date	Notes
1	2s	3 panes of 6 x 1d 2 panes of 6 x ½d	10 August 1911	Downey Head
	2s	3 panes of 6 x 1d 2 panes of 6 x ½d	26 April 1913	Profile Head
2	3s	2 panes of 6 x 1½d 2 panes of 6 x 1d 2 panes of 6 x ½d	8 October 1918	Increase in postage rates
	3s	3 panes of 6 x 1½d 1 pane of 6 x 1d 1 pane of 6 x ½d	17 July 1919	Change in content
	3s 6d	3 panes of 6 x 2d 1 pane of 6 x 1d	7 July 1920	Increase in postage rates; 2d - die I
	3s 6d	2 panes of 6 x 2d 1 pane of 6 x 1½d 1 pane of 6 x 1d 1 pane of 6 x ½d	26 January 1921	Change of content; 2d – die I
	3s	3 panes of 6 x 2d	21 April 1921	(die I and die II)
3	3s 6d	2 panes of 6 x 2d 1 pane of 6 x 1½d 1 pane of 6 x 1d 1 pane of 6 x ½d	2 August 1921	2d - (die I and die II)

Series No.	Cost	Content	1st Issue Date	Notes
3 cont	3s 6d	3 panes of 6 x 1½d 1 pane of 6 x 1d 1 pane of 6 x ½d	29 May 1922	Decrease in postage rates
	3s	4 panes of 6 x 1½d	17 June 1922	Change of content
	3s	3 panes of 6 x 1½d 1 pane of 6 x 1d 1 pane of 6 x ½d	29 February 1924	Waterlows Block Cypher watermark
	3s	[as before]	May 1930	Airmail label included
4	2s	1 pane of 4 x 1½d + 2 labels 1 pane of 6 x 1½d 1 pane of 6 x 1d 1 pane of 6 x ½d	8 February 1924	Printed by Harrisons
	2s	[as before]	31 March 1924	Waterlows Block Cypher
	2s	[as before]	February 1934	Harrisons
5	5s	1 pane of 4 x 1½d + 2 labels 5 panes of 6 x 1½d 1 pane of 6 x 1d 1 pane of 6 x ½d	1 August 1931	Waterlows Block Cypher
	5s	[as before]	July 1934	Harrisons

To produce stamp books at the printers required them to stack the printed sheets in the correct order, with the covers on the outside and the interleaves in place inside. The sheet layout, as described above, meant that from the left there were six stamps upright, then six stamps inverted followed by a gutter, and the same repeated. First, the stack of sheets one booklet deep were stitched down

Above: part of the registration sheet for 1½d panes in stamp books with the advertising label printed later (left)

131

Above: Post Office notices for stamp books

the middle of the sheet in the gutter. Then both outside ends were stitched. This stack was then guillotined in between and across creating 40 books per sheet. The books were then wrapped in bundles and packed into parcels for distribution and sale over post office counters.

Books of stamps were eventually to be sold from machines as well as over the Post Office counter. In 1931, some 25 machines were installed experimentally for the sale of 2s books in various post offices. Most were in London, but there were also machines in Glasgow, Birmingham, Nottingham and Sheffield. Difficulties were experienced with variations in some of the coins (both 1s and 2s being used), especially the Victorian examples.

Interestingly, the Cypher shown on the front cover of stamp books was an anomaly. In script format it followed the style of the monogram of the previous reign including the addition of the letters P O., and did not change to block lettering as for most other Post Office uses.

Rolls

Rolls of stamps (termed coils by collectors) exist so that the public can buy stamps when the post office is shut, or so that businesses can stamp their mail efficiently by using stamp-affixing machines ("to save the labour of the mail room boy's tongue"[3]). Mrs Kermode had first trialled a stamp-vending machine for the Post Office in 1906. She then gained a contract for 12 machines installed from 1907 onwards and formed the British Stamp and Ticket Automatic Delivery Co. Ltd to manufacture and service them. Various patents were taken out by Mrs Kermode for developments to these machines. By 1910 she had 13 official machines in London, Liverpool, Manchester, Edinburgh, Glasgow, Dublin and Belfast. There were also at least 39 private machines installed in such premises as hotels, cafés and clubs.[4]

There were both ½d and 1d machines and the BSTAD made up their own rolls of 1,200 stamps from sheets supplied by the Post Office. These were rolled so that the gum side was outwards as this was found to give greater tension in the machines, and also so that the stamp would be delivered face side up. Sheets of stamps were joined every 12th stamp and then slit by machine and reeled. An early making-up table was constructed by Grovers. The resulting rolls were for endways delivery (after an initial trial with sideways delivery).

In November 1911, Mrs Kermode gained an order for 100 new machines from the Post Office. These held two dispensers, the left for ½d stamps and the right for 1d. By now Edwardian stamps had been replaced by the new Downey Heads, in their different varieties. In the new agreement the BSTAD was to receive 2% commission on sales.

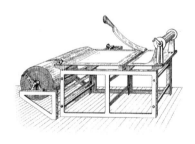

As with stamp-vending machines, rolls of stamps for use in stamp-affixing machines were made up by the private manufacturers. These were in rolls of 1,000 or 500 depending on the machine and had cores of different sizes dependent on the machines they were to be used in. During 1912, the International Stamping Machine Co. Ltd became overwhelmed by their own success in selling machines. So much so that they asked Captain Cecil Norton, MP to ask a question in the House of Commons. In May they had supplied owners of their Fixo stamp-affixing machine some 2,619 rolls or 1,309,500 stamps.

Above: Grover making-up table for rolls

> We are, I must confess, being swamped in the matter of reeling at these offices.

> During the month of June, we sent out in reels 2,021,000 stamps.

> In May, as I have already written you, we sent out 1,309,500, as against 683,000 in the month of March.

> From present indications we expect that this month will run over 3 millions, and that the increase will be constant so, as you can quite appreciate, it is getting a very serious matter for us[5]

Below: inner workings of a stamp-vending machine

Was there any news about the Post Office supplying such rolls themselves? The Post Office were being delayed by an argument with the Treasury over charges to customers for the projected rolls. An agreement had already been come to with Harrisons to produce rolls of both 1,000 and 500 ½d and 1d stamps. They were to receive 1.625d per large roll and 1.15d per small roll. As a result the Treasury had approved charges to the public of 2d per large roll and 1½d per small. Various companies objected to the charge for the small roll as being out of proportion. The manufacturers of machines which took these rolls also complained and so Herbert Samuel proposed to reduce the charge from 1½d to 1d. This required Treasury authority and it had to be admitted that this charge would now be at a small loss. It took 2½ months for the Treasury to give in and grudgingly no longer "refuse Their [Lordships'] assent". It was only then that the Post Office could go ahead and announce their plans.[6]

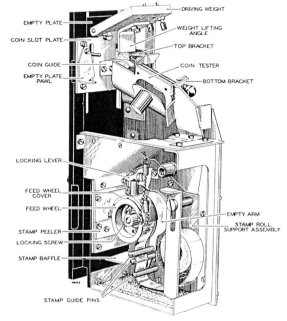

Issue of postage stamps in roll form.

Arrangements are being made for the introduction of rolls containing 1d and ½d postage stamps, made up in eight different ways, suitable for use with various types of stamp-affixing machines, viz:-

Rolls with large cores (about 1¼" diameter).

A containing 1000	1d	stamps arranged for delivery	top end first price	£4 3s 6d
B	"	1d	"	lower end first price	£4 3s 6d
C	"	½d	"	top end first price	£2 1s 10d
D	"	½d	"	lower end first price	£2 1s 10d

Rolls with small cores (about ½" diameter)

E containing 500	1d	stamps arranged for delivery	top end first price	£2 1s 9d
F	"	1d	"	lower end first price	£2 1s 9d
G	"	½d	"	top end first price	£1 0s 11d
H	"	½d	"	lower end first price	£1 0s 11d

The different size of core, and whether it was top end or lower end delivery, reflected the requirements of different stamp-affixing machines. Each type of roll had a "leader" of paper printed in the same colour as that of the stamps contained inside, with the code letter and giving details of content and price. Unlike the rolls produced by Mrs Kermode these were reeled gum side in.

At the outset, all eight varieties would be stocked only at the Chief Post Office London, the London Head District Offices, and the Head Offices at Belfast, Birmingham, Bristol, Dublin, Edinburgh, Glasgow, Leeds, Liverpool, Manchester, and Newcastle on Tyne. 6,000 of rolls A to D had been ordered in March, together with either 4,000 or 8,000 of rolls E to H. These were all made up with Downey Head die 2 stamps. With changes in stamp design, rolls (and books) also changed. The first Profile Head rolls in August 1913 were E and G printed on all-over watermarked paper (Multiple Cypher). From November that year all rolls were issued printed on the chain watermark (Simple Cypher) and from the end of 1914 the printer's imprint was added to the leader.

Wartime production

When Treasury Notes were first printed in 1914 they used Royal Cypher watermark paper intended for postage stamps. Then, for the notes, Joynsons produced a stouter paper of better quality, still with the Royal Cypher watermark. As a result of a change-over to a more distinctive watermark there were almost 228 reams of this paper left over. In 1915 it was agreed that this should not be wasted and it was used to print 1d stamps, eventually made up into rolls.

At the beginning of January 1916 D.G. Ginn, the Director of the firm supplying dry "colour" to Harrisons for printing 1d and ½d stamps, came to see the Post Office.

He says that since the outbreak of War his firm has supplied Messrs Harrison and Sons with all their colour, both for the stamps themselves and for the covers of the books. The colour is manufactured in this country, but the dye is made in Germany and has to be imported.[7]

Above: roll leader for stamp-affixing machines

134

They had a licence to import such dyes but their agent had disappeared and they were in a quandary. It transpired that although Harrisons bought in ink for stamps of 1½d and upwards, they made their own inks for the two lower values, which of course constituted the vast majority of those they printed. The aniline dyes which were a constituent part had come from Germany. This interview was an attempt to bring pressure on the government to grant the ink-makers a licence, needed when more than 25% of material to be imported was enemy produced.

This was trading with the enemy and the Board of Trade would not be moved. They referred the Post Office to British Dyes Ltd, a firm set up by the government. Harrisons provided details so that the dyes might be reproduced.

> The description of the dry colours used in the making of the inks for ½d and 1d Stamps are Red Lake and Green Lake respectively.

> The Red is aniline dyes struck on pure Alumina Hydrate.

> The Red dye really required is known in Germany as Lithol Red but as this has been unobtainable the shade is obtained by a combination of several dyes.

> With reference to the Green, Aniline Yellow is struck on Pure Alumina Hydrate and shaded with Chinese Blue (Ferro Cyanide of Iron).[8]

Samples of green and red dyes were supplied on 7 July 1916 and passed on to Harrisons. Essays in both green and red proved unsuitable. By September it became clear that Harrisons were eking out their supplies of red ink. Ginn's firm, J.W. & T.A. Smith Ltd, had kept Harrison supplied with "small quantities of strong red colour which they mix with weaker red obtained from other sources so as to produce the shade required for penny stamps".[9] However, this had resulted in some pink stamps which had been issued.

There was also the question of the colour used for printing the front covers of stamp books – Persian Red.

In the end Harrisons were able to obtain sufficient colours from material seized and sold as "prize" mixed with the weak colours mentioned. This lasted until mid 1917 when British Dyes were able to produce colours which the Post Office considered "not unsatisfactory".[10]

Postage Rates & their Effects

In general, postage rates were very stable during George V's reign but changes did take place and these had obvious and immediate effects on the contents of stamp books and rolls.

On 3 June 1918, the basic inland letter rate was raised to 1½d from 1d. This resulted in changes to stamp books already seen, and in the creation of four new rolls of 1½d stamps for stamp-affixing machines:

J 1,000 top end
K 1,000 lower end
L 500 top end
M 500 lower end

Statistics for the year 1918-19 give the level of consumption. There were far fewer rolls of 1,000 sold than those of 500.[11]

Value	Code	Delivery	No. of Stamps	Issued
½d	C	Top-end	1000	709
	D	Lower-end	1000	3,174
1d	A	Top-end	1000	279
	B	Lower-end	1000	1,427
1½d	J	Top-end	1000	530
	K	Lower-end	1000	1,956
½d	G	Top-end	500	51,162
	H	Lower-end	500	26,839
1d	E	Top-end	500	14,216
	F	Lower-end	500	10,126
1½d	L	Top-end	500	24,993
	M	Lower-end	500	17,904

From 1 June 1920 the inland letter rate was raised again, this time to 2d Q -1,000 lower end, R – 500 top end, S – 500 lower end.

Until now Mrs Kermode and BSTAD had produced 1,200 stamp rolls for vending machines on a commission basis. Early in 1919 they asked the Post Office to take over this production. In March it was announced that the rolls of 1,000 stamps coded A, C and J (1d, ½d and 1½d), originally intended for stamp-affixing machines, would be used instead but this did not prove satisfactory.

Subsequently, Harrisons produced rolls of 1,000 for use in vending machines marking the leaders "Kermode Roll" and "For use in Automatic Machines installed in Post Offices only. Not for sale to the Public." 2d rolls were also produced for the time that was the letter rate but in May 1922 postage rates were reduced to 1½d again.

Flaws & Errors

Proofs of all plates were taken before they were sent to the printers and brought into use. These were carefully examined and marked up where minor flaws were found, the proof being sent back to the Royal Mint for the flaws to be corrected. Some flaws were more major than others and not all were picked up. This was more likely when the plate was being repaired, rather than initially created. In February 1921, G.W. Stonestreet at the Inland Revenue wrote in horrified tones to W.J. Hocking at the Royal Mint:[12]

> My attention has just been called to a most serious error on the part of your people in repairing a 1½d Unified Stamp Plate which was sent to you for that purpose on 28th October 1919.

> This plate was recently taken from reserve and brought into use again, and after fifteen reams had been printed, one of my Officers, by the greatest good fortune, discovered that a "Halfpenny" stamp piece had been inserted in what was the damaged portion of the plate.

> I am appalled that such a mistake could possibly occur and I will leave you to imagine what would have happened had any of these prints been issued.

Once might be regarded as unfortunate but only two weeks later he had to write again.

> Unfortunately another defective plate has come to light [No. 585/14] for 1½d Postage stamps. You will see from the enclosed proof that the fifth stamp down on the extreme right of the lower pane has the letter F instead of E in the word "halfpence". This plate was sent to you for repair on 17th April 1919 and again on 19th August 1919 and on each occasion the defect appears to have escaped observation.[13]

This error did appear. But it was not the only plate on which it occurs and so must have happened during the moulding of the plates. A note dated 31 December 1919 states that at exactly the same place on the plate, but plate 586/15 rather than 585/14, the same flaw had occurred. Some 192,000 sheets had been printed from this plate before the error had been detected, 131,000 under Control M 18 and 61,000 under O 19.[14] Proofs were now demanded after every repair and both these plates were repaired before re-use.

Printing Continuous Reels

From as early as 1912 the Inland Revenue had been working in conjunction with Grovers, the manufacturers of perforating machinery.

> With a view to obtaining a more satisfactory and economical method of production of rolls of stamps than that in use at present, experiments have been carried out in the Stamping Department for some time past on the design and construction of a machine which would print stamps "in the web", i.e., in a continuous roll, and as a result of these experiments, mechanism of a special design is now being constructed which, it is anticipated, will give satisfactory results. This mechanism requires a printing plate of a special design, the plate being different from the design used for printing stamps in sheets both in its dimensions and in the fact that it requires to be slightly curved.[15]

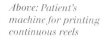

This was the brainchild of J. Patient, Superintendent of the Engineering Branch of the Department of Stamping of the Inland Revenue. Special reels of paper at a specific size had to be ordered (from William Joynson) and a particular plate made. The plate was to be of 200 images of the 1d Medal Head stamp, 3/16 of an inch thick but being stiffened by a thicker nickel deposit than normal. It was also to be slightly concave on the face side, the camber being 1/16 of an inch. The Royal Mint created a master plate in August 1913 and then six working plates from this, though only one of these (338/2) was used for the experiments.

Above: Patient's machine for printing continuous reels

By January 1914, the machinery had been tested on the reel of watermarked paper provided. But the printing surface was not good enough. A further reel of paper was ordered but problems persisted. Over 350,000 stamps were printed and delivered on 26 and 28 March 1914 and immediately cancelled.

A description of the machine's operation was provided by Patient. At each impression of the plate 200 stamps were printed but the machine was so constructed that when printed there was no break between plate impressions.[16]

> 1. The gummed watermarked paper is printed in the web and rewound (at the printing machine) in convenient lengths. At the time of printing, each impression is numbered in the margin, also a hole is punched in each margin for registration purposes at the perforating machine.
>
> 2. Printed rolls stored for print to dry.
>
> 3. The webs of stamps perforated.

The operator then cut the web at every 50th impression for rolls of 500 stamps or every 100th impression for rolls of 1,000 stamps. Then the web was slit and reeled.

But at this point war intervened and experiments were delayed. In the end they were discontinued for the duration of the war because of the difficulty in obtaining a supply of suitable paper and the absence of skilled printers and engineers.

After the war, in 1919, the Merkham Trading Company wrote to enquire when they might expect rolls in a continuous strip from this machine.

> The reason I am writing you just now is, that within a very short time we must manufacture here our Multipost Affixing machines which are now made in U.S.A. and if there is a possibility of sideways joined stamps being available, we could import from America the necessary tools to manufacture the machine here, but if we are not likely to get the stamps joined sideways, then it will be necessary for us to have tools specially made to produce here a perfect machine for the lengthways joined stamps.[17]

This was the first mention of producing *sideways* delivery stamps from this machine. If sideways delivery were required then another printing plate and a different perforating mechanism would be necessary. Eventually, on 9 December, the company were informed that they would be supplied with sideways rolls, though it could not yet be stated whether they would be joined or continuous.

Patient explained that "a new printing plate 192 set with the stamp pieces at right angles to those of the present plate" would be required. The stamp pieces should be in two panes, each 12 x 8 stamps with a gutter between. A new perforating punch box would also be required as well as various other pieces of the mechanism. The same paper could be used but this would produce stamps "with the watermark at right angles to the print."[18] In other words, sideways continuous rolls would have sideways watermarks.

The existing plate 200 set was awkward. To avoid printing on unwatermarked paper (for endways delivery rolls) the existing dandy roll could still be used to make paper but the plate needed to be altered.[19] Rather than create a completely new plate the existing plate 200 set of 1d stamps was cut into three pieces on 13 April 1920 – two of 90 images and one superfluous of 20. The two 90 set pieces were clamped together to form a plate 180 set (two panes of 90 with intervening gutter). This was also better from a printing point of view. The other plates were also cut before 1924 when they were transferred to Waterlows, though no date is given for this.

In the meantime, Harrisons had produced trial rolls for sideways delivery by joining strips from normal sheets. These were successful and so three new types of roll were created:

N   1½d   for delivery left side first
O   1d   for delivery left side first
P   ½d   for delivery left side first

Below: 2d dies – I (C.13) and II (14.12.21) and roll leader

Supplies of each type were to be ready by 5 May 1920 as the Merkham Company wanted to exhibit them with their Multipost machine at the exhibition then at the Agricultural Hall.[20] As these were produced from horizontal strips of 12 stamps the total number of stamps was changed from 500 which would have been difficult to produce to 480. It is not clear if they were demonstrated at the exhibition for it was not until 31 August that the *Post Office Circular* announced that they had been introduced. By that time there were also rolls of 2d stamps – Q (1000 lower end delivery), R (500 top end delivery), S (500 lower end delivery) and T (480 left side delivery).

On the continuous reel machine paper problems meant that it was not until September 1921 that the first 100 "E" rolls (end delivery) were delivered on an experimental basis. Further delays ensued and it was only a year later in September 1922 that it was reported that delivery of 7,000 rolls had been made to Post Office Stores. By May 1923 it was clear that no further experiments would be required to produce sideways rolls from continuous reels. However, by now there was the question of a new contract for printing stamps and continuous roll production was to be incorporated in that.

Changes to 2d and 9d Stamps

In the meantime in 1920, with the increase in postage rates on 1 June, more working plates were required of the 2d value. The printers had complained that the existing plates were out of gauge. When examined it was found that the stamp size was slightly wrong. Dimensions were 0.893 of an inch in height rather than 0.8875. This caused the horizontal perforation gutters to be too narrow and affected all plates, for both sheets and books.[21] To rectify this, a new die for striking leads was made from the existing roller in June that year. A master plate was made from this die and then 18 working plates. In October a master plate was also made for books and a further eight working plates made from that. However, it was only at this stage that it was discovered that there was a defect in the new die – "in hair at back of head – 3 black spots in triangular form" as recorded in the plate register.[22] All work had to stop and the plates could not be used. Yet another new die had to be created from the original head and frame rollers. This was completed by February 1921 and a third master plate for sheet stamps was created in April 1921 with another for

Above: changing colours of 9d from registration sheets

books the following month. Working plates from the latter began printing in July, though those for sheet stamps did not begin until November. Die II, as it is referred to, thus first appeared in stamp books. Postage rates came back down to 1½d in May 1922.

Another change involved the 9d stamp. The printing colour used (agate) had never been liked and was found to resemble "too closely the colour of the obliterating fluid"[23] – in other words it was too dark for the cancelling ink to be apparent. As a result it was changed to green (G.2 essay) and re-registered on 11 October 1922. In September 10,000 sheets were printed with a little more yellow to better match the essay. (The colour of the embossed die for stamping stationery and paper was also changed to green at this time.)

Changing Printers

In 1922, the new Postmaster General was the rising politician, Neville Chamberlain. A résumé was written for him of the various contracts then in place and this gives a good overview of how things stood at the time.[24]

Subject matter	Contractor	Commencement of Contract	Date of termination	Approximate annual payment	Terms
Watermarked paper	Joynson.	1 July 1912	On 6 months notice at any time	£27,000	Actual cost + 10% on cost of production. Maximum payment £54 per 6 chests of paper.
Printing Postage stamps ½ to 1/- (except 6d) Postage due labels Books of stamps and advertisements Entertainments Duty stamps	Harrison	1 Jan. 1911	On or after 31 Dec. *1923* by 12 months notice	£56,000	Actual cost of labour, materials and overhead charges + £7,500 annually for depreciation and interest on capital.
Insurance stamps	Waterlow	1 May 1912	On 6 months notice at any time	£12,000	Actual cost of production + 1s 9d per ream as profit.
Postage stamps 2/6, 5/, 10/-	Bradbury Wilkinson	1 Aug. 1918	On 6 months notice at any time	£500	32s 6d per ream (500 sheets)
Postage stamp 6d and some Inland Revenue Stamps	Somerset House	-	-	-	-
Stamped Stationery	McCorquo-dale	1 Jan. 1911	Already determined as from 30 June 1923	£90,000	Schedule rates + all proved extra costs of production in respect of labour and materials, power, lighting, repairs, maintenance, cartage and office requisites.

The history of the stamp contracts was explained.

> The intention was to invite fresh tenders when the contract had run for the normal period of ten years, but in 1920 trade conditions were still so abnormal as a result of the war that it was decided with Treasury approval to extend Messrs Harrison's contract until the end of 1923 on the terms indicated in the schedule.[25]

It was recommended that notice be given that the contracts with Harrisons and Waterlows would be terminated and invitations for a fresh contract for the whole of the work would then be issued. It was not proposed to change the arrangements with regard to the work at Somerset House, nor with the high value contract.

Chamberlain, ever the businessman, noted at the foot:

> Certainly notice should be given to terminate the Harrison & Waterlow contracts at the end of next year. If I am P.M.G. I should desire to consider the terms of any fresh contract before invitations to tender are sent out.[26]

He was still to be Postmaster General at the time – August 1923 – when the tenders were considered. These had been received from four firms: Thomas De La Rue, Waterlow & Sons, Harrison & Sons, and Bradbury, Wilkinson. At the same time however, there had been an investigation into paper and watermarks and this complicated the estimates provided.

Below: suggestions for a change to all-over watermark

Watermarks & Sheet format

At first, in 1911, the watermark used had been a simple crown but this had to be accurately registered to ensure that one appeared on every stamp. This was soon changed to a watermark featuring the Royal Cypher and a simplified crown. The Cypher was in scroll lettering but still needed to be registered horizontally and was described as a "chain watermark", though known to philatelists as "Simple Cypher". At the beginning of 1923 there was a proposal for an "all-over" watermark (as had been used for a short period in 1913, then termed "Multiple Cypher").

> The watermark is used primarily to show whether the stamp is genuine, and it should be readily visible by holding the stamp up to the light. The form of watermark at present in use.... can only be distinguished, particularly in the case of a cancelled stamp, with great difficulty. The faintness of the watermark

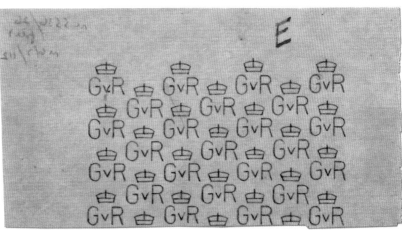

seems to be due mainly to its character – the *"GvR"* being too complicated – and it would be more distinct if simpler in character e.g. "GvR" [with crown above]. There was no difficulty with the watermark in use before the existing one was adopted, a crown – in fairly broad lines.[27]

A number of pencil sketches were produced by Edwin Amies & Son, dandy roll manufacturers from Maidstone, to show the effect of sans or block letters as opposed to a scroll. The over-all watermark was more economical and, known as "Block Cypher" to philatelists, was introduced with the new contract.

This had the effect of reducing the complexity of registering the paper. But at the same time efforts were being made to reduce the size of the paper as well. A suggestion from a certain Mr Swingler, Assistant Superintendent in Leicester, pointed out that there was considerable waste in the existing sheets.[28] The central gutter could be dispensed with replaced by horizontal lines to mark half sheets, in the same way that vertical lines marked quarters. And other margins could be reduced. These points were addressed when considering the four tenderers. The result was to eliminate the central gutter - to be replaced by marginal arrows to indicate half sheets. This had obvious, and major, implications for existing printing plates.

The New Contract

Based on a year's estimated requirements the revised costings were given as:

	£
Messrs De La Rue	40,064
Messrs Waterlow	40,160
Messrs Harrison	42,980

Bradbury, Wilkinson had not been considered because they were not prepared to gum and plate-glaze the paper. Although the cheapest, De La Rue were in a very difficult financial position and also the sizes of their paper were unsuitable. The Post Office were not prepared to take the risk of such a breakdown as would occur if they were bankrupt. So the choice fell on Waterlows at a cost of about £13,000 less than the current contract with Harrisons. The contract would be for 10 years from 1 January 1924 and the Treasury did not hesitate to give their approval. It also covered printing of Health and Pensions stamps, Unemployment Insurance stamps and Entertainment Duty stamps.

They propose to undertake manufacture at their works at Watford, where Treasury Notes and Insurance stamps are printed and where the control of supplies of watermarked paper and of stamp production in all its stages can be carried out without difficulty. It is anticipated that with their experience of stamp printing Messrs Waterlow will soon overcome any initial difficulties and produce stamps fully equal to those manufactured by the present Contractors.[29]

As we have seen Waterlow and Sons Ltd had re-united with Waterlow Brothers & Layton in 1920. New machinery was required. Three new (Payne's) quad Wharfedale printing machines were due for installation at the end of November 1923 with a further two by mid December. They already had a sixth quad Wharfedale by another maker at Watford which was to act as a reserve. Experimental 1d stamps had been printed on it in September using two plates (numbered 603/114 and 604/115) supplied for the purpose. Grovers were to provide one platen, two perforating and one or two slitting and reeling machines.[30]

A new building was also required in which gumming and plate-glazing would be carried out but this would not be ready until 1924. In the interim gumming and plate-glazing would be carried out by Samuel Jones & Co. at Camberwell.[31] By November 1924 Waterlows had six plate-glazing machines, one of which had been used for Insurance Stamp work under their old contract. Three of the remainder had been obtained from Harrisons.[32] It was later stated that four of these machines had cost £1275.[33]

The new smaller size of paper with its all-over watermark and the smaller plates required those plates in existence to be converted – cutting out the centre gutter strips, re-joining them and fitting the margins with arrows to indicate half sheets. The first 1½d plate of the new pattern was begun at the Royal Mint on 20 September 1923. Other existing plates for sheet stamps were sent to them for conversion, beginning the following month. Master plates also had to be converted for new plates from the new pattern to be made. As these plates became available and stocks were required, proofing of the various values began (from 23 December). Some required three or four proofing runs before being pronounced satisfactory.[34]

Denomination	No. of proofing runs required	First proof	Satisfactory proof
½d	3	22 Dec 1923	7 Jan 1924
1d	3	31 Dec 1923	8 Jan 1924
1½d	1	2 Jan 1924	2 Jan 1924
5d	1	14 Jan 1924	14 Jan 1924
9d	2	14 Jan 1924	18 Jan 1924
10d	1	19 Feb 1924	19 Feb 1924
1s	1	25 Feb 1924	25 Feb 1924
2d	1	19 Mar 1924	19 Mar 1924
4d	3	22 July 1924	18 Aug 1924
2½d	2	20 Aug 1924	3 Sept 1924
3d	4	28 Aug 1924	26 Sept 1924

Once printing was underway the output of a four-plate Wharfedale machine was given as 22 reams (480 set) a day, or 22,000 issue sheets. Each machine required one minder and two feeders. The average daily output of a Grover perforator was 28 reams (240 set) requiring three girls to operate each machine, two feeders and one taking off.[35]

As part of the run-up to Waterlows beginning printing they were instructed by Post Office Stores on the use of the control mark on plates for sheet stamps. They were to begin with A and change it twice a year, the number representing the year to be changed on 1 January.

The "control marks" for the year 1924 will therefore be as follows: -

For stamps printed
A.24   From 1st January to 30th April inclusive
B.24   From 1st May to 31st October inclusive
C.24   From 1st November to 31st December inclusive

1.

A 23

2.

A 23

3.

A 23

4:

A 23

Type no .3 approved

~~~ 2/11/23.

Above: proofs from Waterlows of control lettering

On the 1st January, 1925, the mark should be changed to C.25.

The "control mark" should be in bold characters. The letter and figures of which the mark consists, should be about two-thirds of the height of those now appearing on sheets of stamps, but they should be slightly bolder and wider.[36]

Proofs were to be supplied as they were at the beginning of November. Harrisons at this point were on control letter W and a few stamps and postage due labels were printed by them with the W 24 control. However, despite their prior instructions, the official stock-take in 1924 took place on 1 July and the change of control letters was thus reduced to two a year, taking place on 1 July and 1 January from then on.

Changes in Rolls

With the new contract Waterlows agreed to the production of rolls in continuous reels. For this they needed the one and only machine in existence, that at Somerset House designed by Patient and constructed by Grover. This was initially lent by the Inland Revenue to Waterlows, and then sold to them for £650.

The cut plates, in two panes of 90, were transferred to Waterlows, but new master plates were also made for continuous reels by the Royal Mint. These were 180 set for endways delivery and 192 set (two panes of 96) for sideways delivery. Working plates for the ½d, 1d, 1½d and 2d were all prepared by April or May 1924.

Waterlows also produced rolls for use in Kermode machines. On 27 February 1924 they were instructed that these ½d and 1d rolls would now be made up in two sizes of 960 and 1,920 stamps creating four new rolls. In 1927, Mrs Kermode having died, the Kermode name was removed from the leader and in 1928 it was announced in the *Post Office Circular* of 2 July that they would be allocated a code letter to bring them into line with other rolls and they would be sold at face value.[37] These were now:

W	½d	960	Lower End delivery
X	1d	960	Lower End delivery
Y	½d	1,920	Lower End delivery
Z	1d	1,920	Lower End delivery

From November 1930 these could also be sold to the public and the restriction clause was removed. Charges for all other rolls had been abolished on 1 September 1927.

Some higher values were also made up from sheets for use in stamp-affixing machines. These were:

F	2½d	960	Lower End delivery	6 November 1929
C	3d	960	Lower End delivery	14 September 1932

Previous code allocations were no longer valid, as the issue of those rolls had ceased, hence the re-use of these codes. As these new rolls were made up from sheets they had joins, but these were now every 20th stamp, there being no interrupting gutter in Waterlows' plates.

Paper Experiments

Most paper used in stamp printing was based on rag and wood. In the early 1920s in connection with continuous reel printing it was found that a mix of esparto provided a very good base. As a result there were a number of experiments with paper manufacture in 1924 with both Spicers and Dickinsons. On 23 April the latter were provided with a special dandy roll for the watermark slightly different from the all-over Block Cypher by then in use. At the beginning of May Dickinsons made the experimental paper at their Croxley Mill. The constituents were:[38]

Soft cotton	18.75%
Linen	6.25%
Paper	6.25%
Esparto	31.25%
Wood (good colour)	37.50%

Below: roll leader for 2½d

Three other papers from Spicers were made up as well but this (paper D) from Dickinsons was preferred. Waterlows were then given a warrant to print both 1d and 1½d stamps on this paper. On 10 October the finished stamps were then distributed to postmasters as follows (sheets):[39]

	1d	1½d
Manchester	4,000	5,000
Liverpool	4,000	4,000
Birmingham	3,000	3,000
Bristol	2,000	3,000
Newcastle	2,000	2,000
Leeds	2,000	1,000
Sheffield	2,000	1,000
London Chief Office	950	1,000

Postmasters were asked for their comments and particularly if there were any complaints from the public with regard to the tearing of the perforations. Generally speaking the reaction was favourable.

Then in December 1924 an official asked if there were any stamps remaining in store from the experimental printing. If so, could they be made up into rolls? The answer was some 387 sheets of the 1d and 315 of the 1½d. These were made up into experimental joined rolls:[40]

60 1d endways	480	E
60 1d sideways	480	O
60 1½d endways	480	L
60 1½d sideways	480	N

The printers found the paper rather better for reeling than the normal. Between January and February 1925 these experimental rolls were issued to London Chief Office, WCDO and seven provincial offices with the instruction that a questionnaire be filled out when the rolls had been sold. Again, reaction was either neutral or generally favourable.

The result of these experiments was a general change-over from rag to mixed furnish paper in 1927 and 1928 and all values were registered on this.

In 1929 there was another change in stamp printing paper, though not in its constituent parts. Rather, it was decided to change from a plate-glazing finish to having the paper super-calendered. Waterlows had been required to buy four plate-glazing machines for their contract but super-calendering was a cheaper process. Post Office Stores reported:

> a good deal of experimental work had to be done, and it was found expedient not to proceed with this until Messrs Waterlow had fully satisfied the Department that they had got over the initial difficulties of this contract; there was a further delay owing to the introduction in 1926 of a new quality paper for stamp printing, namely a mixed furnish paper in place of an all-rag paper. This experimental work has now been done and a large quantity of stamps – in all some 60,000 sheets – have been printed on super-calendered paper. The results are quite satisfactory and I am satisfied that there is little, if any, lowering in the standard of perfection of printing.[41]

Again, stamps were re-registered on the different paper and Waterlows were compensated for their loss. The saving to the Post Office was estimated at £1,450 per annum.

Wilkinson machine

Methods of prepayment other than stamps were tried out shortly after George V came to the throne. An interesting trial of a slot machine was made in 1912 though it made no progress. Invented by one F. Wilkinson his machine was installed in London Chief Office on 25 January. By inserting 1d in a slot and putting the envelope through the posting aperture and then turning a handle twice a paid die was impressed on the envelope and the letter posted.

Above: envelope paid by Wilkinson slot machine on the first day

Right: trial paid impression (top)

Wilkinson machine in situ

This caused the Post Office a lot of time and labour – clearing the box, date-stamping the letters, accounting for the pennies – out of all proportion to any advantage or saving. The trial came to an end on 31 August the same year.

The paid die used included the place name London EC and a crown. A previous die proposed did not include the place name. Wilkinson was still producing propaganda for his "Stampless Post" in the 1920s.

Meter Franks

From 1922 meter frank machines had been allowed for private firms to prepay postage. There were three manufactures, Neopost, Pitney Bowes and Universal Postal Frankers. The design used was utilitarian and incorporated the wording Great Britain rather than the monarch's head. This caused a number of complaints and already in 1923 there were speci-

Left: suggested use of a King's head design in meter franks

Far left: first artwork for Royal Cypher design

Below: Royal Cypher die for meters

men dies prepared with a version of Mackennal's profile head, thus making the meter mark resemble a postage stamp. Mr E.H. Kinnard, then of Universal Postal Frankers tried out a die in September that year. Some three years later, now with Neopost, he showed these to General Williamson. The latter objected to the use of the King's head and thought there could be complications in international mail if a design were close to that of an adhesive stamp, but not printed in the correct colour.

After discussion with H.T. Howard a new proposal was made incorporating the Royal Cypher and crown. This now resembled the foliate version originally rejected for Post Office use, but also that used on contemporary watermarks. A modified specimen is dated January 1927 and it was introduced on meter dies that year.[42]

Waterlows lose the contract

Waterlows contract was due to run for 10 years. In 1933 they lost the overall contract to Harrisons and photogravure printing, as will be seen (in chapter 17). However, Harrisons were unable to produce rolls of stamps initially in continuous reels by the new method and so Waterlows were asked to continue with the only machine available for such letterpress printing. This was to last until 1935. But Harrisons could, and did, print sheets of stamps from the normal sheet and book letterpress plates used by Waterlows. These had been transferred from January 1934.

One result was that they produced 2½d and 3d sideways delivery rolls of 480 letterpress stamps joined every 12th stamp for use in Multipost stamp-affixing machines.

1   **Alexander, Dr J.** & **Newbery, L.F.** *British Stamp Booklets* 1987-97 p2

2   For details see **Alexander, Dr. J** & **Newbery, L.F.** op cit

3   As coined by Dr Jean Alexander

4   **Homer-Wooff, G.H.R.** & **Jones, P.J.** "British Coil Stamps" *GB Journal* [date] p29

5   POST 33/1949E Postage Stamps: supply in rolls for use in stamp vending machines, part I. International Stamping Machine Co. Ltd to Captain Cecil Norton MP, 3 July 1913

6   *Post Office Circular* 10 September 1912.

7   POST 33/3797A Postage Stamps: colour supplies. Memorandum by Walter G. Gates, 7 January 1916

8   ibid. Harrison & Sons Ltd to Controller, P.O. Stores, 6 April 1916

9   ibid. F.H. Nichols to Controller, P.O. Stores 4 September 1916

10   ibid. H. Sparkes to Secretary, 2 November 1917. Details in **Wilkinson, L.** *Wartime Printing Ink Problems* – www.les-wilkinson.co.uk/article5.shtml

11   IR 79/26 Rolls. Memorandum by H.J. Howard, 3 December 1919

12   IR 79/12 15 February 1921

13   ibid 5 March 1921

14   31 December 1919. Signed A.J. Musto. Information from Leslie Wilkinson.

15   IR 79/26 op cit. Inland Revenue to Royal Mint, 5 June 1913.

16   ibid. J. Patient to Director of Stamping, 3 May 1920.

17   ibid. Merkham Trading Co. Ltd to Stonestreet, 17 September 1919.

18   ibid. J Patient, 3 January 1920

19   ibid

20   IR 83/82 Contracts. W.M. Cook to Secretary, GPO, 3 March 1920

21   MINT 14/53 Stamp dies. Stonestreet to Hocking 11 May 1920

22   POST 52/344 plate 765/8 30 December 1920

23   POST 33/774B Colour of 9d stamps changed due to difficulty in detecting obliterating marks. F.H. Nichols to J.W. Bowen 20 July 1922.

24   POST 33/1738 Postage Stamps: contracts for manufacture, papers, 1922-1933. Memorandum to Postmaster General. 19 December 1922.

25   ibid

26   ibid

27   POST 33/1738 op cit. Memorandum 7 April 1923

28   POST 33/1599B Contracts for watermarked paper. 20 April 1923

29   POST 33/1738 op cit. G.P.O. to Treasury, 17 August 1923

30   POST 52/918 Unified Stamps: Plates and Dies for various issues

31   POST 52/148 20 September 1923

32   POST 52/147 15 November 1924

33   ibid 16 December 1929

34   POST 52/149 Waterlow and Sons: Contract for Unified Stamps

35   POST 52/150 W.M. Cook to Reardon 13 June 1932

36   POST 52/1336 W.M. Cook to Waterlows 22 October 1923

37   Details in: **Wilkinson, L.** *King George V Stamps issued in Rolls* 1998

38   POST 52/766 Dickinson's Experimental Royal Cipher Paper. Dickinsons to P.O. Stores, 10 May 1924.

39   POST 52/745 Esparto Paper: Experimental papers (Spicers and Dickinson) R. Fanshawe to Postmasters, 10 October 1924.

40   POST 52/869 Unified Stamps (1d and 1 d) printed on experimental paper: issue for sale to test public reaction. W.M. Cook to Wevell, 5 December 1924

41   POST 33/1738 op cit. P.O. Stores to Secretary, 10 April 1928

42   POST 33/5103 Franking (Postage meter) machines: dies, impressions, changing of design, Royal Monogram

11

THE ROYAL CYPHER

ON MAIL VANS, CARTS & STREET FURNITURE

The monarch's insignia was obviously of primary importance as soon as George V acceded to the throne. It was needed for so many applications. As far as the Post Office was concerned it was the Royal Mail and therefore the royal initials appeared on many public vehicles and street furniture, such as letter boxes. That used for Edward VII was ornate with interlaced lettering, described as "foliated".

As early as 23 May 1910, the Controller of Post Office Stores instructed the various manufacturers of letter boxes that they should make no more boxes with the Edwardian monogram. The design of the new monogram would be forwarded "in due course".[1] On 14 June, the Keeper of the Privy Purse, Sir William Carrington informed the Post Office that a new monogram for mail carts and letter boxes had been approved. This showed G v R in block letters. But there was a question as to whether this would be suitable for the curved surfaces of pillar boxes and so a series of rough drawings were prepared. Sir Matthew Nathan sent these to Sir Frederick Ponsonby asking if any were suitable. He preferred the most elaborate but thought that the V could be omitted from the others. It was Sir Arthur Bigge who replied. The King still approved his original choice but agreed to the removal of the V.

A few days later there was a complication. The War Office sent the designs which the King had approved for both Royal and Imperial Cyphers. These were quite different, resembling the interlaced lettering of the previous reign. Nathan thought it best to check. He made sure that the Crown was correct, the College of Heralds confirming that it was "quite all right", had the V removed as agreed and submitted the revised design together with the interlaced version from the War Office.

Bigge replied on 19 July:

> Thank you for your letter of the 18th instant, with enclosures, which I have again submitted to the King. On the whole His Majesty prefers to adhere to the design of the Royal Cypher "A", with the "V" omitted, for all the Post Office Vans, etc, instead of the War Office design "B".[2]

That should have been the end of the matter.

On 6 August 1910 Sir Matthew Nathan sent out instructions with regard to the use of the new monogram.

Above: approved block lettering for Royal Cypher with V scored through (top)

With War Office scroll Cypher.

Above: Royal Cypher on mail cart driven by a woman during World War I

Right: final approved artwork for block Royal Cypher

The new design should be adopted for all new vans, hand-carts, letter boxes, etc; for all existing vehicles when they are repainted; and in similar circumstances for all letter-boxes on which the Royal initials have hitherto been painted. Where the letters on existing boxes are in enamel or embossed or cast in metal they need not be changed.

It will not be necessary in all cases to use the Crown.[3]

However, the London Postal Section made the strange suggestion that the existing E in foliate lettering be replaced by a foliate G when vans were being repainted. They used a wide variety of vans (14 in all) sometimes with the Royal Arms (the lion and the unicorn) with or without initials and sometimes the Royal monogram with

crown. The reply was that the new, approved block lettering should be used when the vans were repainted.

Not everyone agreed. Thomas Fairgray in Cardiff pointed out that for other Government applications "His Majesty has approved of the royal cipher to be on the same lines as that of the late King, a more artistic design in my opinion, and much more suitable for letter boxes &c than the initials as shown…… In the absence of the Crown, the block letters G.R. convey little meaning."[4] He was told, very shortly, to use the monogram as approved. Even so, the same question was being raised as late as 1912.

Letter Box Contracts
There were some 11 different standard letter boxes - pillar boxes, wall boxes and a lamp box. The contracts for the different types were spread among three manufacturers.

Pillar Boxes (A and B sizes)	McDowall, Steven & Co. Ltd, Laurieston Iron Works, Falkirk
Pillar Boxes (C size – double)	Andrew Handyside & Co. Ltd., Britannia Iron Works, Derby
Wall Boxes	W.T. Allen & Co., Sherwood Foundry, Mansfield
Lamp Boxes	Andrew Handyside & Co. Ltd.

These contracts were not to change until the 1930s though the Carron Company near Falkirk manufactured B size pillar boxes from 1922. Each company now implemented the instructions about the new monogram though some detail had to be corrected to make them all conform. W.T. Allen, for example had to be told to make the pearls on the crown round rather than oval.

New Developments in Street Furniture

There were a number of new developments during George V's reign. The first came in 1924 when an experimental custom-made telephone kiosk was erected temporarily near St. Michael's Church in Bath, awaiting the opening of a new post office. This incorporated a posting box and a stamp-vending machine. Made of "armour-ply" (plywood faced with steel) it had been constructed by Maple and Co. Ltd of Tottenham Court Road, London.[5]

51. Telephone kiosk No. 4, 1929.

In April 1925 drawings were produced by the Engineer-in-Chief's Office of the new iconic telephone kiosk designed by Sir Giles Gilbert Scott. These incorporated a posting box and two vending machines for ½d and 1d stamps. Eventually 50 (No.4 type) in cast iron were supplied by the Carron Company and they were installed from 1929.

Another development also involved stamp-vending machines. By April 1930 an oval pillar box, similar to the double-aperture C type boxes already in use, was agreed incorporating vending machines. In November that year Andrew Handyside gained the contract, they already making that type. The new boxes came in two sizes. Type D had the same capacity as the large A type boxes and type E was equivalent to the smaller B type.

Above: No. 4 telephone kiosk with vending machines as installed in 1929, originally at Bristol city centre, now preserved at Cranmore Station, East Somerset Railway

Right: Combination letter box and vending machine

Seventy-five of the large D type boxes were ordered, fifty for use in London and twenty-five for use in the provinces. Fifty of the smaller E type boxes were ordered, all for provincial use. Erection began in January 1932*. In 1933, however, because of the difficulty in clearing the boxes, it was decided that no more should be ordered.[6]

No more telephone kiosks (No.4) were ordered either as the siting requirements of telephones and stamp-vending machines did not coincide. As a result, from 1933 such machines were either fixed to the side of an existing pillar box or placed on a free-standing pedestal nearby.

* more correctly by December 1931

1   POST 78/136 Change of Monogram on Letter Boxes from ER to GR
2   POST 30/1907A Royal Monogram: designs for mail vans, letter boxes, kiosks etc part 1. Sir Arthur Bigge to Sir Matthew Nathan, 19 July 1910.
3   ibid. Sir Matthew Nathan to Mellersh
4   ibid. Thomas Fairgray to Secretary, GPO, 29 August 1910
5   **Farrugia, J.Y.** *The Letter Box: A History of Post Office Pillar and Wall Boxes* 1969 p173
6   ibid. p174

12

MAILS IN CONFLICT

THE ARMY AND THE R.A.F., IN WAR AND PEACE

In time of war, one of the most important aspects of maintaining troops' morale is an efficient mail service. Letters from family and loved ones at home are eagerly awaited, as is news from the front to those at home. To provide this was the job of the Army Postal Service. Although its history goes back to 1799 when a postal official was despatched to supervise the postal arrangements for the British troops then in Holland, it was not until the Egyptian campaign of 1882 that an Army Post Office was first properly established.

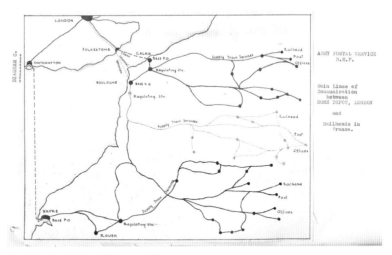

With the reorganisation of the Army after the South African War, a military unit (technically known as the Royal Engineers, Postal Section, Special Reserve) was recruited entirely from postal staff. They were to apply their expert knowledge of postal organisation to conditions in the field.

The Army Postal Service was included, in overall military Field Service Regulations, with those departments of an army "without which the fighting troops cannot be maintained in a state of efficiency".[1]

World War I – Army Postal Service Organisation
A trained force of some 300 men was at once available at the outbreak of World War I and was despatched with the British Expeditionary Force. The great expansion of the Army, however, called for continuous increases in personnel, and by the end of the war the strength overseas of the Army Postal Service numbered nearly 4,000. Each new expedition took out its postal complement and the Dardanelles, Egypt and Palestine, Salonika, East Africa, Italy and North Russia all had a complete postal service.[2]

At the outset, as laid down in pre-war planning, all mails were sent to the Overseas Base Post Office, and there sorted for the various units in the field. Letters and parcels were then taken to the Advanced Base Office near the front by rail and at Railheads were transferred to supply trucks which conveyed them to the troops concerned. Mails generally followed supplies. Field Post Offices (with train) were established with the larger units.

Planning on paper in peace time was neat and clear; reality in war forced changes. Initially, the Base Post Office was established at Le Havre, later moving as far away as Nantes (after the retreat from Mons) and then back to Le Havre. This meant that for mails from Britain

Above: sketch map showing how mails travelled from the Home Depot to the troops at the front (top)

Notice encouraging volunteers to the Post Office Rifles

Above: Home Depot in Regents Park (top)

Troops loading mail on to a train

to reach the army in the field they had to be conveyed by a roundabout route via Le Havre (or Nantes), across northern France to troops which were only 100 miles from London.

When H.M. the King visited the Army in December he expressed his satisfaction with the work. At that time the mails were about 4 days in transit from England to the Front via Havre and 2 days from the Front to England via Boulogne. 2000 bags of mails were being received each day from home; and the staff of the Army Postal Service had increased from 300 to 900.[3]

With the route via Folkestone and Boulogne open it was obvious to send mail that way but there was no suitable accommodation in Boulogne for sorting. So, after Christmas 1914, this work was gradually transferred to the Home Depot in London.[4] By 8 February 1915 all letter sorting for all units in the field had been transferred, with parcels following later.[5]

This speeded up the delivery of mail considerably. After March 1915, with a lorry service between Boulogne, G.H.Q., and the Headquarters of Armies, with branch services to Corps Headquarters

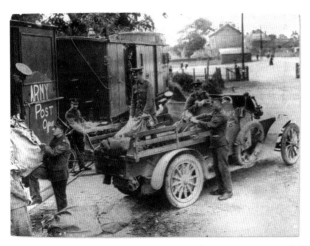

letters which leave London by train at 7.0 a.m. are delivered at each Army, Corps, Divisional and Brigade Headquarters in the Field before 7 p.m. the same day and in some cases earlier; and Headquarters officers and others are now apt to complain if, by any chance, they do not receive their morning papers by post from London on the day of publication.[6]

Mail from troops to home went the same way in reverse and there was also an inter-connected service for army to army mails. Most of the time army units were static but there were also periods of violent movement and disruption which had an obvious effect on the mails. The Home Depot was situated in Regents Park in London and expanded during the war. Built of wood, it came to be what was described as the largest wooden building in the world.

Stationary Field Post Offices were often very short staffed. This became acute in 1917.

There were instances when a total staff of 1 N.C.O. and 2 men were all that could be spared to work an Office serving 50,000 troops, who posted approximately 30,000 letters and received 400 bags of mail daily in addition to transacting a large amount of postal order and registered letter business.[7]

Above: Mail arriving at the railhead, being sorted and delivered, and a soldier in a dug-out (sea view) writing home

Below: First Field Service card with Downey Head stamp

This was obviously totally inadequate and resulted in everyone working long, hard hours.

Forces Mail

For a short time after the outbreak of war soldiers had to pay for their correspondence. However, on 7 September 1914 it was announced that all letters written by soldiers on active service could be sent free to the United Kingdom. Interestingly, this privilege was subsequently extended to mail sent to certain other countries as well (France and Belgium, fairly obviously, but also Portugal, Japan, Italy, Russia, United States, Denmark,

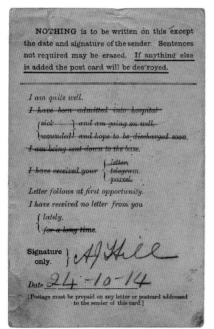

NOTHING is to be written on this except the date and signature of the sender. Sentences not required may be erased. If anything else is added the post card will be des'royed.

I am quite well.

I have been admitted into hospital

(sick) and am going on well

(wounded) and hope to be discharged soon.

I am being sent down to the base.

I have received your (letter
                      (telegram.
                      (parcel.

Letter follows at first opportunity.

I have received no letter from you

(lately.
(for a long time.

Signature
only. } A Hill

Date 24-10-14

[Postage must be prepaid on any letter or postcard addressed to the sender of this card.]

Above: Reverse of Field Service card with printed messages

Spain, Switzerland and Uruguay).[8] In 1915 this was revised several times, only allowing items under 4 oz. free, with varying rates for packets and parcels above that weight. On the other hand, all mail to those soldiers from families and friends in the U.K. and overseas had to be prepaid.

The first Field Service Cards for use by soldiers came with an imprinted 1d Downey Head postcard die in red. On the reverse were printed simple messages which could be scored through as appropriate.

The idea had first been suggested as far back as December 1912 but essays were not prepared until May 1914.

> In order to facilitate communication between soldiers on active service and their relatives at home, and reduce as far as possible the volume of work thrown upon the Censors with the Expeditionary Force, it has been decided to introduce for the private postal correspondence of that Force the specially printed postcard of which a specimen is enclosed.[9]

To encourage soldiers to use them the cost of postage was eventually to be borne by the Post Office. On the outbreak of war the cards went into production and were available at the War Office on 15 August 1914. The first issue, with the wording in black, was issued on 21 August, to be followed by a different printing on 28 September. On 15 October a new type was issued with the wording and stamp both printed in red. Later printings reverted to black, but without the now unnecessary imprinted stamp. Every week each soldier was issued with two cards.

Field Service Postcards were given precedence over ordinary letters, especially during periods of heavy fighting. Whenever possible, special arrangements were made for their collection and despatch

> During the attack on Messines Ridge at the beginning of June 1917 special arrangements were made to enable wounded men to communicate with their relatives. A man of the Royal Engineers Postal Section was stationed at each Corps Casualty Collecting Station with a stock of Field Service Postcards to be used by the lightly wounded as they arrived. Special steps were taken to send them by a late night service to the Army Depot in time to connect with the lorry service to the Base and to England by the morning boat. In this manner the Postcards reached England 12 hours after they were posted at the Casualty Collecting Station.[10]

In February 1916 some 129,000 such cards were being posted daily. In the autumn of 1917, at the close of active operations, the figure was 287,743 and it was stated that "this figure would have been much higher if the return could have been taken during the period of active warfare."[11]

At the end of March 1915 special green envelopes were issued to the troops on the basis of one per soldier per week to enable them to transmit domestic and private letters without them being subjected to local regimental censorship. Each envelope had to bear a certificate from the writer that the contents related only to private and family matters, and it was subject to examination at the Base. They were very popular. In the same week in February 1916 quoted above for Field Service Cards some 1,222,000 green envelopes were posted. By November 1917, the weekly number was 1,379,000. Some were even forged, examples having been found in August 1915 and September 1917.

> In July 1916 the "Green" Envelope changed its colour owing to the difficulty of obtaining supplies of green paper. It was then changed to a white envelope with green bands.[12]

A similar system of privilege envelopes was introduced for the navy in January 1918. Again, the issue was of one per man per week, but only to those on ships in home waters.[13]

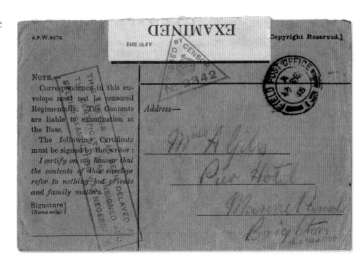

Above: Green envelope censored because the sender had not signed as required.

Censorship

One of the questions considered by the Committee of Imperial Defence in the decade before World War I was, for military reasons, the establishment of postal censorship in the United Kingdom and the Empire. In November 1913 they recognised that to achieve complete success it would have to include all outward and inward correspondence from and to the country. This appeared impracticable. Perhaps strangely, they did not recommend that postal correspondence with an enemy country should be prohibited. (Nevertheless, the Post Office immediately suspended mail services to Germany and Austria-Hungary in August 1914.) But on the outbreak of war there should be "The establishment of a partial or complete censorship of all postal matter destined for specified countries; the Post Office to be responsible for carrying out the censorship, and the Admiralty and War Office, in consultation with the Foreign Office, to be responsible for notifying the Post Office as to what the countries should be."[14] Censorship came under Military Intelligence (M.O.5).

In the event, the situation was chaotic, with only one officer in post to organise matters.

> The General Staff Officer, who should have been responsible for the study of this question in peace, had been given charge of the relatively simple duty of Field Censorship and had vanished with the British Expeditionary Force; the retired officer charged with the far more onerous duties of advising the General Staff on questions of Postal Censorship in general found himself on mobilization literally without staff or buildings, and with a vast quantity of detained mails already accumulated and accumulating in the bowels of the General Post Office.[15]

Gradually things became organised, and staff numbers grew. On 8 August letters to and from enemy countries began to be examined at the Returned Letter Branch at Mount Pleasant. Later this was expanded to other, neutral countries and work took place at Salisbury House in the City of London. This transferred to Imperial House in Kingsway and eventually Strand House, Carey Street, WC2 in April 1916. From 1 December 1915 a branch was established at Dock Offices in Liverpool for transatlantic mail.

The gradual increase of examining and clerical staff, (not including porters, Post Office personnel etc) was detailed in the report[16]:-

Date	Men	Women	Total
3rd August, 1914	1		1
31st December, 1914	110	60	170
30th June, 1915	546	232	778
31st December, 1915	846	607	1,453
30th June, 1916	853	1,706	2,559
31st December, 1916	1,140	2,673	3,813
30th June, 1917	1,070	2,753	3,823
31st December, 1917	1,121	3,079	4,200
4th November, 1918	1,343	3,518	4,861

The number of women employed increased dramatically with the opening of the Liverpool branch. By November 1918 170 men and 1,247 women worked in censorship at Liverpool, the remainder in London.

The main objectives of censorship were to prevent communication with the enemy, the spreading of false reports and to gather information about military or espionage operations and about enemy trade. The basic premise was that "no letter (except official correspondence) should ever be passed without examination to any country having free communication with enemy territory."[17]

At the outset, mails were divided into different categories in a military context[18]:

(a.) *Dangerous* letters, consisting of those containing –
    (1.) Definite political, naval or military information
    (2.) Correspondence to and from addresses on the Black List (this was the counter-espionage Black List, not the later Trade Black List).
    (3.) Offers of service to the enemy.
    (4.) Cyphers and code.

(b.) *Suspicious* letters, viz.-
    (1.) Correspondence indicating unusual relations between persons resident in the United Kingdom and someone abroad.
    (2.) Correspondence indicating payment of money on behalf of residents in the United Kingdom without indication of a business consideration.
    (3.) Letters expressing the intention of Germans to join the British Red Cross organization.
    (c.) *Indiscreet* letters, viz., out-going letters containing pessimistic views.
    (d.) Letters indicating that the writer or some other person was liable to military service in the enemy forces.
    (e.) *Innocuous* letters, and
    (f.) Letters in uncommon languages.

Shortly afterwards a more commercial approach was also introduced. In order to divide the mail up into these categories examiners were to open the cover, one by one, at the short side. After examination the cover was re-sealed with a gummed label bearing the examiner's personal number (in case of subsequent complaint). No portion of the name and address was to be covered, nor the postage stamps, though this often was the case in practice. Slips were prepared for those letters of interest and they were passed to the relevant authorities. Some mail was destroyed immediately; others had passages erased; most continued on their way, if delayed. Examiners each read on average 86 commercial or 110 private letters a day. Their labels were initially printed on pink paper but this soon changed to white.

At the height of censorship activity the average number of letters censored each day was 375,517, weighing about 4 tons. Of these 116,700 were commercial and 258,817 private letters. In addition 117,300 newspaper packets and 2,407 parcels were daily examined, making the average total weight of mail matter, dealt with each day, over 25 tons.[19]

Letters on which the express fee of 2s 6d had been paid were brought by special messenger and after a "careful but speedy examination" they were returned immediately.[20]

These are the statistics for one month in 1918 for letters to and from abroad.[21]

Country	Outgoing - Weight in lbs.	Percentage opened and examined.	Incoming – Weight in lbs.	Percentage opened and examined.
Denmark	1,543	100	834	100
Greece	410	100	192	100
Holland	3,114	100	2,348	100
Norway	1,875	100	1,207	100
Portugal	1,652	100	904	100
Spain	2,247	100	1,411	100
Sweden	1,137	100	982	100
Switzerland	2,682	100	2,213	100
Siam (trade mail only)	108¼	100		
Russia	370	100	85	100
Persia	109	100	15	100
Roumania	7¼	100		
United States of America	30,732	95	37,514	64
Central and South America (excluding British and Allied possessions)	5,799	58	7,764	85
Canada (mails from or to Ireland only)	929	100	835	100

Not everyone saw any point in censorship. The post-war history of the subject quoted with incredulity the Foreign Secretary, Sir Edward Grey's pointed remark of April 1916 "I have always doubted whether interference with *letters* was worth while"[22] A lot of the detail of the voluminous report tended to back this up.

There were essentially three different censorships. One was of mail from Britain going abroad, and vice versa (and also international mail in transit). Another was undertaken by military authorities of mail from the forces. But there also arose a third type – internal censorship – which took place from time to time. The first occasions were perhaps understandable – from April 1915 of mail from the Orkneys and Shetland with their concentration of naval ships.

The justification for inland censorship was given as two-fold.[23]

(1) They may contain communications between two enemy agents in the United Kingdom, one in a district where the information can be obtained, the other in a place more convenient for the despatch of the information to a neutral or enemy country.

(2) Some of them are sure to contain undesirable information, sent by respectable people, without malice, to friends in another part of the country. It is desirable to check such indiscretions, whether on the part of members of His Majesty's Forces or of private individuals, in order that they may not be repeated in communications through any channel to persons in neutral or enemy countries.

A great many short-lived censorships were set up, some in the strangest places. One or two were made permanent, such as Kirkwall in the Orkneys from 1916 and Falmouth from 1917.[24] Some censorship was also covert.

Reviewing the detailed results of inland censorship the conclusion was evident that nothing of great value had been achieved. The author of the report admitted:

There is always a tendency for the intelligence officers of Commands, and especially naval officers, to accept rumours as to the presence of spies in the area for which they are responsible, and to overrate the uses of an inland mails censorship for purposes of protection.[25]

Censorships actually conducted did not discover anything more serious than indiscretion. Their value lay perhaps in fear of detection which acted as a deterrent though some officers in intelligence were zealous, if not paranoid and censors were certainly self-important. In order to conceal the nature and locality of factories which were employed in military work, especially the preparation of munitions of war, business firms were in 1916 prohibited from using paper which indicated that they were controlled by the Government and especially paper which gave illustrations of the factories themselves.[26]

Ireland & the Easter Rising

One aspect where thoughts were not paranoid was that of Irish mail. Fear of revolution or rebellion within the United Kingdom caused preparations to be made. As early as February 1916 a confidential memorandum was sent to Arthur H. Norway, Secretary, GPO in Dublin.

It has been decided that, in the event of active operations in this country private correspondence for all troops in the British Isles whether engaged in the operations or not, will be restricted to postcards and letter packets. This restriction will, however, not apply to official packets. The parcel post will be suspended and no newspapers will be accepted. Should the emergency arise the necessary instructions will be issued by wire from the Central Telegraph Office to all Head Postmasters.[27]

The rebellion began on Easter Monday, 24 April. Norway managed to write a report three days later, getting it out the following day. That Monday he had been called from his office in the General Post Office in Dublin to go to Dublin Castle at about 11 a.m. to talk to the Under Secretary, Sir Matthew Nathan. Both Castle and G.P.O. were attacked a quarter of an hour later.

> So far as I can ascertain, the Post Office was rushed about a quarter of an hour after I left my room. The Instrument room was guarded by soldiers, as since the first days of the war, but the soldiers had, at some subsequent time, without my knowledge, been deprived of cartridges, & were accordingly powerless. They appear to have made some fight & the sergeant was wounded, but I believe not dangerously. The original instructions, given in my presence in the early days of August 1914, were that each man of the guard should have his magazine changed, & cut off closed, & should fire to stop any unauthorized person. I had no reason to suspect any alteration of these instructions.

> At the moment of writing (noon [on Thursday]) the Post Office is still in hands of rebels, & I am without information as to how long it may be so.[28]

Postal services were at a standstill. Although pressed by the Lord Lieutenant, Lord Wimborne, to resume them Norway was adamant that this was impossible.

Above: Telegram informing London of the taking of the GPO in Dublin

> On ringing up the Mail Cart contractors, I received an assurance that they would let no mail cart leave the yard. Apart from that, the streets are in such a condition that all use of them in almost any direction is dangerous. I have myself narrowly escaped being shot – twice yesterday – and I cannot accept the responsibility of ordering Postmen to attempt either collections or deliveries at present.[29]

The telephone service was intact (though only in use for Government and military messages) and Norway was in free communication with the Postmasters of Cork and Belfast. Limerick and Galway were cut off, however. By Sunday he was able to write:

> I have not been able yet to commence a full report, nor would it be of much use to do so until I have seen the ruins of the Post Office, & been able to form some sort of plan for the resumption of services. The surrender of the rebel leaders yesterday may make that possible this morning… Shooting is much less this morning, though a machine gun has been very busy close at hand, & a soldier in this street has just fired, I suppose at one of the snipers who are still on the roofs of many houses. He has just fired again. Big guns are silent today….. Notwithstanding the surrender last night, some parties of rebels still hold out. The machine gun close at hand fires almost continuously. But the worst is over.[30]

He had managed to get a small mail off to England the previous night. When the fighting was over, the extent of the destruction became apparent and it was clear that the G.P.O. building "so recently gleaming from its renovation, would be useless from any operational aspect. With commendable speed, however, a temporary Sorting Office was established within the Rotunda buildings in Parnell Street and sorting and delivery work had begun

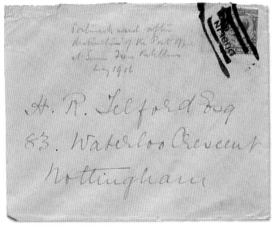

Above: The devastated G.P.O. in Dublin

Mail with a dummy cancellation used in the immediate aftermath.

again by the morning of the 3rd May."[31] Hand cancellers and stamping machines were all destroyed so "dumb" and temporary cancellations had to be used on mail for a period.

From 25 April until 1 May all mail was censored at Liverpool and London to try to identify other rebels. Those prisoners not executed were taken to a camp at Frongoch and to Reading for internment. "The public were warned to address letters to them, c/o the Chief Postal Censor in London…. Outward letters were sent by the commandants in batches to the London censorship for examination and release."[32]

There were considerable difficulties in this censorship.

> Much of the correspondence was in Erse or forms of native dialect and it was found exceedingly difficult to discriminate as to what was and what was not veiled reference to political matters. It is to be feared that the censorship was unduly suspicious and that the Irish prisoners, in accordance with what appeared to be a childish and mischievous temper of mind, endeavoured to set traps for the Censor and so to create a grievance.[33]

A lot of the correspondence was referred to M.I. 5 or the Home Office and there were frequent complaints of delays. In December, 1916, male prisoners were all transferred to Lewes prison and the regulations were considerably relaxed. On 20 March, 1917, it was agreed that this correspondence be controlled by the Governor of Lewes prison. Later, in 1918 more disaffected Irishmen were imprisoned in England but smuggled letters meant that censorship was not a complete system of control.

Correspondence with enemy countries

The Post Office issued a notice in August 1914 stating that communications with United States embassies and consulates in enemy countries were possible through the U.S. Embassy in London. When the Ambassador complained, this method of contacting friends in enemy or enemy-occupied lands ceased. However, other indirect methods were allowed. Correspondence via a neutral country was arranged principally through Thomas Cook & Sons. For occupied Belgium arrangements were made with the Bureau de Correspondence Belge and Mme. Carton de Wiart's bureau.

Mail had to be sent under cover to Thomas Cook at Ludgate Circus in London. The inner envelope had to be left open and unstamped. A postal order for 1s covered the cost of postage to the neutral country and then to the enemy country. Only matters of personal interest could be written. "Cook's packets" were then censored as normal. Incoming mail could be similarly sent but surviving examples are rare.

German Submarine mail

On the other side of the conflict the Germans tried to evade Allied censorship by means of submarines. A certain amount of correspondence was carried to and from the United States by the commercial submarine *Deutschland* for a short time in the summer and autumn of 1916, and that during the years 1917 and 1918 quite a lot of letters between enemy countries and Spain were carried by submarine. A letter was intercepted from the Berlin Post Office sent to the German Post Office in Shanghai stating that the most important posts both ways were to be carried by U-boats.

> On the 29th December, 1916, the Berlin wireless announced that the German Postal Administration would despatch letters by submarine mail to the United States, Mexico, Central and South America, the West Indies, China, the Dutch Indies, the Philippines, &c. All envelopes were to be sent to Bremen and endorsed "Submarine Letter", the maximum weight to be 60 grammes, the additional postage to be 2 marks for each 20 grammes.[34]

Most of South America, except Brazil, thus continued to have some correspondence with the Central Powers until the end of the war.

Prisoner of War Mail

During the first few months of the war correspondence of all prisoners of war, British and enemy, was examined in London by the "Hostile Countries" branch of censorship or at the P.O.W. camps. This was soon concentrated on the normal censorship offices which were provided with a good laboratory to detect secret writing.

For enemy prisoners there were stringent regulations. Only a highly glazed special pattern paper was allowed to guard against the use of secret inks, and no envelope could be used.

> On account of the ease with which secret messages can be sent on photographs and drawings, prisoners were forbidden to despatch these articles, certain specified exemptions being made in regard to photographs specially taken and controlled.[35]

Out-going letters from prisoners of war were censored with the following principal objects in view:-
(a.) To stop the leakage of news to enemy countries;
(b.) To detect complaints of ill-treatment, so that the commandants of camps and officers commanding companies might remedy what was wrong;
(c.) To prevent false accounts of the prisoners' treatment before and after capture from reaching the enemy; and
(d.) To discover breaches of discipline, organized attempts at escape or sabotage.[36]

One result of this censorship came immediately after the end of the war. "The intention of the crews of the German ships interned at Scapa Flow to sink the interned ships was surmised from very clear hints in correspondence and reported more than once to the Admiralty."[37] This discovery clearly did not have much effect.

Women at Work

Women were first employed in the Army Postal Service in May 1917. However, they had been employed in the Post Office for a long time before that and during the War had already been replacing men on the home front.

In late 1915, the Postmaster General announced:

> What I feel is, generally, that in the present state of national affairs all the work of the nation that can be properly done by women ought to be done by women, in order that the men may be set free for the Army and Navy and for work which can only be accomplished by men.....A great deal of the Post Office work – I am far from suggesting all of it – can be efficiently done by women, and therefore it seems to me the policy of extending women's work wherever possible, without undue hardship on the men, ought to be pursued.[38]

Above: Women mail cart drivers during World War I

This rather patronising attitude was typical of male statements of the time. Women were employed on mail delivery duties in urban areas for the first time, driving horse-drawn carts, whip in hand. In late 1915, women working in the Returned Letter Office were gradually allowed to open returned postal packets. There had been a rule in place since 1873 which stated that women were not permitted to do this in case they came across anything indecent in the packets. Women were also employed on mail sorting duties, and, overall, tens of thousands took the place of men.

Their work proved to be successful beyond all expectations; they combined genuine enthusiasm with remarkable aptitude for postal work.[39]

This did not mean that they received the same rates of pay, however. Some duties were regarded as unsuitable – bag carrying, irregular night working. In the Army Postal Service they worked shorter hours and the "normal proportion" of four women to three men had to be altered to seven women to four men. By the end of the war some 139 women were employed there.

The Watch on the Rhine

The Armistice signed on 11 November 1918 ending the "Great War" laid down strict conditions about the evacuation by the German army of invaded territories on the Western Front. In an annex it was stated that "the evacuation of the invaded territories, Belgium, France, and Luxemburg, and also of Alsace-Lorraine, shall be carried out in three successive stages." The first stage was to be completed within five days, the second a further four days and the third a further six, 15 days in all after the signing of the Armistice. Allied troops would enter these territories after the expiry of the periods specified, so the German army was allowed to retreat without hindrance.

It was not until 17 November, therefore, that Allied forces moved forward to occupy that part of Germany on the left bank of the Rhine. Garrisons were to hold the principal crossings of the Rhine at Mainz, Coblenz and Cologne, together with bridgeheads at these points of a 30-kilometre radius on the right bank. Evacuation of these areas, and a neutral zone, was to be completed by the German military within 31 days of the signing of the

Armistice. On 13 December the Allies crossed the Rhine. The British area of control was centred on Cologne; Belgians were to the north and west, Americans and French to the south.

The British Second Army which moved to occupy the area, with 18 RAF squadrons in support, comprised nearly 275,000 officers and men. These troops needed mail.

As the troops advanced eastwards the existing express mail lorry services from Boulogne to Roubaix were extended. The total journey from Boulogne to Cologne, about 300 miles, was performed in seven lorry stages.[40]

In December 1918 a through mail train was established from Boulogne to Cologne but this was slow and irregular. It was decided to establish two airmail services by the R.A.F. on an experimental basis, one for express mails for the headquarters of the First, Second and Fourth Armies from Marquise near Boulogne to Valenciennes and Namur.

This service, to be known as Service A, was to be provided for 10 Handley Page aeroplanes, 5 machines doing a round trip on alternate days from Marquise to Valenciennes to Namur and back. Each machine was to carry 10 cwt. of mails (i.e. a total of 50 cwt. each day) and all mails were to be dropped by parachute until such time as suitable landing grounds were available for Handley Page machines. Machines were to start at dawn and would reach Namur about 2½ hours later, travelling between 60-70 miles an hour.[41]

The second service (Service B) was to be used to carry inter-army official and ordinary mails. This was undertaken by smaller De Haviland aeroplanes between St. Andre, near G.H.Q. in France, and Namur with a stop at Valenciennes. Nine aeroplanes, each carrying 2 cwt. of mails, were to leave both St. Andre and Namur each day at dawn. It was subsequently decided to extend this service eastwards, first to Spa and later to Cologne.

From the outset it was understood that the services were experimental. Regular postal services by aeroplane were not possible, flight being affected by weather conditions (wind, rain, snow and fog) to such an extent "as to make regularity out of the question."[42]

Their work proved to be successful beyond all expectations; they combined genuine enthusiasm with remarkable aptitude for postal work

Below: Route map of the aerial services to Cologne.

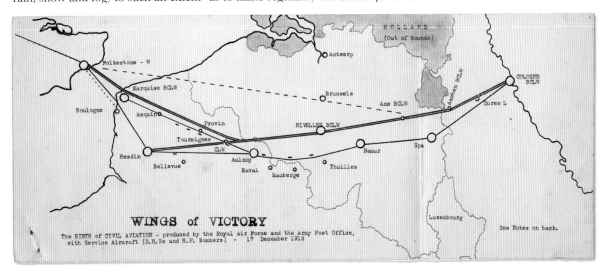

The inaugural flight was fixed for 16 December but bad weather prevented take off. The following day the weather improved and five D.H. 45s took off from St Andre.

> Left about 12.50 and flew in formation via Arras and Douai to Valenciennes. As the flight descended over Valenciennes and was approaching the ground the Handley Page from Marquise flew across and dropped mails by parachute which were seen to land in the middle of the aerodrome. At the same time the machines from Namur arrived and all mails landed at the aerodrome about the same time. Two machines from Hesdin had bad landings – one crashed and another broke its landing wire on some goal posts.[43]

Bad weather prevented most flights over the next two months. In January 1919 the Handley Page bombers were only able to take off from Marquise on eight occasions, two of which resulted in forced landings en route. Structural alterations were required before they could be used for mails. The bombers had to be "fitted with large Post Office parcel baskets (an obsolete pattern dug out of store) which exactly fitted the bomb apertures and were released by the bomb dropping apparatus with parachutes attached."[44] The De Havilland Service B achieved a higher rate of success.

As a result the service between Boulogne and Cologne was handed over to two D.H. 9A squadrons, based at Maisoncelle near Hesdin and at Cologne and these flew through the night. At the same time a new service (C) began on 1 March where the planes left from near Folkestone. Hawkinge aerodrome was free from the London fog and near to the railway and the service was so timed that morning newspapers published in London arrived in Cologne the same day. Mails left Victoria by the 05.45 train arriving at Folkestone at 07.45. They were then collected by motor lorry and delivered at the aerodrome by 8.30. The first service arrived in Cologne before 15.30.

Highly detailed records were kept of all flights and frequent aerial mail service circulars were issued. Special bag labels were printed to show the town of destination and the coded location.

Above: Lorry with mails from Folkestone to aerodrome (top)

D.H.10 conveying first night mail from Hawkinge 14 May 1919 (middle)

Loading the mails at Hawkinge (bottom)

Two pigeons had to be carried with each flight to release with a message in case of forced landing but it took some time for these to be properly trained. Experiments took place in January in East Anglia dropping pigeons from different heights. Two pigeons were packed in a basket with a parachute and dropped successfully on a target at 500 and 700 ft. One attempt without parachute resulted in one dead bird.[45]

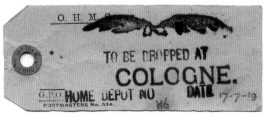

Towards the end, the intermediate stop at Maisoncelle between Folkestone and Cologne was eliminated. The aerodrome at Folkestone was changed to Lympne and that at Cologne from Bickendorf to Marheim. Although the last service by the R.A.F. was on 31 August 1919 it was then continued by Sir Samuel Instone and his Instone Air line as a civilian service. A resumé of the eastward service from Folkestone to Cologne from 1 March to 31 August showed that flights took place on about 80% of days scheduled. The number of individual flights was 922, carrying some 6,157 mail bags with an estimated weight of 61 tons.[46]

Above: bag labels for the Cologne flights

Below: First despatch by night mail

Bottom: Archangel F.P.O. staff April 1919

The experiment had taken place to prove the value of airmail. It was also to keep the R.A.F. intact after World War I in the face of desperate cost cutting. Regulations were very military in nature, as might be expected, with initials proliferating. Local place-names were frequently mis-spelt and everything was recorded in minute detail. No sooner had it ended than its value in an emergency was to be proven.

British Troops in Russia, 1918-19

British troops were already established in supply bases at Archangel and Murmansk in northern Russia before the Armistice was signed on 11 November 1918. Army Postal Service staff arrived at the end of September and with the civil war in Russia between Bolsheviks and White Russians fighting was still taking place. British troops continued to arrive during 1919. These troops obviously had to be serviced with mail and Army and Field post offices were set up with the codes P.B. Sleighs and mail vans were

Above: Archangel post sleigh for Royal Mail

Item sent from P.B. 2

commandeered or built and had the Royal Cypher applied. It was not until 12 October 1919 that the evacuation of these troops was complete.[47]

1919 Railway Strike

Despite building industrial unrest, after continental revolutions and the signing of the Armistice, the national railway strike of September 1919 came as a sudden shock. Already that year, Lloyd George had been confronted with strikes by miners, gas and electricity workers, shipyard workers and dockers which had "triggered off strikes, riots and demonstrations elsewhere and the Clydeside, in particular was the scene of much turbulent activity."[48] Railwaymen had been incensed by a proposal that their wages should be reduced and stopped work on 26 September.

The extent to which the Post Office depended on the railways to transport mails was well illustrated by this strike. There was an almost complete cessation of mails between towns though local collections and deliveries were maintained. The parcel post was suspended, except for local delivery. Some train services did run, however. The South Eastern and Chatham Railway Company established a daily service from Victoria at 8.45 a.m. to Folkestone for Boulogne; and mails for the continent were despatched by it. In addition, mails were despatched from Hounslow by aeroplane to Paris on the Monday (500 lb in 12 bags) and Brussels (1500 lb in 45 bags). In the end, the total carried by Handley Page Transport Ltd to Brussels was 5,450 lb for which they required payment at 3/6d per lb. Aircraft Transport & Travel Ltd accepted 4/- per lb for the 500 lb to Paris. The total cost to the Post Office was £977:14:6 and £100 respectively.[49]

Initially, the authorities had been worried about official government mails to Ireland. A special R.A.F. flight was organised from Kenley aerodrome to take despatches to Bangor, thence by road to Holyhead and by steamer to Dublin.

On 29 September an experimental internal airmail service for public mails was announced between London and Bristol, Birmingham, Newcastle, Manchester and Glasgow. Aeroplanes had been chartered by the Air Ministry. Letters were to be charged an extra fee of 2s per ounce. There was also an R.A.F. service for Government despatches but because of small numbers of private letters these services were subsequently combined. The total paid to civil aviation firms for the hire of the planes was £3497 5s.[50]

Items of mail carried with the extra 2s fee.[51]

For	1 Oct	2 Oct	3 Oct	4 Oct	5 Oct
Glasgow	113	138	113	37	9
Manchester	89	67	49	12	4
Newcastle on Tyne	49	61	49	20	6
Birmingham	45	38	28	11	2
Bristol	19	16	22	5	3

From	1 Oct	2 Oct	3 Oct	4 Oct	5 Oct	6 Oct
Birmingham	25	125	15	35	1	8
Newcastle-on-Tyne		115	161	157	74	
Manchester		91	97	59	11	10
Glasgow		204	217	248	161	45
Bristol	34	59	25	22	4	

This emergency service was discontinued on 6 October with the ending of the strike.

As a harbinger of things to come in the General Strike of 1926 Sir Evelyn Murray, the Post Office Secretary, made a number of suggestions once the strike was over.

Transport and housing of staff. A complete stoppage by the railwaymen and transport workers combined would necessitate the putting into operation of immediate measures for the conveyance of the Post Office telegraph and telephone staff (especially women) to their work if these services were not to collapse. Last week arrangements were worked out for the provision of lorries etc. but this took several days to complete. It is suggested that steps might be taken to earmark transport which would be independent of the Transport Federation and available at short notice. Arrangements might be planned for housing a considerable portion of the essential staff and information obtained as to where mattresses and blankets could be secured.[52]

Above: item carried by aeroplane during the Railway Strike with 2s fee

Striking transport workers would probably bring out "a considerable proportion" of mail van drivers. The possibility of supplying volunteer drivers might be investigated.

Aeroplane mails. In the event of an aeroplane service for Government despatches being started, it should be made available for limited numbers of express letters prepaid with a special fee. Probably the Government despatch service would suffice for mail purposes until a modified train service was resumed. But to provide against a prolonged and complete stoppage of railway communication, it is understood that a scheme for supplementing the Government service by civil machines is being worked out.[53]

There was one exciting event reported in the *Workington News*. On 5 October an airship had delivered mail to Whitehaven.

On Sunday afternoon a small crowd of Whitehaven people had rather a treat. The footpath across the Meadows, through the railway arch and up to The Thicket is a popular Sunday afternoon walk; and those who took that walk on Sunday afternoon partook of the treat. Otherwise it was known to but a few that an airship was to arrive from Barrow at 3.20 and deliver mails "to the south of Whitehaven."[54]

The local postmaster at Barrow in Furness had taken advantage of an offer from the commanding officer at the Walney Island airship station. Some 800 items were forwarded to Whitehaven saving a 24-hour delay.

Mr Davis, the Postmaster and several members of his staff were there and received the mail bags; and then in a very few moments the propellers were set going again and the ship rose quite gracefully and made off back to Barrow.[55]

Letters for Barrow were also carried on the return flight. Weather conditions were described as ideal. Had the strike not come to an end it was proposed that mails for the Isle of Man be conveyed by this means.

Ireland 1920 - 22

"SECRET" – thus the superscription on a long series of memos and reports describing the setting up of official airmail communication within Ireland during the troubled period there from July 1920 through to 1922. Road convoys were often attacked, so towards the end of July R.A.F. flights were instituted to carry military mail in the Cork area. By August a regular service had been set up.

On 10 August, No.2 Squadron, RAF Fermoy was able to report to a Col. D.K. Bernard on the General Staff of the 6th Division at Cork:

During the past week further progress has been made in establishing aerial mails throughout the division.

Mails have been delivered to Killarney, Tralee and Listowel. Landings were effected at Killarney and Tralee and mails collected. The landing ground at Killarney is not very safe, but steps are being taken to improve it.

The landing ground at Limerick is now ready for use, and mails between Fermoy and there will start tomorrow – Wednesday 11th inst.[56]

Below: Official mail carried by aerial mail within Ireland, July 1922

Timings were agreed for planes leaving Fermoy and Limerick on Mondays, Wednesdays and Fridays. Later, this was extended to Oranmore, Tralee and other areas. Instructions and reports were telegraphed backwards and forwards and deeply laughable code words established. Various rather obvious words were used to indicate that an aircraft had left or safely arrived. Nothing could have been disguised. One example sums it up:

The following code word will be used to notify all concerned when the service for any particular day is cancelled:-

"DUDDAY" – Unfit for Air Mail today … (date).[57]

Armoured cars took the mails to and from the landing grounds. If mails had to be dropped an officer would accompany the pilot, mechanics being considered not intelligent enough. If the plane was forced to land somewhere else the pilot had instructions to burn the mails to prevent them falling into rebel hands.

Matters came to a climax in May 1921 when the Custom House in Dublin was attacked by Irish Volunteers. Here, official stamping of documents and stationery took place. A telegram of 26 May announced that the stamping machinery was destroyed. The next day, a report from a distraught Superintendent, T. O'Beirne, came through describing the desperate state. He and his staff had been held at gunpoint but the Volunteers had not got into the safes. After the firing of the building floors had collapsed and the stamping machinery could be seen still standing through open walls. Stamp dies were "all put in a heap on the floor and saturated with petrol".[58] The staff escaped with their lives, though not the raiders.

On 21 June 1921 King George V opened the new Northern Ireland Parliament in Belfast. His speech was placatory.

> I appeal to all Irishmen to pause, to stretch out the hand of forbearance and conciliation, to forgive and forget and to join in making for the land they love a new era of peace, contentment and goodwill. … May this gathering be the prelude of the day in which the Irish people, North and South, under one Parliament or two .. still work together in common love for Ireland.[59]

The situation then improved dramatically and on 11 July British troops returned to their barracks.

> In view of the altered conditions now prevailing it has been decided to suspend the Destroyer and Aerial Mail Services and to forward correspondence by train in charge of Other Ranks Couriers commencing on the 27th instant. These Couriers should be provided with civilian clothes, and should travel in pairs.[60]

Official mails now ran regularly without interruption on the ground. From June 1922, with partition looming and civil war breaking out, a similar airmail service for military and government mail connected Belfast and Dublin (from Aldergrove to Collinstown).

1926 General Strike
"Unlike the unions, the government was united, ruthless and prepared."[61]

This was certainly true of the Post Office, whose workers were, of course, government employees. Preparations had begun as far back as 1923 for the great emergency on the mainland of the inter-war years, and plans were secretly drawn up for men and women to carry out their work efficiently in the event of a general transport strike. Much had been learned from the 1919 Railway Strike. Now extra allowances were to be offered to "bribe" employees to work.

> The allowances we propose are meant to tempt not Postmen only but Sorters as well and more especially and if we do not make them tempting enough we may find ourselves, when the emergency is upon us, short of the staff we need. The alternative is to provide a specially organised char-a-banc service the cost of which would, as the Secretary has said be very much greater.[62]

In London, for those living beyond walking distance (defined as five miles) it was proposed to hire charabancs (long open vehicles with benches) to bring female staff in to work, particularly in the telephone exchanges. Men should make use of bicycles or their own motor cars, for which allowances would be paid. Bedding would be provided in their offices for those who might find this impossible. In the event, the bedding was little used but almost 140 charabancs were hired. These were intended to carry about 6,000 passengers a day but it was found possible "by resorting to overloading" to carry as many as 9,000.

> It does not seem to have been clearly understood that these services were intended for the use of female staff only, except for an occasional man or so to act as guards.[63]

More than 100 volunteer drivers were specially trained for some weeks on a Post Office van lent for the purpose. They were to be used in maintaining road services within London. Trunk road services were planned between London and other main cities for public mail, and for government mail an airmail service would be set up.

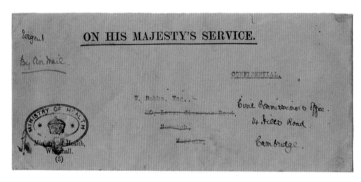

ON HIS MAJESTY'S SERVICE.

Above: Airmail to a Civil Commissioner during the General Strike

Overall, outside the Post Office, a Chief Civil Commissioner was appointed by the Government and he divided the country into 12 districts, with a Deputy Civil Commissioner to run each in the event of a strike. The Commissioners, mostly ex-military men, would have the power to do everything necessary to maintain public services, with transport, food distribution, power etc all under their direct control. The Commissioners' regions were "virtually autonomous, their objectives specific, their resources unlimited."[64] They operated within a bureaucratic culture which understood how to relay information and delegate the carrying-out of commands. The Unions were often in disarray.

The immediate cause of the strike was the threat, a year previously, of a miners' strike. This had been bought off by a temporary government subsidy and an inquiry under the chairmanship of Sir Herbert Samuel, the former Postmaster General. His Commission reported in early 1926 with a number of proposals, but from the miners' point of view "offered only uncertain benefits in return for immediate pain."[65] Their Union invoked a prior agreement with other unions and the TUC General Council held long, but unproductive, talks with the Government. The subsidy was due to run out on 30 April and the mine owners threatened lock-outs.

Telegrams were monitored throughout by the Post Office and copies of particular ones passed on to other branches of the Government. Thus, news of Union intentions, or actions, was immediately known to the authorities through such intercepts.

> On Saturday evening, May 1st, telegrams calling out members of various Unions on the following Monday night began to be handed in, and copies were duly sent to the Chief Civil Commissioner, who with his staff had taken up duty in Whitehall. It was clear that a General Strike would be called.[66]

Even though talks were still going on, the Cabinet issued instructions on Sunday afternoon that the prearranged emergency schemes should be brought into force. Talks duly broke down and the strike began at midnight on Monday, 3 May. The Parcel Post was immediately suspended and a limit put on the weight of letter packets. In London mail van contractors' drivers struck immediately but about 120 of their vans were commandeered. A further 70 were "extracted" from Macnamara's garage the following day and these were all driven by the volunteer drivers previously trained.

Two services were set up for urgent Government mail. One was a Trunk Despatch service by road, the other an R.A.F. airmail service. Various routes had been set up for both at least a year in advance. On 3 May the Home Office issued a memo to Government departments marked "Urgent and Secret".

> With reference to the Home Office Secret letter of the 7th December, 1923 I am directed by the Secretary of State to inform you that the scheme for the conveyance of urgent Government despatches will be brought into operation as from tonight, that is to say the first Air Mail will leave London tomorrow Tuesday morning. Letters for despatch by air mail should reach the Home Office as early as possible in the day, but in any case not later than 10 p.m. They should be sent under cover addressed *Room 101, Home Office,* and should be brought direct to that room by the bearer.[67]

The services started promptly on 4 May, routes and timings having been worked out with military precision. There were no special markings applied to the mail carried and no fees charged. An official comparison of the two services was drawn up.[68]

	Average time of arrival at centres where Civil Commissioners were stationed		Remarks
	P.O. Service	Air Mail	
Bristol	6.30 a.m.	9.0 a.m.	Road Service to London more reliable than Air Mail and preferred by Civil Commissioners.
Cardiff	Road 1.0 p.m. Rail 12.0 noon	9.45 a.m.	Despatches to London by Despatch rider leaving 6.30 p.m. via Gloucester and Oxford
Nottingham	9.0 a.m.	10.30 to 11.0 a.m.	
Leeds	Very irregular 12 to 15 hours journey	11.0 a.m. (by road from York)	Despatch to London by private motor car at 9.0 p.m.
Newcastle	9.0 p.m.	11.0 a.m.	Air Mail used in both directions.
Birmingham	7.0 a.m. to 9.0 a.m.	9 a.m.	Despatches to London by Motor Cycle, journey of 5 to 6 hours
Liverpool	4.0 to 6.0 p.m.	11.30 a.m.	Despatches to London by Motor Cycle via Birmingham.
Cambridge	12.30 p.m.	Noon (Despatch Rider)	Despatches to London by P.O. van.
Reading	Rail 10.0 a.m. Road 4.0 to 5.0 a.m.	10.0 a.m. (Despatch Rider)	

The last despatches by airmail were on Sunday 16 May outward from London and the following day for mails to London.

During the strike there were a few isolated incidents in the East End of London. One or two vans were attacked by mobs and some charabancs had to be diverted to other routes because of hostile crowds. Strike incidents were treated very seriously by the Post Office, and Government generally, with eyewitness accounts recorded in detail, but it was hardly the stuff of revolution.

> Miss Pike, Telephonist, City Exchange, stated that about 6 p.m., while passing through the Bricklayers Arms neighbourhood (Old Kent Road), a mob endeavoured to rush the charabanc and turn the passengers out. They were prevented from doing so by the Police and the charabanc was diverted to another route.

> The charabanc following the one mentioned above was diverted by the Police through some back streets. The charabanc was pelted by a crowd of women with refuse (rotten fruit, tomato, potato). Miss Hume, Telephonist, City, was hit in the face with a piece of raw potato.[69]

Rather than face such hostile crowds, and possible attack, the Post Office arranged for mail bags to be carried from the Eastern District Office sorting office on Whitechapel Road to King Edward Building in the City by the as yet unfinished Post Office underground railway, well over a year before it was officially inaugurated.

> The whole of the mails passing between the Eastern District Office and the King Edward Building were successfully carried yesterday [Monday 10 May] on the Post Office London Railway by means of the battery locomotive and trailer cars. It was not therefore necessary to run any mail vans on this route which it will be remembered was one on which there was a certain amount of trouble last week.[70]

The Emergency GPO Report for Wednesday 12 May ended with: "N.B. A telegram from Mr Bevin is attached." – one of the intercepts sent to Joynson-Hicks, the Home Secretary. It would have been interesting to read the contents, but sadly it is missing from the file.[71] Undoubtedly, it would have intimated that the strike was to be called off. Ernest Bevin was the driving force behind the Strike Organization Committee of the TUC. On the evening of the Tuesday, after exhausting talks, he and the others had decided to terminate the general strike on the basis of a memorandum of understanding negotiated by Sir Herbert Samuel. This was announced to Baldwin, the prime minister, at midday on the Wednesday, but without the agreement of the miners on whose behalf the strike had been called.

As might be expected, the cancellation of the General Strike resulted in a marked increase of telephone and telegraph traffic. It was noted that the additional revenue from London Telephone calls during the strike had been about £8,000 a week.

Postal traffic had been reduced by about 50% but they had still managed to get mails abroad. On 6 May it was reported that

> It is hoped to run a train daily from London to Dover connecting with Steamers to Ostend, Flushing and Calais. This train left this morning at 12.25 p.m. carrying 225 bags of mails. No trains are yet running to Newhaven, but the Boat Service may run occasionally and mails will be sent down by road. 200 Continental bags from Newhaven were brought to London yesterday by road. Part of the American Mail ex "Mauretania" was delivered in London yesterday afternoon. The Indian Mail should be

despatched from Dover to-day. Advance bags were sent to Dover on Monday and about 180 bags were sent by rail at 2 p.m. yesterday. The Indian Mail Officer leaves for Dover with special bags by private car provided by the Ministry of Transport this morning.[72]

Post Office workers were not called out on strike. However, secret plans had been made for the eventuality.

A note in a report, compiled after the strike was over, hints at one aspect which was of interest to philatelists:

The printing of stamps, stamped stationery, postal orders, etc. at Contractors' Works ceased and no deliveries of these items were made to Somerset House: but the available stocks were sufficient to meet all requirements during the period of the Strike and issues proceeded as usual.[73]

Although there seems to be no written record, nevertheless it can be proved that basic letter rate 1½d stamps were printed at Somerset House during the strike period (or in preparation for the strike) in case contractors' deliveries continued to be interrupted. Two sheet plates (numbered 962/80 and 963/81) were transferred from Post Office Stores to the Stamping Branch within Somerset House on 23 December 1925 "for experimental purposes". Both were returned on 26 August 1926. At some point in between they were used to print a limited stock of stamps which can be identified by the marginal control E.26, the typeface and full stop indicating Somerset House printing. This minor variation is the only philatelic consequence of the General Strike.

Above: Control examples from both plates used at Somerset House in 1926.

1   Quoted in POST 47/12 *Army Postal Service, Review of a Year's Work, August 1914-1915*, p1
2   POST 72/211 General F.H. Williamson, *Posts and Postal Services*, c.1931
3   POST 47/12 op cit p5
4   POST 47/11 Major E Gawthorne, *Army Postal Service British Expeditionary Force*
5   POST 47/12 op cit, p7
6   ibid
7   POST 47/11 op cit
8   ibid
9   Quoted in **Dagnall, H.** *The Evolution of British Stamped Postcards & Letter Cards* 1985 pp136-7 [PKT114/1913]
10   POST 47/11 op cit
11   ibid
12   ibid
13   POST 56/57 Report on Postal Censorship during the Great War (1914-1919 p 204
14   ibid p4
15   ibid p6
16   ibid p329
17   ibid p117
18   ibid p296
19   ibid p331
20   ibid p340
21   ibid p332
22   ibid p31
23   ibid p32
24   Details in **Mark, G.** *British Censorship of Civil Mails during World War I, 1914-1919*. pp 125-136
25   POST 56/57 op cit p190

26 ibid p118

27 POST 47/140 Emergency Scheme, Ireland

28 POST 56/177 Easter Rising, Ireland. A.H. Norway, Dublin to Secretary, G.P.O. London. 27 April 1916

29 ibid

30 ibid 30 August 1916

31 **Ferguson, S.** *G.P.O. Staff in 1916* 2005 p41

32 POST 56/57 op cit p215

33 ibid p216

34 ibid p54

35 ibid p210

36 ibid p211

37 ibid

38 POST 115/420, *The Postman's Gazette,* 1915.

39 POST 72/211 op cit

40 POST 47/11 op cit

41 ibid

42 ibid

43 **Gawthorn, Maj.** *Pioneers of Air Mail Service* [1938]

44 ibid

45 AIR 1/1209/204/5/2622 Pts 1-8, Report on Pigeon Dropping on Ground Targets from Aeroplane, 29 January 1919

46 **Gawthorn** op cit

47 Details in **Hopkins, Maj. A.E.** *The British Army Post Office in North Russia 1918-1919* 1965

48 **Rowland, P.** *David Lloyd George - a biography* 1975, p506

49 POST 30/4489 Air Mail: railway strike 1919, inland mails conveyed by aeroplane

50 ibid. 2 January 1920

51 ibid. Compiled from several reports.

52 AIR 5/135 Part III memo by G.E.P. Murray, 8 October 1919

53 ibid

54 ibid. *Workington News* 11 October 1919

55 ibid

56 AIR 5/82

57 ibid. Col. Maxwell Scott, General Staff, 5th Division, Curragh Camp SECRET 8 November 1920

58 IR 80/51 T. O'Beirne, Superintendent, Customs House, Dublin, to Stonestreet 27 May 1921

59 **Hattersley, R.** *Borrowed Time: the Story of Britain Between the Wars,* 2007 p53

60 Quoted without source in **Dulin, Dr. C.I.** *Ireland's Transition: The Postal History of the Transitional Period 1922-1925* [date] p210 – 20 July 1921

61 **Hattersley, R**. op cit p128

62 9 June 1925. POST 65/191. General Strike: Papers comprising industrial crisis bulletins, summarised reports, general council bulletins and correspondence.

63 POST 65/192. General Strike: Papers comprising memoranda, narrative history and emergency reports.

64 **Perkins, A.** *A Very British Strike: 3 May – 12 May 1926* 2006, p212

65 **Perkins** op cit p.82

66 POST 65/192. op cit

67 POST 33/448A Strike Emergency Arrangements: Home Office airmail scheme and London despatch service. From Under Secretary of State, Home Office, 3 May 1926

68 POST 65/192 op cit 21 October 1926

69 ibid. Strike Incidents. Wednesday 5 May 1926

70 ibid. 2nd Emergency Report 11 May 1926

71 ibid. 1st Emergency Wednesday 5 May 1926

72 ibid 1st Emergency Report Thursday 6 May 1926

73 ibid 21 October 1926

13

AN OCEAN OF AIR

AIRMAIL: THE GREAT ADVENTURE

A t the beginning of the 20th century, flying was the great adventure. Soaring into the sky and looking down – it was thrilling to watch, and even more thrilling to take part. The speed and the danger, combined with the rickety contraptions open to the elements, all added to the excitement. There was a sense of freedom. Man was defying Nature.

When one of the best known pioneers, Gustav Hamel in his Blériot monoplane, gave an exhibition flight over Windsor Castle in 1914, George V excitedly noted in his diary:

> Beautiful bright day, mild and hardly any wind. ….Hamel flew here at 12.15 for Hendon, he went up & "looped the loop" 14 times, most interesting & wonderful to see with what ease he did it & it was most graceful. All the Eton boys & many others were on the terrace & were delighted….[1]

Shortly afterwards Hamel was lost in the Channel and never found. It was a dangerous sport, though crashes were often not fatal – the flimsy craft were never that far from the ground. The fact that planes could cross the Channel raised the prospect of them carrying mail overseas. In the nineteenth century this, of necessity, had gone by ship. Now an ocean of air opened up much faster possibilities.

Before the coming of the aeroplane all mail abroad had to go by sea. Across the Channel was relatively short, but to get to America, Africa, Asia or Australia took a very long time. If planes could make the journey instead a great deal of time would be saved.

Ships such as the R.M.S. *Titanic* carried the mail – they were Royal Mail ships. As in the case of the *Titanic,* they had post offices aboard, a Sea Post Office, where mail was sorted. When the *Titanic* sank on its maiden voyage in 1912 all the 3,366 bags of mail and 763 parcels were lost, as were the five postal workers from both the British and American post offices who manned it. The two British workers were J.R. Jago Smith and James B. Wilkinson. Other lines such as the P. & O. also had Sea Post Offices with identifiable postal cancellations. It took 23 days by steamship to India through the Suez Canal.

First Aerial Post

The first aerial post took place at an Exhibition in Allahabad in India in February 1911. Allahabad was then the capital of the United Provinces of Agra and Oudh and lay at the confluence of the Ganges and the Jumna rivers. The Exhibition had opened on 1 December 1910 to last for three months and, as part of this, an aviation meeting was organised by Captain Walter George Windham, R.N. for 18 February. Planes, both monoplanes and biplanes made under licence by the Coventry-based motor firm of Humber, were shipped out from Britain in crates.

Above: the Titanic leaving Southampton and telegram announcing its loss

It occurred to Windham that a special aerial post could help raise funds for a new hostel for Indian students though it was also said that another purpose of such a flight would be to demonstrate the possibilities of an aerial service for a beleaguered town.[2] A special postmark was arranged, as, at the last minute, was a postcard bearing a picture of the biplane in which the mail was to be carried. The postcard cost one rupee and donations were requested for the new hostel for other mail carried.

Flown by Henri Péquet, the chosen Humber biplane took off shortly after 5.30 p.m. on the Saturday from the aviation ground, circled around twice and then flew across the River Jumna south to Naini Junction, about two miles away, at a height of 130 feet. Its speed was about 40 m.p.h. in the air and about 30 m.p.h. when landing, with the entire trip lasting 27 minutes. The large special postmark was applied in magenta on public mail, but in black on privileged mail. In all, some 5,000 to 6,500 items were said to have been included in the mail, the total weight being 200 to 300 pounds.

Above: posting box for Coronation aerial post

A copy of Windham's plane was quickly made by the Humber Company so that it could be exhibited on that firm's stand at the Olympia (London) Air Show from 24 March to 1 April the same year.

Below: poster advertising Coronation aerial post

When he returned home Windham used this experience in India to promote the idea of special mail flights to celebrate the coronation of King George V, and approached the Postmaster General, Herbert Samuel, directly.

Coronation Aerial Post

As in India, the Postmaster General would not agree to a charge for postage over and above the normal rate. But he did agree to the sole use of private illustrated stationery, for which a charge would be made, and also special postmarks. However, when it came to advertising the service, before and during the course of the flights, the Post Office refused to be publically associated. Use of the Royal Cypher, or the words "Royal Mail" was specifically forbidden; "Aerial Mail" was agreed, however, to appear on the side of the aeroplanes.

The scheme which was agreed was for a series of flights between Hendon and Windsor, limiting the mail to the special cards and envelopes which would receive the special postmark. The stationery would be available at principal London stores and special pillar boxes were provided where the souvenir stationery was on sale. These boxes were painted in Post Office red, measuring 4ft high by 2ft square. Stores who took part included Arding & Hobbs, Harrods and Selfridges.[3]

At the insistence of the Post Office the collecting vans were not commercial newspaper vans but rather chartered from Messrs McNamara. These were painted green and bore on the side the words "Aerial Post Collecting Van". There was nothing to indicate a Royal Mail connection.

Cards and envelopes were normally sold with ½d or 1d Downey Head stamps already affixed. The cost was 6½d for the cards or 1s 1d for the envelopes. Both cards and envelopes bore the same design, depicting

a Farman biplane in flight over Windsor Castle. This was the work of William W. Lendon and came in two slightly different versions. In the legend at the foot one said "London to Windsor"; the other had the words "Windsor to London".

However, both cards and envelopes come printed in a variety of different colours. Violet (described as "mauve" by the Post Office) was reserved, generally, for "privileged" mail, that is mail to VIPs. All versions of card and envelope were produced in this format. For postcards with the ½d stamp affixed the London to Windsor version also came in red-brown, dark brown and olive green. From Windsor to London it was only in olive green. For envelopes London to Windsor with a 1d stamp affixed was also printed in scarlet, purple brown, bright green, deep green, deep brown and red-brown. The return version was again only in olive green. There was also a label in violet for newspapers.

Left: artwork for Coronation aerial post stationery;

Above: privilege envelope and postcard flown from Windsor.

Below: rehearsal for the aerial post

Flights were to begin on Saturday 9 September but there was a full-scale rehearsal at the end of August with mail bags being handed over to an aviator, though presumably not flown.[4] Aviators and their machines were assembled. Pilots were E.F. Driver, Clement Hugh Greswell, Gustav W. Hamel and Charles L.A. Hubert. There were two types of plane – a Blériot monoplane and a Farman biplane as portrayed on the stationery design. Ironically, it was the monoplane with Gustav Hamel at the controls which made the first flight, and most of the subsequent ones.

The postmaster at Windsor wrote to the G.P.O. Secretary on 11 September:

> I beg leave to report that the first Aerial Post reached Windsor at 5.13 p.m. on Saturday the 9th inst.

> The aeroplane alighted in the Windsor Castle Grounds about 100 yards from the Frogmore Mausoleum.

> It had previously been arranged that the aeronaut should land on the lawn immediately facing the East Terrace, but through some cause the aviator was unable to manage this.

> When it was seen where the machine had alighted, a cycle Postman was despatched from the East Terrace to Frogmore and returned with the mail and the aviator

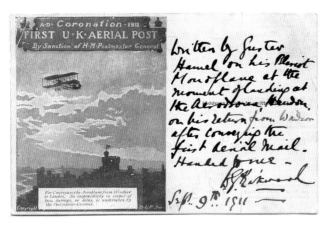

to the East Terrace. The mail was taken over from the aviator and despatched by the cycle Postman to the Post Office, reaching there at 5.33 p.m.

The mail was sorted and the contents despatched to London by the train leaving at 6.0 p.m.; also a special bag was despatched by the same train for Balmoral, containing aerial Letters, Cards, and Newspapers, for H.M. the King and members of the Royal Family.[5]

This was captured on film for British Pathé News, the tiny monoplane and Hamel buffeted by the high wind but landing safely, then handing over the mails. Hamel also pencilled a note of the flight on an unstamped card.

Huge amounts of mail were posted. By the preliminary collection on the Friday before the first flight it is estimated that about 58,000 letters and postcards had been received. Thereafter, a close count was kept of the number of bags and in particular their weight. Equally, the precise times of leaving and arriving were carefully noted. Hubert crashed on 11 September when trying to take off with eight bags of mail and broke both his thighs. This was described as a "matter of regret" in a Post Office report and it was sincerely hoped that no further accident would occur (a marginal note stating that "The Postmaster General's request to the organizing Committee on this point shd have a salutary effect.").[6] Other pilots staged a strike so that Hubert could get compensation.

Flying arrangements were primitive. One delightful example of this is related by Hamel in his book published a few years later.

> Flying from Windsor to London with the 'Aerial Post' in 1911, an aviator [Gustav Hamel] was overtaken by night, and he only picked up his direction by the brilliant illuminations of the White City and the Edgware Road. At Hendon, where he was expected, a number of motor-cars had been ranged with their headlights showing on the field; this enabled him to make a landing quite easily.[7]

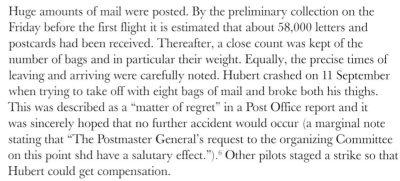

Above: Hamel's card carried on the first flight

Hamel (centre) arriving at Windsor

Images of Hendon aerodrome

This was probably on 18 September with a 6.45 pm return (but this before British Summer Time was created during World War I, so the equivalent in terms of darkness of 7.45 pm today).

In all, from 9 to 26 September there were 16 flights from Hendon to Windsor with 35 bags of mail carried. Normal weight of each bag was about 26½lbs. At the urgent request of the Mayor and other residents of Windsor there were four return mail-carrying flights from Windsor

to Hendon on 17 and 18 September. Only four bags of mail were carried between 21 and 21¾lbs in weight. An estimated 133,000 envelopes and cards were carried, of which only 10,000 were envelopes.

There was also a souvenir Aerial Post edition of the *Windsor Chronicle* published on 15 September. With a specially printed label these were included in the privileged mail bag and flown on 17 September from Windsor to Hendon.

A Post Office view of the novel means of transporting the mails was given by Robert Bruce, Controller of the London Postal Service. After detailing the number of mail bags, amount of mail, expenses etc, he summed up:

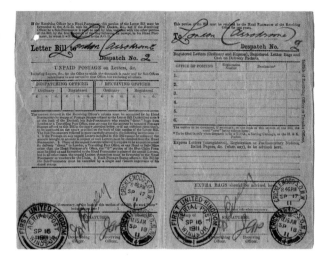

> The experiment has been an interesting one, and has proved that when the conditions are favourable it is possible to send mails from point to point by aeroplane very much quicker than by any other means, but from a practical point of view the Aerial Post has not been a success, as owing to unfavourable weather a large proportion of the special Letters and Postcards have been seriously delayed.[8]

This was the world's first regular airmail service. There were no other serious attempts in Britain before World War I intervened.

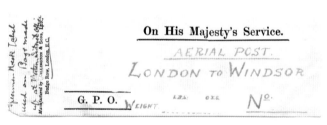

Across the Atlantic

The prevailing winds across the wide expanse of the North Atlantic are from west to east. So it was easier, relatively, for early aviators to attempt to fly in that direction first. Equally, the shortest distance between North America and Europe was also the obvious choice and so the initial point of departure was St. John's, Newfoundland. In 1919, with World War I over and planes having developed significantly in the meantime, several attempts were made to cross the Atlantic by planes carrying mail.

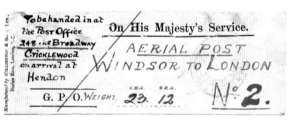

Above: Letter bill for the a flight from Windsor. "Artwork" and example of the special bag label

In the race to be first across the Atlantic there were two different strands. On the one hand three American flying boats were to take a southerly route from New York via Newfoundland to the Azores. Although longer in total the sea crossing was only 1,200 miles. Some 50 warships were stretched out over 2,400 to protect the whole route. They left on 16 May and one succeeded in reaching the Azores 15 hours later, the others having to land in the sea and remarkably managed to power themselves through the water to the islands.

On the other hand, Lord Northcliffe of the *Daily Mail* had put up a prize of £10,000 for the first successful British crossing of the Atlantic. There were several competitors, all deciding to take the northerly non-stop route of nearly 2,000 miles to Ireland using land-based planes. The Sopwith Aviation Company designed and built a biplane in six weeks, fitted with a single Rolls-Royce Eagle VIII water-cooled engine of 360 horse power, called the *Atlantic*. Pilot and navigator were Harry Hawker and Commander K. Mackenzie Grieve. Vickers (Aviation) Ltd entered a modified version of their *Vimy* biplane, a long-distance bomber employed extensively during the war. Much larger than the Sopwith it had two Rolls-Royce Eagle engines. Captain J. Alcock and Lieutenant Arthur Whitten Brown were pilot and navigator for Vickers. Bad weather had delayed their departure. That of the American flying boats spurred them into action.[9]

Newfoundland, not yet part of Canada, was a much more adventurous stamp-issuing colony than most. The Postmaster General, Dr J. Alex Robinson, seemed to act independently in almost cavalier fashion. On 5 April 1919 he approached the Sopwith Aviation Company asking if they would carry a small official mail of not more than 10 letters, assuming they were the first plane to leave. Five days later he agreed that the Company could carry an additional 100 letters and immediately made arrangements for 200 3c stamps to be suitably overprinted at the offices of the local *Daily News*. These were placed on sale at the St John's post office on 12 April and 95 used for franking letters. Each was initialled by the Postmaster General on the reverse, with the exception of a few initialled by the Secretary to the Post Office, William Campbell.[10]

On Sunday, 18 May, Hawker and Grieve in their *Atlantic* took off from Mount Pearl flying field, St. John's at 3.40 pm (local time, and five hours after the Americans had reached the Azores) properly marked and sealed according to the competition rules.[11] They carried a mail bag complete with Letter Bill detailing the contents – 80 ordinary letters, 10 official letters (this scored through), 1 package photos, 6 ordinary (supplementary letters). One of the official letters was addressed for the King, another was from the Newfoundland Postmaster General to the PMG in London. The specially overprinted stamps were cancelled with a machine cancellation of 12 April, the date the stamps went on sale and about the time the first flight was originally expected.

Below: letter carried on the fateful Hawker and Grieve flight showing water staining

Immediately after take-off the undercarriage was jettisoned and the plane climbed through cloud to 10,000 feet. Speed through the night was 105 miles an hour. Both Hawker and Grieve were in cockpits open to the elements. When they were 800 miles from Newfoundland the engine cooling system failed and the water began to boil. They realised they would not be able to reach Ireland. Dropping down to the steamer lane they eventually spotted the small Danish vessel *Mary* heading for Europe. They managed to land safely in the sea and were taken aboard the

steamship *Mary* which unfortunately had no wireless so after a time it was assumed they were lost. Hardly anything was salvaged from the aircraft. After a week they were taken to Scapa Flow, thence to a hero's welcome in London.

However, the *Atlantic* remained afloat and was found later by the American ship S.S. *Lake Charlottesville*.

> It was floating in the sea tail up, and on the top of the tail was a white shirt tied as a signal of distress, near the top of the plane was lashed a brown mail bag which was marked, Newfoundland G.P.O. It contained mail mostly addressed to the King, the mail was very much water soaked and otherwise damaged, but will be turned over to the Authorities in due time.[12]

The mail was taken to Falmouth and reached London on 30 May. The American captain had replaced the soaked-off stamps on the mail, as can be clearly seen on the surviving examples. As far as the unused stamps were concerned (out of the 200 originally overprinted), after various presentations and destruction of defective copies, the 76 remaining were sold at $25 each in aid of the Marine Disasters Fund in Newfoundland.

Now it was the turn of Alcock and Brown. Their converted *Vimy* bomber had arrived on 24 May and was now in competition with a Handley-Page aircraft for an increased prize. Again the Newfoundland Postmaster General announced that mail would be carried. This time the fee was $1 and a 15c Cabot stamp would be overprinted and surcharged, 10,000 being printed. 50c of this $1 was to go to the Marine Disasters Fund.

Above: Letter bill for the Hawker and Grieve flight

After trial flights Alcock and Brown took off on Saturday 14 June shortly after 5 p.m., the mail bag containing 196 ordinary letters and 1 letter packet. The airmen were seated side by side, again in an open cockpit. For the next seven hours they were constantly flying, with a following wind, through banks of fog and cloud making navigation very difficult. At one point they nearly crashed into the sea but managed to climb back to 7,000 feet. About 6 a.m. they climbed to 11,000 feet and obtained an observation of the sun. Shortly afterwards they spotted islands but the mainland of Ireland was still invisible. Then they sighted tall wireless masts which they recognised as Clifden wireless station. In search of a safe landing they came down nearby in what they thought was a field but which turned out to be a bog. Time spent in the air was 16 hours, 28 minutes at an average speed of 110 miles per hour.

Despite their successful flight, Alcock was of the opinion that a flying-boat was more suitable for the crossing than an aeroplane. Both he and Brown were knighted.

In the other direction, east to west, difficulties were much less serious for an airship than an aeroplane. Within three weeks of the first non-stop aeroplane crossing the British airship *R 34* left East Fortune on the east coast of Scotland for America. It was an official experimental flight with an R.A.F. crew. Originally built by William Beardmore at Inchinnan in Renfrewshire for military use in World War I the *R 34* was not completed until war was over. It was 643 feet long and 78 feet, 9 inches at its maximum diameter, with a gas capacity

Above: letter carried on the return flight of the R34

of 2,000,000 cubic feet. There were five Sunbeam 275 h.p engines (but only four propellers) carried in four gondolas under the keel.

After midnight on 2 July the *R 34* left the airship base and less than an hour later was over Glasgow heading out into the Atlantic. Speed was 56 miles an hour but the crew did not experience the extreme discomfort of the airmen. They had excellent meals, music by gramophone, exercise along the keel and wireless communication. After 59 hours they reached Newfoundland but continued for 1,000 miles to Mineola field, New York. The whole voyage had taken 108 hours, 12 minutes.

The airship was moored at Mineola for three days, when it made the return journey to Britain carrying mail from the U.S. Postmaster General. This was much quicker, taking only just over 75 hours.

This flight was the end of mail-carrying flights across the Atlantic for several years, when the German *Graf Zeppelin* airship and others again made crossings with mail. The *Graf Zeppelin* service to South America commenced on 20 March 1932, and flights were also made across the North Atlantic.

To Europe & Beyond

Early pioneering trials and failures are always more interesting than established regular success. The period just after World War I was very much one of trying to extend the boundaries. Perhaps the furthest flung of these boundaries was Australia. Here, again in 1919, the Australian government offered a prize of £10,000 for a pioneer flight from England to Australia, the machine having to be all-British and the aerial journey accomplished in 720 consecutive hours. Two brothers, Ross and Keith Smith, with two crew, chose the same Vickers *Vimy* aircraft as Alcock and Brown and set off from Hounslow aerodrome on 12 November. Their journey had to be a series of many hops and a number of crashes. At Surabaya, in Java, for example, the landing ground was so muddy that the wheels sank in deeply to the point where it was thought impossible to get out again. However, they managed to make a bamboo runway through the mud and carried on, arriving at Port Darwin on 10 December. They completed the flight in just under 28 days, within almost 52 hours of the specified maximum flying time.[13]

Carried with them was a bag of mail. Included was a letter written by Keith Smith in which he mentioned the "very dud" weather which had delayed the start of the flight and "if we get through safely you may be able to get one of the special stamps if they are issued." Commemorative labels were indeed produced and attached to the mail in Australia, but the letters were not delivered until 26 February 1920 when the labels were cancelled with a special postmark. About 130 covers were flown.

Within Europe, there had been the experimental carriage of mail by the R.A.F. from Folkestone to the British forces in Cologne through the first half of 1919. After that ceased, negotiations with the French Post Office resulted in a civilian air mail service from London to Paris carried by machines of Mr Holt Thomas's Aircraft Travel and Transport Ltd. This service began on 10 November 1919, the first public international air service. Letters had to be posted at certain offices in London in the morning to be delivered in Paris that evening, though the inaugural flight was delayed by bad weather and did not arrive until the following day. There was a high additional charge of 2/6d an ounce and this was found to be excessive. Traffic was only 45 letters a day. Almost immediately an "Air Mail/Express" cachet was applied to such mail.

In May 1920 the service to Paris was increased to twice a day and the surcharge reduced (to 2s on 12 May), being drastically reduced to 2d on 22 July. In mid August the express cachet was replaced by a new airmail etiquette in light blue.

The service to Paris was not successful because of high cost in direct competition with the fast existing rail and steamer connections. However, this was merely the first stage in a much wider expansion of airmail. In July 1920 services were extended to Brussels (2d per ounce surcharge) and Amsterdam (3d surcharge). Thereafter, the airmail service slowly joined up with other countries' services to provide airmail routes through Europe. Direct flights were to take longer. An air parcel service was inaugurated to Paris in July 1921 and then to Belgium and Holland in 1922. This was regarded as a success as it combined rapid transit with a simplification of customs formalities, enabling a gain of several days in comparison with the normal parcel service.

Above: 1919 envelope carried on the Ross and Keith flight to Australia with label (top)

First flight to Paris with 2/6d extra fee

> The starting point of the development of the Empire air mail services may be said to have been the utilisation, by arrangement with the Air Ministry, of R.A.F. service flights between Egypt and Iraq in 1921, when it was decided that these flights, which were undertaken as part of the ordinary military training, should be run at regular fortnightly intervals and that they should be used for the conveyance of mails.[14]

Iraq, or Mesopotamia, was a British territory under mandate from the League of Nations since April 1920. It was also in revolt, for which the R.A.F. were required. At that time the ordinary route to Baghdad was via Bombay, Karachi and the Gulf, taking 20 to 23 days from Cairo. By air it took two days. The first consignment of official left Baghdad for London on 28 July 1921, with the return flight from Cairo carrying mail from London arriving in Baghdad on 17 August. This was the beginning of the airmail route to India.

In Britain there were three separate companies operating international air services – Handley Page Transport, Daimler Hire and the Instone Air Line.

It became increasingly clear that, without some substantial guarantee of subsidy, real development of civil aviation was out of the question, and at last, in 1924, the separate Companies were merged into a single Company – Imperial Airways – to which the Government agreed to give a monopoly in regard to Government subsidies, and an agreement covering operations for ten years.[15]

This took place in March 1924 and Imperial Airways Ltd was incorporated as the national air transport company, charged with the development of Empire and European services, including airmail.

An official digest of airmail developments from 1922 to 1929 gives an indication of how international airmail developed, from the standpoint of the British Post Office.[16]

1922	May	An air parcel service to Belgium was instituted but was discontinued by the air company in August 1922, the service having proved unprofitable.
	June	An air parcel service with Holland commenced.
	October	The air mail service between London and Brussels was extended to Cologne.
	November	Reduced fees on air letter & parcels for Holland (letters 2d instead of 3d).
1923	1 May	Air parcels for Paris & Holland – posting facilities extended to branch and head post offices in London and the provinces.
	August	The route from London to Cologne was extended to Berlin.
1924	May	Extension of the route to Berlin was introduced to Copenhagen. A parcel service to Germany, Denmark, Norway and Sweden commenced.
1925	March-May	An experimental service between Cape Town and Durban was operated for 3 months.
	May	The United States internal air service between New York and San Francisco became available. A service between London-Bale-Zurich-Geneva was instituted.
	June	Extensions of the European services to Malmo, Helsingfors, Kovno and Moscow became available.
1926		Services opened from Zurich-Vienna-Budapest-Bucarest-Constantinople and Paris-Prague-Constantinople. The London-Marseilles route was used for connection with P & O boats to the East.
	March	The French service from Toulouse to Casablanca was extended to Dakar in Senegal
	July	Further extensions of the European services from Cologne to Frankfurt and to Munich were utilised for air mails. A parcel service with Switzerland was commenced.
	December	Internal air services in Colombia were made available for air mails.

1927	January	Imperial Airways Ltd commenced to operate a fortnightly service between Cairo and Basra.
	March	A few experimental services (2 or 3 despatches only) were operated by Imperial Airways on the route Cairo-Khartoum-Uganda and Kenya.
	April	The Cairo-Basra service commenced to operate weekly instead of fortnightly.
	June	The parcel service to Belgium which had operated for a time in 1922 was resumed. Arrangements were made to use the Colombian internal service for parcels.
	September	The Canadian air service from Rimouski to Montreal commenced operating in connexion with the arrival of the C.P.R. steamers from this Country. Ordinary business correspondence was selected for conveyance; no air fees were charged and the service was not advertised to public.
1928		Arrangement commenced for posting on board homeward bound P & O packets for transmission by Marseilles-London air service.
	February	Internal air services in the Belgian Congo became available for mails.
	April	Certain reductions in air fees took effect on 30 April following the recommendations of the Hague Air Mail Conference (September 1927).
	May	Parcel services to Denmark, Luxemburg, Norway and Sweden were introduced. The Malmo-London air service was utilised by Sweden for transmission of ordinary correspondence within certain limits of weight.
	June	Experimental night flights were operated from Stockholm to London. New air service in Peru – letters accepted for Iquitos and certain smaller places. New service opened Rotterdam-Prague in connexion with night mail from London via Hook of Holland. A service to Persia – by air throughout – once a week, via Moscow, came into operation.
	July	Insured letter and box service with Switzerland and Holland commenced.
	August	New Air Mail to Biarritz. The French air service from Toulouse to Dakar was extended to South America. Charges on air mail letters for Peru reduced. Parcel services to Austria, Hungary and Czechoslovakia were introduced.
	September	Air Mails for U.S.A. were despatched for conveyance by aeroplane launched by catapult from S.S. Ile de France when nearing New York.
	November	New service to Algeria (from Marseilles by air). Air fees to U.S.A. reduced to 7d per ounce.

Night Flights

The experimental night flights mentioned began on the evening of 20 June 1928. Five flights took place between London and Stockholm flying over Holland and Germany. The last was on 5 September. Sorting took place on board the aircraft and special "Air Post Office" cachets were applied to mail, both English and Swedish indicating the particular flight. Flying by night saved time but also entailed a number of obvious difficulties. Night services then began to Brussels on 19 April 1930 and to Berlin on 14 May (London-Cologne-Hanover-Berlin).

The route to India

The volume of mail carried on these European flights was not very great. It became obvious that the real value of airmail services lay in their use over long distances. Linking the Empire provided great possibilities but it had to be done in stages. The first experiment was the service between Great Britain and India where the volume of traffic was greater than any part of the Empire other than Canada.

In 1922 an exhaustive enquiry was made by the Civil Aviation Advisory Board which went into the technical and financial aspects and made a series of recommendations on preliminary steps. The route should be surveyed; the necessary ground organisation prepared; and "very full" experiments should be carried out. By 1925 there was an agreement for the establishment of a fortnightly service between Egypt and India. The route was then surveyed by Alan Cobham in a De Havilland 50 aircraft, and by way of advertisement he used unofficial descriptive labels on mail carried on the return flight. He left Calcutta on 12 February 1925 arriving at Waddon Aerodrome, Croydon on 17 March. Similar surveys were undertaken by Cobham in December that year on a route via Cairo to Cape Town. On this occasion he had illustrated souvenir cards produced as well as specially printed labels (incorporating his signature).

The Air Minister, Sir Samuel Hoare, travelled in one of three aeroplanes surveying the route from London on 27 December 1926 arriving at Delhi on 8 January. A number of souvenir envelopes were carried. On the return journey labels were applied and a cachet indicating the name of the De Havilland plane – one being the "City of Delhi".

Below: Post Office leaflet for the introduction of the first air mail to India

At the same time the service from Cairo to Baghdad was extended to Basra but had to stop there because of political difficulties with Persia which prevented flights over that country. The first mail for this fortnightly service was accepted in London on 6 January and mail arrived in Basra nine days later. From 14 April the service became weekly.

It was not until Easter 1929 that all the difficulties were resolved and regular flights from London to Karachi could be instituted. For the first flight leaving Croydon on 30 March, Samuel Hoare was again a passenger and he has left a description of the journey.

There were two reasons why I decided to make an African flight. The air mail to India was due to start on March 30th, and I was anxious to make the first journey in a service that Lady Maud and I had practically started two years ago. Moreover, I had not crossed the Mediterranean in a flying boat and I wished to see how the all-metal Calcutta did the sea stage. But there was a second reason for my decision. Whilst the India air mail had always been my first objective in the field of civil aviation, my second was an air service from London to Cape Town. Both these projects had their own peculiar difficulties. In the case of the India service, there was the trouble of arranging flying facilities with the foreign countries along the route, Italy, Greece and Persia. In the case of the African service the almost equal trouble of obtaining financial support from the several British Governments between Cairo and The Cape.[17]

The flight was a series of hops with a change of aircraft at various points. It began at Croydon on Saturday, 30 March (the mail closing at 7 a.m. at the G.P.O. in London) and Imperial Airways produced souvenir envelopes. The air fee was 6d per half ounce.

> As things are at present, the air stages from London to Alexandria are short, the first day to Basle, the second to Naples, the third to Athens and the fourth to Tobruk, on the African coast, three or four flying hours from Alexandria. Already, however, Imperial Airways are planning to telescope this journey into a considerably shorter time.[18]

On the initial trip from Croydon the "Argosy" type airliner carried 12,000 letters and four passengers. This travelled as far as Basle where both mail and passengers were transferred to the railway for the journey to Genoa. There were no regular flights over the Alps until the 1930s. From Genoa a three-engined flying-boat carried the mails and passengers to Alexandria where a further transfer was made to a three-engined Hercules for the remainder of the journey to Karachi. It arrived on 6 April, a journey lasting seven days. Actual flying time was only 56 hours 25 minutes, but Hoare describes many celebratory meals en route including a dinner at Naples given by the Italian pilot General Pinedo. Hoare left the flight at Alexandria to undertake his exploratory African journey.

> A detailed list of the flights indicates just how arduous and difficult these were:[19]

Croydon to Paris	2 hours, 30 minutes
Paris to Basle	2 hours
Basle to Genoa	11 hours, 20 minutes (covered by rail)
Genoa to Rome	3 hours
Rome to Naples	1 hour 15 minutes
Naples to Corfu	4 hours, 30 minutes
Corfu to Athens	3 hours, 15 minutes
Athens to Suda Bay	2 hours, 15 minutes
Suda Bay to Tobruk	3 hours, 15 minutes
Tobruk to Alexandria	4 hours, 30 minutes
Alexandria to Gaza	3 hours, 25 minutes
Gaza to Baghdad	7 hours, 30 minutes
Baghdad to Basra	3 hours
Basra to Bushire	2 hours, 40 minutes
Bushire to Lingeh	3 hours, 50 minutes
Lingeh to Jask	2 hours, 20 minutes
Jask to Gwadar	3 hours, 30 minutes
Gwadar to Karachi	3 hours, 40 minutes

Above: commemorative envelope carried on the first flight to Karachi (top)

"Argosy" airliner from Croydon to Basle (middle)

Flying boat from Genoa to Alexandria (bottom)

Hoare then scouted the air route south of Alexandria towards the Cape, and it seems almost to have been a tourist trip "at first looking down upon the Pyramids amid the green garden of the Nile, and then striking across the arid desert to Wadi Halfa and Abu Ahmed, the scene of Kitchener's greatest achievement, the building of the desert railway."[20] On the way back Hoare picked up the first return flight at Alexandria.

> The determination of General Balbo, Mussolini's chief lieutenant, to see me forced us to land for a ceremonial luncheon at Lake Bracciano.[21]

After another banquet at Naples another flying boat in the bay, an Italian Dornier-Woll, had caught fire and in two or three minutes was completely destroyed. Such hazards were always present.

Once in regular service, passengers were also carried, varying in number depending on the type of aircraft.

> For the Mediterranean service all-metal flying-boats are used, and these have the distinction of being the quietest and most comfortable aircraft on the route. The fifteen passengers' seats are placed in the hull, with a porthole opposite each seat, and a buffet is installed at the end of the cabin. The engines are above the hull, which is metal-covered instead of on each side of it, and this arrangement reduces the vibration and noise to a minimum, so that the passengers can carry on a conversation without undue effort. This is the only English air-line machine in which smoking is allowed.[22]

Sir Samuel Hoare, then Minister for Air, was later to become infamous as Foreign Secretary in 1935 for the Hoare-Laval pact over the Italian invasion of Abyssinia. This was to completely overshadow his earlier achievements in the field of air services.

Right: Airmail stamp issued by India in 1929

The service to Karachi was extended to Delhi by the "City of Bagdad" airliner on 28 December 1929, an inland service set up by the Indian government. For mail to continue beyond that by air required the use of foreign air services such as the Dutch. Their air service to the Dutch East Indies commenced on 25 September 1930, and was made available for air correspondence from Britain for Siam, the Straits Settlements, the Malay States and the Dutch East Indies. The French took mail from Bangkok to Indo-China.

Airmail Letter Boxes

The growing volume of airmail prompted the idea of special letter boxes for its collection. In November 1929 a report was prepared by the London Postal Service justifying this. "One of the sources of difficulty in dealing with Air Mail correspondence in the Foreign Section is its receipt mixed with ordinary correspondence, necessitating somewhat elaborate arrangements to ensure its selection and separate treatment."[23]

The solution was separate letter boxes to be painted blue.

> As a means of inducing the Public to use the boxes, it could probably be arranged to afford a later posting for Air Mails at these boxes than is possible at any of the adjacent boxes or Post Offices. It might be worth considering whether, at the outset, at any rate,

it might be well to have the boxes cleared by a small Departmental motor which could also be painted a distinctive colour and marked with a prominent "Air Mail" design.[24]

The experiment began on 23 June 1930 with the opening of 11 airmail posting boxes in London situated outside:

London Chief Office, King Edward St.
Ludgate Circus B.O.
Moorgate, opposite Britannic House
Royal Exchange
West Central District Office
High Holborn, opposite Staple Inn
East Strand
Charing Cross B.O. (bronze front)
Oxford Circus, north east side
Piccadilly Circus, opposite the Pavilion Theatre
Victoria Station, forecourt

Two more would shortly be opened in front of the Imperial Airways offices in Charles Street, Haymarket (wall box) and outside the Parliament Street B.O. (large wooden wall box). The boxes were mainly type B, medium size boxes made by Carron Co. They were painted "Air Force" blue and surmounted by oval blue enamel signs with "Air-Mail" in white lettering. Charles Street and Ludgate Circus had a B size wall box on a pedestal. Motor vans were also painted blue as proposed. Time-plates and tablet notices were printed on card at the Savings Bank Department. In connection with the blue boxes and vans special airmail datestamps came into use at the Foreign Section in King Edward Building, both handstamps and machine cancellations incorporating the wording "Air Mail".

In 1933, because it was occasionally too full, the airmail box outside King Edward Building was replaced with a larger A type.

In May 1931 the scheme was extended to the provinces with boxes in Birmingham, Liverpool, Manchester, Edinburgh and Glasgow. That in the vestibule of the G.P.O. in Edinburgh was specially constructed of wood "as the Edinburgh Corporation was unable to agree to a bright blue pillar box being erected in front of such a dignified building."[25] Manchester was also individual. At the Head Office there, and at Newton Street sorting office, one of the posting windows was also faced with an airmail blue front. Later, in 1934, at the Thomas Street branch office, because of congestion it was not possible to accommodate a special pillar box in the vicinity of the office. A suitable window box was fixed instead.[26]

Back in 1931 the question arose of providing information about postage rates on the blue boxes. In the end it was decided to replace the existing single notice frame on the door with a larger one. This would contain a notice showing the latest time of posting and the combined postage and air fees. The notice would be printed card and there would be a metal crosspiece vertically placed in the centre to prevent theft. A specimen of the enlarged notice frames for the "B" type pillar air mail posting boxes was first fixed to air box No.13 outside the London Chief Office on 6 April 1932 and then introduced on all other boxes in London.[27] Later it was supplied already fitted by the manufacturers.

Above, top: blue airmail pillar box – B type

Below: larger A type at KEB

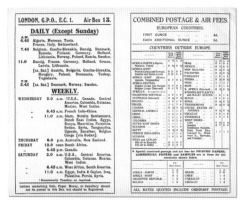

When, in February 1934, the question arose of erecting an airmail box in Tunbridge Wells the Head Postmaster there suggested that an additional inscription would be desirable, indicating that ordinary letters posted in an airmail box might be delayed. This prompted the introduction nationwide of a small enamelled iron plate which had already been applied to some London boxes, reading "AIR MAIL ONLY". They were available from May, having cost 9d each from Messrs Garnier & Co. Ltd.[28]

By 1936 the number of airmail posting boxes had risen to 139 in London and 174 in the provinces. However, with the introduction of the "all-up" scheme to Europe in 1936 and a year later to the Empire, they were no longer required. The last box to be withdrawn in August 1938 was that outside the London Chief Office in King Edward Street, the first to be erected.

Airmail Labels & Pennant

The first airmail labels were light blue in colour. Later this changed to a dark bright blue and books of these were made available from Imperial Airways. They were then also incorporated into standard stamp books. On 25 July 1934 a new airmail label was introduced designed by Theyre Lee Elliott. This image was also used on posters and leaflets and was clearly inspired by Sir Stephen Tallents.

At the same time a special pennant was created to be flown on aircraft carrying mails or related buildings. This, termed a pendant at the time, was approved by the Postmaster General on 17 May 1934.

To Australia and South Africa

Once the service to India had been established the extension to Australia "became only a question of time and money."[29] After prolonged negotiations it was agreed that Imperial Airways would be responsible for the service from London to Singapore, with the section across India being operated by a joint Anglo-Indian company, Indian Trans-continental Airways. This was completed by 1933 with the Australian government being responsible for the service from Singapore to Australia and the mail carried by Qantas. Experimental services were operated to Australia from 4 to 25 April 1931, but it was not until 8 December 1934 that the full direct service was inaugurated, with great ceremony, at Croydon aerodrome. Film was taken of the PMG hand-stamping souvenir mail from the royal family with gusto, with Williamson and other high ranking officials and dignitaries looking on. A special handstamp with an ivory handle was used on this occasion only. Then R.M.A. *Hengist* took to the air at 13.07. Here the new Morris streamlined airmail van also made one of its first appearances.

Above: Airmail letter box double notice (top)

Artwork for airmail pennant (middle)

Airmail leaflet (bottom)

Over 100,000 letters were carried together with parcels weighing 500lb – a total weight of over two tons. This was so great that it was necessary for a second machine to carry part of the load. The mail would reach Brisbane, 12,000 miles away, in 12 days.[30] Until then mail by land and sea would have taken 30 days.

By now the route within Europe had changed slightly, as had the aircraft. 38-seater "Heracles" aeroplanes flew from Croydon to Paris. Thence, the mail was taken by train to Brindisi where a flying boat of the "Scipio" class flew it to Alexandria. From Alexandria a "Hannibal" class aeroplane (similar to the "Heracles" but accommodating only 28 passengers) travelled as far as Karachi and then the "Atalanta" class (with room for 11 passengers) continued the journey via Rangoon to Singapore. Qantas utilised "Dianas" for the final leg.[31]

In the meantime a service to South Africa had also begun. There had been a choice of routes – down the east or west coasts of Africa. The east coast was preferred because, with the exception of Egypt, the planes could follow British territory throughout. A weekly air service from London to Mwanza (Tanganyika) operated by Imperial Airways Ltd was first introduced on 28 February 1931 and was used for air correspondence for Egypt, Sudan, N.E. Belgian Congo (via Juba), Uganda, Kenya and Tanganyika. This branched off from the Indian route at Alexandria.

The onward extension from East Africa had to wait to the end of the year. A preliminary Christmas mail was flown from London [on 9] December 1931, arriving at Cape Town five days before Christmas. The regular service started six weeks later [on 20 January 1932].[32]

Above: 8 December 1934 first through flight cover to Australia

Croydon aerodrome with "Heracles" aircraft and airmail van

Again "Hannibal" class aeroplanes were later used from Alexandria to Kisumu in Kenya and the "Atalanta" class from Kisumu to Cape Town. Decorative envelopes were produced for the various extensions of the air services.

"All-up" Services

A combined air fee and postage of 4d for 1st oz. and 3d for each subsequent oz. was introduced for European countries on 2 June 1930. However, it was not until March 1936 that the first "all-up" service to a European country came to fruition. Air fees were now gradually abolished on letters to various European countries and this principle was then extended to the Empire. From 1937 you could send a letter to anywhere in the Empire for 1½d, a postcard for 1d.

These reductions in fees and increases in services caused, naturally, a great increase in the volume of mail carried. By 1932 exactly four times the amount of mail was carried by air in comparison with 1928, 64 tons in weight or about 3,500,000 letters. In 1934 this figure had risen to 6,000,000 letters and in 1935, 10,500,000, a very rapid increase which, with the acceleration of times, was to continue.

1   RA GV/PRIV/GVD/1914 2 February

2   **Harman, K.** "The World's First Official Post by Aeroplane, Allahabad, India, Saturday 18th February 1911" *Exhibition Study Group Journal* No. 59 Winter 2000, pp52-60

3   Details in: **Field, F.J. & Baldwin, N.C.** *The Coronation Aerial Post 1911* 1934 pp18-19

4   *Illustrated London News* Vol. 139 p 364, 2 September 1911

5   POST 30/2859 Coronation Aerial Mail

6   ibid. Vice Controller A.E. Adeney to the GPO Secretary, 12 September 1911

7   **Hamel, Gustav & Turner, Charles Cyril** *Flying. Some practical experiences* 1914, p104

8   POST 30/2859 op cit. 22 September 1911.

9   See **Dixon, C.** *The Conquest of the Atlantic by Air* for full details

10   See **Dalwick, R.E.R. & Harmer, C.H.C.** *Newfoundland Air Mails 1919-1939* 1953 p5ff

11   ibid p 15

12   ibid p 16 Lt.Com. A.C. Wilvers to the Secretary of the Navy [U.S.] 29 May 1919

13   **Harper, H. & Brenard, R.** *The Romance of The Flying Mail* 1933 p42

14   POST 50/8

15   **Williamson, Sir F.** *The Air Mail Service* P.O. Green Paper No. 1 1934, p4

16   POST 50/7, amended by draft in POST 50/25

17   AIR 19/135 *Ten Thousand Miles in a Fortnight* p3

18   ibid

19   "By Air Mail to and from India" *St. Martin's-le-Grand* July 1929 pp176-181

20   AIR 19/135 op cit p9

21   ibid

22   *St. Martin's-le-Grand* op cit

23   POST 33/2979B Posting Boxes for Air Mail correspondence: special blue boxes erected in London and Provinces, Part 1. 19 November 1929

24   ibid

25   **Farrugia, J.Y.** *The Letter Box* 1969, p100

26   POST 33/2980 Posting Boxes for Air Mail correspondence: special blue boxes erected in London and Provinces, Part 2. Madden, Head Postmaster, Manchester to Postal Service Department, 21 July 1934

27   ibid. Controller, L.P.S. to Secretary, 6 April 1932

28   ibid. Controller, P.O. Stores to Secretary, 13 March 1934

29   **Williamson** op cit p6

30   **Briant, F.H.** "Air mail to Australia: A Landmark in Empire History" *Post Office Magazine* January 1935 p16

31   **Lumley, D.O.** *Air Mail Operation* P.O. Green Paper No. 23 1935 p9

32   **Williamson** op cit p6

14
SPEEDING THE MAILS INLAND
TRANSPORT, SORTING & DELIVERY

There are five main operations in the handling of mail: collection, transport, facing and cancelling the stamps, sorting, and delivery. With the huge increase in mail volumes from Victorian times onwards attention was focussed on mechanising these various aspects to cut down on the number of people required, and therefore costs. The most labour-intensive aspects were cancelling and sorting. Transport was soon mechanised - by train, van or plane. Collection and delivery have remained largely by hand, even today. Machines to cancel stamps were developed towards the end of the 19th century and by 1910 were widely installed in sorting offices. Apart from conveyor belts and lifts there was no other form of mechanisation.

Transport over longer distances inland was by train. But from the station the mails had to be taken to the delivery office and then be delivered. At the beginning of George's reign this was by horse-drawn vehicles or on foot; by the end it was largely by motor van, motorcycle and bicycle. In major cities there was also the problem of traffic congestion and in London this was met by the construction of the Post Office's own underground railway. For rural areas the service depended very much on a small number of dedicated sub-postmasters and their staff.

Great progress was made in speeding up mail handling in 25 years. By the end of the reign sorting offices were much more mechanised and one sorting machine was being tried out. Transport was largely motorised, and even partly by air, and rural deliveries were transformed. The service was modernised and greatly improved, both in towns and to more remote areas.

Motor boat to Foula

One delightful example of improvement of postal services to remote places came right at the beginning of George V's reign. The small island of Foula (Old Norse *Fuglaey* – "bird island") lies some 18 miles west of Walls on the mainland of Shetland. Islanders, then crofters and fishermen, were fiercely independent – still keeping the Julian calendar when the rest of Scotland had adopted the Gregorian in 1600 (England only following in 1752) and thus celebrating Christmas Day (Yule) on 6 January and the New Year (Newerday) on the 13th, even today. In 1911 there were 184 souls; today 30.

The contract to convey the mails from Walls to Foula dated from 1909 and was carried out by Magnus Manson and Laurence Grey, men of Foula. When Manson intimated in August 1911 that he was leaving the island and wanted to transfer the contract to one James Isbister this was brought to the attention of the authorities in Edinburgh. The question was then raised as to whether an improved service was warranted.

> The question of a more frequent service to Foula has not been considered within recent years, and there is no record of any application having been received from the islanders for improved service.

> Owing to the distance (18 miles) the island of Foula is from the mainland and the ex-

posed nature of the sea passage I doubt whether the frequency could be increased even in summer by the use of a rowing and sailing boat as at present. At all times the service is uncertain and during the winter months so hazardous that a crossing sometimes cannot be made for weeks at a time. To improve the frequency of service it would, I think, be necessary to substitute a motor or steam vessel for the present rowing and sailing boat. This change could not be made without increasing the cost considerably and the revenue would not warrant the expense involved.[1]

Nevertheless, the Secretary in Edinburgh thought that the Post Office was not spending the amount of money which was warranted on the Foula service and asked if a motor or steam service would not help the islanders in other ways. Could an outside contractor take it over? This immediately worried the more locally-aware postmaster at Lerwick and he suggested that he ascertain from the Sub-Postmaster on Foula what the islanders' feelings were likely to be. There would be a delay, however "as, at this season, the crossing is liable to be delayed. 19 days elapsed between the last trip and the previous one." He explained that

> The difficulty at Foula is the lack of pier or harbour accommodation at which vessels can lie in stormy weather. The ordinary boat has to be beached when not in use. A motor or steam vessel being larger and much heavier could not be 'hauled up'.[2]

P.P. Gear, the Sub-Postmaster at Foula, confirmed that the islanders would prefer a motor service but "any service provided and run by outsiders would be detrimental to the interests of the islanders apart from mail questions, as was sufficiently proved before the islanders obtained the contract."[3] The loss of the present payment for the mail service would be regarded as a hardship. "Outsiders" and "mainland" of course meant Shetland, not distant Scotland.

Reporting the matter to London, the Edinburgh Secretary accepted that tenders for a motor service should not be invited by advertisement.

> The Islanders have not complained of their present service, and it seems to be quite clear that they would prefer it to an improved service provided by Contractors outside Foula.[4]

The suggested improvement was to twice a week in summer and once a week in winter, being only half that at that time. Nautical advice pointed out that the stretch of sea between Walls and Foula is open to the full force of Atlantic gales, especially in the winter, and that the tides were strong. Local advice was clear that once a week was out of the question in winter and the postmaster at Lerwick questioned whether there was sufficient mail to justify a service twice a week in summer. There was also the question of cost.

While the boat was new, and originally constructed with the possibility of a motor being added in mind, nevertheless it would cost about £100 for all the alterations. The two Foula men who owned the boat asked for an increase from £2 to £3 a trip but eventually settled for £2 15s. After a long exchange of letters it was decided to keep the service at the same level of 39 trips a year but add the motor to the boat. This was agreed in June 1912 and the alterations took place at Scalloway on the Shetland mainland.

> The weight of the boat is now about 18 cwt., about 7 cwt. having been added in respect of the engineering plant.

> The craft is undecked, but an enclosure in the nature of an engine room has been erected at the stern to protect the engine and mechanical fittings. The engine provided is

5 h.p. which should give a speed of fully 6 knots, the boat being light. The propeller is protected by means of a strong iron guard fitted from keel to sternpost. This is intended to prevent damage to the propeller during "hauling" operations at Foula.

The usual lug sail is retained and can be used for auxiliary power or in the event of a breakdown of the motor.[5]

Foula's motor boat service finally began on 29 November 1912, leaving Walls at 9.15 a.m, although it had been delayed for a week because of gales. A congratulatory telegram was sent from Leiper to Gear and a photograph of the boat and crew taken.

In the whole, quite substantial, file in the archives there is only one mention of the total amount of mail per week: 68 letters and 15 parcels. This shows to what extreme lengths the Post Office would go to improve its service.

Road Transport

In 1934, Brig. General Sir Frederic Williamson, Director of Postal Services, looked back on thirty years of progress in road transport.

> The Red Mail Van is the most ubiquitous of vehicles. It is found in the streets of the big towns, at the railway stations at dead of night, in the Devonshire lanes and on the wild roads round Stornoway … Thirty years ago, practically the whole of the Post Office transport service was in the hands of contractors, and the Motor Van was hardly known; but the advent of the internal combustion engine has revolutionised all the conditions of this service. At the present time there is hardly a horse left and the Post Office services every year pass more and more from the hands of contractors to the direct control of the Post Office.[6]

Top: The Foula motor mailboat at Walls on its first day

Above: The Maudslay 50cwt 'Stores 1' van

Before 1919, almost all road mail services were in the hands of outside contractors, such as James Allen and Co., Birch Brothers (both only with horses) and McNamara (with both horses and motors), though all in red livery. The vehicles were driven by men wearing a G.P.O. uniform, even though they were employees of the contractor. They worked longer hours for lower wages than Post Office employees. It was the high cost of these contracted services, combined with increased vehicle reliability, which encouraged the Post Office to own its own motor vehicle fleet. By March that year the total number of motor vehicles *owned* by the Post Office was still only 15 lorries (Stores Department), seven cars and two testing-vans (Engineering Department) and 20 motor-cycle combinations with four tri-cars.[7]

The first petrol-driven vehicle, the Maudslay 2½-ton van for carrying lighter stores, had been bought in 1906 and was put into service in January 1907. It was an immediate

success saving about 22% of the cost of horse hire. It continued to give economical service up to 1925 when it was sold back to the makers. In 18 years it covered nearly 300,000 miles.[8] Even before World War I Major C. Wheeler of the Stores Department had visited the Ford factory in Detroit in America and been impressed. But it was not until after the War that serious steps were taken to create a Post Office fleet. Most road transport continued to be contracted out, either borne on motor vehicles or often on horse-drawn ones.

First, in 1919, some 54 ex War Department Ford model T (7 cwt) vans were purchased cheaply to begin the Post Office's own fleet. British design and manufacture was to be preferred, however, and an order was placed with G.W.K. Company of Maidenhead for 100 8 cwt light vans. These were delivered during 1920 but were a disappointment. They had a unique system of power transmission, a friction drive, and for this there was no adequate maintenance and service infrastructure. As a result, more than 600 Ford vans were supplied to the Post Office between 1921 and 1925, Fords having the necessary country-wide service system.

Top: the Post Office van fleet in 1919

Above: BSA 4¼ h.p. Engineering motor cycle combination

As an alternative to the American Ford, Wheeler "induced the Morris Motor Co. to build a suitable vehicle for trial on mail work" and impressed on them the necessity of organising a service system throughout the country.[9] In 1924 the Morris Commercial L and T types were introduced and specified for nearly all vehicles under two tons capacity for both the postal and telephone fleets – the result of political pressure to buy British. By the 1930s there were well over 2000 Morris vehicles in service, the small Morris Minor being introduced in 1931.

Not all were well cared for. The Chief Motor Transport Officer in the Post Office, Captain A. Hudson, noted laconically, with reference to the drivers:

> In addition to the rota of drivers, provision has to be made for reserve drivers to take a turn at the wheel, and there are cases where one vehicle may be handled by 20 or more drivers. Thus a minimum of personal interest in the vehicle may be expected, with difficulties in fixing responsibility for careless handling. Such conditions react unfavourably on maintenance costs.[10]

The Red Vans described by Williamson at the outset did most of the postal work. They came in three sizes – large, intermediate and "baby". But from 1924 solo motorcycles were also used for postal deliveries.

> These three 2¾ h.p. machines were adapted for postal use by the provision of a wire mesh rear pannier that was capable of containing a load of around 70 lb of mail. By the following year around 400 motorcycles of various makes were in use on both delivery and collection work. These tended to take the place of the rural cycle posts. It was

estimated that one postman with a motorcycle could cover the same ground as two postmen on pedal cycles.[11]

In 1931 the Motor Transport Branch of the Post Office Engineering Department was established together with workshops as part of the Stores Department. Thus, by the end of George V's reign there had been a huge increase in the number of motor vehicles owned by the Post Office for various services:[12]

Postal services	6204
Engineering services	5030 (excluding 550 trailers)
Telegraph delivery	264
Stores Dept transport	57

As Williamson had noted, this was a revolution.

Trains & Travelling Post Offices

Within Britain, the mails were transported long distances by train, the routes established in Victorian times. From as early as 1838 they had also been sorted *en route* in a series of Travelling Post Offices, a network of which covered the whole country. All the main functions of an ordinary sorting office were performed in a T.P.O. and all classes of postal packets, except parcels, were dealt with. Parcels, of course, were also carried by train. Until November 1915 there were also parcel-sorting carriages but this ceased because of prohibitive cost. Mail bags were taken by ordinary trains on other routes.

In 1928, there were 80 T.P.O.s throughout Great Britain, plus four in Northern Ireland (and 12 in the Irish Free State).[13] The carefully interconnected system was based on the main rail arteries from London: T.P.O. services went Up to London or Down from it and were thus named.

> A Travelling Post Office consists of one or more letter sorting carriages, with or without mail storage vans, attached to a train. In four cases …. all the vehicles forming the train are devoted entirely to Post Office business.[14]

The four special trains mentioned travelled through the night:

Below: Loading vans at a railway station.

London, Midland and Scottish Railway.
Down Special T.P.O.

Euston	dep. 8.30 p.m.
Aberdeen	arr. 7.52 a.m.

Up Special T.P.O.

Aberdeen	dep. 3.25 p.m.
Euston	arr. 3.55 a.m.

Great Western Railway
Great Western T.P.O. Down

Paddington	dep. 10.10 p.m.
Penzance	arr. 6.21 a.m.

Great Western T.P.O. Up

Penzance	dep. 6.48 p.m.
Paddington	arr. 3.50 a.m.

The L.M.S. *Down Special* was the subject of the famous G.P.O. film, *Night Mail*. Each T.P.O. received mail at the station from which it started its journey, at various stopping stations and also while running at full speed by means of trackside apparatus. Mails could be posted by the public later at the stations for an extra fee of ½d per item.

Sorting carriages and stowage vans varied in length from 42' to 70' but most were classified as 50 feet or 60 feet vehicles. Each railway company had a mail contract with the Post Office and was responsible for the "construction, maintenance and replacement of all sorting carriages".[15]

> One side of a sorting carriage is occupied by pigeon-hole sorting fittings, and separate groups of pigeon holes, of appropriate sizes, are used (a) for registered letters, (b) for small letters, (c) for long letters, newspapers and packets. On the other side of the carriage are rows of iron pegs (for suspending the mail bags into which the sorted correspondence is placed according to destination); the apparatus fittings; and other necessary equipment.[16]

To protect the staff from injury, the edges of shelves, tables etc were covered with horsehair padding. All the carriages were steam-heated and, by this time, had electric lighting installed. There were also electric urns to make tea, lavatories *en suite* and in some cases, wardrobe cupboards.

Down Special T.P.O.

For sorters on the *Down Special* work began at Euston at 7.15 p.m. Vans arrived continuously from London sorting offices and rail termini. Mails were despatched, not only from London, but forwarded from about 70 provincial offices in surrounding counties, and the Channel Islands.

> As the hour of departure approaches the contents of the station late-fee posting box are handed in, and at the last minute members of the public hurry to post their letters in the late-fee box on the train.[17]

On leaving Euston at 8.30 p.m. on its 540-mile journey the *Down Special* to Aberdeen was made up as follows:

Locomotive
Liverpool stowage van
Manchester stowage van
Preston stowage van
Stranraer stowage van
Aberdeen stowage van
Aberdeen apparatus van
Two Aberdeen sorting carriages
Three Glasgow sorting carriages
Glasgow stowage van.

Vehicles were detached en route, the first two at Crewe and the third at Preston. The Stranraer van left at Carlisle and the Glasgow vehicles at Carstairs Junction. However, additional carriages for Glasgow and Edinburgh were attached at Crewe and Carlisle. The train stopped at Rugby, Tamworth, Crewe, Preston, Carlisle, Carstairs Junction, Stirling and Perth, at no time for more than 10 minutes. Mails were received, or despatched, by apparatus (or both) at some 33 intermediate stations to Aberdeen.

The bag-exchange apparatus was first invented in the middle of the 19th century. It enabled the transfer of mail either for sorting or delivery without the train having to slow or stop and thus speeded transport considerably. Heavy leather pouches protected the mail from damage. The pouches, with mail weighing 50 or 60 lbs, were hung from the lineside standard.

> Shortly before the train reaches the standard, the apparatus officer in the T.P.O. opens the sliding door outside which the carriage net is fixed. By means of a lever inside the carriage he extends the net which takes the pouches off the lineside standard. The pouches drop into the net and fall through the open doorway on to the floor of the carriage.[18]

A similar operation took place in reverse to despatch the relevant pouches.

Despatches were also made, especially at Crewe, to connect to other T.P.O.s which started from there, or passed through. Of the 39 postal workers on board, 17 left at Crewe to return to London on the *Up Special*. Others came on board to work the section from Crewe to Glasgow.

When the King was at Balmoral a special despatch was made up to catch the train to Ballater leaving Aberdeen a few minutes after the arrival of the T.P.O. This was then taken from Ballater to the Castle by road. "So, having handled His Majesty's mails all the way, the T.P.O. finishes with the despatch of His Majesty's personal mails."[19]

Above: Travelling Post Office booklet featuring part of the bag exchange apparatus.

Below: Route of the Post Office railway

Post Office (London) Railway

Road traffic was congested in big cities. In order to transport mail quickly to and from the main sorting offices and railway stations in London the Post Office built an automatic electric underground railway. It ran over six miles on a narrow 2 ft gauge from Eastern District Office in Whitechapel through Liverpool Street Station, then the East Central District Office (King Edward Building), Mount Pleasant Sorting Office, West Central District Office at Holborn, Western District Office at Wimpole Street, Western Parcels Office at Baker Street arriving at Paddington District Office connecting with the railway station. The trains were driverless and controlled by staff in the stations.

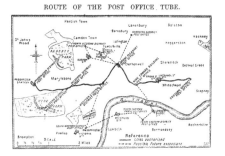

ROUTE OF THE POST OFFICE TUBE.

The original detailed plans had been drawn up by Harley Hugh Dalrymple-Hay for the Engineer-in-Chief's office in 1912. On 22 March that year trials of electric powered railways took place in Chelmsford by the British and Colonial Pneumatic Tube and Transport Company. Later, in January 1914, there was a further Post Office trial on Plumstead Marches where Dick Kerr and Co. Ltd built a short experimental track and a timber building for use as a station. From this "valuable data were obtained on matters concerning

Above: Trials of electric trains on Plumstead Marches, January 1914

electrical control, braking, speeds, curves, and so on."[20] Illustrations were featured in the *Illustrated London News*.[21]

Although work began in 1915 it was not completed until 1927. Work on the tunnels was completed early and art objects were stored there to save them from air raids during World War I. Electrification did not begin until 1924. The first 90 wagons produced by English Electric were four-wheeled and had a rigid body. These were soon replaced by wagons with bogies, introduced in 1930. The cars of four containers had a motor at each end

Mail was first carried on a short stretch during the General Strike of 1926 and it was brought into use for the Christmas mails in December 1927 but the railway did not fully open until 2 January 1928.

Inland Air Mails

In 1934 a number of air routes within the United Kingdom began to be used for airmail without surcharge. However, these were not the first attempts at internal airmail, though previous experiments had largely been over the sea to Ireland. The first was on 1 May 1924 from Belfast to Liverpool and was carried on intermittently until 2 June. Mail was carried in that direction only and about 1,000 lb was carried in total. A fee of ½d per 2 ounces was charged in addition to postage.

Then, during Liverpool Civic Week in 1928 an experimental airmail service was operated by the Calcutta flying boat, again between Liverpool and Belfast but in both directions. The service lasted for two weeks from 24 September but many flights were not made due to inclement weather. There was an air fee of 1d per 2 ounces.

Railway companies already carried letters up to 2 oz for an additional fee in order to expedite delivery. Rates for the Railway Letter Service had varied, after 1928 being 3d. In 1933, the Great Western Railway instituted a passenger air service from Cardiff to Plymouth and it was agreed that they could carry "railway letters" on these flights for the same fee. A 3d private railway letter stamp featuring an aircraft was designed by G. Sawyer and printed by Waterlows for use on mail carried by the company. The first official flight was on 15 May. One week later the service was extended to Birmingham. This service came to an end on 30 September. A few other companies also tried their luck but none was successful. Other labels produced included some for the Portsmouth, Southsea and Isle of Wight Aviation Ltd who flew covers privately on 2 February 1934.[22] From 7 to 12 May the same year there was even an Air Post Exhibition "Apex" at the Horticultural Hall, London. A variety of strange methods of transporting airmail were tried out in connection with this.

More seriously, at this time the Post Office was looking at what possibilities new internal air services might have for mail transport.

> Conveyance by air in a small country like the British Isles offers comparatively little advantage over the ordinary mails, especially when the time required for road transportation between the Post Office and the aerodrome at each end of the flight is taken into consideration.[23]

However, to isolated islands over sea channels surface mails were often poor and therefore a different matter. Complementing the much earlier Foula motor mailboat, the first internal service to benefit from airmail was to the Orkneys. Existing surface connections were slow.

An experimental, but official, air mail service was inaugurated on 29 May 1934 between Inverness and Kirkwall in the Orkney Islands for ordinary light weight letters (limited to 2 oz.) and postcards. As the official digest put it "This development marked the first use of air transport for the conveyance of correspondence not specially charged, labelled or marked for air conveyance."[24] It was operated by Highland Airways Ltd and souvenir envelopes and vignettes were prepared for the first flight.

At the same time, a more general inland air mail service between London and Glasgow was being contemplated. Williamson wrote to head postmasters of the cities and towns concerned informing them of the plans and asking for information about the quantity of mail which might be available.

A meeting of the main railway companies (London, Midland & Scottish; Great Western; Southern etc) was held with General Williamson on 6 June to discuss forthcoming air services. It was agreed that Railway Air Services Ltd would carry mails at the flat rate of 6d per pound on routes serving London, Birmingham, Manchester, Douglas, Belfast, Glasgow, Liverpool, Cardiff, Plymouth, Bristol, Southampton and Cowes on an experimental basis from 20 August. A surcharge on ordinary postage rates would act as a deterrent so it was proposed that the minimum rate would be the same as a surface letter, i.e. 1½d for the first two ounces but that each ounce above that would be an extra 1d. Treasury sanction was sought for this, and given, but with a proviso.

As you know, the delay here [at the Treasury] was due to some apprehension on our part at the decision reflected in the Inverness-Kirkwall service to abandon the policy hitherto followed of regarding air transport for mails as a luxury service for which the user should be called upon to pay the extra cost involved.

I understand … that the Post Office view is that the time has now arrived when, both from a postal and general point of view, it is desirable to regard inland air transport as a legitimate means of accelerating postal traffic, and that you should be free to use that method at your discretion. We should not wish to dissent from this view provided you are satisfied … that you will not be forced as a corollary to extend the principle to continental air services which, with a minor exception, are, of course, not run by British Companies. …It is, of course, understood that if you contemplated at any time an extension of the principle to continental or extra-European traffic, you would bring us into the picture.[25]

Above: Post Office railway control room (top)

First rigid body train (middle)

Bogie wagons in tunnel (bottom)

Above: Cover carried on the ill-fated first flight from Glasgow, signed by the pilot, John Lock (top)

Cover from London to Kirkwall connecting with the Inverness flight.

This, of course, is precisely what was to happen over the next two or three years.

Special envelopes were printed and a great deal of publicity was provided for the new services. The first day, 20 August, coincided with the day of issue of the first photogravure stamp, happily the 1½d, which was then used on much of the mail. When the day came, however, disaster struck. Newspaper headlines of that day read: "Thrill for new air mail passengers: A Terrific Bump; Passengers thrown out of seats; A Head through the Emergency Exit" (*The Evening Citizen*). "Air Mail Ordeal over Channel: Battle with Gale; Forced to land at Manchester" (*The Evening News*).

The first plane from Renfrew Aerodrome, a four-engined RAS Mercury piloted by Captain John Lock left shortly after 9.30 a.m. flying into a "wall of mist". It arrived at Belfast (Aldergrove) already 20 minutes late. It then took off again into a gale. Over the Irish Channel they experienced their "terrific bump".

Sir Harold Hartley, vice-president of the L.M.S. Railway and chairman of Railway Air Services, was thrown up through the emergency roof exit, his head and shoulders smashing the canvas open.[26]

Other passengers hit the baggage rack, though none was seriously injured. The plane arrived at Manchester, again 20 minutes late, and stayed there. The mail was taken on by train. Other services that day suffered similarly.

After such a disastrous beginning the services settled down but they were not a success, largely because of poor timings. Very little advantage, if any, was gained by sending letters by air and the aircraft left Glasgow and London far too early in the morning for mail to be ready. An internal report noted that "Apart from the opening day the public have adopted a rather apathetic attitude towards the new services."[27]

It took the London to Glasgow service as an example.

The plane leaves Croydon at 3.10 p.m. calling at Birmingham, Manchester (here it connects with a shuttle service – mails and freight only – to the Isle of Man and Belfast) Belfast and arriving at Glasgow at 7.30 p.m. the latest hour of posting in London is 1.0 p.m. At no place does the correspondence arrive in time to be delivered the same day.[28]

In the reverse direction the latest hour of posting at the Head Office in Glasgow was 6 a.m. As a result the volume of mail was negligible. The only place really to benefit was the Isle of Man.

The experiment ceased on 30 November when a new policy was brought in. In future, the Post Office would use at its discretion any regular flying service for the conveyance of first class mail "if by so doing the correspondence would be materially accelerated in delivery. No extra charge would be made to the public, and they would not be required to mark the letters specially for air conveyance."[29]

As a first step an agreement was made with Hillman's Airways Limited to convey mails between London, Liverpool, Belfast and Glasgow. This began on 1 December using De Havilland "Dragon" aircraft. On the same date the Inverness-Orkney air mail service was extended to include letter packets (in addition to light letters and postcards) and Wick and Thurso were brought into the service.

Blue Airmail Vans

The first blue airmail vans were introduced in connection with airmail pillar boxes in 1930, and the transport of mail by air overseas. The estimated cost of the London service at the time was £731 per annum. Initially, two new Morris Minor vans were adapted and painted Air Force blue, and the existing van employed on airmail duties was replaced with one also painted blue. On the side of the vans there was gold lettering, outlined in black, for "Royal Mail" and the Royal Cypher. There was also an oval, airmail sign on the roof. Strangely, the lettering on this was in red on black on the first vans. Shortly after their introduction Williamson indicated that he wanted to see a luminous (daylight) roof sign as an alternative.[30] The Stores Department sent two double-sided plaques, one in flame on black, the other blue on black. When Williamson saw them he definitely preferred the blue colour.[31] These were introduced shortly thereafter.

Above: Streamlined airmail van used for publicity purposes (top)

10 cwt, 70 cubic foot Morris airmail van leaving the Customs House, Croydon Aerodrome, 1933

It was not until 1934 that a special van was mooted, at the same time that internal air services were being envisaged. Col. Banks, the new Director General, suggested that one or two special air mail vans should be constructed for publicity purposes. "He has in mind that the body of the van should be in the shape of an aeroplane gondola and painted blue."[32] Rather than the gondola-shaped body, an aeroplane model or badge "symbolic of speed" on the roofs of existing vans was suggested as an alternative by Williamson and Tallents. Banks, however, still wanted to have "if only one effective looking van produced – with a more stream lined effect".[33] He had his way.

Three companies were asked if they would undertake the task of creating "rough designs for special coachwork on (a) a Morris Six-cylinder private chassis (b) a Morris 15 cwt commercial chassis."[34] Treasury approval was obtained for the supply of eight Minor and two 105 cu. ft. Vans for air mail services in London.

> The Postmaster-General desires one of the Minor Vans to take the form of an advertising car – a special body mounted on a standard 15 cwt chassis. Several

Above: Hey-Dolphin "Flier" cancelling machine in a London sorting office (c1914).

contractors have been consulted, designs received, and competitive estimates obtained. The Director General, The Controller, L.P.S. and the Public Relations Department have examined the designs submitted and have selected that of Messrs Duple Ltd – whose quotation too is lowest. The total cost of this car will approximate to £360 but there may be a small additional cost for special fitments.[35]

The vans were supplied by the beginning of November but as the streamlined version was to be used for publicity purposes, not only in London but also transferred to provincial towns, one more van was purchased to act as a reserve. The extra cost of the streamlined van was £250 over that of a modified Minor airmail van.

From late 1934 the streamlined van would appear at special events such as the launch of the Australia service at Croydon aerodrome or various exhibitions. In 1938, when the blue airmail pillar boxes were to be abolished, it was in Glasgow for the Empire Exhibition, having covered about 30,000 miles in the previous four years. It was then converted into an ordinary 105 cu. ft. van and painted red. By now, there were 26 Minor vans, one 105 cu. ft. van and one 250 cu. ft. van in operation on airmail services in the London Postal Region. All were repainted the standard red before being absorbed into the ordinary motor fleet.[36]

Above: 1939 New Zealand express stamp showing the streamlined van

There is one stamp which features the streamlined van. Strangely, it is a New Zealand express stamp issued in August 1939. Quite how, or why, is not clear.

Cancelling the stamps

Stamp-cancelling was the first mail-handling operation to be mechanised, the first installation dating from 1857. A number of experimental machines were tried out in the Victorian period but by the reign of George V the design of stamp cancelling machines had stabilised. Better features of one design tended to be incorporated into those of other manufacturers.

By 1922, three makes of machine dominated the cancelling field – a continuous impression machine manufactured by Krag Maskinfabrik in Norway, and single impression machines made by the Universal Stamping Machine Company and the International Postal Supply Company, both of American origin. Mail processed by single impression machines could be readily counted.[37] From 1927, Krag also had a single impression version in service.

International Postal Supply Company machines had been on trial since the late 19th century. It had been formed by, among others, George Hey and Matthew Dolphin (Hey's brother-in-law). Production machines of their "Flier" came into service from 1914.

The Universal Stamping Machine Company had been formed in 1908 in New York by the Maxim brothers (of machine gun fame). By 1910 initial trials on two of their models had taken place in London. In late 1913 the faster version was installed in London EC, London Inland Section, Doncaster, Glasgow, Manchester and St. Albans. The slower model went first to Croydon and Stockport.

A number of other manufacturers were also tried out including Alma, Cummins, Michelius and Klüssendorf.

Mount Pleasant Sorting Office

In 1934, Mount Pleasant in London was the site of the largest letter sorting office in the world, dealing with over 17,000,000 letters, packets, newspapers and circulars every week. Some 3,500 staff were employed despatching 11,500 bags of correspondence every day.[38]

On Friday, 2 November the Duke and Duchess of York opened the new reconstructed building, housing the Inland Section Sorting Office, the Postal Stores Depôt and the administrative offices. After speeches, the Duke operated switches which set the new German Zwietusch conveying equipment in motion. Afterwards, the Duchess, smiling, tried her hand at sorting *Post Office Magazines* to divisions and operating the stamp cancelling machine fitted with a special commemorative one-day slogan.

Mount Pleasant was an example of the extensive building programme carried out by the Ministry of Works on behalf of the Post Office in the inter-war years. Most effective were the public areas of offices which were now increasingly airy and pleasant to be in, and this was part of a deliberate plan of improvement.

Transorma Sorting Machine

To get to its destination, mail needed to be sorted more than once. Initially, after collection, it had to be primary sorted to destinations – towns or areas often far distant. Nearer the delivery point it needed a secondary sorting to get it to its office of delivery. There, it had to be sorted yet again down to the postman's walk. The farther the distance it had to travel the more often it was likely to require sorting. It was clear that machinery would save time and labour, ideally if it sorted mail from its point of collection right through to its final destination.

It was the enthusiasm and leadership of one man which brought about the installation of a sorting machine in a British sorting office. This was Brig. General Frederic H. Williamson. Born on 16 December 1876 he joined the General Post Office on 16 October 1899. He worked his way up rapidly in the central Secretary's Office and during World War I was Director of Army Postal Services (Home), hence his military rank. On 7 July 1922 he was appointed to the new post of Director of Postal Services controlling the Home Mails Branch and the Foreign & Colonial Branch. He was to galvanise investigations into speeding the mails. Later, in 1933, he was knighted and retired in 1937.

Above: Mount Pleasant sorting office (top)

The Duke and Duchess of York operating the cancelling machine with a commemorative cancel (bottom)

Prior to this, lack of manpower during World War I had stimulated ideas for various machines to replace them and a committee was set up to investigate. By 1922 several schemes had been examined but none seemed to offer a promising way forward. All were basically conveyors rather than sorters.[39] As the man in overall charge, Williamson gained first-hand knowledge of the necessity for some form of mechanisation and of the failures so far.

He probably saw the prototype Dutch Transorma sorting machine in 1927 when he attended the U.P.U. Airmail Conference at The Hague. Delegates to the Conference were invited to a demonstration in Delft. After this there was an approach to the Federation of British Industries. At a meeting in January 1928 with 13 firms the Post Office explained its needs with regard to the handling of small letters. Only three firms submitted proposals; only one was regarded as promising, that of Jackson & Co. A trial was set up in the London S.E. office with their prototype and tests were carried out for two years until October 1931. Then the apparatus was dismantled as yet another failure.

At this point, in the middle of 1932, Williamson became Chairman of what was now the Mechanical Aids Committee of the Post Office. Immediately, things began to move. The first working Transorma machine had been installed at Rotterdam in 1930. It had been invented in Holland in the 1920s by two engineers, J.J.M.L. Marchand, a former Dutch postal official and Professor J.C. Andriessen of the Technical College at Delft. Its name came from an amalgamation of TRANsportation and SORting of mail, together with the initials M and A of its inventors.

Visits were arranged to see the Rotterdam prototype, and another system in Berlin. Transorma manufacturers met Williamson in London. By now British officials had despaired of any successful British invention. It was thought that trying a foreign machine which worked might force some manufacturers to come up with a British alternative. So the Transorma machine was taken

Top: The Transorma machine at Brighton

Middle: Transorma operators

Bottom: Letter sorted on the first day, 7 October 1935, with operator ident d in magenta.

seriously. Detailed British Post Office criticisms of the first working machines resulted in improvements were first put into practice in the second machine at Rotterdam. After the usual, but relatively short, bureaucratic delays two revised version Transorma machines were purchased and installed as a trial at the small office at Brighton.

The Transorma could perform either primary or secondary sorting in one operation, but not both. Outward primary sorting would take a letter from Brighton to its town or area of delivery; inward secondary sorting would sort it to a box for a street or firm for the postman to deliver. The operation was purely mechanical. There were five positions at each machine for the operators.

An operator, called a Transormist, sat at his position on the upper floor of the machine. Letters were presented to him in a tray. Lifting one in his right hand, with his left he keyed a three number code representing the address – either town if outward or street or firm if inward. For outward operations there were 250 codes to be learned, for inward far fewer.

Having coded the address the operator dropped the letter into a slit. His coding set the pins on a carrier which then transported the letter on a moving chain of 75 carriers until it reached its correct box when the carrier opened and dropped the letter into the box.

The machines began full operation on 7 October 1935. They were very loud and described as a "Hungry Monster". Each operator had a key which impressed an identifying letter or number (idents) in red on to the letter. This was to check any missorts. Although the machines were to remain in successful operation for more than 30 years they were not the future path of sorting automation.[40]

A Rural Delivery

In the autumn of 1934, the daily journey of the red mail van from the village of Drymen round the banks of Loch Lomond to Rowardennan was rather romantically recorded by an English staff member for the *Post Office Magazine*.[41]

> A duty sheet is prosaic and on it one cannot expect much more than "5.35 a.m. collection from Drymen S.O. and Catter Letter Box: 6.20 a.m. receive mails from Balfron Motor at Blane Smithy and transfer collection." But between these points we saw sun-splashed whitewashed cottages with grey slate roofs, and the blush of rowan, and black cock and pheasants, and, in the distance, Ben Lomond.

Top: "Little red van" on the banks of Loch Lomond

Bottom: Early morning mail collection from Drymen Station post office

The van was then driven by John Angus up the east side of the loch through tiny hamlets with "soft Highland names" to Rowardennen, the end of the road. Illustrations showed Miss MacGregor, the sub-postmistress outside the Drymen Station post office (now Croftamie), lochside views and the inside of Rowardennan Sub Office, described as having one of the smallest telephone exchanges in the country.

This was a far cry from the backward rural service, often still on foot and horse, at the beginning of George V's reign, and a vital life-line.

1   POST 33/199B Lerwick. Foula and Walls mail packet service, contract. W. Dickinson to Secretary, GPO Edinburgh, 4 December 1911

2   ibid J.D. Leiper, Postmaster, Lerwick to the Surveyor. 18 December 1911

3   ibid P.P. Gear, Sub-postmaster Foula, to J.D. Leiper 30 January 1912

4   ibid. G.W. Bedford, Secretary, Edinburgh to Secretary GPO 23 February 1912

5   ibid J.D. Leiper to Surveyor 29 November 1912

6   **Williamson, F.H.** "Red Vans" *Post Office Magazine* January 1934 p6

7   **Wheeler, Maj. C.** "The Development of Mechanical Transport in the G.P.O." *St Martin's-le-Grand* 1933 p172

8   ibid Part III *St. Martin's-le-Grand* Vol. XLIII 1933 p170

9   ibid Part IV p272

10   **Husdon, Capt. A.** *Post Office Motor Transport* P.O. Green Paper No.28 1936 p6

11   **Stray, J.** *Moving the Mail ... By Road* 2006. p26

12   **Hudson** op cit p4

13   Listed with timings in POST 18/13 List of Travelling Post Offices, Sorting Carriages and Mail Bag Duties, 1928

14   **Rowden, J.J.C.** *The Travelling Post Office* P.O. Green Paper No.24 1935 p3

15   ibid p6

16   ibid

17   ibid p9

18   ibid p7

19   ibid p12

20   **Carter, Maj. W.G.** *Post Office (London) Railway* P.O. Green Paper No. 36, 193.. p3

21   *Illustrated London News* Vol. 144 p 165, 31 January 1914

22   See **Redgrove, H.S.** *The Air Mails of the British Isles* 1940

23   POST 33/4432 Air mail services of railway companies: proposed change by Post Office in its inland air mail, parts 1 & 2. D. Banks to Treasury, 3 July 1934

24   POST 50/7 Imperial & Foreign Air Mail Services. Summary

25   POST 33/4432 Air mail services of Railway Companies: proposed change by Post Office in its inland air mail. F.P. Robinson, Treasury to Banks 11 July 1934

26   POST 33/4590 Air Mails: inland services London-Liverpool-Belfast-Glasgow. September 1934

27   ibid

28   ibid

29   POST 50/7 op cit

30   POST 33/2979B Posting Boxes for air mail correspondence: special blue boxes erected in London and the provinces, part 1. W.C. Burns, P.O. Stores, M.T. Section to F.H. Williamson, 16 September 1930

31   ibid. Note to Burns 23 September 1930.

32   POST 33/4709 Blue air mail letter boxes, vans: London introduction, abolition. 12 March 1934

33   ibid. 29 June 1934

34   ibid. 28 July 1934

35   ibid. A. Hudson, Engineering Dept. To Personnel Dept., 22 September 1934

36   ibid. 18 August and 1 November 1938.

37   For details see **Peach, J.** "Cancelling Machines: Who made them, how they worked and what they printed – 3. 1910 to 1933" pp E1-34 in **Muir, D.N. (Ed.)** *British Postal Mechanisation: A Handbook* 1993-

38   "Mount Pleasant New Sorting Office – Ceremonial Opening by the Duke of York" *Post Office Magazine* December 1934, pp544-5

39   **Muir, D.N.** "Early British Sorting Machines" ppC1-12 in **Muir, D.N. (Ed)** *British Postal Mechanisation: A Handbook* 1993-

40   Full details of construction, operation and idents in **Muir, D.N.** *The Transorma at Brighton* 2006

41   **Briant, F. Heathcote** "Bonny Banks of Loch Lomond" *Post Office Magazine* April 1935 pp114-6

15

CELEBRATION

OF EMPIRE, POSTS & STAMPS

T oday, there are upwards of 12 new issues of Royal Mail special stamps a year. In all the 25 years of King George V's reign there were only three *in total*. Then, events, great and small, passed without philatelic celebration, or even notice. There were enough definitive stamps in circulation to meet postal needs. On international mails, commemorative stamps of limited validity had been banned by the Universal Postal Union up to 1920 - though that regulation had lapsed at that year's U.P.U. Congress in Madrid when Spain issued stamps for the Congress itself. So it was not until 1923 that any serious suggestion was made of issuing a commemorative stamp in Britain.

British Empire Exhibition

The occasion was the British Empire Exhibition held at Wembley. After World War I – with the addition of German colonies and parts of the Ottoman Empire mandated by the League of Nations – the British Empire was at its greatest extent, covering a quarter of the globe. The diversity and extent of the Empire was celebrated by a great exhibition to be opened by the King on 23 April 1924. All the Dominions, India and groups of smaller colonies built pavilions in a 216-acre site featuring their daily lives and work in natural settings. Built of ferro-concrete were huge Palaces of Engineering and Industry, and a Stadium for sporting events.[1]

The Government Pavilion was designed by Maxwell Ayrton and took eight months to complete. Within it was the Post Office gallery where there were working machines to convey messages – pneumatic tubes, telegraphs, telephone equipment and a demonstration of the automatic pick-up system for mail bags from travelling post offices. There was also a working model, one inch to one foot in scale, of the Post Office underground railway, then being built in London.

Above: The Post Office gallery in the Government Pavilion with the model of the Post Office underground railway (top)

Around the exhibition site there were two post offices (a head office and a branch office in the Palace of Engineering), a number of stamp vending machines and various posting boxes. In many of the pavilions Frank Godden, the stamp dealer, had organised displays of classic and later stamps of the countries concerned. This clearly would have been an attraction for the King. According to *The Times*

> The displays of the Ceylon and Newfoundland Pavilions attracted the close attention of the King, whose collection of Imperial postage stamps is the finest extant, on one of his visits to Wembley. His Majesty commented particularly upon the array of the scarce and beautiful pence series of both the possessions.

A number of essays and proofs were also on show, and on the stands of both
De La Rue and Waterlows in the Palace of Industry. Waterlows also produced
an attractive advertising label featuring the Palace of Industry, printed in a large
number of colour standards. King George visited the Exhibition on several
occasions, especially in May when the weather improved, conscientiously taking in
all the pavilions (and showing round visiting royalty from Romania and Italy).

There were to be a total of 17,403,267 visitors passing through the turnstiles by 1 November.

Philatelic Commemoration

The first intimation that this exhibition might be commemorated by special stamps came
in April 1923. Then it was confined to special postal stationery and postmarks. Sir Evelyn
Murray, Secretary to the Post Office, proposed: "Stamped Postcards, Stamped Envelopes
and possibly Letter Cards, available for postage inland or within the British Empire, to
be placed on sale at the Exhibition Post Office. No special adhesive stamp to be issued."
These were not to be on sale elsewhere "but this of course will not prevent Stamp dealers
from obtaining them." The imprinted stamp should be larger than the ordinary definitives
and "include besides the King's head some illustration characteristic of the Dominions."
However, he concluded "Is it advisable to exclude adhesive stamps?"[2]

By May it was decided that:

> The stamped stationery to be sold will consist of postcards with the 1d and 1½d stamp
> and envelopes and letter-cards with the 1½d stamp. If there is no special difficulty in
> obtaining supplies, adhesive stamps of the values 1d and 1½d will also be issued.[3]

Despite the fact that the Exhibition was due in April the following year there seemed little
urgency in getting any designs. It was not until 17 November that Murray wrote to Sir Cecil
Harcourt Smith, Vice Chairman of the British Institute of Industrial Art and Director of the
Victoria & Albert Museum. Harcourt Smith was also a member of the newly established
Royal Mint Advisory Committee on the Design of Coins, Medals, Seals and Decorations
where he was described as a "vigorous-minded man".[4] Murray informed Harcourt Smith of
the proposal to issue stamps and asked for advice on artistic design from the Council of the
British Institute of Industrial Art. They created a small sub-committee and made a number
of recommendations stating that "In view of the commemorative nature of the stamps it
would be an advantage if the terms of reference were enlarged so that the designs need not
necessarily include a portrait head which it is thought may unduly restrict the opportunity
of obtaining a fine result."[5] This showed a lack of understanding.

At the same time the Treasury wrote to Murray reminding him of the existence of the
standing Royal Mint committee which was felt to be the appropriate body to deal with
designs. News of the idea had also reached the King whose views were typically forthright.

> The King has heard of the proposal to issue a commemorative stamp at the British
> Empire Exhibition and although His Majesty is not very much in favour of stamps of
> this sort, because the whole idea is un-English and is copied from America, the King
> thinks that if it is to be done at all, it should be done properly. Assuming therefore
> that the Post Office has approved of the general idea, His Majesty hopes that a really
> competent Committee will be appointed to assist the Master of the Mint with the

designs. The King is of the opinion that it is a waste of time to put people on the Committee who do not know anything about stamps or designs, and trusts that you will see that a thoroughly good Committee is appointed. His Majesty would like Mr E D Bacon, CVO, Buckingham Palace, put on the Committee in the interests of the Philatelists' Society.[6]

The Royal Mint Advisory Committee had been established in April 1922 with its members appointed by the King. Two of those members, Sir Cecil Harcourt Smith and the Earl of Crawford and Balcarres (Trustee of the National Portrait Gallery and the British Museum, and son of the great stamp collector and bibliophile), were to serve on the ad hoc stamp committee. Others mirrored the Royal Mint appointments - from the Royal College of Art (Professor Anning Bell), the LCC Central School of Arts and Crafts (F.V. Burridge). From the Post Office came Brig. General Williamson and Murray who acted as Chairman.

On 16 January 1924, only three months before the opening of the Exhibition, the newly formed British Empire Stamp Committee held its first meeting. There were to be two stamps of 1d and 1½d to bear the portrait of the King as in the intaglio high value Seahorses. The words "British Empire Exhibition 1924" had to form part of the design and the design itself was to be symbolic of the British Empire. The Committee decided to invite eight artists to submit designs. An "honorarium" of 10 guineas would be paid to each and 90 guineas in addition for any design which was accepted.

Those invited were:
John D Batten
Eric Gill
George Kruger Gray
F.C. Herrick
Harold Nelson
F. Richards
Noel Rooke
E.W. Tristram

Only five submitted designs (Batten, Gill, Nelson, Rooke and Tristram). Herrick did not create any stamp designs but he had designed the Egyptian-style lion used to advertise the Exhibition. He had also created lettering, very closely based on Latin inscriptions on Trajan's column, for use on posters. Eric Gill submitted four designs in two sets of two. In a long letter he explained that he believed "Elaborate pictorial designs are untrue to the notion of a postage stamp. A postage stamp, as the name implies, is primarily a stamp. A 'picture' stamp is an absurdity - especially when it is remembered that it will often be obliterated by the postmark or disfigured by dirt."[7] One set of designs was the "British Empire as a business proposition". The 1½d version featured various mechanical implements on the left with a sheaf of corn on the right, the two connected by a telegraph.

Above: Lion symbol designed by F.C. Herrick, and the 1924 Exhibition map

Left: Harold Nelson's unadopted design featuring St George and the Dragon

Below: Selected design by Eric Gill not liked by the King

Gill's other set was headed "The Empire viewed historically". The 1½d design he described as follows: "The Empire is a thing fought for and to be fought for. The British Lion is an attitude of defiance."

Designs by others featured emblems of the British Isles and Empire, that by Rooke being an engraving on wood. Subject to amendments two designs were recommended by the Stamp Committee on 19 February – a design by Harold Nelson featuring a British lion for the 1d stamp and Gill's mechanical implements design for the 1½d.

Below: Accepted artwork by Harold Nelson, and revised version

Gill wrote at length explaining how very few alterations were possible, though some were undertaken.

Sir Cecil Harcourt Smith recommended that altered design as it stood. "After all we felt, and I think the Committee in general felt, that the real charm of Gill's design lies not so much in the composition of the fields as in the beautiful lettering which surrounds it."[8] Nelson amended his design, particularly with regard to the background (where the sea became land), and both were then submitted to the King - whose views were unsurprising. Stamfordham wrote on 28 February:

His Majesty very much likes the 1½d design by Mr Harold Nelson; but, I am sorry to say, the King cannot think Mr Gill's 1½d design (which I understand is recommended by the Committee) at all attractive. His Majesty rather likes the design of Mr Harold Nelson's 1d stamp, St George and the Dragon; but, as the choice of this would give both designs to one artist, the King would be in favour of having Mr Nelson's 1½d design, as chosen by the Committee, for both the 1d and 1½d issues, with of course different colours for the two stamps.[9]

Although this lost the services of a great, if cantankerous, typographer we may be thankful, in this instance, that it did.

Harold Nelson, born in Dorchester in 1871, had studied at the Lambeth School of Art and the Central School of Arts and Crafts. His chief work was in book illustration and he had exhibited at the Royal Academy and other establishments since 1899.

In the same letter quoted above the King went on to suggest that the stamps might be sold considerably above face value, at 1/- and 1/6d respectively, the premium being given to the King Edward's Hospital Fund. He referred to the 1890 precedent when, on the occasion of the Jubilee of the Penny Post, an envelope and postcard were sold at a similar amount with the considerable proceeds going to the Rowland Hill Benevolent Fund. This caused Murray to consult Sir Otto Niemeyer at the Treasury, sending him a memorandum on the subject. In his covering letter he wrote: "The suggestion, I happen to know, emanates from the King's private stamp collector."[10]

Above: Harold Nelson

Murray derided the proposal and hoped that Niemeyer would agree.

> The issue of special stamps for commemorative purposes and their sale at fancy prices is a well known device in many foreign countries for the purpose of raising revenue for special or general purposes. But I should regard it as beneath the dignity of Great Britain. If we embark on devices of this kind, there are many simpler means of manufacturing rarities for philatelists which would no doubt command fancy prices and swell the Post Office receipts.[11]

Happily, Niemeyer agreed, in equally strong terms. Referring to the 1890 precedent he said that "it seems to me to have been wholly illegal and I cannot believe that Parliament, through the Public Accounts Committee, would accept it in modern conditions."[12] The King eventually accepted defeat.

Production

Waterlow & Sons Ltd had just taken over the contract to print the low value definitives and they represented to the Post Office that they had the right to print the new commemoratives. Nevertheless, as the stamps were to be printed recess it was regarded as supplementary to the main contract. Waterlows quoted:

Engraving original die and supplying printing plates for 1d and 1½d denominations	£130 0 0

Printing
Initial orders:

1 million 1d stamps	£120.16. 8
½ million 1½d stamps	£62.10. 0

Subsequent orders were quoted slightly lower for printing one million stamps.

J.A.C. Harrison was now working for Waterlows and he was entrusted with engraving the recess dies for the adhesive stamps. Plates (120-set – two panes of 60) were also to be made by Waterlows rather than the Royal Mint and printing would take place at their plant in Clifton Street, London E.C. rather than their Watford works.

Below: Recess head die proof

It was only on 5 March that Waterlows were given Nelson's artwork and instructed to proceed immediately with the engraving of the recess dies. The only recess head die was that contained within the original Seahorse master die, but the Mint were able to make a roller from that of the head alone. Harrison then engraved the frame and design around this. Matters proceeded apace and proofs of the 1½d die were submitted to the King on 27 March. These were returned approved four days later and by 3 April Waterlows were rolling in the stamp image on printing cylinders. Only one plate of each value was created. They began printing the

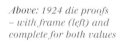

1½d on 11 April and the 1d on the 14th. Special watermarked paper suitable for recess printing had been obtained from Joynsons.

Above: 1924 die proofs – with frame (left) and complete for both values

There then came the question of perforation. Back in January Sir William Waterlow had said that perforation as in definitive stamps would require a new perforating box, costing about £60. But for such a small quantity and recess printing he would not recommend such comb perforation. Rather he could provide - at no extra cost - "cross perforation" in any size of stamp. "Cross perforation [normally termed 'line perforation'] is not quite so satisfactory at the corners of the stamps but he thinks it would give quite good enough results." Here only a single line of perforations is utilised horizontally and the sheets are turned to provide the vertical sides, cutting the corners imperfectly. Although a 1mm diameter hole was specified Waterlows did not have this and offered a much smaller pin.

Initial supplies, which were put on sale on 23 April, were perforated in this manner, with no special box being supplied by Grovers. However, line (or cross) perforation caused difficulties when the sheet stamps were split and coiled into rolls for stamp vending machines, and generally perforation was not up to standard.

Stamp Vending Machines

There were two post offices at the Exhibition where, on average, some 400,000 stamps a week were being sold. This pressure on counters needed to be relieved and representations were made for the provision of stamp vending machines. Immediately, a number of problems were obvious. The stamps were larger than standard and would not fit existing machines; the 1½d stamp would require two coins rather than one, requiring a change of mechanism; and the perforations needed to be improved so that the gripper pins in the machines would work. Clearly, the stamps also had to be made into rolls at an extra cost.

Above: Commercial first day cover

As far as the machines were concerned, these were supplied by the British Stamp & Ticket Automatic Delivery Company (BSTAD), the Director of which, Mrs Georgina Kermode, had died in September 1923. They had formerly installed a machine at the House of Commons Post Office to sell 1½d stamps and this had worked satisfactorily. It was still available and others could be supplied in a few weeks. Experiments in the Engineer-in-Chief's office proved that adjustments could be made to the machines to accommodate the larger stamps. Special machines were ordered from BSTAD in due course.

Waterlows' quotation for creating the rolls from sheets was too high but the BSTAD had previously made up rolls for their own machines for a long time and offered to do so again at the price paid to Harrisons before the contract passed to Waterlows. This was later increased from 3¼d to 6d because of various difficulties.[13] There now only remained the question of perforation.

The only solution was to purchase a new Punch Box for comb perforation from Grovers. That firm's Technical Director, F.B. Woolford advised that to ensure satisfactory results a "split box" was needed, costing £63 and taking three weeks to make. On 30 May the Post Office agreed the figure, eventually paying half.

> The split box can be adjusted and is designed to overcome the exceptional difficulties due to the abnormal expansion and contraction of the paper in the recess printing process. Messrs. Waterlow are prepared to guarantee that its use will result in the stamps being perforated evenly and at perfectly regular intervals.[14]

Grovers made a point of measuring a sheet of stamps themselves, not accepting dimensions supplied by the Post Office, and then built a narrow split box to perforate the entire width of the double pane of stamps.[15] Through June and July stamps continued to be perforated line at Waterlows' Clifton St works but at the end of July the split box was ready and installed in Watford. Thenceforward, stamps were printed at Clifton Street but perforated in Watford.

The BSTAD had made various experiments in creating rolls with cancelled sheets of stamps during May. They were then supplied direct by the Post Office. However, it was not until 1 August that the first finished rolls were despatched to the Exhibition post offices for immediate use, although the vending machines did not go into operation until the 4th (after the August Bank Holiday). The rolls, of 1200 stamps each, were vertically delivered and joined at every 10th stamp.

There were five (double – for both 1d and 1½d stamps) "official" stamp-vending machines. These were located outside the Head Post Office, outside the Branch Office at the Palace of Engineering, in the Post Office exhibit in the Government Pavilion, and one in each of the two telephone call office kiosks - one in the amusement park at the North Entrance and one at another kiosk near the South West entrance. All rolls supplied for the machines outside the two post offices were comb perforated. The others were supplied by BSTAD with "Kermode" rolls made up from stamps (some line-perforated) purchased by them from the London Chief Office. In addition to the five pairs of "official" machines four pairs of patent Brookers machines were also in use and controlled by BSTAD under licence from the Post Office. They were also supplied with stamps by BSTAD. Some sideways delivered coil stamps have been identified and these may have come from these machines.[16] Locations of these machines are not clear, but one may well have been at, or in, the Canadian Pavilion.

A total of 220 rolls of 1d and 75 rolls of the 1½d stamps were supplied by BSTAD for the two Post Office machines. Of these 22 rolls of the 1d and 16 of the 1½d were recorded as remaining unsold at the end of 1925.[17]

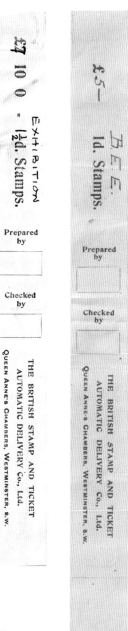

Above: BSTAD roll leaders for the 1924 Exhibition stamps amended in manuscript.

Above: 1924 Wembley postcard used with the Exhibition lion machine cancellation

Stamped Stationery

The stamped postal stationery (postcards, envelopes and lettercards) also produced were printed letterpress by McCorquodales. Although also supplementary to their contract they were supplied at contract prices with the exception of the "A"-sized envelopes. These were charged at 6/8d per 1,000, an increase of 1/3d. Ordinary "A" envelopes were embossed with stamps and gummed, folded and completed on a specially designed machine. This could not be adapted for flat-printed stamps.

In March, McCorquodales' quoted approximate prices for the production of dies for the printing of stamped postal stationery[18]:

Cutting, engraving and making two complete original dies for 1d and 1½d stamps respectively	£25.0.0.
24 working dies @ 4/6 each	£5.8.0.
Total approx.	£30.0.0.

The two master letterpress dies were engraved by Mr MacDonald of Thomas MacDonald & Sons (Engravers) Ltd. Working dies were prepared from these for McCorquodales' by the Nickeloid Electrotype Company of New Street Hill, London EC4.

Items issued at the Exhibition (with sales compared to ordinary versions elsewhere from May to October) were:

	BEE	Ordinary
1½d "A" envelopes	75,000	2,734,000
1½d Lettercards	50,000	6,639,000
1d Inland postcard (stout)	100,000	1,405,500*
1½d International postcard (thin)	12,000	- **

*also 25,190,660 thin postcards
**old stout 1½d issued

Sales & Public Reaction

The stamps and stationery were to promote and advertise the British Empire Exhibition at Wembley. Their issue was not primarily intended as a money-making exercise. As a result, sales of the stamps etc were initially confined to the Exhibition site, making them an added attraction. Later, stamp dealers could obtain supplies from postal headquarters.

In the *Daily Telegraph* on 1 May, in his weekly philatelic column, the great philatelic writer Fred Melville found the design appropriate and pleasing, and better engraved and printed than the standard definitives.

The stamps were printed in sheets of 120, contained in two panes (10 rows of six stamps for each pane). These panes were separated before the stamps were delivered to post office counters. Waterlows delivered the following amounts of stamps during 1924:

1d
Good	=	8,143,620	Singles
Waste	=	1,096,380	Singles
	=	9,240,000	

1½d
Good	=	6,046,200	Singles
Waste	=	433,800	Singles
	=	6,480,000	
Total	=	15,720,000	

Actual sales are more difficult to determine as the 1924 stamps were also available during 1925, and even into 1926. Sold during the 1924 Exhibition season (from 1 May to 31 October 1924) were 7,250,000 1d stamps, and 5,692,000 1½d stamps, though this excludes the first week.

It was not until the stamps had been issued and sales commenced that it was discovered that Waterlows had numbered the sheets. Waterlows had been in the habit of numbering sheets of stamps produced for the colonies. These numbers, at the top right hand corner were in addition to the control letter and year which had always been at the bottom of the sheet. On discovering this P.O. Stores immediately asked Waterlows not to print them and those already numbered were removed from sale.

Postmarks

Special postmarks were in use at the Exhibition. In February the Design Committee, examining drawings from the Engineer-in-Chief's office, recommended the inclusion of the diagrammatic "Egyptian-style" lion created by F.C. Herrick for advertising posters. This was then used in both handstamps and machine cancellations. Steel counter dat-estamps were in use at the Palaces of Engineering and Industry, and at the sorting office in the Stadium. Occasionally, one was available for events in the Conference Hall (and one was inscribed "Wembley Park" for use at the N.W.D.O.). For registered mail there were also oval rubber handstamps with the lion. For parcels there were also circular pictorial rubber handstamps and non-pictorial rectangular rubber cancellations.

Slogan machine cancellations had been in use in various towns around Britain since 1922 to advertise the Exhibition. They were also widely used throughout the Empire.

Again in 1925

The Exhibition closed on 1 November 1924, though the Exhibition post office remained open for some time. It was clear, however, that it might re-open the following year and stamp vending machines, for example, were stored on site. By December, Sir Travers Clarke of the Exhibition Committee was writing to Murray confirming that there would be another exhibition in 1925 and asking that stamps be issued again, if possible four rather than two. It was not until 9 February 1925 that Murray responded, saying that "We propose to re-issue the stamps of last year, altering the date in the design from 1924 to 1925, and I have been informed

Below: Initial sketch (top) and artwork (bottom) for the Palace of Engineering datestamp.

unofficially that the King approves this proposal."[19]

Waterlows were immediately informed and asked to have the dates altered on the recess master dies and plates. Specifications were exactly as before except that the sheets were to be "well and efficiently comb perforated". This necessitated Harrison re-engraving the die. Rather than start again from scratch he took the original master dies and, at the appropriate point with the numeral "4" of "1924", hammered out a very small area of the metal from the rear of the die. He then re-engraved a "5" in place of the "4" and, at the same time, corrected the slightly damaged leaf surround. From these altered master dies new transfer rollers were taken and new plates made, again only one of each value. The cost of altering the dies and producing the new plates was £50.

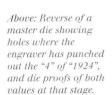

Above: Reverse of a master die showing holes where the engraver has punched out the "4" of "1924", and die proofs of both values at that stage.

Below: Completed die proofs of the 1925 designs

Stationery and rolls were also produced as in 1924 and post-marks were re-introduced. The Exhibition re-opened on 9 May but to rather less fanfare. By 31 October, when it closed, 9,699,231 people had visited, just over half the previous year's total.

Stamps and stationery supplied by the contractors in 1925 were:

Description	Quantity	
1d stamps in sheets	45,800	sheets of 60
1½d stamps in sheets	23,900	sheets of 60
1d stamps in rolls	249	rolls of 1200
1½d stamps in rolls	74	rolls of 1200
Inland Postcards, Stout	750	parcels of 100
International postcards	30	parcels of 240
"A" Postage Envelopes	250	parcels of 220
Letter Cards	350	parcels of 100

Revised Postal Arrangements

In 1925, the building previously known as the Palace of Engineering was re-named the Palace of Housing and Transport and became the Head Post Office, while the Palace of Industry Head Office became the Palace of Industry Branch Office. The Head Office (for a short time back in the Palace of Industry) eventually closed on 19 November.

Where in 1924 there had been five "official" vending machines at the 1925 Exhibition there were seven "official" pairs of machines: two at the entrances to the new Head Office; two at the entrances to the Branch Office in the Palace of Industry; two in the Post Office Exhibit in the British Government Pavilion; one in the Imperial Airways Exhibit in the Palace of Housing and Transport. The telephone call office kiosk installations of the previous year were apparently not re-used.

Rolls had been produced by both BSTAD and Waterlows for the 1925 stamps. Those made up by Waterlows often caused problems in the BSTAD machines, partly due to poor joining and partly because the shrinkage of the paper in printing was slightly different. Poor maintenance was also blamed. The total number of vending machines in use at Wembley is not certain, although the additional machines in the Government Pavilion seem to have been single, but on 19 September 1928 the Stores Department reported that 11 wooden SVM cases and six pedestals had been recovered from the Exhibition. They were sold for £3 10s.

The first British commemoratives had been a success, though the lack of fresh designs for the 1925 versions caused dismay. Nevertheless, four years were to elapse before the next commemorative stamp issue. Left-over paper was used to print the new Imperial Reply Coupons.

International Postal Union Congress (I.P.U.C.)

On Friday, 10 May 1929, the Prince of Wales opened the ninth Congress of the Universal Postal Union, the first to be held in London. The King was still convalescing in Bognor from a very severe illness, though news of his impending return to Windsor appeared in the same newspapers as reports on the opening of the Congress. This was to be the occasion of Britain's second commemorative issue of stamps.

Left: Dignitaries involved in the Congress (including Brig. Gen. Williamson top left)

Below: Civil Service Commission Building, Burlington Gardens (top) and a plenary session of the Congress (bottom)

The opening ceremony took place in the Royal Gallery of the House of Lords. Subsequent meetings of the over 180 delegates and "attachés" (including delegates from Soviet Russia which did not have full diplomatic relations with Britain) were held over the next two months in the Civil Service Commission Building, 6 Burlington Gardens, London W.1. Proceedings were conducted wholly in French, the language (even today) of the U.P.U.

Founded in 1874, the Universal Postal Union controlled and regulated all international exchanges of mail. It held a congress every four to six years, sometimes with intermediary conferences, where detailed regulations were discussed and agreed. Prior to the London Congress there had been an important airmail conference at The Hague in 1927 and agreements there were to be incorporated into the basic Convention in London. Apart from extensive detail, perhaps the most important innovation resulting from

the London Congress was the introduction of the category of "small packets" internationally, in effect a small parcel post by letter mail. It was agreed that these could be up to 1 kilogram in weight, charged at 15 centimes per 50 grammes, with a minimum charge of 50 centimes. All internationally agreed rates were given in theoretical gold francs and centimes which were then translated into the local currency. As Britain was host, Brigadier General F.H. Williamson, Director of Postal Services, was made executive President of the Congress and gave the opening address. During the Congress the mandated state of Iraq signed the Convention, and the newly created Vatican City State "adhered" to all the rules. The Irish Free State sent delegates independently for the first time.[20]

Stamp Issue a "Tradition"

The previous Congresses had been held in Madrid (1920) and Stockholm (1924). Both Spain and Sweden had issued sets of stamps to mark them, Sweden issuing two sets as it was also the 50th anniversary of the U.P.U.'s foundation. According to a memorandum prepared by Captain D.O. Lumley of the Secretary's office "Tradition would therefore seem to require some sort of special issue in connection with the London Congress in 1929."[21] He suggested that either there should be a complete range of stamps from ½d to 1/-, or a more limited range, as for Wembley, but of ½d, 1d, 1½d, and 2½d. The adoption of either of these

> would mean a considerable increase of stamp revenue which might be devoted to the payment of the cost of entertaining the Congress. It is understood that Sweden made over £30,000 from the sale of her Stamps and that the hospitality – often very lavish – which she offered at Stockholm, cost her nothing at all in consequence. There is probably more to be made from the issue of a whole series of stamps than from the issue of only a few; but the issue of values other than those commonly used would probably result in advantage only to the pockets of stamp dealers.[22]

This theme of revenue-raising, and covering costs, was taken up by the Postmaster General, Sir W. Mitchell-Thomson, when he wrote to the King asking for his approval.

> It has become a recognised custom for the country in which the Congress is held to issue a commemorative series of postage stamps, and I should propose to follow this precedent; although the British Post Office has been averse to the production of commemorative issues, it must be admitted that special stamps, through their sale to philatelists, would yield a revenue which would go far to meet the considerable expenses of holding the Congress and entertaining the foreign delegates.[23]

He proposed setting up a committee to obtain designs. The King approved but, after making sure that his head would be part of the design, decided not to nominate any member of the committee.[24] He did not comment on the idea of making money out of stamp collectors. Enquiries of the stamp trade had elicited the notion that 20,000 people would buy a £1 stamp, considerably increased if the issue were restricted to one year. At this time there was no £1 denomination on sale.

Problems with a "Committee of taste"

Unlike the Royal Mint there was no standing Committee to advise on stamp designs. That created for the Wembley stamps had been disbanded, their work done. The Postmaster

General asked the Earl of Crawford and Balcarres, now Chairman of the Royal Fine Arts Commission, if he and other members of the RFAC would be members of a committee. This would be together with Post Office and other representatives who would provide technical expertise. Unfortunately, artistic temperament was offended. While the Commissioners recognised that they lacked such technical knowledge to undertake the task on their own, they did not wish to be part of a committee of which they were only one or two members. Despite entreaty, they refused to take part. The position was summed up succinctly by the Postmaster General in a letter to Lord Crawford:

> ...frankly, I do not understand why your colleagues should feel that the inclusion of other persons, who are concerned with the technical rather than the aesthetic side of the problem, should be a bar to their assisting. It seems to come to this, that the Commission cannot function without expert assistance and will not function with it; this is a very unfortunate impasse, especially as it will mean that in setting up my Committee of taste, I shall, I suppose, have to regard membership of the Royal Commission, which was expressly constituted as arbiters of taste, as a positive disqualification.[25]

Crawford did recommend a number of people who he thought might be willing to serve, two of whom had been on the 1924 Committee. In the end the new Committee consisted of: Sir G. E. P. Murray (Chairman – Secretary to the Post Office), Sir Cecil Harcourt Smith, F. V. Burridge, and Professor Anning Bell (all on the previous Committee); with Sir Frank Short, a noted engraver and Campbell Dodgson, the head of the Print Room at the British Museum.

Their first meeting was held on 8 November 1928 when they decided to invite nine artists to submit designs, together with the printing firms of Waterlows and Bradbury Wilkinson. They were asked to consider printing techniques to be used. In the case of the £1 stamp they decided on recess or line engraving. For the low values, they were for the first time given the option of photogravure. Waterlows had recently demonstrated this process to postal officials at their Watford plant. Stamps being printed for San Salvador had impressed and they said they could guarantee uniformity of colour, a problem which had previously been a hindrance.

Above: Designs submitted by Eric Gill

Below: Designs submitted by Edwin Arnold (left) and Miss E.M. Jackman of Bradbury Wilkinson

Prices were quoted well in advance of letterpress stamps and there were a number of requirements for the design. The Committee decided to postpone a decision as to printing method which as a result effectively killed the possibility.

In the instructions to artists were various requirements as to King's head and legend. However, for the £1 stamp it was desirable that any design "should be either of national significance or should be symbolic of

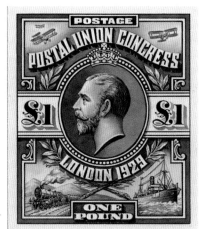

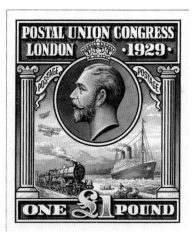

the assembly which it is intended to commemorate."[26] The same fees would be offered as before.

Artists who submitted designs were: L. Doman, F.W. (John) Farleigh, Eric Gill, Harold Nelson, Eric Ravilious and Noel Rooke. Both printing firms also complied with three staff artists from each preparing artwork. These were considered by the Committee on 12 December when two designs by Farleigh were chosen for the ½d and 2½d stamps and one by Ernest Linzell of Waterlows for the 1d and 1½d stamps. Farleigh was 28 at the time and a teacher of art at the Central School of Arts. Linzell was nearing 60 and had designed a number of banknotes and stamps for his employers.

Right: F.W. (John) Farleigh

For the £1 stamp they chose Harold Nelson's design of St. George and the Dragon (subject to a few alterations). This was a reworking of a design Nelson had first submitted unsuccessfully for the Wembley stamps. It was agreed that during the process of engraving the plates the engraver should confer with Sir Frank Short and the artist.

The modifications were minor – sharpening the contrasts around the head of St. George and removing the word "Revenue" as per the original instructions. Nelson returned the amended design to Harcourt Smith on 2 January 1929. At the latter's suggestion "Revenue" was replaced by "One Pound" and Nelson noted:

> by slightly lightening the ground at the back of St. George, and the reduction of some of the light passages, I have brought the whole design more into harmony – I like your suggestion of a second colour and imagine that if the stamp could be printed in the right shades of say green and red it would be most effective.[27]

Above: Revised accepted artwork by Harold Nelson

When he saw it Murray agreed with the revisions and liked the substitution of "One Pound". Two colours would create great problems of registration and so the suggestion was dropped. However, the King was now extremely seriously ill and it was thought he might not survive. With little time available, Murray was forced to speak to Stamfordham who undertook, quite exceptionally, "to try and induce the Queen to approve the designs on the King's behalf."[28] A rather larger sized photograph showed the detail more clearly on the £1 and this size Murray preferred.

Happily, Stamfordham was able to reply the following day:

> I have submitted to the Queen the accompanying designs of stamps which the Postmaster General proposes to issue on the occasion of the International Postal Union's Congress in May next: and Her Majesty feels sure that they may be regarded as approved by the King. No doubt in due course the Postmaster General will be kind enough to give the King specimens for his collection. With regard to the other point upon which you consulted me, after speaking to the Doctors I feel confident in saying that in no circumstances would the King be able to attend the Congress in May next; therefore it would be quite in order to approach the Prince of Wales in order to secure His Royal Highness's presence on that occasion.[29]

Suffering from septicaemia, and before the days of penicillin, the King was not well enough to travel to Craigweil house at Bognor to begin his convalescence until a month later. Coincidentally, 6 January was the first day for six weeks when he could even speak to his wife, and to Stamfordham only the next day.[30]

Production

Given the time constraints it was decided that the 1d and 1½d letterpress dies (both of the same design by Linzell) would be engraved by Harrison, as would the recess £1 die, but the ½d and 2½d letterpress would be engraved by less able Royal Mint staff – which was to cause problems. The ½d was allocated to Charles G. Lewis, the 2½d to Thomas E. Storey. The letterpress low values were to be printed by Waterlows and the recess £1 by Bradbury Wilkinson.

There was also the question of which head to use. For the £1, as with the Wembley recess stamps, it would come ultimately from the Seahorse high values. For the letterpress lower values Herbert Evans of the Royal Mint "pointed out that the designs would not admit of the use of the 1d head, and suggested that the head at present used for the 5d stamp ("No.2 Coinage Head") [sic] which is modelled on the 1d head and is considered better than the 1½d head, should be used."[31] He meant the Medal Head II not the Coinage Head, showing that even involved experts got confused as to which head was which.

For Farleigh's designs a head with tint lines was required; for the Linzell one a head with no tint lines. To achieve this the Mint took the Medal Head II transfer roller of 6 April 1913 and ground off the tint lines from one impression. Storey then rolled in a head on to a 3" piece of Sellars transfer steel and proofed this, supplying it to Harrison at Waterlows.[32] This was sent to Waterlows on 10 January.

First proofs of the engraved Farleigh designs for the ½d and 2½d were received from the Royal Mint in mid-January. The 2½d needed the "9" of "1929" to be redrawn; as it stood it resembled a "0". With the ½d there were greater problems, however. Several letters of the wording needed to be improved, but the real problem was with the crown. It was small, touched the King's head inside the oval and appeared to be balanced precariously above it. Despite improvements it needed complete re-drawing which, after some discussion, Farleigh did and Lewis created a totally new die bringing the crown very nearly outside the oval for the King's head. The white lines within the numerals of "½" were also widened. The new die was approved by the artist on 4 February. It was only after Farleigh had redrawn the word "Postage" on the 2½d and a third die engraved that this was approved on 21 February.

Above: First and final die proofs of the ½d and 2½d values

Harrison, with his greater experience, fared better on Linzell's 1d and 1½d dies. As there were two denominations with the same design he first created a master die with the values blank. Proofs from the Royal Mint were forwarded to the Post Office on 24 January. Apart from minor amendments toning down the background Union Flag the two working dies with values inserted were approved on 19 February.

On 1 March, the Committee met to consider colour proofs. These had been prepared by Waterlows from 4-set blocks of the four values, though the 2½d was from the second die which had not been approved. Inks were divided into those "fast to light" and those "not fast to light". For the ½d there were seven shades of green; the 1d seven shades of red; the

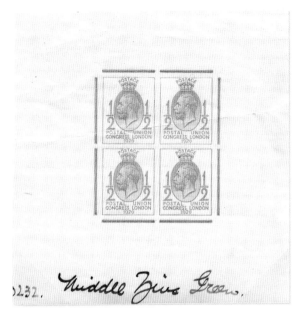

Above: Colour trials (4-set) of the four values

1½d six shades of brown; and the 2½d eight shades of blue. The present standard colours for these values were included in each case. The Committee selected:

½d	0236 – Middle Chrome Green
1d	0189 – Permanent Vermilion
1½d	0324 – Chocolate Red Brown
	or
	0082 – Art Brown
2½d	0270 – Steel Shade Blue

The choice of shade for the 1½d was left to the Postmaster General who decided on chocolate red brown.

Waterlows then, on 11 March, produced trials of the approved dies in the selected colours. However, these lacked depth and richness in colour in comparison to the previous versions. There then followed a long series of attempts to get the colours right. The Controller of Stores, H. Sparkes, visited Mander Brothers the ink manufacturers to discuss the difficulties and they then supplied sample stamps from different inks from their Wolverhampton works on 22 March. Yet more trials followed and colours were approved selected from essays of varying dates through March.

In the meantime, the Royal Mint were preparing the letterpress plates. The same process in their creation was followed as for definitive stamps (described in Chapter 4). Master plates for sheet stamps were made first from leads struck from the approved working dies and completed during February: ½d – 15th; 1d – 25th; 1½d – 27th; 2½d – 28th. Working nickel plates were then grown from these masters. Initially supplied were four each of the ½d, 1d and 1½d plates, and two of the 2½d. Because of time constraints and the amount of work most of these had to be proved at Waterlows' Clifton St. works rather than at the Royal

hot fast

B.B.91 fast Indian Red.

267. Sky Blue

Mint. The first four ½d plates were sent to Waterlows Watford plant on 14 March.

When printing began Waterlows found that these plates were "picking up" – i.e. applying too much ink to the paper, causing blotting. They had to be returned to the Mint where it was decided to grow new plates rather than attempt to correct these. This caused a delay until four more plates were supplied on 5 April. Further plates for all values were supplied later in the same month. To deal with what was now a backlog of work overtime was required and extra payment demanded, though this was not paid.

An enquiry by the Post Office concluded:

> There is no doubt that the trouble with the first batch of ½d plates threw the programme both at the Mint and at Waterlow's entirely out of gear. At the same time, I do not think that Messrs Waterlow used every effort to meet the Department's requirements until considerable pressure had been brought to bear upon them.[33]

Print requirements of sheet stamps to be delivered by 3 May were:

½d	870,000 sheets
1d	315,000 sheets
1½d	750,000 sheets
2½d	36,000 sheets

Despite production difficulties sufficient quantities were distributed and available for sale on the first day, 10 May.

In all, the Royal Mint produced twelve ½d working plates for sheet stamps, eight 1d plates, seven 1½d plates and four 2½d plates, though not all were used, several being destroyed at the time as unsatisfactory.

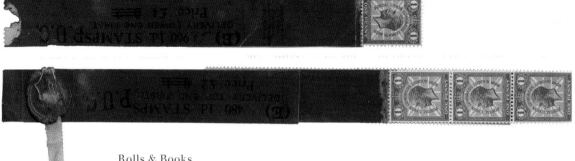

Rolls & Books

There was never any suggestion that there should be commemorative postal stationery for the P.U.C. issue. However, the low value stamps (with the exception of the 2½d) were to be issued in both rolls and books. These formats necessitated special printing plates. Roll stamps were printed in continuous reels from plates of 180-set or 192-set depending whether they were end, or side, delivery. Side delivery rolls provided stamps with sideways watermark. Master plates 90-set or 96-set were created for each value and then used to grow one working plate of two panes for each value. They were sold for use in private stamp-affixing machines or inserted into Post Office vending machines according to type.

Above: Roll leaders B and E overprinted PUC

Sales were later quantified as:

Rolls	No. of stamps	Value	Plate set	Delivery	Use - machine	Rolls Issued
B	960	1d	180	Bottom End	Affixing	952
D	960	½d	180	Bottom End	Affixing	2,993
E	480	1d	180	Top End	Affixing	5,916
G	480	½d	180	Top End	Affixing	11,811
K	960	1½d	180	Bottom End	Affixing	3,245
L	480	1½d	180	Top End	Affixing	2,847
N	480	1½d	192	Left Side	Affixing	38,077
O	480	1d	192	Left Side	Affixing	4,653
P	480	½d	192	Left Side	Affixing	43,458
W	960	½d	180	Bottom End	Vending	14,555
X	960	1d	180	Bottom End	Vending	15,373
Y	1920	½d	180	Bottom End	Vending	7,628
Z	1920	1d	180	Bottom End	Vending	8,219

As with standard definitive versions the plate format for books was quite different. These were 264-set if for stamp panes of six, or 176-set if four panes of four with two blank labels for advertisements. However, each pane was inverted (or tête-bêche) in relation to its neighbour, thus causing inverted watermark varieties on 50% of the stamps. This was to allow efficiently and economically for the essential margins to the final stamp panes. Master plates and two working plates were made for each type but there were the same problems

Below: Proofs of typography for the stamp books

with the first ½d plates as with the sheet varieties and so two more had to replace them. There was also one extra 1½d 264-set plate.

Two types of stamp book were issued – 2s containing 6 x ½d, 6 x 1d and 10 x 1½d (one pane of 6, and one of 4 with two advertisement labels); and 3s containing 6 x ½d, 6 x 1d and 18 x 1½d (three panes of 6). Cover and interleaving advertisements were sold through the Sells agency to offset the cost of production. Printed letterpress in black they varied in the five editions of each book (numbered 103 – 107 for the 2/- and 168 - 172 for the 3/-books). Messrs Sells suggested that in order to attract advertising the covers ought to have a particular title or be printed in distinctive colours. Proofs of the 2/- cover were submitted by Waterlows in shades of red and blue bearing the title "Postal Union Congress, London 1929" in different formats. One version of typography was chosen for both and a particular blue for the 2/- book with red for the 3/- version.

Numbers sold of the five editions were: 2/- 2,453,839 and 3/- 2,500,269.

The £1 St George & Dragon

The £1 stamp featuring St George and the Dragon by Harold Nelson was to be printed recess by Bradbury Wilkinson at their works at Raynes Park, New Malden. On 8 January, immediately after the Queen had given her approval, Sparkes, Cook and Tydeman of the Post Office Stores Department visited the works and informed H. Leslie Hendriks, the Managing Director, that their artists had failed with the designs they had submitted. On seeing Nelson's design Hendriks "expressed considerable admiration"[34] and admitted its superiority to his artists' designs. These had generally shown methods of postal transport.

Above: Initial engraving of the £1 value with the design "laid in"

> This is rather a satisfactory tribute from the firm which will in fact engrave the £1 stamp and who have a pretty wide knowledge of the productions of other countries. It will be an added inducement to them to put their best work into it.[35]

It was arranged for the paper to be supplied gummed as pressing after printing detracted from the brilliance of the inks. Samples printed with the latest British dyes were shown described as of "special brilliance". The Seahorse dies would be supplied for the engraving of the head and J.A.C. Harrison was seconded to engrave the die, and they would make the one plate. Sir Frank Short from the Design Committee would be consulted during the course of the engraving.

Costings were quoted for the work:

Item		Cost
Original engraving		£89.10. 6
Printing Plate	20 set	£14. 7. 6
Printing: 50,000 stamps	50,000 stamps	£15.15. 0
incl. perforating, warehousing, counting and controlling.	100,000 stamps	£25. 0. 0
Total		**£144.12.12**

Rather than Bradbury Wilkinson's rotary line perforator a special comb box was suggested but at a one-off cost of £38 but this was rejected. Approval was given however for a proposal that the £1 stamp be printed on paper bearing a special watermark similar to that adopted for the high value National Savings Certificate. The watermark consisted of a large Royal Cypher, GVR, in script with a crown above. Each stamp would bear one centred watermark.

Above: Artwork for the £1 watermark

Below: Colour trials from the £1 die

The first proofs were ready on 25 January. These were both taken from a soft steel die, printed in blue, with the design "laid in", i.e. cut in outline only with no shading or depth. One was completed in blue wash in order to give an impression of the final effect. Three days later there was a discussion between Harrison, Nelson and Short where Short seems to have suggested cross-hatching to give depth to the design (but not the background to the head).

A total of 16 colours were proofed with the completed die together with a final one in full

black. This had been requested by Short as he felt this would sharpen the contrast and accentuate the darker parts of the engraving. At their meeting on 1 March the Design Committee duly chose black as the colour. In the meantime Bradbury Wilkinson had made the plate 20-set and this was approved on 21 February. They were told to proceed with curving the plate for mounting on the cylinders, and chrome facing in order to prolong its durability.

During March, a second die was engraved and two single prints with extra wide margins were taken from it in late April which were presented to King George V for inclusion in the Royal Collection.

20 reams of the specially watermarked paper were delivered by Portal and Sons and Waterlows gummed 9,173 sheets of it prior to printing. Bradbury Wilkinson then printed 3750 sheets of 20 stamps each, of which 5,660 stamps were waste, leaving a total print of 69,340 stamps delivered.

Condemnation

When the stamps were issued, on the opening day of the Congress, there was universal condemnation of the designs, especially the lower values. The ½d was variously described as "appearing to reflect its price" *(Daily Chronicle)* and "more like a patent medicine Customs stamp than a British postage stamp" *(Morning Post)*; the 2½d was "more fitting for a beer bottle label" according to Albert Harris, Editor of the *Philatelic Magazine,* and in general of the letterpress stamps "the less said the better" *(The Times)*. Nelson's £1 design was better received, though it was regarded more as a bookplate.

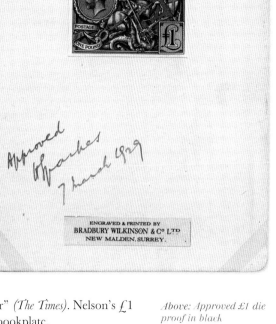

Above: Approved £1 die proof in black

Philatelists huffed and puffed about the high cost and the *Philatelic Magazine* stated:

> The criticism the unnecessary One Pound value has evoked was anticipated by the Post Office, and there is reason to believe that it was included in the set with the deliberate object of testing the demand from collectors. Obviously the sales of the low values are no guide on this point, but the inclusion of an extreme value that is not necessary for ordinary postal work does definitely throw light on whether a commemorative stamp is worth while from the cold and calculated monetary point of view. The official attitude towards commemorative stamps has undergone a complete change in the last few years and if the sale of this series – and of the £1 value in particular – reveals that the Post Office can secure additional revenue by this means we think there is little doubt that British stamp designs will change more frequently in the future than in the past.[36]

There were to be no more commemorative stamps for six years.

Final sales figures for the low values were:

Single stamps	½d	1d	1½d	2½d
In Sheets	589,797,840	274,777,200	658,920,960	26,782,800
In Books: 2/-	14,723,034	14,723,034	24,538,390	
3/-	15,001,614	15,001,614	45,004,842	
In Rolls	58,020,960	36,525,600	22,758,720	
Total	**677,543,448**	**341,027,448**	**751,222,912**	**26,782,800**

The £1 stamp remained on sale generally until May 1933 and was still available from London Chief Office up to July 1937. A final sales figure was given of 66,788.

Delegates' Privileges & Congress Post Office

Delegates to the Congress were guests of the British Government. As such, everything from hotels to excursions and receptions was paid for. All postal, telegraph and telephone services were also free from the Congress building, including all those overseas. Out of more than 180 delegates and attachés only one was a lady, predictably from the U.S.S.R.

Special stationery in the form of notepaper, envelopes and labels were supplied for the use of delegates. They bore emblem of the London Congress in the form of an oval within which was the Royal Badge and the wording in French, and came in a variety of colours.

For the identification of delegates a metal enamelled badge was designed on the model of the Jockey Club badge, with a buttonhole attachment for gentlemen and a safety pin attachment for ladies. The national colours and the monogram of the Universal Postal Union were worked in. It proved very popular with the delegates who wore it constantly.[37]

Two inkwells (for black and red ink) were sunk into delegates' desks and a special souvenir blotting pad was intended to be taken away.

Above: Special notepaper for the use of delegates

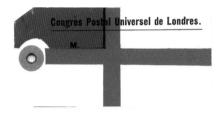

A post office was set up in the Congress building, open from 9 a.m. till 6 p.m. It opened on 6 May and closed on 3 July.

> A letter box, specially constructed so as to harmonise with the general decoration, was set up in the hall and cleared in time for the daily despatches. Parcels, which owing to accounting difficulties, were treated as letters, were handed over the counter. All packets thus collected were franked with stamps of the special Congress issue and obliterated with the Congress date-stamp. Great use was made by the delegates of the Air Service, the mail to South America showing a decided increase.[38]

There were three principal excursions for delegates with Edinburgh and Stratford on Avon amongst the destinations. One of the Congress postal officers accompanied the parties and collecting any correspondence, franking it out of a small stock of PUC stamps carried for the purpose. Such postal privileges in total cost £657 13s 3½d.

Telephone calls were also free. A 20 x 50 two-position switchboard was set up in the building to serve as the Congress Private Branch Exchange. The number was Gerrard 4040. Two of the telephonists were French-speaking and a supervisor at the Gerrard Exchange was German-speaking. Three telephone cabinets were installed again specially painted to harmonise with the overall decoration. In total, there were 4294 local calls, and 442 trunk calls (60 inland, 20 Irish Free State and 362 continental). Cost was £198 17s 11d though this only included the British share of the cost of foreign calls.

Top: Specially printed bag labels in national colours

Bottom: Crown handstamp for official mail

To cancel mail there was a special double ring steel datestamp and rubber handstamps for parcels and registered mail. There was also an oval crown for official mail and a frank for telegrams. Special registered labels were provided as were specially printed bag labels in the national colours, with similar much larger gummed labels for returns from abroad.

---

1   For details see **Knight, D.R.** & **Sabey, A.D.** *The Lion Roars at Wembley* 1984

2   POST 52/985 Unified Stamps – British Empire Exhibition issue. Murray to E.A. Francis 30 April 1923

3   ibid Memorandum by F.H. Williamson 8 May 1923

4   **Frayling, Sir C.** "Continuity through change: the Royal Mint Advisory Committee" in **Clancy, K. ed.** *Designing Change – the Art of Coin Design* 2008 p.41

5   POST 33/4840 Stamps postage: special issue, British Empire Exhibition, Committee appointed. Cecil Harcourt Smith to Sir Evelyn P Murray 29 November 1923

6   ibid copied with letter from Treasury to Murray 10 December 1923

7   ibid Eric Gill to Murray 31 January 1924

8   ibid Cecil Harcourt Smith to Murray 26 February 1924

9   ibid Stamfordham to Murray, 28 February 1924

10 T160/192 Murray to Niemeyer 11 March 1924

11 ibid. Memorandum 11 March 1924

12 ibid. Niemeyer to Murray 12 March 1924.

13 POST 52/953 Stamp Rolls – for selling machines – British Empire Exhibition issue. BSTAD to GPO 28 August 1924

14 ibid. Memorandum by W.M. Cook, 29 May 1924

15 Grover documentation MP 102/122A

16 **Alexander, Dr J** "The Wembley Sideways Roll" *The GB Journal* Vol. 48 No. 1 January/February 2010 pp 18-23

17 Summarised in: **Pendlebury, A. and Allen, G.** *Special Stamp History No. 1: British Empire Exhibition* (unpublished, National Postal Museum) 1996.

18 POST 52/953 op cit. H. Sparkes to Secretary 29 March 1924

19 POST 52/985 op cit

20 *L'Union Postale Universelle: Sa Fondation et son Développement 1874-1949. Mémoire.* 1949, pp 169ff

21 POST 52/986 Unified Stamps: Postal Union Congress (London) issue. 9 May 1928. Lumley was later a delegate to the Congress.

22 ibid

23 POST 52/986 op cit. PMG to Stamfordham 25 May 1928

24 ibid. Stamfordham to PMG 26 May 1928; Stamfordham to Murray 23 July 1928.

25 POST 33/2903A Universal Postal Union Congress 1929: commemorative postage stamps. Sir William Mitchell-Thomson to Earl of Crawford, 25 July 1928, and quoted with commentary in **Griffiths, A.** *Special Stamp History No. 2: 1929 Postal Union Congress* 1998 p.5

26 ibid. 13 November 1928

27 ibid. Nelson to Harcourt Smith, 2 January 1929

28 ibid. Murray to Harcourt Smith, 5 January 1929

29 ibid. Stamfordham to Murray, 6 January 1929.

30 **Pope-Hennessy, J.** *Queen Mary* 2000 edition, p545

31 POST 52/986 op cit. Memorandum by W.M. Cook, 8 January 1929

32 Royal Mint Work Order Instructions

33 POST 52/986 op cit Memorandum, 29 April 1929

34 ibid. Memo by Cook, 8 January 1929

35 POST 33/2903A op cit. Murray to Harcourt Smith, 9 January 1929

36 *Philatelic Magazine* 22 June 1929

37 POST 33/2513 Universal Postal Union: London Congress 1929

38 ibid

16

TALLENTS TO DEVISE

PUBLIC RELATIONS & THE G.P.O. FILM UNIT

Stephen Tallents was aptly named. He was an early, remarkably skilful, enthusiast for publicity and managing public opinion. Born in 1884 he began his career as a civil servant in 1909 in the Board of Trade. After being badly wounded serving in the Irish Guards in World War I he worked in various government ministries and was in charge of food rationing on the home front. From 1920 he was in Ireland at that critical period in Anglo-Irish history, becoming Imperial Secretary for Northern Ireland from 1922 till 1926. Then, he was secretary to the Cabinet Committee dealing with the General Strike.

Left: Sir Stephen Tallents

It was at this point that Leo Amery, Secretary of State for the Colonies, chose Tallents to be the first Secretary of the Empire Marketing Board, because of his reputation for "initiative, vision and great driving power".[1] The Empire Marketing Board (EMB) was set up in May 1926, with a budget of £1 million a year, to develop and market food and goods produced in the Empire, and to "bring the Empire alive". It was Tallents' interest in selling the idea of Empire that formed the rest of his career. He organised press and poster campaigns, exhibitions, Empire shops, and radio talks. With Frank Pick from London Underground some 800 posters were produced. But perhaps most influential was the creation of the EMB Film Unit led by John Grierson. Innovation and experimentation were the guidelines.

From 1931, Tallents also served on the Telephone Publicity Committee of the Post Office, set up when Major Clement Attlee was Postmaster General. With Imperial Preference agreements signed in Ottawa in 1932 the Empire Marketing Board was no longer needed and it came to an end the following year. But the then Postmaster General, Sir H. Kingsley Wood, immediately wanted Tallents' services. The high-level post of Public Relations Officer was established for him and when he transferred to the Post Office he brought Grierson and the Film Unit with him, to create the GPO Film Unit. In a speech to his erstwhile colleagues Tallents claimed that he would now "sing the EMB's song in a strange land".[2] One of his first achievements, however, was the creation of a Post Office "badge".

Post Office "Badge"

While still at the Empire Marketing Board, Tallents wrote to G.H. Taylor of the Post Office Telephone Publicity Department saying he felt "the need for a single dignified design, which could be used throughout your telephone publicity in the same way as we use our emblem of the Crown and the initials 'E.M.B.'"[3] He suggested as an artist Macdonald Gill (variously spelt, as with Mackennal) who had prepared various Empire maps for the EMB. This was agreed at a fee of approximately £20. Shortly before taking up his GPO post Tallents wrote again to confirm that Gill was willing to undertake the work.

Macdonald (Max) Gill was the architect and designer brother of the more famous Eric Gill whose typeface (Gill sans) he then used in his design. Well-known for his Empire posters, in the early 1920s he had also drawn various maps of the London Underground. Less well-known, but highly relevant, was his experience in designing the badges for war graves.

In January 1934, Gill submitted six designs on tracing paper for what was described as a GPO "monogram" or "badge". Most incorporated stylised birds' wings with the letters G.P.O. surmounted by a crown. The accepted version (No. 6) had no wings but only a crown (with eight pearls on either side) over the letters GPO within a double circle. Type was in Gill sans, unlike the other designs which used a serif font. Artwork was supplied on 1 February and this was then used in publicity such as press advertisements. However, it was felt it could be improved. Tallents wrote to Gill on 30 April:

> Such criticisms as I have heard, and they have not been numerous, have been (1) that the crown seemed a little to overweight the lettering, and (2) that the adjustment of the inner circle to the outside letters might be improved – perhaps that a single circle would be more effective.[4]

In Gill's preliminary sketch (No.6) he had suggested alternatives or variants of the bounding lines. He now tried out a number of variations omitting the inner or outer line. The newly appointed Director General of the Post Office, Col. Donald Banks, suggested that a post-horn be included and this was passed on to Gill in June. This post-horn was that used in the jack, or standard, flying on mail ships and aircraft.

At the beginning of July Gill submitted "a design … for the G.P.O. Badge incorporating the bugle." On the original artwork he noted that the "P" should be better centralised. For the sake of legibility he thought it best to limit the number of pearls to seven a side.

Above: First Badge artwork by Macdonald Gill, and used on van advertising (top)

Suggested posthorn design and two forms of crown

> In the many cases in which I have designed crowns for the War Graves Commission I have varied the number of pearls in deference to the size and the demands of the material. These designs have received the King's assent and approval.[5]

Although this was intended for a Post Office Board meeting in July it was postponed until October. In the meantime the drawing of the strap and horn was simplified. Nevertheless, the new design "did not altogether commend itself" to members. Tallents, a member of the Board, was asked to consult the newly-established "Poster Group" and come back with a revised drawing.

As a result of their advice Gill produced a drawing on 19 November based on the original No. 6 sketch but without the outer circle or post-horn. This was approved by the Poster Group and Tallents submitted it to the Post Office Board where it was also approved on 5 February 1935. It gradually came into use through 1935 and the beginning of 1936, when it was first used on the *Post Office Magazine*.

Public Relations

Giving a lecture to the Post Office Telephone and Telegraph Society in 1934, Tallents presciently observed:

> We ought to know, better than we do, how the Italian, German and Russian governments are setting about their deliberate task of speaking to their peoples through the various channels of modern publicity.[6]

He did not use the emotive word "propaganda". Rather he went on to define three "direct and legitimate purposes of Post Office publicity" – the selling of its services, ensuring that its services were correctly used, and the creation of goodwill. Contrasting the publicity of a government department with commercial advertising he said that "It must make its publicity truthful, clear, attractive and in harmony with its surroundings."[7] In order to achieve this, his specially created public relations department had set about commissioning artists to create attractive posters, exhibitions and films. There were also temporary "Post Office Shops" at various shows or fairs with a model postal train (gauge 1¾" – an exact miniature of the original Royal Scot No.6100) and model sorting office to illustrate postal operations, and various publicity leaflets. Not only were these directed at Post Office staff, and their customers, but some were to be used as educational tools in schools. However,

> the effective practice of publicity involves experiments, and a proportion of experiments are bound to go wrong. Mistakes in Post Office publicity are much more readily observed and traced than mistakes in purely commercial advertising; and an institution like the Post Office is permitted little cupboard space for skeletons.[8]

19 xi 34 *MacDonald Gill*

Above: Final accepted Badge artwork

Posters

The "Poster Group" had been set up in April 1934 to advise on subjects and artists for Post Office posters, especially for schools. It consisted of: Kenneth Clark, newly Director of the National Gallery and Keeper of the King's Pictures; Clive Bell, a writer on art and literature (and married to Vanessa Bell, an art critic and sister of Virginia Woolf); and Jack L. Beddington, Publicity Officer for Shell-Mex (and thus creator of many highly regarded posters).

It had been foreshadowed by Tallents' work at the Empire Marketing Board. When that was under threat of extinction he conducted a campaign laying out his underlying beliefs. Scorning the luxury of private art, he called for "the encouragement of a national rather than a private art, and the patron who gave that encouragement would know that

Above: Schools posters by H.S. Williamson, 1934

he was not merely satisfying a noble taste but was fulfilling one of the great needs of his country".[9] This was now to be put into practice with the Post Office as patron. For Tallents, this was a crusade.

Under the Telephone Publicity Committee, later renamed the Post Office Publicity Committee, posters had already been commissioned to promote telephone and telegraph services, and also for airmail. Now its purpose was to be expanded to influence and educate, and create goodwill.

At the first meeting of the Poster Committee, in May 1934, members examined roughs by H.S. Williamson, Principal of the Chelsea School of Art, for a set of school posters on the theme of "Overseas Communications". Williamson was called in to the meeting to hear the Committee's rather critical views. Present was John Grierson who offered Williamson help to resolve some of the problems, telling him that the GPO Film Unit had been able, by special treatment "to vitalize such scenes as the departure and arrival of air mail planes" and undertook to show him his material on the subject and on shipping at the London docks.[10] This was to result in the first set of four educational posters, free to schools, royal size (20 x 25 inches) showing: the relays carrying the King's Messenger in 1482; mails for the packet boats arriving at Falmouth in 1833; mails being loaded at London docks in 1934; and air mails for the Empire being loaded at Croydon in 1934. The public could purchase the posters individually for one shilling or all four, plus the two leaflets written to accompany the set, at three shillings. To a fanfare of publicity in the press and on radio, the scheme was launched in late November 1934. Some 25,000 sets of posters and leaflets were distributed in the first issue.

It was intended that a second set be issued in April 1935 but this, in the end, was reduced to a single map poster by Macdonald Gill - *Post Office Radio-telephone Services*.

By the summer of 1935, Tallents could look back with considerable satisfaction at his achievements. He could also look forward to further success since new school posters, designed by Edward McKnight Kauffer, John Armstrong, Clifford and Rosemary Ellis, and Vanessa Bell and Duncan Grant, as well as numerous 'selling' posters, by Austin

Cooper, Barnett Freedman, Douglas England, Andrew Johnson, Peter Morgan and others, were already in the pipeline.[11]

The "selling" posters were to help the public to understand how the Post Office worked, and to publicise particular services. Among these services were, in particular, the telephone, and a series of posters were created for a "Telephone Week" in October 1934. Some 270,000 posters were issued for use on vehicles, pillar boxes, in post offices and in shops and on trams and buses throughout the country. There were also half a million postcards printed reproducing these. Edward McKnight Kauffer was one of the well-known artists employed. Airmail was similarly treated and included work by Theyre Lee-Elliott. One particularly attractive strip poster for the side of mail vans was for "Cheaper Parcel Post" designed by Barnett Freedman.

Helping to understand how the Post Office worked came in the practical campaign to "Post Early". As Tallents put it

> All of us deplore certain habits of the public – their habit, for example, of holding up their parcels and their letters to the last moment. It would increase our efficiency, decrease our costs, and secure a better service to the public if these habits could be changed.[12]

This led to the first poster commission for Graham Sutherland in March 1934. Sutherland was then teaching engraving two days a week at the Chelsea School of Art and was both a friend of Tallents and a neighbour in Kent. He had already been prominent in designing posters for Shell and had been picked out by Clark as being the best in that field. Sutherland's resulting design, unfortunately, was rather uninspired, and uninspiring, showing a postman on his rounds looking at a letter.

The "Post Early" campaign was also to lead to eventual controversy. Tallents admitted that a civil servant did not readily understand the artist's point of view, nor that the latter needed a certain liberty. Equally, artists did not easily appreciate the limitations and responsibilities of government. This potential clash now became real.

In July 1934, Tallents had written to Vanessa Bell, wife of Clive Bell:

> Your husband said … a satirical poster would be to your liking and looked doubtfully towards us to see how the Post Office would take the idea. So far from alarming me, it opened out a new line of publicity to me. It seemed to show a new means of enlisting the help of the public. Instead of merely commanding them to post early, we will show how ridiculous they look, and what inconvenience they suffer, when they post late. Instead of protesting against rudeness to our telephone operators, we will show how foolish an angry man at the telephone looks. From time to time, our Post Office walls shall be a mirror of the public's folly. This should amuse the public, and delight our staff, who cannot individually answer back their more tiresome customers.[13]

Above: Parcel poster by Barnett Freedman (top)

Used on a mail van outside Bush House, London (middle)

"Post Early" poster by Graham Sutherland (bottom)

This did not seem to strike Tallents as naïve. Nor was he to foresee that the difference in attitude between civil servant and artist might also be reflected in a difference in taste. Bell completed her design of what became known as *The Last Minute* poster in March 1935. A month later, it was approved by the advisory group and prints of this were available in early 1936, but were not issued.

By this time, Tallents had left the Post Office and his successor was not of his artistic persuasion. Argument about *The Last Minute* was to lead to the abolition of the Poster Group in September 1937. Looking at the design today, one is struck most immediately by its resemblance to a painting (and not a very good one at that) rather than a printed publicity poster. It shows a quiet counter girl with irate, pushing customers, all portrayed in dull, rather gloomy colours. A later commentary revealed that it had been regarded at the time by the Post Office Board as unsuitable and especially disliked "not because of its method, but because the treatment of the subject chosen was quite out of keeping with Post Office requirements. ... The enthusiasm for it simply shows that the Group has failed, like some of the artists, to grasp Post Office atmosphere and requirements."[14] However one looks at it today, it is difficult to disagree.

Tallents moved to the B.B.C. as a Controller in October 1935 and later returned as a civil servant to government work. Subsequently, he was twice President of the Institute of Public Relations and died in 1958.

Above: "The Last Minute" by Vanessa Bell (top)

Artwork for unused poster of the P.O. Underground Railway by Edward Bawden

Before he left the Post Office he provided his successor, Colonel Tristram Crutchley, with a memorandum which alluded to the problems the latter would later face.

We have had some excellent letterpress posters, for example the strips for vans and related double crown designs for the sixpenny telegram and night telegraph letter (Austin Cooper) and the cheaper parcel post (Barnett Freedman). This part of the poster work is running on sound and promising lines which may well be continued. On the other hand, the pictorial designs so far secured, though many of them are respectable, are on the whole disappointing in comparison with other work done by the same artists in other fields. The disappointment may be partly due to a belief by the artist that a government department is sure to want a conventional design….. It may be due to the nature of some Post Office material. It may in some cases be due to laziness on the artist's part. But the main difficulty seems to be that we have not by present methods succeeded in getting our artists under the skin of Post Office activities.[15]

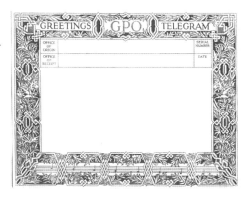

Greetings Telegrams

Decorative greetings telegrams were first issued on 24 July 1935. Initially, it was merely a decorative border printed in red and gold, designed by Mrs Calkin James. However, when this was withdrawn on the last day of the year a new version was issued designed by Robert Gibbings. This was more obviously celebratory including baby, sailing ship and wedding bells in the design. The first particular greetings form came on 14 February 1936 for St Valentine's Day. Printed in multicolour this was designed by Rex Whistler with various cherubs. Each of these telegrams had specially printed envelopes.

G.P.O Film Unit

"One remembers looking at a sorting office for the first time and thinking that when you had seen one letter you had seen the lot".[16] Thus John Grierson of the G.P.O. Film Unit. But it was his job to present this material, on the face of it not very exciting, in an interesting and popular shape.

Grierson had come to prominence at the Empire Marketing Board with his film *Drifters* of 1929 about the Scottish herring fleets. This had had its first showing in 1930 at the London Film Society. Tallents described the occasion. He and Grierson were in the audience.

> We watched the drifter leaving harbour and facing the open sea; the crew in their cabin and on deck, the captain on the bridge; the herring shoals pursued by dogfish below the surface; the shooting of the nets and the pause from labour which followed it; toiling men hauling the nets inboard on a rough sea, under threat of a gathering storm; the silver fish pouring on to the deck, into the hold; the drifter's return to port through the storm; the unloading of its catch at the quayside.[17]

Above: Greetings telegrams by James (top), Gibbings (middle) and Whistler (bottom)

The film was shown before Sergei Eisenstein's great *Battleship Potemkin* and was at least as warmly applauded as that Russian classic. Still a silent film, it was to have a great influence on other film-makers. It was through this that documentary films were launched. From then until the closure of the Empire Marketing Board Grierson supervised the production of more than one hundred films. The Post Office was among the departments for which the E.M.B. Film Unit was making films. Two of them were by Stuart Legg, *The New Operator* (1932) and *Telephone Workers* (1933). This probably helped Tallents to convince the Post Office to take over the entire Unit and the film library.

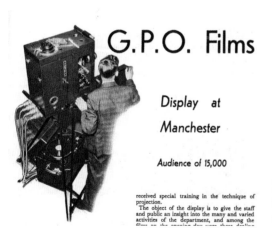

Above: G.P.O. Film Unit advertising

Work did not suddenly stop with the change of name. There was an overlap in the films being made. At the moment of transition the most important of these were *Song of Ceylon* for the Ceylon Tea Propaganda Board and *B.B.C. – The Voice of Britain* for the B.B.C. Basil Wright's film on Ceylon was his outstanding personal achievement. It was described as a gentle and poetic film. That for the B.B.C. was by Stuart Legg and was the most expensive film the Unit ever made (costing £7,500). Harry Watt was another member of the small team, now to be joined by others. Perhaps the most important of these was the Brazilian Alberto Cavalcanti who, after experience in studios in Paris, joined in 1934. Grierson recruited Cavalcanti as someone who could stimulate the innovative use of sound. (Al Jolson's *The Jazz Singer* had revolutionised the cinema in 1927.) Now a new sound studio for the GPO Film Unit was acquired in Blackheath at the same time as more spacious offices at 21 Soho Square. However, even here some of the members worked from desks in the corridors.

A friend of Grierson's, the contemporary film critic and writer Forsyth Hardy, wrote a short history of the G.P.O. Film Unit for the archives. It provides an insight into the atmosphere and beliefs of the time.

> ·Within the G.P.O. Unit 'experiment' was the watchword," wrote Roger Manvell, and added that that word "acted like magic in the mid-thirties. You were just nowhere if the film you had just made or the film you were planning was not an experiment in something." The formal experimentation moved along three main lines, represented by the preoccupations of Cavalcanti, Lye, and Watt…. sound, animation, story and characterization. During the years 1933-37 there was also movement away from the simple description of work and workers to a broader sociological analysis of the underlying and surrounding human conditions.[18]

No attempt was made by the Unit to produce first feature films. Efforts were confined to "shorts" varying between one and three reels in length and taking 10 to 30 minutes to show. Earlier films were essentially silent with commentaries added. Having control of sound would add a new dimension to their experimentation and the experimental use of sound was to become a characteristic of G.P.O. films.

Key appointments were made by Grierson. His resulting team has rather derisively been described as being mostly "over-earnest upper-middle-class Cambridge graduates."[19] When Basil Wright told him that W.H. Auden wanted to join the unit he was urged to bring him in at once. Similarly Grierson asked the Royal College of Music if they had a bright young student who could write a little incidental music for a forthcoming film. Benjamin Britten then also joined. Grierson, a Scot, put the rationale simply. If they wanted music

> we find it cheaper to have it written for us. If we want natural sound, the producer drives out and gets it. If we want to orchestrate sound we sit in the sound van and arrange the re-recording as we think best. If we want to play with sound images, or arrange choral effects, or in any way experiment, we have no one's permission to ask and no considerable overheads to worry about, because we do most of the work ourselves.[20]

Above: G.P.O. Film Unit introductory image

Films produced about Post Office activities included: Evelyn Spice's *Weather Forecast* (1934) about the collection and dissemination of weather information; Stuart Legg's *Cable Ship* (1933), on repairing submarine telephone cables; *Six Thirty Collection* (1934) in which Edgar Anstey and Harry Watt described the collection, sorting and dispatch of the early evening mail at a large London post office; *Under the City* (1934) where Arthur Elton collaborated with Alexander Shaw describing the maintenance of telephone cables under London's streets; and Harry Watt's *Droitwich* (1934) on the erection of the tallest radio mast in Britain.

Six Thirty Collection was probably the first documentary film to use authentic sound though it was still described by its maker, Harry Watt, as "unadulterated boredom".[21]

> Grierson believed that every film-making unit should have an artist who could experiment and not be held to account for everything he did. At the G.P.O. this role was filled first by Len Lye, the New Zealander, who brought *Colour Box* to Grierson and Cavalcanti and who made *Rainbow Dance* (1936) and *Trade Tattoo* (1937) for them. In these two films Lye combined recognisable figures with abstract elements moving rapidly on the screen in syncopation with jazz. ....[22]

There is no obvious reason why the Post Office should make a film about coal mining. Although Grierson was born in the village of Deanston near Doune in Perthshire he spent his boyhood in Cambusbarron near Stirling, partly a mining community. His mother had run a soup kitchen for striking miners. Coal was then of great importance in Britain. It was used in power generation, rail and marine transport and in homes all over the country – but it was hardly of immediate relevance to the Post Office. Nevertheless, one was made. Shooting for the film was done by several members of the Unit and given to Legg to assemble. Auden wrote a madrigal which was sung by female voices as the miners returned to the surface. *Coal Face* appeared in 1935 and is of great importance as a precursor.

Such diffuse experimentation could not last forever. The new Postmaster General Major Tryon thought that it was time to "slow things up and consolidate".[23] A financial committee was appointed and unsurprisingly reported "that the raising of the level of social consciousness and the interpretation of the drama of everyday life had little connection with the advertisement of rates for the parcel post and the virtues of the new telephone system."[24] The Committee concluded that, when existing commitments had been met, the G.P.O. Film Unit should confine itself to strictly Post Office activities. Tallents left. Yet its finest achievement was still to come.

"Night Mail"

Who can forget the famous opening lines of Auden's poem in *Night Mail?*

This is the Night Mail crossing the border
Bringing the cheque and the postal order,
Letters for the rich, letters for the poor,
The shop at the corner and the girl next door.

Above: Still from "Night Mail"

And yet, the verse was almost an afterthought. The film began life humbly enough as a record of the journeys of the Postal Special travelling post office between London and Scotland, during which letters were collected, sorted and delivered by apparatus at points along the route. Grierson's friend Hardy was asked to undertake the journey initially and give his impressions.

> The experience certainly gave me an understanding of the physical demands made on the postal workers who worked in shifts – Scotland to Carlisle, Carlisle to Crewe and Crewe to Euston. Their sorting had a kind of rhythmic fascination as the letters found their niches in the panel in front of each sorter, the process interrupted occasionally by an indecipherable address or an obscure location. I can still recall the thump of the leather bound bags of mail hurtling into the collecting van at the front of the train.[25]

It was Grierson's decision, naturally, that the northward journey should be shown – the Down Special of the London, Midland and Scottish Railway from Euston to Aberdeen. Amongst the most memorable shots of the film are those of the soft, rounded Border hills in the grey light of early morning. Visually, the film also gains immensely from the "aerial shots as the train sped northwards through the dusk or the fleeting shots taken of its illumined windows as it thundered through silent stations."[26]

There was a script of sorts by Wright, though it was Watt who created most of the human scenes. Both were credited, amidst considerable acrimony, with being producers. The film's "authenticity and narrative strength" would come from "the well-practised glances, glares and behavioural tics of the travelling post office's staff."[27]

Chick Fowle and Jonah Jones were cameramen and Pat Jackson and W.H. Auden assistants. Filming could be dangerous. On one occasion the bag-exchange apparatus was to be filmed from the train. Watt later described the scene.

> Chick Fowle volunteered to hang out of a window, just behind the catching net, with a hand-held camera. It was bloody dangerous. ... Pat and I hung on to his legs and prayed. All we could see was Chick's tensed bottom. The run-up to the change-over position was endless. The train seemed to be going faster and faster, and I could see

that ugly great black bag hanging on its sinister arm, and rushing inexorably at Chick's head. There was a sudden, frightening crash as the pound landed in the van ahead of us, and a faint "OK" from Chick. We hauled him in….[28]

According to Wright, it was Grierson, when seeing a rough assembly of film, who said: "There's something missing. What we haven't got here is anything about the people who are going to get the letters. We've only the machinery of getting the letters from one point to the other".[29] This was the origin of the addition of Britten's music (the score written in 48 hours) and Auden's poem. The latter was frequently revised because of Watt's opposition. Verse was often discarded, either because it did not fit or because the verbal images were too strong for the pictorial equivalent. Finally, it was written to the rhythm of the clattering train. Stuart Legg spoke the rapid passages and Grierson himself gave emotion to the closing lines.

Night Mail was an immediate success from its first public showing at the Arts Theatre, Cambridge in early 1936, and that success was repeated all over the world. Recently, the original has been digitally remastered by the British Film Institute. After this success Grierson was to resign from the GPO in June 1937.

In later life, Grierson's secretary, Phyllis Long, recorded her recollections of the Film Unit and its personalities.

> The Film Unit was a marvellous and exciting place to work. Salaries were never more than at bread-line level, especially for the young trainees who received only 30/- a week when they started, but the atmosphere, friendliness, being made to feel that we were all making a contribution, more than compensated.[30]

Above: "Night Mail" poem by Auden

From Post Office Establishment books, on the other hand, one can glean that Grierson's salary was £900 a year, raised to £950 at Tallents' insistence[31]; Tallents' was £1,641 11s.

Phyllis's view of some of the people involved[32] –

John Grierson Tough, imaginative, far-seeing, single-minded, concerned only to maintain the Film Unit's position as the premier film unit and to maintain its high standards of craftsmanship. He sought to provide opportunities for young film-makers….He was quick to spot those who showed promise; those that did not, he quickly despatched….

Harry Watt Not a favourite of mine. He was rough, tough, noisy and very bossy, but he quickly learned his craft and made many successful films. He would often argue with Grierson.

Basil Wright A very shy person…His instructions were always given in clear precise tones, or carefully hand written.

Alberto 'Cav' Cavalcanti 'Cav' was not an easy person to get along with. Highly emotional, prickly, demanding, and expecting always to have immediate attention given to his demands….We all loved 'Cav'.

Len Lye I remember him coming into the office and telling us about his technique and that he was going to make some short colour films for us. I think we all thought he was a bit cranky, until we saw the results. He was given a completely free hand with all his work.

W.H. Auden He was always hard to pin down, not a good time keeper and incredibly untidy and forgetful.

Benjamin Britten He only came to the office occasionally, disdaining to speak to any one except Grierson and Golightly [an office staff member].

1   POST 121/431 Sir Stephen Tallents, Public Relations Officer: appointment papers. J.H. Thomas to Kingsley Wood 14 August 1933

2   Quoted in **Barden, M.** *Post Early,* 1993 p7

3   POST 122/8388 GPO Monogram. Design of crown. 16 March 1933

4   POST 122/8391 GPO Monogram. Proposed revision.

5   ibid 2 July 1934

6   **Tallents, S.** *Post Office Publicity* P.O. Green Paper No. 8, 1935 p4

7   ibid p7

8   ibid p3

9   **Barden** op cit p7

10 ibid p13

11 ibid p13

12 **Tallents** op cit p10

13 **Barden** op cit p18

14 ibid p 22. 15 October 1937. Crutchley to Director General

15 ibid p18

16 **Grierson, J.** *The Story of Documentary Film* quoted in **Ellis, J.C.** *John Grierson: Life, Contributions, Influence* 2000, p5

17 **Ellis, J.C.** op cit quoting Tallents.

18 POST 108/91 "History of the GPO Film Unit" by Forsyth Hardy 1990

19 **Anthony, S.** *Night Mail* 2007 p29

20 POST 108/91 op cit

21 **Anthony, S.** *Night Mail* op cit p22

22 POST 108/91 op cit

23 Quoted in **Anthony, S.** *Night Mail* op cit p79

24 POST 108/91 op cit

25 ibid

26 ibid

27 **Anthony, S.** *Night Mail* op cit p30

28 **Watt, H.** *Don't Look at the Camera* 1974 p84 (quoted in **Anthony, S.** *Night Mail* op cit)

29 POST 108/91 op cit

30 POST 108/298 Personal recollections of the GPO Film Unit by John Grierson's secretary Phyllis Cain, 1985

31 POST 121/430 Grierson, John, Chief Film Officer, GPO Film Unit; appointment papers

32 POST 108/298 op cit

17
THE KING'S STAMP
PHOTOGRAVURE PRINTING & THE SILVER JUBILEE

"We celebrate the present under the spell of the past."[1]

King George V celebrated his silver jubilee in May 1935, over several days. The huge crowds wherever he went, and the outpouring of popular feeling, astonished him. Essentially a modest man, he had shortly before innocently remarked, when resting at the Duke of Devonshire's house on the south coast, that the local parson seemed such a fine fellow: "He filled his church to overflowing every Sunday we went to it."[2] Now he was overwhelmed by the affection shown. There was a speech to Parliament, a service of thanksgiving at St. Paul's, a review of the Fleet and open carriage tours everywhere. There was also an exhibition of stamps at the Royal Philatelic Society's premises which he found time to visit.

He wrote to his friend Count Albert Mensdorff, the former Austrian ambassador:

> I do indeed appreciate all the love and affection which my people are expressing, from all over the world. The festivities will entail a lot of extra work, and I shall be pleased when they are all over, I hope I shall survive them. I remember so well both Queen Victoria's Jubilees and can't yet realise that I am having one now.[3]

The first suggestion for special stamps to be issued came from the Colonial Office. In January 1934 an internal memorandum noted that they were constantly having to refuse permission to Colonial Governments to issue new stamps, on the ground that no particular reason had been shown (other than extracting revenue from the stamp-collecting public). It was accepted, however, that important anniversaries were a legitimate "excuse".

> On the 10th of May 1935 H.M. will celebrate the 25th anniversary of his accession to the throne & it seems to me that, particularly in view of H.M.'s personal interest in philately, no better opportunity for a general commemorative issue could be found.[4]

A single design might be chosen to be used by each colony or dependency. The first step would be to ascertain the intentions of the GPO and then the views of the King. However, when they wrote to the Post Office in February they received a condescending, and disheartening, reply.

> As you may have heard we are about to produce a new issue of stamps which will embody certain modifications of the present design. We have reason to think that the King would not favour the production in this country of yet another new issue. The answer to your enquiry whether the Postmaster General has any similar proposal under consideration as regards this country is therefore in the negative.[5]

As the Colonial Office official tartly noted "The fact that a slight change is being made in the existing design of the U.K. stamps does not appeal to me as a good reason for not considering a proposal to commemorate a jubilee."[6]

Above: Photographs used for essays by Lafayette, Vandyk and Downey

New Definitives printed in Photogravure

The modified stamps the Post Office letter referred to were as a result of the ending of Waterlows' printing contract in 1933. Tenders had been sought from various printers which included the possibility of printing the low value stamps in photogravure. This was not a new process for stamps generally – the first postage stamps printed thus were those of Bavaria in 1914 – and photogravure had been used by British stamp printers for foreign and other types of stamps. But it had not been used with British postage stamps.

Its first use in connection with the GPO had been with the 6d National War Savings stamp of 1918. This had been printed by Waterlow Brothers & Layton who had already printed the third series Treasury £1 currency note of 1917 (featuring St George & the Dragon and designed by Bertram Mackennal) which included photogravure to print part of its security features. By 1933 Harrisons were also experienced with photogravure for postage stamps having printed (with Dutch assistance) stamps for Egypt in 1922 and subsequently. They had also printed Savings Stamps from 1921. Photogravure by Waterlows was also considered for the PUC low values in 1928. The process had not been introduced for British postage stamps, however, because of concern about uniformity of colour – not only during the printing run but even within one sheet. For Savings Stamps this might matter less. Its major advantages lay in rapid rotary printing though it was not immediately cheaper than letterpress.

Eric Harrison, of Harrison & Sons Ltd, was interrogated by postal officials in May 1933. Comparisons were first made between flat-bed and rotary letterpress machines. The Controller of Post Office Stores said he was doubtful if the present quality of print could be maintained on a rotary press and asked which Harrison had in mind at their new premises at High Wycombe. Harrisons had been considering two machines, one by the Victory Kidder Company and the other of their own design. The perforating would be done separately on the web. Harrison then admitted that stamps produced by photogravure lacked "uniformity in colour, etc. although he thought that owing to differences in design there would be somewhat less variation with Unified Stamps than with National Savings Stamps."[7] An experimental print run over six to eight weeks would cost between £500 and £1,000.

Leaks about the new tenders had led to speculation about new stamps in the press. This worried the Postmaster General, Kingsley Wood, about what the King might think. He therefore wrote to head off any untoward criticism.

> In case His Majesty may have noticed the references in the Press to the question of the new contracts for the printing of our postage stamps and especially to the possibility of some alteration in the design, I think that perhaps I ought to explain the position.
>
> As the present contracts for the printing of our postage stamps expire at the end of this year, tenders have been invited for surface printed stamps exactly similar to those at present in use. The firms invited were, however, informed that the Post Office was prepared to consider tenders for any alternative printing processes which gave results as satisfactory as those laid down in the specifications.
>
> Tenders have been received for stamps to be produced –
> (1) by surface printing on flat-bed machines sheet fed – as at present;
> (2) by surface printing on rotary machines reel-fed
> (3) by the photogravure process;
> (4) by recess or intaglio printing on rotary machines.

No decision has, of course, been come to as yet and no change would be made without His Majesty's consent.[8]

A series of essays had been produced with a solid background to the King's head. On 8 March five different heads had been essayed in photogravure (in three different colours for the basic rates) using the Mackennal frame design for the 1½d, on both coated and uncoated papers (numbered specimens A to G). These showed:

Left: March 1933 photogravure essays with various photographic portraits

A. Photograph of the Coinage head plaster model
B. Wash drawing of the Coinage head die proof
C. Wash drawing of the Coinage head die proof with light background
D. Near full-face photographic portrait by Lafayette (c. 1932)
E. Three-quarter photographic portrait by Vandyk (c. 1932)
F. Three-quarter photographic portrait by Downey (1910)
G. Photograph of the Coinage head plaster model with light background

Subsequently, on 19 April, the Royal Mint created special copper electros of the 1d, 1½d and 4d existing designs but with a solid background, printing letterpress essays in blue. Finally, in May Waterlows produced experimental prints of the same values with solid backgrounds but printed in the correct colours for the denominations. These were again in letterpress.

The Postmaster General had a number of audiences with the King and on 1 June noted:

> I saw the King this morning. His Majesty was very pleased with the improvements suggested in the colour printing etc. of the stamps (including the solid

Above: April 1933 letterpress essays

Left: Recess essays by Bradbury Wilkinson

249

background), and was very impressed with the photogravure process. He would like the suggested trial by photogravure to take place.

As regards the head, he prefers the head in specimen "B" i.e. the portrait redrawn in tone from a print of the die of the current stamp.

He does not wish any change to be made in the higher value stamps.[9]

There is no note as to the King's views on the other photographic portraits but, as with the subsequent Silver Jubilee stamps, he preferred to keep the effigy of his now deceased friend, Bertram Mackennal. As a result, the experimental print run of photogravure stamps at Harrisons was arranged, to compare with an experiment on the Miehle press in letterpress which had already taken place.

The Photogravure Process

Eric Harrison provided a memorandum describing how the photogravure process worked. Firstly, a design is created in tones of grey, with any line work eliminated. Of this a photograph is then taken and enlarged to form the negative. At this stage any parts of the stamp that are required to appear white in the finished stamp, such as the lettering, have to be carefully retouched with opaque to eliminate tone.

The next stage is the stepping-up of a multiple positive of 480 stamps precisely uniform, and positioned the same size as the finished product. A special camera is used for this purpose, the negative being placed in the camera and a powerful stable light projected through the negative by means of mercury vapour lamps. The stamp is focussed upon a sensitised plate fixed into an apparatus, which enables the plate to be moved either horizontally or vertically and with the utmost precision by the operator by means of hand-operated mechanism and dials for registering movement per thousandth part of an inch either way.[10]

A multiple positive of 480 images is created in this manner, each image being exposed for about 20 seconds. The next stage is the production of the carbon tissue, described as a "gelatine resist" through which the etching of the copper cylinder took place. This tissue on a paper backing is first placed in a vacuum printing frame behind a 200-line screen and exposed to arc lamps. Where the light penetrates the screen the gelatine becomes hardened and these lines then provide the cell walls to hold the ink.

The cylinder is now etched:

The effect of the etching fluid has been to etch into the surface of the cylinder a series of cells; where the fluid has penetrated readily through the gelatine resist the cells are deeper and become shallower and shallower to effect the whole range of tones.[11]

After cleaning the cylinder is reading for proving and retouching to eliminate flaws which might have occurred due to any particles of dust.

When printing from a photogravure cylinder the cylinder is revolved, receiving a full supply of very fluid ink.

A steel doctor blade, the sharpened edge of which runs on the surface of the cylinder with a reciprocating motion, returns all the surplus ink to the trough. The ink is now only contained in the cells that have been produced by the etching which are below the surface of the cylinder itself. The deeper cells contain more ink, and, therefore, produce the darkest tone and so on right through the range. The paper is impressed by means of a cylinder or roller covered with rubber, with great pressure upon the cylinder so inked, and effects the printing operation.[12]

It is clear from this description that the process is very effective in reproducing tones, but not sharp simple lines. These are all made up of cells and appear very uneven under any magnification. In contrast, letterpress or recess dies are composed of lines and can only show tones by varying sizes of dots.

Harrisons won the contract, for a minimum of ten years, to begin on 1 January 1934. It was on 26 July, 1933 that they were told that the photogravure process would be adopted for their contract. On this basis, Harrisons purchased another factory – at High Wycombe. They then equipped this with completely new machinery which cost over £40,000 and this had to be installed, tried out and perfected before manufacture could begin. This was to take many months and the Post Office instituted a weekly visit to the new premises to check on progress from April 1934.

The new machinery consisted of printing machines, perforating machines and gumming and other plant. Four rotary printing machines were ordered from Timsons Ltd of Kettering at a cost of £10,000. These were described as having "several new features" without any further elucidation.[13] Some 13 rotary perforating machines were ordered from Grovers "of entirely new design" also costing £10,000. These were to cause considerable trouble. Then there was the supply of cylinders and the other plant. All this was to take time and a great deal of money. New factory, completely new machinery, radical change in printing process – there were echoes here of the problems with Harrisons' first contract in 1911. And so it proved, though this time it was not entirely unexpected.

Above: Rotary perforating machine by Grover

Reviewing the history later (referring to rolls of stamps, though it applied to everything) a report to the Treasury stated:

> although the necessary machinery was ordered promptly there was delay in delivery of it by the manufacturers and when it was installed some months were occupied in making adjustments and modifications and in experimental runs.[14]

At the first conference to review progress on 16 April 1934 one of the printing machines had been erected and was under trial with a cylinder which showed the portrait of a film star. The first two rotary perforators had been delivered for sheet stamps. There were separate machines for perforating rolls.

> The machine for endwise rolls has been delivered, that for sideways rolls is ready for delivery. The slitters on all the perforators are considered unsatisfactory for the purpose but Mr Warne says that he can readily put this right.[15]

Above: Grover machine for rolls

The following week they were already trying out a full cylinder of 1½d stamps but ominously due allowance for the stretch of the paper was causing problems with the size of the stamps. Cylinders were to continue to cause problems as were the rotary perforators. After a full-scale trial at the beginning of June it was decided to try out "commercial printers" which were rotary, but sheet-fed rather than reel. Three of these were then used, described as B.T.1 machines. It is possible that they were of German manufacture as a German fitter is noted as erecting the third machine. Both types of machine were used to print the initial supplies of the 1½d stamp which went on sale on 20 August. Output on the B.T.1 machines was about one third of that on the Timson. Perforation was sheet-fed for both at this point, with the reel from the rotary machines being chopped into sheets beforehand. Two of the B.T. machines had "given out" by 11 October and were then taken off stamp work.[16]

Creating the Gravure Stamps

The King had chosen essays with his head created from a tonal wash drawing based on the Coinage head die. How the artwork was built up was later described in a note by A. Tydeman of Post Office Stores.[17]

Firstly, a black impression was taken from the master die used for the letterpress stamps. This was then photographically enlarged and the lines in the oval and head bleached out to leave only a shadow impression. One of Harrisons' artists then worked this up as a "wash drawing".

> This work consisted mainly of eliminating the line-work, and substituting tone, with the addition of such alterations as the darkening of the background in the centre.[18]

This wash drawing then became the standard for the King's head on all the stamps, thus using a version of the Coinage head for all gravure designs. Perhaps the King had a wry smile remembering all the trouble about the size and form of his effigy in the original profile stamps, when he had not been able to understand why one head would not fit all frames. Now, with the solid background, it would.

The artwork was now photographed down to stamp size for the production of photographic plates and then the multipositive was created as described above.

Apart from the King's head there were five basic frame designs. The Dolphin 1½d letterpress die had been supplied in November 1932 and the wash drawing created was used for all the March 1933 design essays. The Oak & Laurel leaves 1d die was provided on 7 June the same year and die proofs of the three other frames (Mackennal Wreath, Eve Pillars and Wreath) were supplied on 27 July.

At the beginning of July Harrisons ran off some 40,000 sheets of 1d and 1½d designs printed in photogravure. Kingsley Wood then arranged an audience of the King on Saturday 22 July when he showed him the results. Two blocks of the 1½d design survive in green and brown (with the new version of the Coinage head) which the King approved on that day.

Through October and November Harrisons worked on proofs of the other designs and values but there was still the question of whether the new version of the Coinage head should appear in the 1d and 2½d values in place of the large Medal head. To be certain of the King's wishes essays were also produced incorporating this old version. On 13 December Kingsley Wood again wrote to the Sir Clive Wigram, since 1931 the successor to Lord Stamfordham as the King's Private Secretary.

Above: Wash drawing artwork for gravure stamps

> When I saw the King with reference to the new issue of stamps, His Majesty decided in favour of the retention of the present designs, modified only by the inclusion of an opaque background, but he expressed a preference for the smaller instead of the larger King's head which at present appears in the 1d and 2½d designs. The contractors have since been working upon designs which would admit of the smaller head being included without materially changing the remainder of the stamp.

> I enclose specimens of the results which, apart from the substitution of the smaller head, merely shew a larger and, to my mind, less insignificant crown and certain minor changes in the scroll work.[19]

He asked if the King preferred the new designs or the old. The same day, Wigram replied saying that the King much preferred the new alternative - and could he have the designs for his collection? It had to be explained that there were no designs as such because of the process used, but essays (approved and unapproved) were later supplied. One each of the different designs was proofed in the various colours required. Five sheets dated February 1934 using the 1d and 1½d values in various colours are in the Royal Philatelic Collection in a trial layout for cylinders – two panes, one of 9 x 20 and one of 12 x 20. This layout is described as not being adopted.

The Silver Jubilee

All this work on new definitives is what had caused the dismissive reply to be sent to the Colonial Office with regard to their proposed commemorative issue for the King's silver jubilee. However, in April 1934 the Government grasped with enthusiasm the idea of a national celebration. Kenneth Rose, in his biography of the King, notes that, even if inspired by respect and affection, this nevertheless owed something to political opportunism.

> A display of patriotic enthusiasm would both encourage support for the Government at the approaching general election and warn the dictators not to provoke a proud and undivided people.[20]

Politicians were ever thus. However, this official celebration gave the Post Office cause to reconsider the issuing of special stamps. Even so, it was not until Bacon, now knighted for his philatelic services, had indicated that the King was "warmly favourable to the idea"[21] that reluctant postal officials were forced to act. This was, in effect, a royal command.

Wigram followed this up immediately with a note from Buckingham Palace stating that the King "quite approves that the portrait on the present stamps"[22] should be used. This was to be ignored, apparently deliberately, as the following day a detailed internal Post Office memorandum on required actions on the stamps said:

> Other questions to be settled in this connection are (a) whether the existing King's head is to be retained or whether an alternative is preferred, and (b) whether pictorial matter should be introduced, or the frame designs should be on the present conventional lines. Excellent reproductions of considerable artistic merit both of portraiture and of pictorial matter can by obtained by the photogravure process.[23]

This was despite the King's clear preference and his previous rejection of other portraits submitted for the new definitives.

Having told the Colonial Office so emphatically that there would be no stamps Kingsley Wood now had to retract, and he wrote immediately admitting that the previous letter was "misleading".[24]

Rather than create yet another committee to obtain designs this task was entrusted to Sir Donald Banks, the Director General, and Sir Stephen Tallents - who involved Kenneth Clark from the National Gallery. Only three months before the "Poster Group" had been set up to advise the Post Office on subjects and artists for posters. Tallents and Clark were the driving force behind it and were now to act on stamp design as well.

Tallents met Clark at the National Gallery to discuss possible designs and designers. As his notes make clear, Clark

> was strongly of opinion that for the purpose now in view pictorial designs would be unsuitable. He suggested that the best effect was likely to be obtained by working a somewhat larger King's head into a symbolical and decorative design which might be different for each denomination. The designs might symbolise, for example, agriculture or shipping, or industries of various kinds; or alternatively they might symbolise the Dominions.[25]

He suggested as artists Stephen Gooden, Rex Whistler and Macdonald Gill, and that Nelson and Linzell might be invited again. Otherwise, he was very critical of the designs submitted for the P.U.C. stamps. He then made the intriguing suggestion that some architects might be in a position to submit suitable designs and promised to make enquiries. This was to prove crucial.

The size of the stamp caused quite considerable discussion within the Post Office.[26] Bacon had originally suggested that a larger size than the standard might be appropriate. However, any different size had cost implications, both in terms of paper and perforating machinery, as had been seen with the previous two issues. In the end it was decided to ask the artists to produce designs twice the size of normal definitives which it was easy to print in photogravure in sheets of 120 rather than 240. Artists' instructions stated that the designs

Left: Classical submitted design by Edmund Dulac for Silver Jubilee stamps

should be "of an appropriate kind" suggesting that they might include depictions of royal homes, buildings, scenes and events of Imperial significance, or perhaps historical scenes such as the King's 1911 coronation. Another theme was taken from Clark, being designs which were "symbolical of various national industries, or the development of land, air, sea and electrical communications during the last 25 years".[27]

Artists invited were those proposed by Clark, together with Edmund Dulac and the printing firms of Bradbury Wilkinson, Waterlows and Harrison & Sons. Gooden refused in emphatic terms describing photogravure as a "cheap and nasty" technique. Whistler was delayed but the others had submitted designs by 17 September with Hugo Fleury and L.D. Fryer (representing Waterlows), Linzell (Bradbury Wilkinson) and C. Hayden (Harrisons).

These designs were referred to Clark, but he thought none suitable. Other artists were now invited – F.J. Sharman, Trevor Morris, John Farleigh, Norman Howard, S. Kennedy North and Barnett Freedman. An alternative size was offered and so those who had previously submitted designs were asked if they would like to try again. The result was a further 20 designs with only Sharman not providing any.

Although apparently not appreciated by Clark, the most artistic designs were submitted by Dulac and Whistler, both using images of classical allusion. Others featured methods of transport, images of industry or royal buildings such as Windsor Castle, Buckingham Palace and even Balmoral. Linzell, in one sketch, had the opening bars of "God save the

Above: Submitted design by Rex Whistler (top)

Accepted lithograph by Barnett Freedman (middle)

Freedman's version of Vandyk portrait design

King" though Howard, most inappropriately, showed the Cenotaph.

At the end of October, Banks, Tallents and Clark considered the new designs. Clark thought that the only successful one was that by Barnett Freedman which would probably produce a satisfactory stamp with a few minor modifications. It was agreed that a modified version should be sent to Harrisons for essaying. Freedman later provided a detailed description for transmission to the King.

The fundamental idea in designing the Silver Jubilee Commemoration Postage Stamp, was firstly, to obtain an effect of dignity and simplicity:- that the design and the lettering should be clear and legible, so as to give at once the function of the new issue, and that the complete stamp should be essentially classical in character.

Secondly, I have used only the very simplest forms of symbolism, the main themes being the Laurel Leaves and the Olive Branches, the Laurel for Triumph and Reward, and the Olive branch for Peace and Goodwill.

The Royal Crown is depicted in each of the four denominations but the Laurel and Olive branches have been interchanged in various forms, with the addition of the Oakleaf and acorn (symbolical of strength and stability) so that with the difference of each denomination-colour, there is also a subtle change of design, without alteration to the fundamental character of the stamp.[28]

The lettering used was Walbaum Roman, originally a German font from the beginning of the 19th century.

Clark's suggestion at the outset that architects might be able to provide suitable designs had proved fruitful. Freedman, when he left school, had been a junior draughtsman with a monumental mason and had then been in a firm which did work for architects. At the same meeting with Banks and Tallents at the end of October further sketch designs by the Post Office Engineer-in-Chief's Office were also shown. These all used the rejected portraits tried out in the definitive essays. One, portrait in format, showed the Vandyk photograph in a simple frame. Referring to this somewhat pompously, and in typically patrician fashion, Clark "thought that a stamp of this kind would

Above: Essays in different sizes of Freedman's Vandyk portrait design

not be inappropriate for the occasion and, at any rate, could not be criticised on artistic grounds."[29] It was agreed that after he had modified his own design Freedman should be asked to redesign this rough sketch, keeping the overall layout. This was to result in one of the most beautiful stamp designs never to be produced. Expertise in technical drawing was clearly a useful background.

Essays were created in different formats using Freedman's original design and his reworked portrait design. The latter Vandyk portrait came in two different sizes; Freedman's original landscape design was essayed with both the Mackennal head and different versions of the Vandyk photograph. All types came in green, red, brown and two different shades of blue, termed "ultramarine" and "turquoise". These were shown to the King on 22 November when he approved the original Freedman design, with the Mackennal head (unsurprisingly)

257

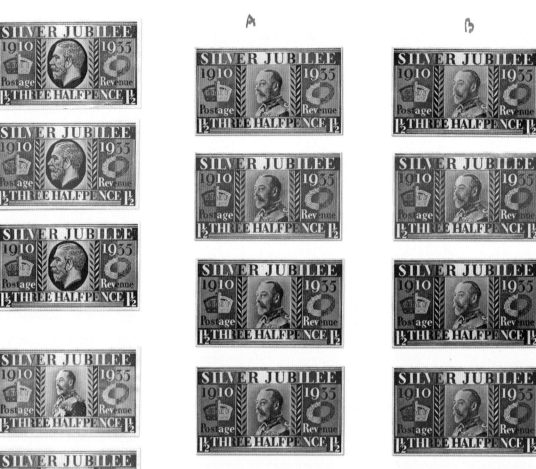

A   B

Above: Essays of Barnett Freedman's accepted frame design with Vandyk portrait in different sizes, and the accepted Mackennal profile

but in a slightly smaller size. There is no record of what the Post Office thought at losing, yet again, the opportunity to replace the Mackennal profile.

Harrisons had been awaiting this decision impatiently. Because the stamp was going to be a different size, no matter which design was chosen, they were going to require new perforating punch boxes. For reasons which are not immediately obvious these were to be manufactured by Harrilds, rather than Grovers (who supplied Harrisons' other perforating machinery), and a total of 12 boxes were ordered at a cost of some £2,000.

Freedman had supplied the artwork to Harrisons in the form of a large lithograph. Essays were now modified over a period to gain the delicate balance of tones which the artist was

Darker oak. Leaves in upright panels made to stand out better. Shading in larger panels improved.

Second + approved proof.

28 March 1935

approved

2 apl/35 Approved by Director General but not initialled – see Mr Kidner's letter of 2 apl 1935.

aiming at and it was not until the beginning of April 1935 that all values (½d, 1d, 1½d and 2½d) had been approved. Even then there was still some confusion with regard to the shade of blue. The final 2½d essay was in "turquoise" – it was approved subject to this being changed to "ultramarine". That for the 1d was described as being "superior in mellowness of tone to any of the others".[30]

Above left: Approved essay for the 1d Silver Jubilee stamp

The stamps were issued on 7 May, the 6 May being a public holiday. They replaced the standard definitives until stocks were exhausted. Overprinted versions went on sale the following day in the postal agencies of Morocco and Tangier.

Jubilee Stamp Books

To produce postal stationery would have required the imprinted stamps to be printed letterpress, regarded as quite possible but the designs had been created specifically for the tonal photogravure process. So none was created. Sales of the issued stamps in stamp books were more immediately practicable, though these would still require separate, specially-formatted printing cylinders.

As with the Postal Union Congress issue there were two types of book, being sold at 2s and 3s. The former contained three panes of 4 x 1½d stamps and one pane of the ½d and 1d.; the latter was made up of five panes of 1½d stamps, and again one each of the other values. There were four editions of the 3s book (numbered 294 to 297) and seven editions of the 2s book (298 to 304). Again following the PUC precedent there were no 2½d stamps in booklets, but a pane of airmail labels was included.

That the Silver Jubilee stamps were larger than normal meant larger books. Freedman was asked to design the front cover which for once would not include any advertising, although pages of advertising were again sold inside.

Freedman was briefed about the cover design in early January, and seems to have delivered his design in the latter part of February. It followed the pattern of the stamps but he noted that he had replaced the usual cover title "Book of Stamps" with the words "Postage Stamps" which he thought brought greater clarity. One book was to have a red cover, the other blue which would make "the whole production lighter and fresher".[31] The books should also be bound in coloured thread to match the cover. Both Freedman's design and his ideas were warmly received by the GPO.

A special postal order was also designed by Freedman though this passed largely unnoticed, and there was also a commemorative home safe for the Savings Bank.

Jubilee Sales

Final sales totals for the Silver Jubilee stamp books were reported as: 3,503,089 of the 2/-, and 2,001,790 of the 3/-. Total sales overall were:

Stamps/values	½d	1d	1½	2½d
- in sheets	331,381,680	128,376,600	407,793,600	14,184,960
- in 2/- books	14,012,356	14,012,356	42,037,068	-
- in 3/- books	8,007,160	8,007,160	40,035,800	-
Total :	**353,401,196**	**150,396,116**	**489,866,468**	**14,184,960**

For the overprints issued in Morocco, supplies to agency postmasters and sales to stamp dealers combined were:

Overprints	Currency	½d	1d	1½d	2½d
Morocco Agencies	British	72,000	51,600	47,040	57,840
"	Spanish	213,600	89,640	82,920	130,680
"	French	81,000	42,960	46,440	58,440
Tangier	British	83,280	53,040	95,400	-
Totals issued		449,880	237,240	271,800	246,960
Totals overprinted		450,829	253,919	272,042	247,193

Barnett Freedman

Tallents described Freedman as being born in 1901 of "humble parentage" in the East End of London. His parents were Jewish-Russian political refugees. When he was nine he had to go to the London Hospital where he spent four years being treated for a rare form of heart disease. He started work at 15 and, by attending night classes at art school, through Sir William Rothenstein won a scholarship of £120 a year to the Royal College of Art in 1922. Here he met the likes of Edward Bawden and Eric Ravilious.

After leaving the RCA in 1925 he was employed as an illustrator and lithographer but the years were lean and in his own words "he starved".[32] Tallents mentions in particular his book illustrations of Siegfried Sassoon's *Memoirs of an Infantry Officer* of 1931 for Faber & Faber. His first work for the Post Office was in illustrating the redesigned Annual Report for 1934.

Later, he was to be the official war artist to the B.E.F. in France in World War II. He served as artist to the Admiralty 1941-6 (given the rank of Captain) and participated in both the Boulogne evacuation and the Normandy landings. He died in 1958.

Public Reaction

There was a great deal of publicity surrounding the announcement of the Silver Jubilee stamps. Press conferences were held in London and in 35 provincial centres. A GPO film was made, *The King's Stamp,* directed by William Coldstream which told the story of the creation of the stamp (with Freedman sketching while puffing a pipe in the back of a taxi) and then showed printing at the new works in High Wycombe. This section was in colour and was the first record of Harrisons' works.

Block of 3 from sheet printed in turquoise (colour not approved). Some of these stamps got into circulation owing to an incorrect issue.

The result was wide coverage in newspapers and newsreel footage. Philatelic reaction was more critical. *The Stamp Collectors' Fortnightly* considered them "cheap" and that "judged by comparison with some of the beautiful photogravure stamps issued by foreign countries, this English effort will probably be regarded by most collectors as disappointing".

Above: "Prussian Blue" versions of the 2½d

The 2½d Silver Jubilee "Prussian Blue"

Essays for the Silver Jubilee stamps included two shades of blue for the 2½d value. One was termed "ultramarine", the other "turquoise". The final proof of the accepted design was printed in "turquoise" and was approved, but the colour was to be changed to "ultramarine". In late March 1935, when printing proof sheets of the 2½d, Harrisons printed a considerable number of sheets in the "turquoise" shade, now known to philatelists as "Prussian blue". This mistake was discovered when three sheets were sent to Post Office Stores Department for inspection. All those remaining at Harrisons were then cancelled and destroyed.

However, a total of five, or possibly six sheets, were still at P.O. Stores. During a period of intense work the Superintendent of Warehousemen there accidentally placed four of these sheets with his good stock. Subsequently, at least three of these were despatched to Upper Edmonton Post Office on 25 June. They went on sale about 2 July and were all sold, but nobody noticed until September when Stanley Gibbons Ltd contacted the Post Office to enquire about a find. It is not clear if the fourth sheet also went to Edmonton or to another office. This inadvertently created a famous philatelic rarity.

Production of Photogravure Definitives

Work on the photogravure definitives at Harrisons new works at High Wycombe was severely disrupted by the necessity to produce the Silver Jubilee commemoratives. The various processes were of course the same. The first operation was for the reels of paper to be gummed.

> The length of paper on a reel is 1½ to 1½ miles and the gumming is done continuously, after which the gummed paper is passed through a special machine to fracture the surface of the gum in order to counteract the tendency to curl. Only pure gum Arabic is used as the gumming agent. The paper is then super-calendered under considerable pressure to ensure a satisfactory printing surface. The final operation is for the reels to be slit to the correct width for the printing machine.[33]

The next operation was printing, done on rotary machines.

> The inks used are of a special character, unaffected by light, free from lead and insoluble in water. The reels of printed stamps are now taken to another rotary machine which delivers them duly perforated and sheeted.[34]

That was the theory, but problems with the rotary perforators meant that many of the stamps had to be perforated in sheets.

It took a long time for the letterpress stamps to be replaced by the new photogravure designs, and the process was not in the end completed. Not only sheet stamps were required, but also books and rolls with their own printing cylinders. It is indicative of the amount of trouble Harrisons were having in that the registration sheet of the 1½d was taken from cylinder 97. Harrisons had to print stamps on their letterpress machines until the photogravure printings were sufficient, and emergency printings of letterpress rolls continued at Waterlows until problems at High Wycombe were overcome.

One small point of detail was noted on 27 July when Harrisons stated that in future all control marks printed on both the Timson Rotary and the BT1 machines would appear on the left hand side of the stamp sheet, as opposed to the bottom margin. This was because of the use of the blanket impression cylinder. Later, in November, the mark was moved up one stamp so that it was alongside the third, instead of the second, stamp from the bottom of the sheet.[35]

At first the gutters, or margins, between the stamps on the sheet followed the example of the letterpress stamps. However, Harrisons found it very difficult to register the reels of printed stamps with the rotary perforators. The first mention of a way round this came on 16 August when it was said that "To overcome the present difficulty (Perforations being too close to the printed surface) new cylinders are being prepared having a printing surface of such dimensions as will neutralise the tension on the Rotary Perforators." What this meant was an increase in the size of the gutter between stamps and a corresponding slight decrease in the size of the stamp image.

On a visit to Harrisons' plant at High Wycombe on 4 October postal officials were shown sheets of the 1d with the guttering increased from 0.0625 very marginally to 0.07 inch. Guy Harrison stated that for photogravure printing it was usual to allow gutters 50% wider than for surface printing. It was hoped to start printing on 16 October and to produce 150,000 sheets a week. Later, in 1935, the gutters were increased several times again to 0.095". This meant that some values were issued in more than one size. Authority was given on 8 January for the 0.095" gutter, but only provisionally for six months.[36]

Colour designations and dates of first issue of the photogravure definitives were:

Below: the issued photogravure stamps

Value	Colour	Registration Date	First issued	Gutter	Notes
½d	Deep Green	5 November 1934	17 November 1934	0.07	Sheets; 1st print of this value
		26 January 1935		0.075	Stamp books
		12 July 1935		0.095	Sheets
		26 July 1935		0.095	Sideways rolls (24 x 10) 1st print
		11 July 1935*		0.095	Stamp books
1d	Deep Scarlet	24 August 1934	24 September 1934	0.0625	Sheets; 1st print of this value
		8 November 1934		0.07	Sheets
		26 January 1935		0.075	Stamp books
		11 July 1935		0.095	Stamp books
1d *cont*		1 August 1935		[0.095]	Endways rolls (20 x 12) 1st print
		19 March 1936		0.095	Sideways rolls (2 panes of 10 x 10)
1½d	Brown Lake	29 August 1934	20 August 1934	0.0625	Sheets; 1st print of this value
		15 January 1935		0.07	Endways rolls (20 x 12)
		26 January 1935		0.075	Stamp books (panes of 6; panes of 4 with gravure advert)
		26 March 1935**		0.08	Sheets
		18 July 1935*		0.095	Stamp books
		20 January 1936		0.095	Endways rolls (20 x 12)
		16 March 1936		0.095	Sideways rolls (2 panes of 10 x 10)
2d	Orange Vermilion	17 December 1935	19 January 1935	0.075	Sheets
		2 April 1935		0.095	Sheets
		2 April 1936		0.095	Sideways rolls (2 panes of 10 x 10)
2½d	Deep Ultramarine	1 March 1935	18 March 1935	0.095	Sheets
3d	Deep Violet	1 March 1935	18 March 1935	0.095	Sheets
4d	Deep Green Slate	18 November 1935	2 December 1935	0.095	Sheets

Below: the issued photogravure stamps

Value	Colour	Registration Date	First issued	Gutter	Notes
5d	Orange Brown	3 February 1935	17 February 1936	0.095	Sheets
6d	Deep Solferino		not issued		
9d	Deep Olive Green	15 November 1935	2 December 1935	0.095	Sheets
10d	Cerulean	17 February 1935	24 February 1936	0.095	Sheets
1/-	Raw Umber	5 February 1935	24 February 1936	0.095	Sheets

*printed

**inscribed as printed 18 January 1935

However, this does not tell the whole story. Harrisons had great trouble aligning the printing cylinders for rolls with the rotary perforating machines. Waste was up to 50%. At the end of 1934 some 1d and 1½d continuous rolls were printed at the intermediate size. Then at the beginning of 1935 ½d, 1d, 1½d and 2d rolls were printed at the smaller size but there are no registration sheets for these. In addition, as far back as May 1934 Harrisons had asked "whether a difference of 2/1000" in the width of each stamp would be permitted" for sideways rolls but it is not clear if this was agreed.[37] Issue dates of early to mid February 1935 for the small size ½d, 1d and 1½d stamps may have come from rolls first. The registration of sheet stamps for those values at that size is either much later or did not take place.

Stamp books were also delayed by cylinder difficulties and did not appear until 1935. One version had the advertisements on stamp panes also printed in photogravure in a vain attempt to save time.

Proposed New Values

Denominations of stamps depend upon postage rates. In 1935 parcel post rates were due to increase. This would require new stamps at 7d and 8d. Instead of just providing new versions of the given frames the Postmaster General thought it best to ask for completely new designs "which would harmonise with the present series but show some improvement in dignity & general appearance".[38] Tallents was to be consulted. Thus began what turned out to be a forlorn exercise.

Clark and Tallents then examined the modern stamps of some other countries, particularly Sweden, as kept in the Post Office "Berne" collection of stamps supplied by the Universal Postal Union. Clark suggested that the new 8d stamp should be yellow and the 7d either brownish pink or pale grey. These seemed the only colours free, given those already allocated to other denominations. As a guide to artists Clark gave his comments on designs in the present series:[39]

1. The 9d stamp was the most respectable and the least open to criticism.
2. The 1½d stamp was the most amusing and the most open to criticism.
3. The 1d stamp was the best balanced design in the series.

There was a delay through the summer, partly because the printers were busy preparing the other values. Then at the end of October a number of artists were approached to provide designs. These were:

Barnett Freedman
Robert Gibbings
Stephen Gooden

Agnes Miller Parker
Eric Ravilious
Graham Sutherland
Rex Whistler

Stephen Gooden reiterated his opposition to photogravure printing and refused to submit designs, as did Eric Ravilious, and nothing was heard from Rex Whistler. This prompted a few caustic remarks from Clark.

> It is unfortunate that the most talented artists invited always behave so stupidly, and some day if there is a protest against new stamps issued by the Post Office, I think that his fact ought to be made known.[40]

He would think of other possible artists although this does not seem to have happened. Freedman and Gibbings submitted one design each, Agnes Miller Parker (now Mrs Agnes McCance) two designs, and Graham Sutherland a total of eight. Six of these were lithographic prints in three colours, the other two were hand-painted with only the King's head a print.

However, these were to come to nought. Work was interrupted by the death of the King and no new designs were created thereafter, although values prepared in existing frames (5d, 10d and 1s) were issued in February. The 6d value had to be in doubly fugitive ink for revenue purposes but prolonged experiments failed to find one suitable for photogravure printing and so this denomination was never issued and the letterpress type continued in use.

Left: Submitted design for the proposed 7d stamp by Graham Sutherland

Left: Submitted design for the proposed 7d stamp by Barnett Freedman

Below: the 6d letterpress printed by Harrisons

---

1 King George V's speech to both Houses of Parliament, Westminster Hall, 9 May 1935 (written by G.M. Trevelyan), quoted in **Cannadine, D.** *G.M. Trevelyan: A Life in History* 1993, p237

2 **Rose, K.** King George V, p.395

3 ibid

4 CO 323/1274/5 G.L.M. Clauson, 30 January 1934

5 ibid H. Napier to Lee, Colonial Office 28 February 1934

6 ibid

7 POST 52/988 Unified Stamps: Photogravure issues. 5 May 1933

8 POST 33/4972 Postage stamps: printing by photogravure process introduced, new issues. PMG to Sir Clive Wigram, 11 May 1933

9 POST 52/988 op cit. PMG to Secretary, GPO. 1 June 1933

10 ibid. Memorandum. 30 June 1933

11 ibid. résumé. 29 June 1933

12 ibid

13 POST 52/174 Harrison & Sons Contract for Unified Stamps – reports of weekly conferences at contractors works

14 POST 52/527 Rolls from Waterlows during currency of Harrisons contract. A.F. Kidner to Treasury, 4 December 1935

15 POST 52/174 op cit 16 April 1934

16 ibid. 11 October 1934

17 POST 33/4972 op cit Tydeman to Secretary, GPO. 29 December 1933

18 POST 52/988 op cit. 29 June 1933

19 POST 33/4972 op cit Kingsley Wood to Wigram 13 December 1933

20 **Rose, K.** *King George V* p394

21 POST 33/4646 H.M. the King: Silver Jubilee Stamp, arrangements Banks Memorandum. 8 June 1934

22 ibid. Wigram to Banks 13 June 1934

23 POST 52/989 Unified Stamps Silver Jubilee issue. W.M. Cook memorandum 20 June 1934

24 CO 323/1274/5 op cit Sir Kingsley Wood, PMG to Secretary of States for Colonies, 15 June 1934

25 POST 33/4646 op cit A.R. Kidner memorandum 20 July 1934

26 Details are summarised in **Bates, S.** *Special Stamp History No. 3: 1935 Silver Jubilee Issue* 1998 p 4

27 POST 33/4646 op cit A.R. Kidner memorandum 20 July 1934

28 POST 52/989 op cit A Note by the Artist on his designs for the Silver Jubilee stamp. 26 January 1935

29 POST 33/4646 op cit A.R. Kidner memorandum 25 October 1934

30 POST 52/989 op cit R. Fanshawe to A.R. Kidner 29 March 1935

31 Details in **Bates, S.** op cit

32 **Rogerson, I.** *Barnett Freedman: the graphic art* 2006 p15

33 POST 52/519 memorandum on gravure, 1934

34 ibid

35 POST 52/1336 Unified Stamps in sheets – Control marks. W.M.Cook note 19 July 1934; and Harrisons to P.O. Stores, 2 November 1934

36 POST 52/527 Rolls from Waterlows during currency of Harrisons contract. W.M. Cook to Mr Dell, 8 January 1935.

37 POST 52/174 Harrison & Sons contract for Unified Stamps – Reports of weekly conferences at contractors' works 25 May 1934

38 POST 33/4972 op cit. Instructions to artists, A.R. Kidner to R. Fanshawe 18 October 1935

39 ibid. Memo by Sir Stephen Tallents, 27 June 1935

40 ibid. Kenneth Clark to A.R. Kidner

18

IN MEMORY
LEGACY & PROPOSED MOURNING STAMP

"Spirit of well-shot woodcock, partridge, snipe
  Flutter and bear him up the Norfolk sky:
  In that red house in a red mahogany book-case
The stamp collection waits with mounts long dry.[1]"

King George V died towards midnight on 20 January 1936 at Sandringham. Upright, always mindful of duty, meticulous about dress, he had been conservative in nature, and despite his great affection for his father, of a Victorian rather than Edwardian era. In contrast, his son was "modern", careless of duty, uninterested in kingship or the crown, though handsome and apparently easy-going, with a gift for public relations which made him very popular.

Edward's VIII's huge popularity was largely based on ignorance. Those who knew him well did not trust him to last. They described him as obstinate, extraordinarily immature and mean with even quite small sums of money, though not with Mrs Simpson. Frances Donaldson, his biographer, paints a picture of a man completely self-obsessed and totally unwilling to face up to reality.[2] Childishly, he always wanted his own way, or whatever Wallis Simpson wanted. He also had strong, unconsidered political views which he dangerously voiced. While reform was undoubtedly necessary, his was very much a case of change for change's sake, rather than for any considered reason.

Mourning Stamps Proposed

Nearly everything the new King did was in deliberate, and striking, contrast to his father. In one respect, however, he wished to honour his father's memory – how better than with an issue of stamps? A letter had appeared in *The Times* suggesting the issue of the basic letter rate definitive, 1½d, with a black border, and correspondence continued mentioning a similar issue for the death of President Hindenburg in 1934. A more recent example had been the mourning stamps for Queen Astrid of Belgium in December 1935, which had borne a charity premium.

Now it transpired that the King George V Jubilee Trust was to be converted into a Memorial Fund and that King Edward VIII, who as Prince of Wales had played a large part in setting up the Trust, favoured a special issue of 1½d stamps to be sold at 2d, the surplus proceeds going to the Fund.

On Saturday, 25 January the Director General, Col. Banks phoned the Post Office Stores Department at midday asking them to furnish designs at the earliest possible moment.[3] Harrisons were immediately informed and rounded up staff who worked

Above: Photogravure definitives in mourning colours

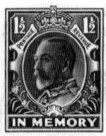

Above: "In Memory" essays

through Saturday night and all day Sunday. On Monday they had produced essays of the 1½d photogravure definitive in mourning colours of black and violet.

Two days later they had adapted this design, replacing the wording THREE HALFPENCE with IN MEMORY and a border of rosemary instead of the dolphins. The Mackennal profile head was also replaced with the Vandyk portrait which had been rejected by King George for use in both definitives and the Silver Jubilee commemoratives. A series of essays were produced in the standard brown and in various shades of grey, on both coated and uncoated papers. This was 29 January, the day after his funeral. Later versions modified the design slightly and were printed in February and March and a number of other stamp-size ideas were tried but not essayed. The possibility of a charity issue, although rejected in 1924, was regarded as reasonable and practicable.

However, after his initial enthusiasm, and as with so much else, the new King proceeded to create difficulties. The Jubilee Trust met on 5 February and examined the first essays. When these were shown to the King he rejected them. Further essays were seen at the Trust's next meeting on 12 March when it became the Memorial Fund. Thereafter, nothing is recorded as happening and Harrisons submitted their final bill for their unsuccessful work on 9 April. It was to be a harbinger of things to come with the Edward VIII stamps.

Philatelic Legacy

Philatelically, George V left a rich legacy. Some of Britain's best-loved stamps were produced under his guidance. In terms of design, however, his son wanted a contrast - simplicity and modernity. Rather than appear in ceremonial uniform he chose for his stamps a design by a 17-year-old schoolboy. The photographic portrait, by Hugh Cecil, utilised the possibilities of the photogravure process much better than the sculpted Mackennal head, however recreated by printers' artists. There was no decoration other than value and crown, and the word "Postage". When issued in September 1936 it caused a storm of argument amongst artists in the national press, particularly between Eric Gill and Edmund Dulac.

On Edward's abdication in December his conscientious brother wanted to be seen to return to the stability of his father. This was reflected in the design of his postage stamps. His portrait was sculpted as before and not photographic as with Edward, and he specified that his stamps should show some "ornamentation" - which provoked the ever-argumentative Gill to write from Rapallo in Italy:

> The abdication of Edward the VIII and the accession of the Duke of York to the throne may be taken to represent a return to previous conceptions both in art and politics ... it was symbolical of Edward VIII's short reign that the kingship, like the postage stamps, had been deprived of some of those ornamental accessories on account of which thrones and postage stamps had become ridiculous. I think the designs prepared for Edward VIII leave much to be desired in other respects but not in respect of their

plainness ... I do not believe there is in reality any such thing as ornament except in the sense in which we call a sergeant's stripes "ornaments", or as a medal is called a "decoration", that is to say something proper and appropriate to the person or thing decorated. All other sorts of ornament are redundant and foolish unless they spring from the exuberance of the workman ... and even then a decent restraint should be observed..... Now in the case of the postage stamps ... if you say: please add some curlywigs or dolphins or roses or dandelions or shells or corinthian columns, or something ornamental, I can only say: but why?[4]

Above and left: Royal Mail miniature sheets for London 2010 Festival of Stamps

269

George V most emphatically would not have agreed. And nor did George VI. His stamps, with national symbols as decoration, clearly deliberately hark back more to his father's designs rather than follow the simplicity of his brother's. So did the first Wilding definitives of the reign of Queen Elizabeth II which followed. It was not until the classic sculpture of the Queen by Arnold Machin in 1967 that design again reached the heights of the Victorian Penny Black. Of that, especially when printed recess, George V would have undoubtedly approved.

Centenary Celebrations

In 2010, to mark the centenary of King George V's accession and to celebrate the London 2010 Festival of Stamps in style, stamps and miniature sheets were issued featuring some of the famous designs of his reign. Both values for the British Empire Exhibition lion, and two of the Seahorse values, were reprinted recess, the images taken from the original dies and proofs. His portraits, both Downey and Mackennal, were combined in another design and the Festival saw a special stamp with his profile head together with the classic Machin head of the Queen. The P.U.C. £1 was also reprinted in facsimile format. Perhaps these too would have received the philatelist king's "warm approval".

1   *On the Death of King George V* by John Betjeman quoted in: **Rose, K.** *King George V* p.406
2   **Donaldson, F.** *Edward VIII* 1974.
3   Detailed in **Allen, G.** *Stamp History No.3a: 1936 Proposed George V Memorial Issue* 1998
4   POST 52/992 Unified Stamps: George VI issue. Eric Gill to Tydeman, 27 December 1936

INDEX

ILLUSTRATION ACKNOWLEDGEMENTS

All illustrations are copyright Royal Mail 2010 except as listed here.

Page

1   Portrait. *H.M. The Queen*

2   Colonial Silver Jubilee *H.M. The Queen*

7   Post Office Mauritius *H.M. The Queen*

8   Tilleard *H.M. The Queen*

9   Catalogue *H.M. The Queen*

10   Hejaz *H.M. The Queen*

11   Bacon, German New Guinea overprints *H.M. The Queen*

12   Pitcher artwork *H.M. The Queen*

13   Treasury Competition *H.M. The Queen*

16   Embossed *H.M. The Queen*

17   Albums *Crescent Lodge, London*

22   Tyrian Plum cover *H.M. The Queen*

27   Royal Mint *The Royal Mint Museum*

32   Mackennal *National Library of Australia*

34   Mackennal Lion *H.M. The Queen*

35   Mackennal Lions *H.M. The Queen*

36-7   Mackennal artwork *H.M. The Queen*

53   Diagrams *Geoffrey Eibl-Kaye*

60   Offset Downey Heads *British Library*

62   Lettering *Royal Philatelic Society, London*

65-6   Models, medals, coins *The Royal Mint Museum*

68   Plaster model, coin *The Royal Mint Museum*

69   Mackennal approved *H.M. The Queen*

70   Plaster models, medals *The Royal Mint Museum*

72   Approved Medal drawing *Royal Philatelic Society, London*

73   Eve 4d drawing and reverse *Royal Philatelic Society, London*

85-6   Coins *British Museum*

86   Phaethon *Pictures Collection, State Library of Victoria*

        Olympic medal *The Royal Mint Museum*

87   Mackennal Seahorse *H.M. The Queen*

90   Eve Seahorse *Royal Philatelic Society, London*

104   Pitcher artwork *H.M. The Queen*

125-6   Postage Due colours *H.M. The Queen*

134   Roll leader *Dr Jean Alexander*

139   Roll leader *Dr Jean Alexander*

145   Roll leader *Dr Jean Alexander*

152   K4 kiosk *Julian Stray*

162   Cancel *Morten Collection*

170   Ireland airmail *Private Collection*

178   Posting box *Windsor & Royal Borough Museum*

191   Blue airmail pillar box *Julian Stray*

217   Roll leaders *Dr Jean Alexander*

228   Roll leaders *Dr Jean Alexander*